Praise for
His Name
George Flo

'An intimate, unvarnished and scrupulous account
of his life . . . brilliantly revealing.'
New York Times

'Since we know George Floyd's death with tragic clarity, we
must know Floyd's America – and life – with tragic clarity.
His Name Is George Floyd is essential for our times.'
Ibram X. Kendi, author of *How to Be an Antiracist*

'A wondrous feat of vivid writing and deep reporting, from
the way it leads the reader through George Floyd's final fateful
day on earth, to its masterly account of Floyd's hopes and frustrations
in the larger context of race in America.'
David Maraniss, author of *Barack Obama: The Story*

'In this age of misinformation, where the victims of police
killings are made out to be the problem, this humanising of Floyd
is necessary . . . Samuels and Olorunnipa's greatest triumph is
placing Floyd's life in the context of white supremacy.'
Observer

'We have come to know George Floyd as a symbol but have
known little of George Floyd the man. In a monumental
work of reporting and storytelling, Robert Samuels and
Toluse Olorunnipa reveal who George Floyd was in life, and
the extent to which his death was the result not just of the
callous choices of a single police officer but of four hundred
years of societal decisions to devalue Black life.'
Wesley Lowery, author of *They Can't Kill Us All:
The Story of the Struggle for Black Lives*

'An expertly researched and excellent biography,
a necessary and enlightening read for all.'
Atlantic

'Deeply reported, expansive, and empathetic – gives readers a
clearer understanding of a man who tried, against the steep odds
of systemic racism, to lead a full, peaceful life in America.'
Top Ten Non-fiction Books of the Year – *Time*

'Detailed, vivid and moving.'
Washington Post

'A much-needed portrait of the life, times, and
martyrdom of George Floyd, a chronicle of the racial
awakening sparked by his brutal and untimely death,
and an essential work of history I hope everyone will read.'
Henry Louis Gates, Jr., author of *The Black Church*

'A vivid, necessary portrait of a Black man in America,
in all its nuance, tragedy, and fullness.'
Abby Phillip, CNN anchor and senior political correspondent

'Masterful, thorough and even-handed.'
Associated Press

'A sobering, deeply intimate account of George Floyd's life
and all that he had to carry and contend with as a Black man
coming of age in America. In a remarkable feat of reporting,
Robert Samuels and Toluse Olorunnipa help us come to know
Floyd as a full, rich, complicated human being.'
Alex Kotlowitz, author of *There Are No Children Here*

'A deeply reported biography . . . Vivid storytelling
drawn from interviews with family and friends reveals
how the clouds of poverty, addiction and racism that preside
over America often loomed over and got the better of
Floyd . . . A sobering and essential work.'
New Statesman

'Excellent, important . . . A novelist seeking to create a character
whose life exemplifies the challenges facing African American males
could scarcely find a better model than Floyd.'
Times Literary Supplement

'Robert Samuels and Toluse Olorunnipa deftly wade through
a history of stolen labor, stolen land, stolen wages, and stolen
dreams in *His Name Is George Floyd*, to lead readers to a life
stolen on a Minneapolis street. The writing's clarity,
smoothness, and compelling analysis expose the wrenching
structural racism that made Floyd's murder possible.'
National Book Foundation

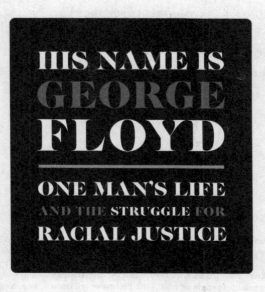

HIS NAME IS GEORGE FLOYD

ONE MAN'S LIFE AND THE STRUGGLE FOR RACIAL JUSTICE

Robert Samuels *and* Toluse Olorunnipa

PENGUIN BOOKS

TRANSWORLD PUBLISHERS
Penguin Random House, One Embassy Gardens,
8 Viaduct Gardens, London SW11 7BW
www.penguin.co.uk

Transworld is part of the Penguin Random House group of companies
whose addresses can be found at global.penguinrandomhouse.com

Penguin
Random House
UK

First published in Great Britain in 2022 by Bantam Press
an imprint of Transworld Publishers
Penguin paperback edition published 2023

A CIP catalogue record for this book
is available from the British Library.

ISBN
9781529176414

Typeset in 10.23/14.26pt Sabon Next LT Pro by Jouve (UK), Milton Keynes
Printed and bound in Great Britain by Clays Ltd, Elcograf S.p.A.

The authorized representative in the EEA is Penguin Random House Ireland,
Morrison Chambers, 32 Nassau Street, Dublin D02 YH68.

Penguin Random House is committed to a sustainable future
for our business, our readers and our planet. This book is made
from Forest Stewardship Council® certified paper.

Contents

Contents

INTRODUCTION
Flowers

I LOVE YOU."

George Perry Floyd Jr. would express the same sentiment to men, women, and children; to relatives, old friends, and strangers; to romantic partners, platonic acquaintances, and the women who fell somewhere in between; to hardened hustlers and homeless junkies; to big-time celebrities and neighborhood nobodies.

Floyd said the phrase so often that many friends and family members have no doubt about the final words he spoke to them. He would end phone calls with the expression and sign off text messages by tapping it out in all caps.

"All right, whatever, man," De'Kori Lawson said when he first heard Big Floyd, as he was known to friends, say those words. "I'll talk to you later, man."

As the decades passed, he came to appreciate Floyd's earnestness as they lost people to gun violence, drug overdoses, police brutality, and other trapdoors awaiting young Black men like them as they came of age in a harsh, often loveless reality.

"D, I love you, bro," Floyd told his friend during their final phone call in the spring of 2020.

"I love you, too, man," Lawson replied by this point.

"We always said we were going to give each other our flowers before we died," Lawson recalled. "And that right there lets you know what type of person he was."

Over the course of Floyd's final weeks, the fractured state of the world revealed the importance of sending love and flowers to friends while they were still alive. By the spring of 2020, the COVID-19 pandemic was raging, killing thousands of Americans each day, shutting down scores of businesses, and leaving millions of people out of work. Floyd, like many Black Americans, proved particularly vulnerable to the pandemic's merciless assault. He had been diagnosed with an asymptomatic case of the virus and had lost his job after the Minneapolis club where he worked as a security guard was forced to close.

With most of the country on lockdown, Floyd spent much of his time on the phone, catching up with old friends and checking in with relatives back in his hometown of Houston. He had left Texas for Minneapolis three years earlier, hoping to reset his life and break free from addiction, but he had only just changed the area code on his cell phone from Houston's 832 to 612, a signal of his renewed commitment to his adopted hometown in the Twin Cities.

One of those calls was to his brother Terrence, whose two-year-old daughter reminded him of his own beloved little girl, Gianna.

"My little niece, oh man," Floyd said over the phone, marveling over baby pictures Terrence had posted online. "When I get right, I'm going to get Gianna down here, and you bring baby girl, and we can have our play dates."

"I'm with it," Terrence responded.

"All right, bro, I love you," Floyd said before hanging up.

Floyd's comment about getting "right" could have referred to any number of things at that point in his life. His attempts to stand on his feet in Minnesota—with the goal of ultimately securing custody of Gianna—had often resulted in his getting knocked to the ground. He was constantly tripping over both his own mistakes and obstacles beyond his control, not least of which was a pandemic that had caused his income stream to dry up.

Floyd's emotional declarations were nothing new to his siblings. As a teenager, Floyd would stop to give his sister Zsa Zsa a hug and tell her he loved her before leaving their house with his friends—just quietly enough to keep the other kids from overhearing.

Floyd had grown up singing love songs karaoke-style with his sister LaTonya, and when they spoke for the last time that May, they reminisced by belting out her favorite tune—REO Speedwagon's 1980 hit "Keep On Loving You": "*And I'm gonna keep on lovin' you / 'Cause it's the only thing I want to do . . .*"

As a young man, Perry, as family called him, had outsize aspirations—to become a Supreme Court justice, a pro athlete, or a rap star. By the time his world came crashing down in the months before his death, he had been chasing more modest ambitions—a little stability, a job driving trucks, health insurance. Still, in his dying seconds, as he suffocated under a White police officer's knee, Floyd managed to speak his love.

"Mama, I love you!" he screamed from the pavement, where his cries of "I can't breathe" were met with an indifference as deadly as hate.

"Reese, I love you!" he yelled, a reference to his friend Maurice Hall, who was with him when he was handcuffed that Memorial Day evening.

"Tell my kids I love them!"

These words marked the end of a life in which Floyd repeatedly found his dreams diminished, deferred, and derailed—in no small part because of the color of his skin.

Like millions of Americans, we watched in horror as the video depicting Floyd's murder replayed on news programs and social media feeds in the summer of 2020. The visceral footage set us on a deeper mission, one to find out not just about the fateful nine minutes and twenty-nine seconds he spent gasping for air, but to pull back the curtain on the lifetime of striving that had come before, and to understand the heartbeat of the historic movement for civil rights that followed.

That mission took us to places we could have never imagined as we pursued two essential questions: Who was George Floyd? And what was it like to live in his America?

In answering those questions, we ducked gunshots after spending time with his roommate at George Floyd Square, the Minneapolis memorial that sprouted up at the intersection where he was killed. We sat for Sunday dinner with his large extended family, dining on the blueberry cobbler and candied yams he had once relished. We got haircuts from his barber, with whom he shared his deepest internal turmoil. We traversed Houston's Third Ward with Floyd's closest friends, listening as they laughed over old memories and cried out their grief over a life cut tragically short. We went to church with his brother and to tarot readings with his girlfriend as they tried to make sense of it all, and then sat with them while they broke down when they couldn't. Floyd's loved ones responded with a level of candor and transparency that gave us a vivid sense of his humanity. Their memories helped reveal the suffocating systemic pressures Floyd ultimately could not escape, even as he tried repeatedly to reset his life and overcome his past.

In all, we conducted more than four hundred interviews to craft this portrait of Floyd's distinctive American experience. We spoke with all six of Floyd's siblings, as well as with his aunts, uncles, cousins, nieces, nephews, lovers, friends, employers, teachers, coaches, teammates, cellmates, roommates, counselors, mentees, and more. We also interviewed scores of people who did not know Floyd directly but who possess an intimate knowledge of the societal forces that buffeted his path. Dozens of policymakers, professors, police chiefs, and other experts helped describe the American institutions that shaped the course of Floyd's life. Our reporting journey also led us to eyewitnesses, community advocates, civil rights leaders, city councillors, mayors, governors, senators, and the president.

After traveling for over a year through Houston; Minneapolis; Washington, DC; and beyond—walking the streets where Floyd watched friends die, standing on the fields where he chased athletic stardom, listening to the mixtapes on which he rapped his insecurities, reading the diary entries where he agonized over his sins, sitting in the treatment centers where he sought redemption—we ended up with a sense of George Floyd's motivations, his limitations, and his soul.

Yet the more we learned about Floyd's journey, the clearer it became to us that his life also provides a tangible example of how racism operates in America. Floyd's story, and the story of his family, encapsulates many of the compounding and relentless traumas that have characterized the Black experience for four hundred years. Here, we have documented Floyd's struggle to breathe as a Black man in America, a battle that began long before a police officer's knee landed on his neck.

When George Floyd took his first breaths in 1973, the strictures of Jim Crow–style discrimination in America had given way to what would become a more enduring and insidious kind of racism, a systemic version that would calcify just beneath the surface of American society. The foundations of his story were laid centuries before his birth, with successive generations of ancestors battling the evils of slavery, abusive sharecropping, legal segregation, and intergenerational poverty from the Civil War through the civil rights era.

As he came of age in the 1980s and 1990s, Floyd experienced the residue of that overt racism as it burrowed within American institutions, entrenching itself in a manner that was on the surface more palatable but still produced the kind of racial stratification more indicative of a caste-based system than a meritocratic democracy.

Growing up in one of the nation's most diverse metropolises, Floyd lived in a neighborhood that was racially segregated because the government designed it to be so. The crumbling Cuney Homes housing project, Houston's oldest, was a modern sand trap of poverty from which Floyd struggled to escape. He attended segregated schools in Houston's Third Ward, where the public education system funneled Black students into underfunded classrooms—and drove some, including Floyd, to believe athletics were the only route to success.

Police were a ubiquitous presence in Floyd's life, harassing, arresting, and threatening him from childhood through his final moments. In all, he was detained more than twenty times over the course of his life, including by at least five officers later charged with breaking the laws they were entrusted to enforce. Floyd spent almost a third of his adult life behind bars, during an era of mass incarceration that disproportionately targeted Black men for nonviolent drug crimes and decimated entire communities.

Derek Chauvin, the officer who killed Floyd, spent decades operating in a policing system in a country that imprisoned more people than any other. We have devoted a chapter to analyzing his American journey and the history of the police department that trained him to use deadly force.

While Floyd had long feared dying at the hands of police, his struggle to stay alive became more multifaceted as he suffered from a range of maladies that disproportionately cut short Black lives. In addition to COVID-19, he battled claustrophobia, high blood pressure, anxiety, and depression—ailments that for the most part went untreated—along with drug dependency.

Floyd readily acknowledged his own missteps and the mistakes that made redemption that much more difficult for him. He cried to friends about decisions that he regretted and the despair he sometimes felt.

"I've got my shortcomings and my flaws," he said in one video posted to social media. "I ain't better than nobody else."

Living our own American journeys as Black men has helped us understand Floyd's essence and relate to his experiences—his insecurities over his size and skin tone, his awareness that his mere presence sometimes sparked fear in strangers, his nervousness during police encounters, his feeling that, as he once articulated, "people quick to count you out, man, but just so strict on counting you in." We hoped to place Floyd's experiences within the context of the myriad forces that operated in the background during his forty-six years, never absolving him of responsibility or making excuses for his actions.

As journalists with more than three decades of combined reportorial experience, much of which was obtained at *The Washington Post*, we have chronicled the impact of politics and policy on American life, from the White House and Congress to union halls, cattle ranches, college step shows, and racial justice protests across the country. We have had access to the *Post*'s vast historical archive of political journalism, which has helped us to analyze the broad set of policies that affected Floyd's life, from the nineteenth-century black codes that made it illegal for his enslaved ancestors to learn to read to the twentieth-century drug laws that criminalized his dependency. We also benefitted from the *Post*'s most valuable asset: its journalists. This biography would not have been possible without the original reporting from the award-winning *Post* series "George Floyd's America," which included more than 150 interviews about Floyd's life and circumstances.

Reflected in the pages that follow is some of the journalism our colleagues produced along with us for that six-part series, which featured Tracy Jan's reporting about housing policy, Laura Meckler's story about Floyd's academic journey, Arelis R. Hernández's piece about Floyd's interactions with police, Cleve R. Wootson Jr.'s article about Floyd's experiences in prison, and Griff Witte's analysis of the historical backdrop of Floyd's life arc. Dozens of other *Washington Post* journalists, notably Holly Bailey, who covered the uprising in Minneapolis and Chauvin's murder trial, also contributed to the journalism that served as the foundation for this work.

The picture that emerged from the series and our subsequent year of reporting is that of a man facing extraordinary struggles with hope and optimism, a man who managed to do in death what he so desperately wanted to achieve in life: change the world.

During the fiery summer of activism that followed Floyd's demise, his name would be uttered by presidents, prime ministers, and the pope. His picture would appear on murals and in museums around the world. And his posthumous celebrity would force both those who knew him intimately and strangers who only saw him die to try to reconcile the man, the symbol he became, and the systems that hobbled his ambitions and stunted his chances.

Lawmakers, police departments, and corporations would invoke his name as they rushed to publicly associate themselves with the fight against racial injustice. Congressmembers would affix his name to legislation aimed at addressing the ills of American racism.

His name would become a rallying cry for a movement that declared that lives like his matter. White suburban moms would march in the street alongside poor Black boys to demand that their country treat them equally. Together, they would shout, "Say his name!" and then they would jointly respond to the prompt with anger, frustration, and resolve.

His name, they would declare, is George Floyd.

PART I

Perry

CHAPTER 1
An Ordinary Day

I T'S MEMORIAL DAY. Y'ALL wanna grill?"

George Perry Floyd Jr. wasn't particularly skilled at flipping burgers, but he was glad when his friend Sylvia Jackson suggested the diversion. The coronavirus pandemic had left him jobless and listless, a shadow of the gregarious man his friends and family once knew. He had been trying to avoid spending more time in the darkness, feeding the addiction he could not seem to escape.

Jackson's modest home in North Minneapolis served as a family-friendly refuge. In May 2020, Floyd would spend most days on her couch, watching *iCarly* and *Mickey Mouse Clubhouse* with her three girls. Other times, he'd help her craft TikTok videos in hopes that one day they might go viral.

"Let's do this one," she'd say, before dancing in her kitchen to the music of Mariah Carey's "Fantasy." Floyd would stare at the camera with mock-seriousness.

They were often joined by two friends who had worked with them at the Salvation Army, a quarantine quartet meant to keep one another company as they waited for the world to go back to normal. Jackson, thirty-two, rolled her eyes as Floyd would go on about chopped-and-screwed music, the hip-hop genre that emerged from his Houston hometown. In the evening, Floyd would talk throughout whatever movie they were watching, then shower her with questions about the plot afterward. Her daughters loved camping, so they sometimes set up tents and slept under the stars. Other nights, they'd throw some hamburgers and hot dogs on the grill and play music, which was the plan on May 25, 2020, the day George Floyd would die.

That day, Jackson had to work an eight-to-two shift as a security guard, so she tasked Floyd with picking up some lighter fluid and charcoal. She handed him the keys to her car, a 2001 navy-blue Mercedes-Benz SUV, and $60 to pay for supplies.

"I'll be back home around three," Jackson told him.

Jackson trusted Floyd; she had loaned him the car several times before. Floyd had no other plans, so he called his friend Maurice Hall around ten a.m. to see if he wanted to hang out. Many of Floyd's friends warned him about Hall, forty-two, who had been sleeping between hotels and his vehicle, dealing drugs while trying to avoid arrest warrants. Floyd had tried for years to move on from using, but Hall provided some kinship during this empty part of his life. The two men would smoke weed or ingest pills, which Floyd would chase down with Tylenol to dilute the impact.

This was not the life either had envisioned when they left Houston's Third Ward for Minneapolis, seeking sobriety and opportunity. Hall told Floyd that he felt he had exhausted his options. Outstanding warrants had driven him underground, and he didn't want to turn himself in to police—he was a father now, with freckled, curly-haired children, and he couldn't stomach the idea of being locked up far away from them. Floyd could empathize with Hall's predicament: he felt guilty being so far away from his young daughter, Gianna.

On the other end of the line, Hall told Floyd he had a day's worth of errands and suggested they complete his to-do list together. Hall was eager to jump into the Benz—he had been borrowing a friend's old truck ever since a woman he had hooked up with in his hotel room had driven off with his ride, taking his clothes, shoes, and video games with her.

Hall suggested that Floyd meet him at a LensCrafters at the Rosedale Commons shopping center off Interstate 35 in nearby Roseville. Floyd could then follow him back to his hotel to exchange vehicles.

"What do you mean I can't come in?" Floyd said to the sales representative when he arrived, turned away by the store's COVID-19 protocol.

Hall bought a pair of clear-framed glasses and then stepped outside, where he saw Floyd dressed in a dirty tank top and blue sweatpants.

"What up, gator?" Hall said, and the two shook hands.

It was close to noon by this point, so they stopped at a Wendy's across the street. Hall ordered a burger with onion rings; Floyd got a Dave's Double. After they carried the food to the Benz and unwrapped the sandwiches, Floyd took out his phone to show Hall a new trend in the world of Southern hip-hop.

"You know about sassa walking?" Floyd asked.

The men ate their burgers and watched music videos of the emerging sound—it contained the heavy, gritty beats of chopped-and-screwed songs, but rappers laced lighter, faster rhymes over the tracks. Some of the videos demonstrated the dance itself, which combined salsa steps with pelvic thrusts.

"It's gonna be big," Floyd said.

Next, they went to drop off Hall's borrowed truck and chilled in his hotel room at the Embassy Suites in Brooklyn Center, just on the other side of the Mississippi River. They ate Cheetos as Hall waited for some buyers to pick up drugs.

After someone came to pick up pills, Hall wanted to show off how successful he had become. He pulled out $2,000 in cash, telling Floyd he had made that much money in a single night. The display was more than a simple flex; Hall thought he might have a solution to Floyd's lingering malaise and hoped Floyd could use his connections in Houston to help boost his drug business. He said he believed he was offering Floyd a great opportunity. Floyd wasn't working; Hall had a bustling clientele, ready to pay.

But Floyd didn't give the idea too much thought, Hall recalled. He didn't want the drug game to be a part of his life ever again. He knew he was a bad hustler. And his last stint in prison had been so traumatizing that he was terrified of what might happen if he got caught up in it anew.

Hall also had to deliver drugs to buyers in different parts of the city, which was another reason he was happy to have Big Floyd around. Hall had become increasingly paranoid about driving himself to drug deals and thought Floyd could take the wheel. They made their way to another hotel twenty miles south, in Bloomington, where they ate sandwiches and drank Minute Maid Tropical Punch. Hall remembered Floyd smoking weed, snorting powdered fentanyl, and taking Tylenol.

As Hall fielded calls from potential buyers, Floyd was busy having conversations of his own. One of the people Floyd was communicating with that day was Shawanda Hill, his former lover.

"I want to see you," she texted him.

Back on the north side, Jackson returned to her house to find no charcoal, no lighter fluid, no car, no Floyd. Concerned by her friend's absence, she called to check in.

"Where are you?" Jackson asked.

"I'm about to see my girl," Floyd said. "I'll be back tonight."

Evening was beginning to fall, and Hall still wanted to drop off clothes at the dry cleaners, get a new cell phone, and shop for a tablet. He thought he could pick one up at a corner store on Minneapolis's south side called CUP Foods, which was known as a spot for buying and selling electronics for cheap. Floyd was a familiar face at CUP—managers said he'd stop by once or twice a week.

He told his old lover that he was on his way to the store. Hill, forty-five, was thrilled at that news—she needed to buy a new battery for her cell phone anyway, and she hoped to sneak a little Floyd time before picking up her granddaughter, whom she had promised to babysit that day. Hill boarded the #5 bus and headed down to the corner of East Thirty-Eighth Street and Chicago Avenue.

Hall and Floyd got to CUP Foods first. Hall walked to the back of the store, outside the view of the security cameras, and bought a tablet for $180. The manager said they needed some time to clean its hard drive, so instead of waiting around, Hall and Floyd headed about a mile north, to Lake Street, where Hall bought himself an iPhone 7.

It was close to seven thirty p.m. when the two friends circled back to CUP. Floyd parked the Benz across the street, and Hall went inside to pick up his tablet. He walked down the store's long, narrow aisles and past rows of fruits and vegetables to the electronics section, where locked glass display cases showcased tablets, laptops, and prepaid cell phones in bright green boxes. The cashier told Hall he needed to give him a refund because he had been unable to clear off the old files. Hall was still trying to figure out if there were any other options when Floyd came in a few minutes later. Floyd meandered around the front of the store, fumbling with cash in his pocket and saying hello to almost every employee he came across.

Floyd made his way through the aisles, passing display shelves that offered Oreo cookies and Little Debbie snacks. He then grabbed a half-rotten banana and said something to a teenage cashier, before bending over in a fit of laughter. The cashier, whose father was one of the store's owners, looked puzzled but shrugged it off and pointed his finger with a get-a-load-of-this-guy smirk.

Christopher Martin, another teenager behind the register, immediately noticed Floyd's size—six foot six, 225 pounds, bulging biceps—accentuated by the snugly fitting black tank top he was wearing. Martin asked him if he played baseball.

Floyd stuttered and rambled for a moment before responding that he played football. Martin, tall and slender with light-brown skin, had seen drunk and high customers come into the store before, and he thought Floyd might be under the influence.

Around that time, Hill walked inside and glimpsed Floyd's muscular silhouette.

"Oh my God, Floyd," she said.

"Baby," Floyd said, "I was just thinking about you."

He wrapped his arms around her, and she kissed him where her lips met his body: on his chest, at the valley of his tank top.

Hill, though, was surprised to see Floyd dressed that way, knowing his mother had taught him to look presentable when he was out on the street. Hill asked why he was wearing a tank top and baggy pants.

"I've been moving," Floyd explained. And before all the errands with Hall, Floyd said he had been playing basketball.

Floyd suggested that maybe they could head to a park and catch up. After Hill told him that she needed to watch her granddaughter, Floyd offered to give her a ride over there. Hill smirked.

"I was thinking I was going to get me some," she recalled.

Hill and Hall had never met each other before, but the trio ended up leaving the store together. Before they left, Floyd also bought a pack of menthol cigarettes.

"He gave him the money, I saw them take the money," Hill said. "They give him the cigarettes, and they give him the change. We walked out the store, went in the car, we were in the car, and we talked like, I don't know, a good eight minutes ..."

Back inside CUP Foods, Martin lifted the $20 bill above his head and held it up against a light. He noticed it had the bluish hue of a $100 bill and suspected it was a fake. He took the bill and showed it to his manager, who asked him to go outside and summon Floyd back to the store. Because Floyd was a regular at CUP, the manager figured it was a mistake that an old customer would be willing to fix.

Inside the Benz, both Hill and Hall sensed the day's errands were catching up with Floyd. While they were chatting, he started to fall asleep in the driver's seat—a trait his friends said was typical. Hall grew nervous. Because the corner was known for gang activity, he didn't want to draw the attention of any police.

"We gotta go from here," Hall said.

Just then, Martin and another teenage employee from CUP walked up to the car on the passenger's side. They told Hall that the boss wanted to see them because the money was counterfeit.

"I didn't give him that," Hall said.

The cashiers pointed to Floyd, who was still slouched over, struggling to stay awake, as the culprit.

"Floyd, did you really do that?" Hill asked in surprise, since Floyd was not known to cheat people out of money.

"Why is this happening to me?" Floyd said, before brushing off the requests to go back inside. Martin gave up and walked away with the other employee.

A few minutes later, Martin returned to the car with two other employees, again asking Floyd to come back inside. But Hill and Hall thought Floyd was too exhausted to understand what was happening.

"We kept trying to wake him up," Hill recalled.

She searched her pockets but didn't have any more cash on her. She apologized to the employees and promised that Floyd would speak to the manager as soon as he woke up.

After a few minutes, Floyd gathered his bearings. He shook himself and patted his pockets for the car keys.

"Floyd, look, that little boy said that money wasn't real," Hill told him. "They about to call the police."

They already had. She glanced across the street and saw two police officers walking into the store. Minutes later, they stepped out.

"They're moving around a lot," one of the officers said to his partner as they approached the car. He gripped his flashlight.

Inside the vehicle, Floyd had started to panic, still searching for the keys. Hall was panicking, too, knowing he had drugs in the car that he needed to hide.

"I'm stuffing and tucking," Hall recalled. "So, the next thing you know, the cop is on his side, all you hear is—boom!"

At the sound of the flashlight hitting the window, Floyd turned to the officer with the terrified look of a man whose mama had told him what could happen when a Black man encountered the wrong police officer.

CHAPTER 2
Home

FOR AS LONG AS anyone can remember, George Perry Floyd Jr. had wanted the world to know his name.

He was young, poor, and Black in America—a recipe for irrelevance in a society that tended to push boys like him onto its margins. But he assured everyone around him that, someday, he would make a lasting impact.

As a child, he had a simple way of letting people know when he wanted to be taken seriously: he would touch them on the forearm and look into their eyes to ensure he had their full attention. So his sister Zsa Zsa stopped what she was doing one day when thirteen-year-old Floyd rested his hand right above her wrist.

"Sis," he said. "I don't want to rule the world; I don't want to run the world. I just want to touch the world."

Zsa Zsa stood in stunned silence as Floyd walked off without elaborating, another tactic he used when he wanted to drive home a point. But she wasn't surprised. Floyd had always seemed to be trying to go somewhere, to find something different, to outrun his circumstances in order to reach a better place. In the hours after he was born at Cape Fear Valley Hospital in Fayetteville, North Carolina, on October

14, 1973, his mother marveled at his lanky limbs, zeroing in on the legs that had been running in place inside her womb. Stretching out from under a slender frame, those legs seemed to constantly be in motion, even from his first moments.

Barely a year later, and only days after he had begun to walk, Floyd had taught his feet how to chase his body with increasing speed. There was not much room to run around inside his family's tiny mobile home, so Zsa Zsa devised a game to take advantage of every inch of the cramped quarters.

Zsa Zsa, about seven years old at the time, would pick up her shirtless, diaper-clad brother and place him at the far end of a narrow hallway, telling him to stand still as she turned and walked to the other end. After a few paces, she would spin around with dramatic flair, landing on her knees as she faced him. Then, she would tap her palms against her thighs, signaling it was time for the game to begin.

"Come on running, come on running!" she would shout, beckoning Floyd to dash down the hallway.

Floyd, smiling and exuberant, would follow the command, toddling from side to side but never halting his forward motion before tossing himself chest-first into his sister's outstretched arms.

Zsa Zsa would catch him under his armpits and redirect his momentum upward, lifting her giggling younger brother over her head as she stood up.

In these moments, Zsa Zsa would glimpse pure joy radiating from her brother's face.

Back then, the Floyds lived at the Sleepy Hollow Mobile Home Park in north Fayetteville. Floyd's mother, Larcenia, and father, George Sr., had returned to North Carolina, the state where their ancestors had toiled for generations, after an attempt to chase stardom in New York had ended unceremoniously in the early 1970s. On their marriage certificate, she had listed her occupation as "Singer," an aspirational answer that belied her true source of income: domestic work. He had written down "Musician," though his musical talents had not produced the kind of stability the couple had desired as they raised two young daughters in crowded apartments in high-poverty neighborhoods like Crown Heights, Brooklyn, and Jamaica, Queens.

The one-way trip back to North Carolina had landed the Floyds closer to their roots and closer to their large families. There was hardly enough space in the Sleepy Hollow trailer for a family of five, especially one with an active one-year-old who liked to chase his toy truck around the confined lodgings.

Known to everyone as "Cissy," Larcenia Floyd had grown up in Goldsboro, one of fourteen children of H. B. and Laura Ann Jones, and she would occasionally take Floyd, Zsa Zsa, and their six-year-old sister, LaTonya, there to visit extended family and glimpse country life. As they drove, the cityscape of Fayetteville's bustling Hay Street would give way to quiet cotton fields, dirt roads, and tobacco farms. Upon arriving at their destination, they would encounter the three-room shack where Floyd's mother had grown up. The dilapidated structure was not much bigger than the trailer in Fayetteville, but it sat on an expanse of arable land that Floyd's sharecropping ancestors had tended for decades, surrounded by a coterie of cows, pigs, chickens, and an assortment of fruit trees.

Minutes after arriving, he would strip down into a more comfortable state, naked except for a diaper, with an empty milk bottle hanging from his mouth and his bare feet slapping against the wood floor.

"He was a pesky little rascal," recalled Floyd's aunt, Kathleen McGee. "But we all loved him."

As a toddler, Floyd paid little attention to the tokens of extreme poverty that marked his family—that had marked his people for generations—instead fascinating himself with the novelties of rural life.

Given the lack of running water inside the shack, Floyd would stand on a short platform outside and press down as hard as he could on a pump to unleash water from the ground, as Cissy had done as a child, and as Laura Ann still did, proudly, as a grandmother in her fifties. Barely potty trained, Floyd did not complain when his sisters took him down a narrow pathway to make use of the putrid outhouse that served in lieu of a modern plumbing system.

In Goldsboro, he was surrounded by feminine affection, doted on by his grandmother, mother, two sisters, and nine aunts. Two of Cissy's teenage sisters, Angela and Mahalia Jones, were especially enamored of their young, energetic nephew. The twin girls thought he resembled Flip Wilson, a comedian whose one-hour variety show on NBC was briefly one of the highest-rated programs in the country in the early 1970s. The most popular character on *The Flip Wilson Show* was Geraldine Jones, a sassy, flirtatious Southern woman whom Wilson portrayed by wearing a wig and colorful dresses. Speaking in a high-pitched voice, Wilson would send the live audience into hysterics when he delivered the character's signature lines.

Angela taught her nephew to mimic Geraldine Jones's catchphrases.

"What you see is what you get!" Floyd would shout, basking in the squeals of laughter he had sparked. "The devil made me do it!"

Realizing how easily he could make the people around him laugh, Floyd began to develop a reputation as a playful jokester, a trait that he would hone for the rest of his life.

Meanwhile, Selwyn Jones, Cissy's youngest sibling, who had been mercilessly bullied in school because of his freckled face and stutter, tried to toughen up his nephew. He would wrestle with Floyd in the yard outside the shack, not letting up on the boy who, in the summer of 1976, was just a few months shy of three years old.

But the roughhousing did not change the fact that Floyd was a mama's boy through and through. When he tired from scurrying around, he'd wrap an arm around his mother's leg or jump into her lap, bathing her in a flurry of kisses.

"Oh, kiss this other side," she'd say, playfully turning her opposite cheek to face him. "This side just got numb."

After obliging, he'd let his head settle against her chest until he drifted off. Cissy would let a smile creep across her face as she looked down at her firstborn son and rocked his sleeping body. Young Perry was healthy and growing, was curious about the world, and had the kind of love for his mother that stood out even then to family as something divine.

But as Cissy Floyd's trips to Goldsboro became more frequent and turned into extended stays, her sisters could see that something was amiss. Outwardly, she kept up appearances, cooking her signature dishes and cheerfully offering advice to her younger siblings, but in private, she confided to some of her sisters that she was hurting. Floyd's father had begun to fade from the picture, chasing his musical dream and the unsettled life that came along with it.

In the mid-1970s, George Perry Floyd Sr. spent increasing time performing as a guitarist for the Chocolate Buttermilk Band, a Fayetteville-based group that performed funk and R&B covers and played backup for Teddy Pendergrass, James Brown, and other artists. Cissy Floyd told her siblings she did not want to be the long-suffering wife of a wandering musician. As their relationship fell apart, she prepared to live as a single mother of three.

But it didn't take long for Cissy Floyd—tall, attractive, and sociable—to find love again. By 1977, she was dating a man named Philonise Hogan, who was stationed at Fort Bragg army base near Fayetteville. Their relationship lasted long enough for the couple to decide it was time for her to see his hometown.

Cissy and her children arrived in Houston and soon settled in a home that wasn't much bigger than the trailer they had left, a shotgun-style house on Tuam Street that the landlord had somehow managed to subdivide into two units.

Residents had nicknamed the neighborhood "the Bottoms," a reference to both its low-lying location on Houston's south side and its position on the socioeconomic ladder of the racially segregated city—it was the poorest section of one of the poorest wards in Houston. Due to a combination of discriminatory government housing policies, the enduring economic legacy of slavery and sharecropping, and the caste-like social order that governed America's race relations, almost everyone living in the Bottoms was Black.

By the late 1970s, Houston's Third Ward had lost much of

the luster that had made it the city's epicenter for Black culture and commerce for most of its history. When Houston was first incorporated in 1837, formerly enslaved Blacks had settled in its southeast quadrant—the third of the city's original four wards. After World War I, Blacks flocked to the area, tripling in population between 1910 and 1930 and supporting a wide range of thriving businesses.

But by the time the Floyd family arrived, middle-class Blacks were moving out of Third Ward, leaving behind a deteriorating neighborhood increasingly characterized by government neglect. The most prominent example of that neglect was the Cuney Homes housing project, where the Floyds secured a unit not long after landing in the Bottoms.

The 564-unit complex of low-slung brick buildings just southeast of Houston's downtown had opened in 1940 and was in a state of disrepair by the time the Floyd family arrived four decades later. The demographic makeup of Cuney Homes had hardly changed since it was first built—with a population that was 99 percent Black and most residents living well below the poverty line.

Inside, the buildings trapped heat during the summer and let in cold during the winter, so it was common to see scores of neighbors hanging outside on porches, under awnings that jutted from their shared roof. The porches opened onto grassy courtyards, with diagonal footpaths that connected the similar-looking apartment buildings.

Neighbors called the community "the Bricks," a reference to the masonry material of its facade and, for some, to the hard-knock life its residents endured. Wary of outsiders but fiercely loyal to fellow neighbors, the denizens of Cuney Homes watched one another's children grow up tossing basketballs into old milk crates that had been tied to telephone poles. Impromptu barbecues took place on humid summer evenings, with everyone within earshot invited. Children would ride their bikes in bunches through the neighborhood, sometimes branching off to explore the University of Houston or Texas Southern University, both just a short pedal away.

Boisterous dice games took place in front of the units against the concrete porches, as mice and roaches scurried between the dumpsters out back. As the 1970s turned into the 1980s, hustlers, junkies, and prostitutes became increasingly common sights in the alleyways and courtyards, with the sounds of gunshots and police sirens punctuating the night. The crack era had come to Houston, and the brick-shaped packages of cocaine being trafficked through Cuney Homes brought a wave of new problems.

Despite the challenging living conditions, Houston had started to feel like home for the Floyds. Zsa Zsa—who initially had cried every day after they first moved from North Carolina, telling her mother that she missed her friends, her aunts, and her husky-shepherd mix, Candy—had begun to warm up to her new environment. She and LaTonya were making friends in the housing project, where there were hundreds of children of similar means.

Floyd had begun elementary school and was developing the Texas drawl that he would keep into adulthood. As he searched for his voice, it did not take him long to start repeating the neighborhood's unofficial mantra, even if he was not yet fully aware of its meaning.

"One roof, one family," he would say, repeating the motto

of the older men in the Bricks who bonded over the shared struggle and communal culture of the townhome-style projects.

Meanwhile, his mother's home cooking had become the source of much fanfare across Cuney Homes, and hungry neighbors had in turn added an honorific to her name, spontaneously descending on unit 112-F when they learned "Miss Cissy" was making one of her famous soul food dishes—rice and beans, mustard greens and turkey necks, spaghetti with pork chops, and made-from-scratch corn bread that was as sweet as cake. She never turned anyone away, once even cooking dinner for a drunk man who had wandered into the Floyds' unit thinking it was his.

"You don't have to leave until you're ready to leave," Miss Cissy had told him while he sobered up on the couch.

But even with this sense of community and camaraderie, Miss Cissy, who had grown up surrounded by her real family, still felt a certain loneliness as she tried to build a life 1,200 miles away from the tobacco farms where she was raised. Worried that Zsa Zsa, LaTonya, and seven-year-old Perry Floyd would never have the kind of big-family experience she had had with her twelve siblings, she began looking for ways to convince her sisters back in North Carolina to move to Houston.

In the fall of 1981, Miss Cissy seized on the news that her younger sister Kathleen had planned to travel with her husband and two daughters on a cross-country road trip from North Carolina to Long Beach, California. She convinced the family to make a stop in Houston and then set out on a mission to get them to end the road trip there and settle in Third Ward.

She pitched Houston as a dynamic, fast-growing city—its population had grown almost 30 percent during the 1970s, to 1.6 million. The Texas Gulf Coast dwarfed eastern North Carolina both in its size and in the reach of its opportunities. Most importantly, she said, the children could all grow up together.

When it wasn't clear if the sales pitch was working, Miss Cissy spoke to her sister privately, in more candid terms.

"I don't have anybody here," she said softly.

"That's all I needed to hear," Kathleen McGee recalled from Houston, forty years after she and her husband ended their cross-country road trip midway.

The McGees initially lived with the Floyd family, giving Miss Cissy and her sister a chance to reminisce on their days growing up together in Goldsboro. They would laugh about the trouble they had gotten into in the 1950s as they tried to outsmart their parents, and the spankings they had received when their high jinks went awry.

Kathleen's daughters, Shareeduh and Tera, also brought stories from North Carolina. Shareeduh, about ten years old at the time, would tell her cousins about how their grandmother had assembled a veritable zoo on the farmland where she lived, with peacocks, pheasants, chickens, and other animals. There was even a monkey, though no one seemed to know how or why it had been acquired.

Floyd, now eight years old, would listen intently to the stories from the land of his ancestors. As Miss Cissy and his aunt Kathleen described what life was like for them when they were his age, they occasionally used the memories to drive home lessons for the present—admonitions that their own mother had passed down as she suffered under the harsh caprices of Jim Crow racism. The Jones family had often been cheated of their wages by White landowners after a season of sharecropping, and the message Miss Cissy imparted to her children mirrored the one she had been given as a young girl: don't give White people even the slightest opportunity to think you have done anything wrong, because they will make you pay for it.

Floyd's grandmother had also stressed education as a pathway out of poverty. At the beginning of the 1970s, they remembered, Laura Ann had instructed her twin daughters to fight their way onto a school bus after White students had tried to block integration efforts by intimidating their Black would-be classmates with taunts and insults.

Zsa Zsa, who had attended school in mixed classrooms in North Carolina in the years after her aunts had helped integrate the school system, had asked her mom why her new school in Houston was still segregated, with only Black students.

"Baby," Miss Cissy explained, "this is the ghetto."

"When I grow up, I'm going to be somebody special," Floyd sang along with his second-grade classmates in February 1982. *"Somebody special is who I'm going to be."*

It was Black History Month at Frederick Douglass Elementary School, and Waynel Sexton, a White teacher standing in front of a group of all-Black pupils, was leading the class in an aspirational song as part of a four-week curriculum celebrating African American culture and achievements.

Sexton, in her midthirties at the time, had grown up in Borger, Texas, a small, predominantly White town about an hour south of the Oklahoma border. Teacher Corps, a federal program designed to prepare educators to work in low-income communities, had placed her in Third Ward in 1970, just as Houston's public school system was sending hundreds of White teachers into all-Black schools, part of a court-mandated effort to speed up desegregation.

Each February, Sexton would teach her students about Jim Crow discrimination, sometimes using her own experience growing up as a White child in the 1950s and 1960s to explain the concept. She told the students in Floyd's class about a trip she had taken to the city with her family, when she saw segregated water fountains for the first time at a Neiman Marcus department store.

"There was a fountain that said 'Colored' and a fountain that said 'White,'" she said. "I thought it was going to be colored water. I just wanted to drink out of that fountain so badly. I thought it was going to be rainbows."

Floyd and the other students laughed.

Her naivete as a child stood in contrast to many of the students she was teaching, who experienced the vestiges of Jim Crow that had persisted into the 1980s in their daily lives. Though it was no longer openly advertised through "Colored" signs, police dogs, and burning crosses, there was little to shield the Douglass students from the fact that they were attending an underfunded all-Black school, living in a segregated ward, and dealing with many of the same indignities that had vexed their parents and grandparents.

Seeking to combat that feeling of generational stagnancy, Sexton put together a curriculum designed to engender a sense of Black pride and potential. In one lesson, she encouraged the students to envision their own lives following in the mold of historical African American icons such as Benjamin Banneker, Mary McLeod Bethune, and Charles Drew.

She handed Floyd and his classmates green, black, and red cardboard paper—colors of the pan-African flag—and explained the "Future Famous Americans" assignment. They were to write a short essay and draw a picture describing what they would be when they grew up.

The responses gave insight into how the seven- and eight-year-old children saw themselves in the early 1980s. Many of the girls wanted to be nurses, ballerinas, and teachers.

"When the bell rings, the children will leave. I will rest," one aspiring teacher wrote.

Police officers, musicians, and professional athletes were heavily represented among the boys, despite Sexton's efforts to highlight Black men who had been successful in other spheres.

One kid said he wanted to be president, writing an essay that reflected both the economic malaise of the last years of Jimmy Carter's presidency and the antigovernment ethos of President Ronald Reagan's first term.

"I will lower the prices of food. I will lower the prices of gas," he wrote. "I will not make that many budget cuts."

Floyd had been intrigued by a lesson about Thurgood Marshall, who had worked as a lawyer to end segregation in public schools and was serving as the nation's first Black justice on the Supreme Court at the time. For his assignment, he wrote that he also wanted to sit on the highest court in the land.

"When I grow up, I want to be a Supreme Court Judge," he wrote. "When people say 'Your honor, he did rob the bank,' I will say 'Be seated.' And if he doesn't, I will tell the guard to take him out. Then I will beat my hammer on the desk. Then everybody will be quiet."

He drew a picture of a robed judge with brown skin and a curly black Afro seated behind a large desk with a gavel in his hand.

In the essay, Sexton noted, Floyd had made appropriate use of punctuation and capitalization, with clear penmanship. He had spelled every word right—though eraser marks on the page showed that he had initially transposed the *d* and *g* in "judge," before correcting himself. The work was in line with the kind of student Floyd was at the time, Sexton recalled four decades later.

"He was a sweet boy," she said, noting that while the school had allowed paddling, Floyd largely stayed out of trouble. "He liked to go outside and run and jump, but he wasn't a difficult child at all."

When Floyd finished second grade, he was academically on par with national benchmarks, an achievement in a school where almost all the students qualified for free or reduced-price lunch, and many had trailed key metrics since kindergarten.

In a yellow-paged notebook, Sexton marked down the scores that Floyd and his twenty-three classmates had received on the Iowa Test of Basic Skills, a standardized exam they took at the end of the school year. Floyd had earned a 3.1 in reading, meaning his capabilities were representative of a standard student in the first month of third grade.

"He was right on level," she said.

He had earned a 3.1 in math and a 3.3 in reading comprehension.

Still, Sexton had been teaching at Douglass long enough to see even the brightest students "get lost" as they grew older, she said. They were often swept up in the vicissitudes of a neighborhood where the challenges of short-term survival could shroud the long-term benefits of an education.

She had reason to fear that Perry Floyd might end up as one of those students. In the same notebook where she had underlined his middle name and marked his test scores and grades, she had written down his address and a phone number for his mother. Next to the phone number she had added the word "neighbor." In a school where most of the students were poor, Sexton had come to know that the "neighbor" label signified an especially impoverished household, one in which the student's family could not afford a telephone.

Originally named Third Ward School, Douglass Elementary had opened after the Texas legislature passed a law in 1870 to create schools for Black children following the end of the Civil War.

The establishment of the first colored school in Houston enticed some Black families to relocate to Third Ward, and government officials in Texas soon concentrated similar facilities in the neighborhood in a bid to create a racially homogenous community cordoned off from the city's White neighborhoods.

In the 1920s, city officials opened the colored Jack Yates Senior High School and the Houston Negro Hospital in Third Ward, while closing or stripping funding for schools and facilities on the west side of the city that had previously catered to Black residents. The moves served to induce middle-class Black families who lived on the predominantly White west side to move to Third Ward.

When Houston prepared to build its first federally funded public housing project in the late 1930s, city leaders saw an opportunity to further entrench the racial segregation scheme they had designed for a diverse city that had been somewhat integrated at the turn of the twentieth century. They named the project after Norris Wright Cuney, a prominent Black politician who was born enslaved in 1846, and located it in the heart of Third Ward.

When Cuney Homes opened in 1940, it housed hundreds of Black porters, maids, chauffeurs, and other low-wage workers. Some of the residents had been forced to move from Houston's oldest Black community because city leaders wanted to raze their dwellings and develop Whites-only public housing in Fourth Ward, where more desirable tracts bordered downtown. One result of the so-called slum clearance was that domestics and drivers living in Cuney Homes had to cross Alabama Street—once the line separating Black neighborhoods from White ones in Third Ward—to work for White families but had to return to their side of town by sundown.

The White residents who lived inside Third Ward began moving out of the area after Texas State University for Negroes was constructed across the street from Cuney Homes in 1947. In response to a Supreme Court ruling that threatened to force the University of Texas to accept a Black applicant from Third Ward, the state legislature opted to instead create the historically Black college (later named Texas Southern University) to preserve segregation in higher education.

By the 1950s, Houston had joined most other major American cities in using federal housing dollars and policies to successfully segregate its population with enduring efficiency. Blacks, locked into urban ghettos, were often prevented from escaping even when they had the means. Redlining and restrictive covenants blocked Black families from accessing the home loans and real estate that would form the foundation of generational wealth for their White counterparts.

Much of the discrimination was sanctioned by the federal government, and the consequences have been lasting. An almost thirty-point disparity in homeownership rates between the two races has endured from the 1950s into the twenty-first century. In large part due to that disparity, the typical White family has consistently owned ten times as much wealth as the typical Black family, a gap that only widened over the course of Floyd's life.

Shortly before the Federal Housing Administration financed the Whites-only Levittown development of 17,500 homes in Long Island, New York, it backed the Oak Forest subdivision of almost five thousand homes in northwest Houston in 1946, the first such project to ban Black applicants.

When the Fair Housing Act of 1968 made that kind of blatant racial discrimination illegal, many middle-class Black families jumped at the opportunity to finally begin building wealth. They moved to neighborhoods with better amenities, often in the suburbs, leaving behind places like Third Ward. Their departure forced many businesses and services to shut down in Black communities, which quickly became exclusively low-income. The vicious cycle of disinvestment and decline would persist into the twenty-first century, as African Americans remained the most segregated racial group in the country.

Less than a month before George Floyd was born, President Richard Nixon decried many of the nation's public housing developments as "monstrous, depressing places—run down, overcrowded, crime-ridden, falling apart." He was less concerned that America's housing projects were also largely located in racialized slums, instead defending the rights of suburban residents to keep these developments far away.

By the time Floyd and his family moved to Cuney Homes a few years later, it suffered from many of the problems Nixon had described, ones that officials at all levels of government seemed content to ignore.

In the early 1980s, kids growing up in Cuney Homes repurposed a popular jingle from a Toys"R"Us commercial, creating a special version reflecting life in the Bricks.

"I don't wanna grow up, I'm a Cuney Homes kid," they would sing. *"They got so many rats and roaches I can play with . . ."*

Floyd initially struggled to make friends in the insular community. He was a quiet kid, and the residents were known to be wary of newcomers. It was not unheard of for outsiders to be accosted for showing up uninvited.

Floyd would spend hours by himself, tossing a basketball against the redbrick exterior of his building as if shooting it into an invisible hoop. He'd bite his fingernails as he passed the time alone.

As he grew taller and became more athletic, however, neighborhood kids and some teenagers would recruit him to join their pickup games. In the heat of competition, Floyd saw the hardened expressions of his young neighbors fade into easy smiles. Soon, he was being invited to hang out with them off the court as well. One of the kids, Gregory Lamont Dotson, gravitated toward Floyd because they were both tall, agile, and particularly gifted on the basketball court. Dotson lived in Cuney Homes and would come by to find Floyd when it looked like a game was about to start.

They would often be on the same team, using their size and power to own the court. Noting their similar height and complexion, other kids took to calling them the "twin towers." Floyd and Dotson embraced the moniker off the court as they spent more time together.

"Floyd and I was like brothers," Dotson recalled years later. "From the Cuney Homes to school, we were never apart."

Floyd started hanging out at the local YMCA, joining the Southside Cowboys peewee football team and signing up to play in an official youth basketball league, where he would compete against kids from across the city. The games were intense and personal, preparing the prepubescent boys for the high school rivalries between Third Ward and Fifth Ward students who competed for bragging rights within Houston's two largest historically Black communities.

Floyd was the starting center, and Dotson was the power forward. The duo helped the YMCA team dominate their league of fifth graders, beating their Fifth Ward competitors multiple times during the season.

After practice, Floyd, Dotson, and some of the other basketball players would hang out at the Blue Store, the local convenience store across the street from Cuney Homes. Officially named Scott Food Mart, it had gotten its nickname due to the blue paint of its exterior wall, which served as the backdrop to conversations, fights, and a disproportionate amount of police activity. Inside, it sold snacks, candy, beer, tobacco, lottery tickets, and other corner-store staples. It did not sell produce, but for those Cuney Homes residents without cars, it served as the closest option for groceries in the food desert that had formed around the Bricks.

Floyd and his teammates were standing inside the store

one day when they spotted a familiar-looking kid who was short, dark-skinned, and thin as a rail.

"That's the little dude from Fifth Ward," one of the Cuney Homes players said, identifying the boy as a point guard for their crosstown rivals.

Floyd's teammates planned to rough the boy up a little to let him know it wasn't a good idea to traipse through their turf by himself. But Floyd, who didn't like the idea of a group of ten-year-olds beating up a much smaller kid for no reason, objected and stood between his friends and the boy.

"No, man," he said. "Y'all tripping."

Floyd and Dotson decided to walk over and chat up the kid. When they learned that he had just relocated from Fifth Ward to Cuney Homes, they offered to escort him home. It was a chance for them to hear more about their new neighbor and to protect him from the guys who had not yet fully abandoned their plan to harass him.

He told them his name was Milton Carney, adding that everyone called him "PoBoy."

The nickname, short for "poor boy," was one that the other kids—also poor—used to delineate his particularly conspicuous poverty.

When they got to PoBoy's unit, Floyd tried to recruit him to join the Third Ward's YMCA squad. He assured PoBoy that the other guys would have a change of heart once he crossed over to become their teammate. Some of the players who would lose playing time to him might complain, Floyd acknowledged, but they could figure that all out later.

"Man, you ain't got to worry about them," Floyd said. "They can be mad."

PoBoy eventually agreed to join the team and would

become part of a squad of boys Floyd hung out with around the Bricks, at the Blue Store, and at Ryan Middle School, where they played basketball after enrolling as sixth graders the following year, in 1985.

"We was just glued to the hip," PoBoy recalled years later. "He always was the biggest person on the team, and I always was the littlest person."

PoBoy, who didn't have any biological siblings, started referring to Floyd as his brother, with the two spending almost every afternoon together. He was more talkative than Floyd and, despite being scrawny, was quicker to pop off at the mouth or jump into a fight with other kids. Floyd, who turned heads at Ryan Middle School as one of the few students who stood confidently above six feet, often found himself trying to cool his friend's quick temper. The alliance worked well, as PoBoy's smooth-talking ways helped Floyd meet girls, and Floyd's more laid-back demeanor kept his friend from getting into too many skirmishes. But the partnership faced a dilemma a few months after they started middle school, when PoBoy's mom told him she was moving back to Fifth Ward.

When they realized the impending move would require a transfer out of Ryan Middle School, Floyd came up with an idea. He told PoBoy to come over to his house.

When Miss Cissy had met her son's friend for the first time, she had been bewildered by his strange nickname, which sounded like an insult.

"Why they call him PoBoy?" she had asked.

"Because he skinny, Mama," Floyd had responded. "Look how little he is."

She gave the kid a once-over, accepting the point.

"Well, got to give him some of this country food."

But now, Floyd was proposing a more permanent position for his friend at their dinner table.

"We don't want to split up," Floyd told his mother. "Can Po just stay over here with us so he can still go to Ryan?"

To their surprise, she agreed. Miss Cissy called PoBoy's mom and worked out an arrangement where he would sleep over on school nights.

"I told you, man," Floyd said to his friend as they prepared to begin rooming together. "My mama got us."

At the time, Floyd's household was already overflowing with occupants. Miss Cissy had given birth to two more sons after arriving in Houston—Philonise Jr. and Rodney—whose hefty appetites added to an already stretched grocery budget. Her relationship with their father, whom she had moved to Houston to be with, had proved ephemeral, and she found herself trying to make ends meet as a single mother of five. The cost of caring for her family often exceeded the income she earned working at Guidry's Fast Food & Game Room, a popular burger joint located just outside Cuney Homes.

Veronica DeBoest, a neighbor who noticed the challenges the Floyds were facing, would occasionally take bags of food over from a charity summer lunch program that had been set up for kids in Third Ward. When the program had leftovers, DeBoest would take a backpack full of sandwiches, cereal, milk cartons, and fruit snacks and pour the contents out onto Miss Cissy's dining table.

Things were especially tight for Miss Cissy in the mid-1980s, as President Reagan pushed to scale back federal aid to the indigent, including cuts to the federal school lunch program and other welfare aimed at supporting low-income children. During his inauguration in 1981, Reagan had declared that "government is not the solution to our problem; government is the problem," pledging to slash the social safety net for families like the Floyds.

Following through on that pledge over the ensuing years, he campaigned for reelection by asserting that the strategy had worked. It was "morning again in America," he boasted in 1984, pointing to the rapid rise in economic growth that had followed his program of tax cuts and other supply-side policies. The nation's economy expanded by 7.2 percent that year, the highest total in more than three decades, but the boom times mostly eluded communities like Cuney Homes, where Miss Cissy continued to struggle financially.

In fact, much of the growth was benefitting those who were already wealthy, while people in public housing and on public assistance were deemed undeserving "welfare queens." Reagan's tax legislation eliminated most deductions for consumer loans but protected the deduction for mortgage interest, further skewing the benefits of the tax code toward people who owned their homes rather than toward renters like the Floyds. Meanwhile, the minimum wage held steady through most of the 1980s at $3.35, as Reagan opposed the kind of increases that could have benefitted Miss Cissy and the other fast-food workers at Guidry's. While the wage gap between Blacks and Whites had been shrinking during the 1970s, it increased during the 1980s: average annual income rose by 3.5 percent during Reagan's first term, according to a study by the Urban Institute, yet Black families saw their income fall by 3.7 percent.

As Miss Cissy put in more hours at work to keep the household afloat, she often left her teenage son in charge of his younger brothers. Floyd, who had grown up eating food cooked by Zsa Zsa when their mom was away, began to take responsibility for feeding Rodney and Philonise, who went by PJ.

While Floyd knew he couldn't replicate the mouthwatering meals his older sister had made for him when he was their age—seasoned potato wedges, chicken-fried steak patties with lettuce and Miracle Whip, and pitchers of cherry Kool-Aid with sliced lemon—he still took his task seriously.

When his brothers grew tired of Floyd's banana-and-mayonnaise sandwiches, he tried his hand at the gas stove in the apartment's tiny kitchen. He was not a very good cook, and Rodney and PJ—both barely old enough to have started elementary school—let him know it.

Floyd was fixing a breakfast of eggs, toast, and bacon one day when the apartment started to fill with the scent of burning meat. The overcooked food did not stop Floyd from confidently presenting his creation to his brothers.

"Here's your plate," he said, handing Rodney the meal.

"It's burnt," Rodney replied, before lifting a blackened strip of bacon with his fork. Taking a bite, he scrunched his face in disgust and then threw the charred remnants to the floor.

"What are you doing?" Floyd asked, noting that he had put a lot of time into cooking the breakfast.

"Your food is nasty," Rodney said curtly, before turning to his other older brother. "PJ could make that better than you."

Rodney and PJ laughed, leaving the breakfast uneaten and their older brother irritated.

"That's why I don't like watching y'all," Floyd said.

When it was time to clean up, Floyd would appeal to his brothers' competitive nature.

"Hey, you guys going to wash the dishes, right? Time yourselves."

He'd then officiate as they raced each other to clean up the dishes and wipe down the kitchen.

Unable to afford laundry detergent, they would use the same dish soap to wash their clothes in the bathroom sink on school nights. After thoroughly kneading their socks and underwear against the sink and squeezing out the filth, they would hang them over the water heater, hoping everything would dry before the next morning. When that didn't work, they would put the clothes in the oven, an improvised speed dryer for kids without access to laundry machines.

Seeing himself as the man of the house, Floyd would sometimes intersperse life lessons into those chores and other daily mundanities. Even as PJ sometimes competed with him for dominance—like when he would try to grab the biggest piece of chicken from the table before his older brother— Floyd wanted to show his siblings how to navigate a world in which their very bodies could be viewed by strangers as a threat.

"Why do you do that?" PJ asked him one day after he observed Floyd enter a room and greet each person one by one, shaking their hands and exchanging brief pleasantries.

"I can't go in a room like you, because of my size," he replied. "People look at me and they're nervous and scared. So I open up to them and let them know I'm okay. I'm a good person."

In the rugged world of Houston's south side in the 1980s, day-to-day survival could sometimes feel like something worth celebrating. The crack cocaine epidemic was ravaging the

Bricks with the twin vices of addiction and violence. Nationwide, the homicide rate for Black males aged fourteen to seventeen more than doubled between 1984 and 1989, according to a Harvard study that linked the increase to the spread of cocaine. Floyd grew from an eleven-year-old boy to a sixteen-year-old adolescent during that tumultuous stretch, avoiding much of the drug game's perils due to his focus on sports. But away from the courts and fields, trouble seemed to lurk on every corner.

In the late 1980s, Houston's Fox television affiliate, KRIV, started an investigative unit that reported on the growing problems of crime and drug use in the city with documentary-style flair. Its ominous title, *City Under Siege*, reflected the prevailing view about life in Houston's urban core during Floyd's teenage years. The KRIV reporters profiled addicts, followed cops on drug raids, and conducted jailhouse interviews, with much of the activity centered around Third Ward. In the period before reality television, Floyd and his friends would watch the show each Sunday evening, checking to see if any of their neighbors had been featured among the besieged or the besiegers.

Miss Cissy tried to spare her children from the kind of lifestyle that might land them on such a show, stressing the importance of focusing on their education and etiquette. She would force them to read books, preside over impromptu spelling competitions, and sometimes publicly correct their grammar.

"Hey, you can speak this ghetto language, but you got to speak the King's English," she'd say.

There was one message that she emphasized specifically to her carefree, go-with-the-flow eldest son, who by age fourteen had become a popular figure in the neighborhood: stay out of trouble, and respect the police.

As Reagan's war on drugs ramped up, a growing number of young men in the Bricks were falling into the crosshairs of the Houston Police Department's narcotics squad. Nicknamed the "Jump Out Boys" by folks in Third Ward, the plainclothes officers were known to speed through the housing project, hop curbs, and fly out of their cruisers to search the pockets of any boy hanging outside.

That kind of aggressive policing, which was happening throughout the country, had inspired the rap group N.W.A— short for Niggaz Wit Attitudes—to release the song "Fuck Tha Police" in the summer of 1988, decrying racial profiling and law enforcement corruption in vulgar terms. Like millions of other young boys who felt they could relate to its defiant tone, Floyd and his crew appreciated the song's sentiment. But Miss Cissy had taught her sons a different standard for dealing with the authorities: always comply, always be respectful, make it home alive.

They were young Black males from the lowest socioeconomic bracket, a status that she knew left them susceptible to a gauntlet of potential hazards. A simple mistake could cost them their freedom; a moment of carelessness could cost them their lives.

"Growing up in America, you already have two strikes," she told Floyd and his brothers. "And you're going to have to work three times harder than everybody else if you want to make it in this world, because nobody is going to look out for you. You're going to have to look out for yourself."

The origins of that sentiment could be traced back across two centuries of abuse and exploitation in Floyd's family line, where the raw, limiting power of racism had left a permanent sting. From the first moments they arrived on America's shores, Floyd's ancestors had formed the roots of a family tree poisoned by the compounding impact of racial oppression that had endured through generations.

Miss Cissy knew better than most that Floyd would have to battle to outrun that history, that he would forever be chased by the ghosts of the past that had been closing in on him from the moment he was born.

CHAPTER 3

Roots

Born enslaved in 1857, George Floyd's great-great-grandfather Hillery Thomas Stewart spent his childhood working without pay in the sizzling fields of Harnett County, North Carolina. But by the end of the nineteenth century, after more than thirty years working as a free man, he had managed to amass five hundred acres of his own farmland. The expansive acreage in Grove Township was a source of pride for Stewart's family—a symbol that hardworking free Blacks, if allowed ownership over their labor, could achieve self-sufficiency and success in the American South.

Neither his birth into bondage nor his inability to read had prevented him from becoming as wealthy as many former slaveowners who had once reigned over Harnett County with braided-leather whips. Back in 1860, for example, less than 2 percent of White farmers in North Carolina held more than five hundred acres of land. After emancipation in 1865, Stewart and his family soon climbed the ladder of upward mobility that had been denied to them during slavery.

Working alongside his twelve siblings during the brief Reconstruction period in which Blacks received some federal protection from racial terror and discrimination, Stewart came to understand the long-term value of owning the kind of land his family had nourished without compensation for generations. In the late 1860s and into the 1870s, the Stewart family's fifteen-member crew constituted a workforce that would have rivaled that of an upper-middle-class slaveowner in eastern North Carolina. Census records show that all the Stewarts above the age of eight were engaged in work as "farm laborers." The Stewarts' long days of pulling cash crops from the earth were no doubt tempered by the fact that the fruit of their efforts now accrued to their own coffers instead of to a merciless master.

As a teenager, Stewart had displayed a knack for independence and industriousness, his descendants said. Working with his father, he learned the intricate science of crop harvesting and had an intuitive sense for whether a plot of land would yield profit. In 1888, Stewart married an eighteen-year-old woman named Larcenia, with whom he would have twenty-two children. Following his father's example, the large family turned farmland into steady revenue, eventually using their earnings to purchase tracts of property along the east side of the Black River near present-day Coats, North Carolina. The portfolio of properties would have made him one of the largest Black landowners in that part of the state, according to property records from the Harnett County Register of Deeds.

"He was the first Black man in Harnett County to own five hundred acres of land," said his great-granddaughter Kathleen McGee.

His wealth attracted a measure of acclaim and, with it, the collective ire of his White neighbors. Behind his back, they called him "the rich nigger," according to family history that passed down through several generations. The vitriol signified his White neighbors' discomfort with the level of prosperity he had achieved. It would not be long before Hillery Thomas Stewart would come to know the risks of openly defying the racial order that had governed America with ruthless efficiency from its earliest days.

In 1748, a twenty-year-old reverend's son named Charles Stewart boarded a fifty-foot sailboat in Scotland headed for the New World. Stewart, who was White, had grown up as a Presbyterian Scot and, perhaps seeing little future for himself in a country dominated by the British government, decided to join the mass migration of Europeans heading to North America in the mid-eighteenth century.

Like many new immigrants of limited means, Charles Stewart began his time in colonial America as an indentured servant, working without pay to cover the cost of his voyage. After toiling as a cattleman for about a year, he was released from servitude and married a Welsh woman named Hannah Kirk, according to written and oral family history. The young couple did not have much, but the speed with which they were able to build a comfortable life spoke to the promise that America held as a land of opportunity—at least for its White residents. The two settled on Neills Creek, near present-day Coats, North Carolina, and soon secured cheap land for farming tobacco, corn, potatoes, and other crops. Their decision to leave behind family and country was validated as they transitioned into a middle-class life characterized by the ownership of land, furniture, and fellow human beings.

The family's wealth only grew as America declared its independence and fought a bloody war against the British. Before he died, Charles Stewart deeded most of his estate to his youngest son, James, in 1805. The list of properties Charles granted to James "for his advancement in this life" included "one negro woman named Cloe," according to a copy of the deed.

A first-generation American born a year before the signing of the Declaration of Independence, James Stewart quickly established himself as one of the richest men in southern Wake County—his vast plantation was located just across the border from Harnett County. His net worth increased tenfold between 1850 and 1860, when records list his occupation as a farmer—though his jump in wealth coincided with his growing involvement in the increasingly lucrative slave trade. Stewart used his fortune to spoil his ten daughters and one son, while making money as a slaver by separating Black parents from their children on the auction block.

Slavery had become crucial to the broader family fortune, as the wealth it produced passed down to successive generations. By 1860, Charles Stewart's grandson Joseph Stewart claimed ownership of fifteen enslaved Blacks, Census figures show. While the record does not list the enslaved by name, the gender, color, age, and location of one of them match that of Abram Stewart, the father of Hillery Thomas and the great-great-great-grandfather of George Floyd.

The fate of both groups of Stewarts—the slaveholding Whites and the enslaved Blacks who bore their owners' surnames—hung in the balance as the 1860 presidential election sought to address the national agitation over the brutal system of bondage that underpinned the South's economy.

When Abraham Lincoln, who had opposed expanding slavery, won the race, Southern Whites immediately began planning a revolt. Joseph Stewart was one of the thousands of slaveowners who took up arms and pledged allegiance to the new Confederacy. In 1862, he left his home to join the Confederate forces, enlisting as a corporal with North Carolina's Thirty-First Infantry Regiment.

For the next three years, Union and Confederate troops engaged in vicious combat, with the death toll rising unabatedly. When the Confederate Army surrendered in the spring of 1865, Joseph Stewart was among the thousands of White masters across the South who had to inform their enslaved namesakes that they were no longer bound to them as property.

Since the first Africans had arrived in colonial Virginia in 1619, about ten million Black people had been enslaved in America, contributing more than four hundred billion hours of unpaid labor to the nation's economy. Hillery Thomas Stewart and his family were among the four million who were still alive, and suddenly free.

Emancipation had granted the enslaved Stewarts freedom, but with no land or money, their options were limited. State laws passed in the aftermath of Nat Turner's deadly slave rebellion in 1831 had forbidden enslaved Blacks from learning to read, limiting their job prospects when slavery ended. Like most freed Blacks at the time, the Stewarts continued to work on White-owned farms, now as sharecroppers receiving pay and lodging in exchange for their labor.

The wealth the Stewarts were able to accrue was notable given the circumstances and limited support available to former slaves across the South. Sensing that freed Blacks would need some level of assistance after the Civil War, Congress had set up the Freedmen's Bureau, which was ostensibly designed to help freed Blacks transition from slavery by providing legal support and other protections, but in North Carolina it proved to be of little use to Black families like the Stewarts.

After the war, which had decimated crops across the state, both Whites and Blacks faced the ills of poverty and starvation. The Freedmen's Bureau issued more than five hundred thousand rations in North Carolina between July and September of 1865. But almost all the government-funded provisions went not to freedmen and -women but to the White relatives of deceased Confederate soldiers, according to the National Archives and Records Administration. Less than 1 percent of the aid went to freed Blacks—about five thousand rations for a population of more than three hundred thousand people.

Despite the lack of federal aid, Hillery Thomas Stewart and his family had amassed $100 in personal property and $70 in land by 1870, a net worth equivalent to about $3,500 in today's currency. It was not a large amount, but in 1870 that level of wealth would have put the Stewarts in the top 5 percent of Black families in the South, according to an analysis of Census records by Loren Schweninger, a history professor emeritus at University of North Carolina–Greensboro. In his book *Black Property Owners in the South: 1790–1915*, Schweninger documented that only 4.8 percent of Black families owned any land in 1870, and only forty-one thousand of the South's nine hundred thousand Black families, or less than 5 percent, had a net worth of more than $100. Five years after the Civil War, the average Black person in the South controlled $76 of wealth, compared to $2,034 for Southern Whites.

But by the end of the nineteenth century, an increasing number of Black landowners were beginning to close the gap.

Hillery Thomas Stewart stood as one prominent example, and his acquisition of hundreds of acres of land became an unwelcome development in Harnett County just as the arc of the nation's political universe was bending back toward White hegemony.

Reconstruction had essentially ended after Republican Rutherford B. Hayes agreed to withdraw the last federal forces from the South in exchange for a favorable resolution to the stalemated 1876 presidential election. North Carolina and other Southern states were free to enforce restrictive Jim Crow laws that criminalized a range of behaviors by Black residents, from intermarriage to sitting in Whites-only train cars.

Against that backdrop, Stewart's landholdings became a target of unscrupulous businessmen and local officials, according to family oral history and local news accounts from the time. Stewart had envisioned passing the real estate down to his descendants and creating the kind of generational wealth his ancestors could only have dreamed of. Instead, the land was taken from him before he could make even one intergenerational transfer.

In a series of transactions involving complex financial instruments that Hillery and Larcenia Stewart were purported to have signed their names to, the land was stripped from George Floyd's great-great-grandparents in the early 1900s. They would have been unable to read the agreements, and it is not clear if they understood their ramifications. Some of the documents included technical clauses that allowed the property to be sold off at auction if the Stewarts failed to follow them to the letter.

"But if default shall be made in the payment of said bond, or the interest on the same, or any part of either, at maturity, then and in that event it shall be lawful ... to sell said land herein before described, to the highest bidder for cash," one of the documents read.

In order to keep the hundred-acre tract of land covered by the agreement, Hillery Thomas Stewart would have had to pay off the $350 bond it secured—more than $10,000 in today's currency—by January 1, 1905, which at the time was less than nine months away. He never did, and the farmland was auctioned off at the county courthouse. It joined at least four other tracts that were removed from his ownership, until he was propertyless.

In 1920, the Harnett County government sold the remainder of Stewart's landholdings. The April 15, 1920, edition of the *Harnett County News* reported that the twenty-four-acre property in Grove Township was set to be auctioned off due to unpaid taxes. Hillery Thomas Stewart, the paper said, had not paid the property's $18.83 tax bill for the previous year. His descendants have disputed that allegation, pointing to the history of Black land loss due to fraudulent tax auctions.

The land was certainly worth more than the disputed tax amount. An ad placed in the same newspaper that day by England Realty and Auction Co. declared, "Wanted: Farm Lands," highlighting the strong demand for arable property at the time.

"If you have a farm or other real estate you wish to turn into quick cash, we would like to hear from you," the ad read. "Farm lands are selling better now than ever before. The sooner you sell, the more you will get."

The average cost of an acre of farmland in Harnett County reached a record $62 in 1920, up 240 percent from the previous decade, according to the U.S. Department of Agriculture.

The twenty-four acres Stewart lost that year over $18.83 in allegedly unpaid taxes would have been worth about $1,488, the equivalent of more than $20,000 today. If Stewart had not lost the hundreds of other acres he owned previously, including more than two hundred acres the local sheriff sold away at a previous tax auction, his net worth in 1920 would have exceeded $30,000—roughly $400,000 in modern currency.

Stewart's land loss was emblematic of what was happening across the South at the time. Between 1910 and 1997, Black farmers lost control of more than 90 percent of their farmlands, according to the Department of Agriculture. Much of the land was taken through fraud, deception, and violence—and almost all of it ended up under White ownership, where it remains today.

In North Carolina and throughout the South, the seizure of Black-owned land was part of a broader movement of political and economic reprisal that took hold between the end of the nineteenth century and the early years of the twentieth century. From the 1896 *Plessy v. Ferguson* Supreme Court ruling sanctioning racial discrimination to the murderous looting of Tulsa's Black Wall Street in 1921, the message to Blacks was clear: America was, and should forever be, a White man's country.

More than two thousand people had gathered at a rally in Grove Township on Friday, November 4, 1898, just four days ahead of the state and local elections that Southern Democrats had cast in explicit racial terms. A large American flag flew high overhead with the words "White Government" emblazoned in bold letters over the Stars and Stripes.

Joseph Stewart, the former Confederate soldier and

owner of his Black namesakes, had helped organize the event, which was designed to build support for the "White man's ticket" of Democrats and push back against some of the political and economic gains Blacks had been making in the region. During Reconstruction, Stewart had taken to politics, joining his comrades in shifting the fight for white supremacy from the battlefield to the ballot box.

"Whenever a man was found who favored negro rule or carpetbag domination, he found in Joe Stewart an implacable enemy," his friend D. H. McLean wrote in a sketch of his life decades later.

Determined to push back against Blacks' postwar gains in political influence, Stewart saw the 1898 elections as a pivotal opportunity to endow his racist views with the power of policy-making. Now fifty-seven years old, with a lengthy beard and balding pate, he gazed out over the crowd with piercing blue eyes. He had composed a special anthem for the campaign rally.

Two dozen young White men and women began singing his lyrics to a version of "Rally 'Round the Flag, Boys" to great applause, according to an article in *The County Union* newspaper:

> *Negro and pie is now all the cry,*
> *Shout, shout the joyous notes of freedom*
> *With young Oliver and old Dr. Cy,*
> *Shout the joyous notes of freedom.*
>
> *Our rights forever, hurrah! Hurrah!*
> *Down with the Negro, raise the stars and Stripes.*
> *O! we'll rally 'round the flag boys,*
> *We'll rally once again . . .*

> *We'll oust the nigs in Newbern and*
> *Wilmington, too,*
> *Shout, shout the joyous notes of freedom,*
> *Greenville and Kinston are coming in too,*
> *Shout, shout the joyous notes of freedom . . .*

The racist song continued with additional references to candidates in the upcoming elections, with more vitriol directed toward Black North Carolinians and those who supported them.

The reference to ousting Black political leaders in Wilmington was more than a whimsical flourish. Wilmington did not have scheduled municipal elections until the following year, but the very same week, White men in that city were planning an insurrection against the biracial Republican-Populist government that had grown out of the political alliance between small farmers, Black voters, and White transplants from the North.

Wilmington had been a source of angst among racist Whites in part because it had become a mecca of sorts for Black cultural and political advancement. Blacks in that part of eastern North Carolina freely served as doctors, businessmen, aldermen, magistrates, and in other top posts—to the growing irritation of wealthy Whites who had once claimed exclusive access to elite society.

A group of White men in the city had drafted a "Declaration of White Independence," saying, among other things, that they would no longer submit to Negro political power and that Whites should be given jobs currently held by Blacks.

On November 10, 1898, they launched a bloody attack on Wilmington's historically African American neighborhoods, shooting and beating residents over the course of several hours. The uprising reportedly killed at least a dozen Blacks and terrorized thousands, with rioters demanding that the bodies of the slain be left in the street as a warning to others.

By four p.m., the city's Republican mayor, police chief, entire board of aldermen, and other elected officials from the biracial governing coalition had handed in their resignations, fearing for their lives and hoping to end the bloodshed. At the time, more than one hundred armed men were roaming the corridors of city hall. To complete the coup d'état, the men who had drafted the Declaration of White Independence selected new city leaders from among their own ranks.

Before the riot ended, thousands of Black residents who had witnessed the carnage gathered their belongings and fled Wilmington—packing the roads from the city and running into the neighboring swamps outside town. Others, including Black businessmen and leaders, were banished from town by the new government.

Wilmington, which had been a predominantly Black city before the riot, saw Whites reclaim the majority almost overnight. It would be decades before the city elected another Black person to office. The riot, which received broad news coverage throughout North Carolina, would have stood as a warning to Hillery Thomas Stewart and other successful Blacks about the futility of trying to live on equal terms with their White neighbors.

At the state capitol, North Carolina legislators were preparing to show what could be done with the kind of political power the Wilmington rioters had just seized. After Democrats won control of both chambers of the legislature during the 1898 elections, they quickly instituted the white supremacy agenda they had campaigned on. Following in the footsteps of other Southern states, they passed Jim Crow laws requiring more severe racial segregation and put in place curbs on voting that would cut off Blacks' access to political power for generations.

Led by a Wilmington legislator who had been installed after the coup, North Carolina passed a new voting law in 1899 that mandated a poll tax, and a constitutional amendment in 1900 required a literacy test for all prospective voters. To protect the rights of poor Whites who couldn't read, the amendment included a "grandfather clause" for illiterate voters whose lineal ancestors were eligible to vote as of January 1, 1867.

The changes helped secure White hegemony across the South for decades. North Carolina's George Henry White, the sole Black member of Congress at the beginning of the twentieth century, lamented the turn of events during one of his final speeches on the House floor.

"This, Mr. Chairman, is perhaps the Negroes' temporary farewell to the American Congress," White declared on January 29, 1901, a few weeks before he left office. "But let me say, phoenixlike he will rise up someday and come again."

No other Black person from the South would serve in Congress until 1973, the year George Floyd was born.

When Hillery Thomas Stewart lost his land and wealth during this era of White backlash at the beginning of the twentieth century, he was physically, politically, and legally powerless to contest the forces of racial hate and history. As a Black man who could not read, he would have been barred from voting for the judges, county officials, and local sheriffs who were responsible for enforcing real estate laws and upholding property rights.

Driving home the skewed power dynamics of that era, Joseph Stewart had campaigned in 1898 to be Harnett County's register of deeds, a position that would have given him authority to sign off on land deals and settle real estate disputes. He was defeated by another white supremacist candidate, who went on to oust the Republican incumbent and sign the very deeds that stripped Hillery Thomas Stewart of his landholdings.

Though he lost his bid for register of deeds, Joseph Stewart returned to his role as a local postmaster general and continued to act as a top organizer in Harnett County Democratic politics. His descendants and relatives would go on to be business executives and community leaders.

As the White Stewarts continued to gain wealth and influence in successive generations, their Black namesakes were forced to start over, essentially from scratch. After losing his land, Hillery Thomas Stewart soon fell ill and lived the rest of his life in poverty. He battled a case of arteriosclerosis and was diagnosed in 1927 with cardiorenal syndrome, which he lived with for a decade before dying on October 20, 1937, at the age of eighty.

His children told their children that he suffered from another untreated malady: depression. He spent the last decades of his life demoralized over the loss of his land and his inability to pass on wealth to his descendants.

His death certificate said he had been engaged in a single profession for sixty-five years: "dirt farming." He was buried in that same dirt, leaving nothing to his children but the cautionary tale of his life as a former slave who had once known wealth but died a pauper.

*

Hillery Thomas Stewart Jr. had few options but to work on White-owned farms for meager wages after his father's death in the fall of 1937. The tenant farming system that developed across the South in the decades after the Civil War maintained much of the economic structure that had been in place during slavery. In rural North Carolina, it was one of the few employment options available for landless Blacks, and it became a family business of sorts for the descendants of Hillery Thomas Stewart Sr. in the decades after his land loss.

Under the system, White landowners would rent small tracts of their farms to Black tenants, along with the necessary seed, equipment, and food. The tenants would begin the season indebted to the landowner and spend the next few months harvesting the crops in an attempt to pay off the debt and earn an income. At the end of the season, the tenant family would typically sell its crops at a price determined by the landowner and learn whether they had worked hard enough to cover the expenses—which were also set by the landowner.

Sharecropping was ripe for abuse, and many Black families were stuck in an economic sand trap that left them hardly better off than their enslaved ancestors. At the end of harvest season, White landowners often told their tenants that, after tallying up the expenses and the crops, they had come out even—or, worse, that they were further in debt. Black tenant farmers in the early- and mid-twentieth century would have had little legal recourse to challenge their employers and often were forced to choose between accepting the abuse or picking up and moving with their families to another farm.

On September 14, 1924, Hillery Thomas Stewart Jr.

married Sophell Suggs, a sturdy churchgoing woman who cleaned the homes of White families for fifty cents an hour.

When she wasn't at church, Sophell could be found caring for the children of her White employers. Some nights, she would plait her daughter's hair into a French braid and cover it with a stocking cap before kissing her and telling her the hairstyle would have to last for the next week. Then she would leave before dawn the following morning to make breakfast for the family she worked for, always entering through the back door. She would continue her domestic duty as a live-in maid and nanny until the following weekend.

Hillery Thomas Stewart Jr., a quiet man known by family as Tom, spent almost all his time sharecropping and raising pigs on farms owned by others. As the couple's work obligations kept them mostly away from their home, few were surprised when their only daughter, Laura Ann, revealed to her family that she was pregnant at age fourteen.

Upon hearing the news, Laura Ann's father and two half brothers, John and Lawyer Stewart, jumped in a pickup truck and went to find the man responsible. When they encountered twenty-year-old Henry "H. B." Jones, they informed him that his presence would be expected at the church on Millers Chapel Road at a time and date of their choosing. Towering over the five-foot-eight Jones, they let him know he did not want to find out what would happen if he didn't show up.

"You messed that girl up, you going to marry her," they told him.

On March 8, 1940, George Floyd's grandparents H. B. and Laura Ann were married at the Millers Chapel African Methodist Episcopal Zion Church in Goldsboro, in the first shotgun wedding in the family's history. Their daughter Mildred was born exactly two months later.

Though she had to drop out of school in seventh grade, Laura Ann Jones took after her paternal grandmother in industriousness, humility, and fertility. So, it seemed fitting that she named one of her ten daughters Larcenia, after the woman who had once owned hundreds of acres of North Carolina farmland alongside her formerly enslaved husband and their twenty-two children.

But that land had left the family long before H. B. and Laura Ann Jones were joined in holy matrimony. With only grammar school educations between them, their options for providing for their growing family were limited. Shortly after their marriage, they began working as sharecroppers.

The couple, who bore fourteen children over a twenty-six-year span, were an attractive target for unscrupulous landowners looking to capitalize on the lucrative but labor-intensive work of tobacco harvesting. Such a large family represented a potentially productive and cohesive workforce—one that would find it difficult to move away if it disagreed with the property owner's rules or calculations.

On the White-owned farms of Goldsboro in the 1950s, members of the Jones clan as young as five years old would traipse through fields at sunrise. They would walk behind a tobacco harvester—a four-legged contraption on wheels that combed through rows of tobacco plants—picking up fallen leaves. When it rained, the juice from the tobacco leaves would drip down their faces, stinging their eyes. But the storm clouds at least offered a brief reprieve from the stifling Carolina sun.

The work started in the predawn hours, with the older

Jones children taking the tobacco leaves down from the barn where they had been hanging overnight. Before heading to school, they would lay the leaves on the ground to absorb moisture from the morning dew. Then, they would pack the softened tobacco into a backhouse for additional conditioning before wrapping it in sheets to be warehoused for sale.

When they got home from school, they would often try to drag out their homework to delay an afternoon return to the now-sizzling fields. A collective groan would emerge from their shack when their father would pop his head in to check on their progress.

"You finish your homework yet?" H. B. would say. "Okay, you got five more minutes!"

During afternoon sessions in the field, the Jones family would start the arduous harvesting process from the beginning—picking the leaves by hand off the seemingly endless rows of planted tobacco stalks, looping them in a bunch with string, and then hanging them on a long stick. Their hands moved swiftly and robotically as they repeated the task thousands of times. An adult male worker would take the bunched leaves and suspend them high in the multitiered barn to be air-cured. There, the leaves would hang until they transformed from dark green to golden brown.

During occasional thirty-minute breaks, the Jones children would snack on peanuts, Pepsi, or a honeybun. Then they headed back into the fields to pick up where they had left off. When Laura Ann saw her children starting to get exhausted or frustrated, she would tell them stories about their grandfather or other family members to help pass the time. She would also tell them about her life and how getting pregnant and dropping out of school at fourteen had limited her options and landed her under this broiling sun in her forties. She reminded her thirteen surviving children about her wish to see them all graduate high school, encouraging them to achieve what she never had.

H. B. and Laura Ann sometimes worked out an agreement with the landowners before a harvesting season: if the family worked particularly hard and exceeded an elevated quota by the end of the season, they could own some of the additional tobacco they had picked. They would use the funds from the sale of the extra tobacco to give their children small payouts and rewards—incentives to encourage hard work.

The Jones children would use the money they received from sharecropping to buy clothes for school, a stark contrast to their middle-class peers, who at the time were enjoying Elvis Presley, drive-in movies, and other pleasures of postwar prosperity.

One year in the 1960s, H. B. Jones gathered his kids together to inform them of an especially promising deal he had bargained with the White landowner. To unlock the deal, they would have to produce a massive quantity of tobacco for their employers, he said. But once they had done so, they could sell as much of the additional tobacco as they could pick and keep all the proceeds for themselves.

The entire family worked overtime that season, with each laborer committed to the vision of achieving their father's deal. At the end of the season, the hundreds of hours they spent in the fields appeared to have paid off—they had met their quota. The Jones children went to bed that night thinking of all the ways they would spend their modest windfalls.

The next morning, they awoke to the smell of burning wood and tobacco. They looked outside to see what was left of the gabled frame of the tobacco barn engulfed in flames. As the devastated family watched the barn burn to ashes, they thought of all the expenses they had already mentally allocated from their expected bonuses—school costs, unpaid loans, overdue home repairs.

"We had pissed away the whole year," recalled Selwyn Jones, the youngest of Laura Ann's children.

He said he was told years later by the landowner's son that the barn had been insured, contrary to what the man had told the family at the time. The landowner had figured he could profit more from burning his own barn than from allowing his workers to experience one season with extra pocket money.

"He quadrupled his money," Selwyn Jones said. "He got his money from his tobacco. Then he got the insurance money for that barn of tobacco. And then he had my mama and daddy pay him back for that barn of tobacco for the next five years."

Despite working harder than they ever had, the Jones family ended that season deeper in arrears. They were trapped in a cycle of backbreaking work and crushing debt, producing ever more wealth while the fruits of their labor seemed to disappear into the rich, dark soil.

As had been the case a century earlier, the benefits of their hard work were flowing up to the families entrenched at the top of the social hierarchy. The White farmers and executives of North Carolina's massive tobacco industry were thriving like never before.

The period between World War II and the early 1970s represented a boon for cigarette makers. Despite scientific studies and a 1964 U.S. Surgeon General report categorically linking smoking to lung cancer, top tobacco companies launched a joint public relations campaign to raise doubt about the science and convince an increasing number of Americans that smoking was cool. Researchers later found that the tobacco companies targeted a disproportionate amount of their marketing efforts at Black Americans, running ads for menthol cigarettes in Black-owned magazines like *Ebony* and *Jet*.

Tobacco was marketed not only as a status enhancer but also as a stress reliever, and there were few groups more susceptible to stress than Black Americans during the era of Jim Crow discrimination. Upward of 60 percent of Black men identified as smokers in 1963, the highest rate of any demographic group. The highly addictive product offered people beset by mental health issues a temporary escape from their anxieties, even as it poisoned their bodies.

There was a lot of money at stake. In 1950, North Carolina farms yielded 850 million pounds of tobacco. Americans smoked more than 350 billion cigarettes that year—an average of more than 3,500 per adult—spending more than $3.5 billion. By 1963, when over 40 percent of all Americans were smokers, producers were selling more than five hundred billion cigarettes annually, or more than 4,300 for every adult in the country.

The tobacco industry, powered by the work of thousands of Black sharecroppers across North Carolina and elsewhere, was a key engine of economic growth in much of the country. It was so politically powerful that Congress created a price-support program to guarantee growers a minimum fee for the lucrative cash crop. But Blacks in the South remained largely locked out of political power, as they had been for the past half century. They had few avenues to bargain for fairer treatment and few allies with influence willing to take up their cause.

The tobacco barons were cultivating soft power as well. In 1924, James Buchanan "Buck" Duke—the chief executive of American Tobacco Company, the world's largest producer—donated $40 million to Trinity College in Durham, North Carolina. The college quickly rebranded as Duke University. It received another $67 million in 1925 when Duke died and left half of his estate to the school. The donations, which would be worth more than $1.4 billion in modern currency, funded an endowment that became one of the largest in the country.

Even if the Black Joneses had tried to complain about their treatment at the bottom rung of the tobacco business, few in power at the time were willing to confront an industry that had become so critical to America's commercial, political, and cultural spheres.

George Floyd's grandparents' only recourse was to move—and several times they found themselves packing up their belongings and relocating to another dilapidated shack on another White man's farm, hoping against hope that he might be true to them.

The home where the Jones family eventually settled consisted of a front room, a back room, and a main room. It had no indoor plumbing or running water and only sporadic bouts of electricity.

The fetid outhouse set back more than a hundred feet from the building forced a choice each time nature called. Some of the children opted to use a bucket nearby instead of making the trek down the unlit, mosquito-riddled passageway. And because the single outhouse shared by as many as fifteen people was inevitably oversubscribed at times, H. B. Jones had fashioned it into a two-seater that allowed for simultaneous use.

The home itself spoke to the lack of progress in the family's economic condition since Hillery Thomas Stewart Sr. was born in an only slightly humbler hovel on a slave row more than a century earlier.

"It wasn't even a shack," recalled Selwyn Jones. "It was just a platform with wood around it."

During the coldest winter nights, they would chop pieces of wood off the frame of the structure to help kindle a fire. Even the White landowner had given up on the property.

"If anything ever happens, just let it burn down," he had told the couple when they moved in, their descendants later recalled.

Bathing thirteen children in a house without plumbing was tiresome, time-consuming work ahead of long days in the fields. Waking up before dawn, Laura Ann would direct her children to fill a tin tub by pressing down on the outdoor hand pump to extract water from the ground before heating it for their baths. Sometimes, when it was particularly hot or cold outside, the boys would tell their sisters not to throw out their bathwater after they had finished. Since girls were usually cleaner, they figured, they could save a trip to the hand pump by reusing the water.

The children also shared mattresses, with as many as five people sleeping hip-to-hip in one bed. While the sleeping arrangements regularly produced fights over the limited personal space, they also allowed for body warmth in a home that lacked proper heating. On a particularly cold winter day in January 1958, the landowner had warned the family against burning a fire—threatening them with expulsion if he saw even a plume of smoke emanating from the shack.

Laura Ann had just given birth to a son named Frank, and the family was bundled together trying to keep him and themselves warm.

Frank Jones didn't survive the night.

His death certificate said he had contracted pneumonia. He was thirty-five days old.

The impoverished and oppressive conditions forced Laura Ann Jones to figure out how to cope with both the debilitating pain of tragedy and the compounding impact of everyday antagonisms. On trips to the grocery store, she noticed that White grocers would always sell her meat that was bordering on spoiled and near-rotten vegetables—the kind of casual racism that she figured was not even worth complaining about.

Instead, she planted summer and winter gardens in the fertile soil behind her home and used the fresh produce to create delicacies that her children relished. Over time, she built a chicken hatchery and bought a dairy cow, so she could always have ingredients to make meals from scratch. She would collect the eggs that rolled down to the bottom of the coop and store them next to glass jars she had filled with colorful preserves. The fruit trees on the land provided a broad assortment of flavors.

"Peaches, pears, plums, apples, grapes," her granddaughter Shareeduh McGee Tate recalled. "She would make jellies and preserves from all of that."

Laura Ann taught her daughters how to cook Southern soul food, using age-old techniques for turning inexpensive or unwanted ingredients into delicious meals for many.

Larcenia was an especially fast learner. She would quickly internalize her mother's homemade recipes for things like chitterlings, biscuits, and cobblers and then use what she had learned to create her own specialized cuisine, using her siblings as taste testers.

One day, Larcenia called over her sister Angela and some other siblings to check out a new "delicacy" she had created using eggs, green peppers, and hot sauce. When she noticed she had a rapt audience, she introduced the creation with the flair of Julia Child describing a boeuf bourguignon.

"It was probably just an omelet," Angela Jones Harrelson recalled of Cissy's creation decades later. "But we looked at it like, 'This is amazing.' You know, we didn't have that type of stuff."

"Oh, it's not going to burn," Laura Ann said, trying to coax her daughter to stand still under the hot comb.

Seven other girls were lined up waiting for their turn in this custom of transforming tightly coiled Afros into straightened hair that surrendered to gravity.

For the Jones sisters, it involved a stove, hair grease, and a sizzling-hot metal comb coursing from the nape of their necks to the ends of their curls. Inevitably, the girls' heads would shy away as the heated comb closed in, frustrating their mother's efforts.

"Hold your head up!" she would snap. "I told you to sit still. I'm not going to burn you."

As she styled the girls' hair, Laura Ann would remind her daughters about how to comport themselves in front of White people.

She would reiterate the rules they had heard so many times:

Always address them as Mister or Missus, followed by a last name. Never go through their front door. Never raise your voice at them. Don't forget to add "sir" or "ma'am" after every response.

These lessons in submissiveness were her best attempt at protecting her children from the racism that dominated the rural South in the 1960s. If the highway billboard outside of town declaring "Welcome to Ku Klux Klan country" hadn't driven home the point, Laura Ann Jones would make sure her children understood the dangers they faced on account of their dark skin and coiled hair.

"When I look back on it, she was just trying to protect us because she didn't want us to get in trouble," her daughter Angela recalled. "Because she didn't have no money to fight anything for us or go to court. Because we knew we wouldn't win anyway."

Laura Ann was also trying to avoid the swift penalty that White sharecroppers often threatened when they felt their tenants were becoming uppity: eviction. As it was, the Joneses could barely afford to stay in the three-room shack.

As successive tobacco seasons passed without any positive change in the family's financial status, H. B. Jones decided to take on another job, as a cook at a popular barbecue spot. He had served in the army during the Korean War and figured he could use the cooking skills he had picked up to earn some money on the side. At Wilber's Barbecue, which was still segregated deep into the 1960s, H. B. joined an all-Black team of cooks who remained out of sight while an exclusively White staff of waitresses served patrons.

When he pulled off Highway 70 and arrived at Wilber's for his six p.m. shift each day, he would walk by a fading "Whites Only" sign on the building's facade. He would bypass the front door and enter through the back, then spend the next twelve hours roasting pigs overnight.

The extra income was helpful, but the family remained financially strained. Laura Ann often found herself having to ask her White employers for small loans to cover everyday expenses and to deal with unexpected family emergencies. She had taught herself how to play the piano, and she would offer her talents to local churches on Sundays—usually receiving a small fee for her services.

Despite Laura Ann working more than full time from adolescence, her wages in the Jim Crow South rarely exceeded $60 a week. The family seemed to be going deeper into debt each year, no matter how hard they worked. Sometimes, it would take four or five years to pay off a loan of $200 or $300 to White landowners, who invariably demanded interest at rates rivaling modern payday lenders.

When Laura Ann couldn't afford Christmas gifts for the kids, she would take them for a drive through the nice side of town. They would gaze at the well-appointed homes, lit up with holiday decorations. Sometimes, her children would spot a tear in her eye as she marveled at the displays of a kind of wealth she would never know.

"My mama worked her ass off," Selwyn Jones said decades later, holding back tears of his own. "And died with nothing."

Laura Ann's children did eventually all graduate from high school, fulfilling her dream. When they received their diplomas, several of them realized that staying in Goldsboro would only commit them to a life of hard labor and poverty.

Dr. Martin Luther King Jr. was captivating national

audiences at the time with his dream of equal treatment for Black Americans, but the Jones children recognized that it would be a long while before their small town in Wayne County, North Carolina, would abandon its racist roots and transform into an "oasis of freedom and justice." At least three of them entered the military, eager to be deployed away from their hometown. Others were drawn to the cooler northern climate and accepted live-in domestic jobs in places like New York, New Jersey, and Washington, DC. Larcenia followed some of her older sisters northward, joining the tail end of the Great Migration of some six million Blacks from the rural South to the urban North and West during the twentieth century. In the late 1960s, she took a live-in job in New York, earning about $3 an hour to care for a White family.

It was there, five hundred miles away from home, that she met a musician who hailed from Clinton, North Carolina— just across the county line from Goldsboro. In a metropolis of almost eight million people, it seemed an act of Providence had led her to George Perry Floyd Sr., a man whose family history so mirrored her own.

Floyd's great-grandfather Carlyle Floyd was born enslaved around 1854 and spent his first eleven years in bondage on the Floyd plantation in Robeson County, North Carolina. His owner, a wealthy man named Francis Floyd, passed away in 1856, leaving his expansive estate to his wife and twelve children.

Because Francis Floyd's thirty-two slaves could not be evenly split up as easily as his 1,500 acres, his heirs opted to sell some of them and apportion the proceeds equally.

Five years after the Civil War ended, Carlyle worked as a field hand for Francis Floyd Jr. in White House, North

Carolina. Two years later, Carlyle married a woman named Kitty Pittman. Their descendants would continue the family tradition of working on White men's farms for the next seventy years.

In the mid-twentieth century, the Black Floyds would be mainstays in the African Methodist Episcopal Church in Robeson County, known for their musical talents. By the time Carlyle's great-grandson George was eight years old, he almost always had a guitar strapped to his back and regularly played gospel music alongside his sisters and brothers. The large family would perform together during Sunday services and would later sell their music on cassette tapes under the moniker the Gospel Souls.

George could play guitar by ear, his daughter Zsa Zsa recalled.

"His sister Annie McLaurin would sing and blow the roof off the church," she said.

George's youngest brother, Ike Floyd, would also impress the congregation with a soulful voice that belied his years. He would go on to become a lead singer for the disco-inspired Brooklyn, Bronx & Queens Band and briefly sing backup vocals for the Manhattans, a discography that reflected the diversity of his adopted hometown of New York City.

George Perry Floyd Sr. was chasing his own musical dreams when he left North Carolina for New York at the height of the Motown era. The tall, striking woman who caught his eye could have been mistaken for one of the Supremes. He immediately recognized her accent and charm. He would quickly come to appreciate her easy familiarity in the kitchen. She was drawn to the tall, smartly dressed musician with large hands and a strong appetite.

They were two lifelong North Carolinians trying to make it in New York, and their connection was instant and deep.

They married on March 28, 1969, in Brooklyn, where Larcenia had recently given birth to two daughters. She had given the firstborn the same first name as the glamorous Hungarian American actress Zsa Zsa Gabor. The second, born a little over a year later, was named LaTonya.

Larcenia had already returned to North Carolina when she gave birth to her third child, George Perry Floyd Jr., in 1973.

The arrival of a namesake son did not heal the fissures that were already beginning to emerge in the elder George's relationship with Larcenia. Even though his musical career had stalled, he remained a "rolling stone," his children later recalled. Selwyn Jones said his brother-in-law had begun drinking heavily and living the life of a young, single musician rather than behaving like a father of three.

"He wanted to do all the things that you didn't want your husband to do," he recalled. "So, my sister got tired of that. And she moved on."

When Larcenia loaded up her children for their journey to Houston in 1977, she told them that the purpose of the road trip was to meet her new man's parents—though she wasn't sure if she would ever come back to North Carolina. She was leaving behind a state where her ancestors had toiled for decades under an unforgiving sun, picking untold millions of dollars' worth of corn, cotton, and tobacco. They had never lived luxuriously, had never been bankrupted by an act of God, had never broken any just laws, and had even served their country in the military—and yet, their descendants remained impoverished.

By contrast, the White family who had owned and abused them had gone on to produce a line of business owners, political leaders, county executives, and scholars. Like Larcenia Floyd's ancestors, the White Stewarts had come with nothing to North Carolina centuries earlier. While they had amassed generational wealth and influence, she had to grapple with the fact that she was leaving the state empty-handed, a thirty-year-old single mother of three.

As she traversed the Carolina highway lined with tobacco fields much like the ones where she had spent her childhood, she looked forward to a fresh start in a new city. She glanced over at her three-year-old son, the great-great-grandson of Hillery Thomas Stewart Sr., a boy who as a man would one day make his own journey to an unfamiliar city seeking redemption from a troubled past; a man who would cry out for her departed soul as he was being murdered in that new city by a White police officer.

His alleged crime would be purchasing tobacco with a counterfeit $20 bill.

CHAPTER 4

Lessons

O N A BRISK MID-DECEMBER day in 1992, the Jack Yates Senior High School football players walked across the University of Texas at Austin campus, taking in postcard views of college life: wide fountains, manicured trees, sun-drenched buildings, and the 307-foot UT Tower. The minimetropolis of Texas's largest public university was quiet, as most of its 49,250 students had left for winter break.

George Floyd and the rest of the Yates Lions made their way to Texas Memorial Stadium, where they were set to compete in the 1992 Texas Class 5A Division II state championship game—the highlight of a high school career that had been dominated by sports.

Floyd, a nineteen-year-old letterman in basketball and football who had sprouted up to nearly six and a half feet tall and filled out to over two hundred pounds by his senior year, was no stranger to college campuses and arenas. He had played football in front of tens of thousands of fans in Houston's Astrodome and dribbled down the basketball courts of Texas Southern University—but UT's stadium and surrounding collegiate environment were on another level, he told his teammates as they walked onto the field. It was the biggest athletic stage he had ever set foot on.

Floyd looked out over the seventy-eight-thousand-seat football stadium, admiring the arched entrances and soaring height that gave it the look of a Texan Colosseum. The stadium had played host to then president George H. W. Bush, who had given the 1990 commencement address at the University of Texas. He used his remarks to hail the school's first-class facilities and to encourage the thousands of graduates in attendance to take advantage of the great privilege their education afforded them.

"In short, you face the best of dilemmas, a wealth of opportunities—opportunities born of democracy," he had told the mostly White crowd. "To graduate from college in America is to be as free as any man or woman can be."

Floyd and the other students at his predominantly Black high school had received a very different message about the pathway to wealth, opportunity, and freedom. At Yates, which suffered from crumbling facilities, aging textbooks, and other vestiges of segregation, gifted athletes like Floyd came to see their bodies as the means to escape poverty. Yates excelled in sports, achieving statewide recognition even as its academic record flagged—the result of a system that concentrated impoverished students with significant needs in underfunded classrooms.

For Floyd, this meant the pinnacle of his high school career was a trip to a university where he was welcomed to compete in its stadium but would not be considered qualified to enroll in its classes. That dichotomy was on his mind as he stood on the stadium's turf, stretching and warming up in the minutes before his final high school football game. Ralph

Cooper, a Houston radio jockey who had traveled to Austin for the game, spotted Floyd from the sideline and walked over to see what was behind the young man's pensive demeanor.

"What are you all going to do today?" Cooper asked him.

"Me and my teammates are going to win the game," Floyd responded.

The conversation quickly shifted away from football. Floyd told Cooper how impressed he was by the university and its facilities, adding that he was disappointed to not be in a position to get an athletic scholarship to a school like this.

"Now I see what some of you all were talking about," Floyd said, a reference to Cooper's gentle, persistent, and largely unsuccessful efforts over the years to get some of the Yates athletes to focus more on their academics.

Cooper had occasionally interviewed Floyd on his local sports radio show and knew that he had been struggling with his schoolwork. Floyd had failed the Texas Assessment of Academic Skills at least twice and had just one more opportunity to pass the three-part proficiency test as a senior or risk not graduating.

As he spoke to Cooper, Floyd looked wistful and a little forlorn, in contrast to his usual upbeat self. His teammates mostly wore stern expressions, as if mentally preparing for battle, or busied themselves with repetitive pregame rituals to keep their nerves at bay. A few of the freshmen who knew they would be unlikely to see the field were goofing off, untroubled by the sense of responsibility and purpose the older players had. But Floyd looked as if the game had already been decided and its key moments already played.

"Well, you've still got a chance," Cooper told Floyd, partly to cheer him up and partly to snap him back into the moment.

He then suggested that two years at a junior college might provide a rehabilitative pathway to a Division I school.

Floyd took in the advice and thanked him before returning to his stretches as the minutes ticked down toward kickoff.

Peering down the field through the fog, Floyd could see his opponents warming up eighty yards away. The Temple High School Wildcats had traveled an hour from Temple, Texas, a mostly White, middle-class town of about fifty thousand.

Temple's players wore shiny blue pants and white jerseys that fit snugly around their modern shoulder pads—a contrast to the hand-me-down uniforms that hung loosely from the Yates players' frames. Noting the slick artificial turf and forecast for rain, some of the Wildcats were changing out of their surface cleats to backup pairs—high-top Nikes with better traction. The Yates players had only one pair—weathered PONY brand turf shoes that had first been worn years before.

As kickoff approached, Floyd put on his helmet, strapped on a pair of maroon receiver gloves, and joined his teammates in a huddle before an estimated crowd of twenty-five thousand that included college scouts, news crews, and seemingly everyone from Third Ward.

"What's that word when you go to Yates?" one player shouted to his teammates, before awaiting the expected response.

More than sixty adolescent voices bellowed back in unison: "State! State!"

Floyd had walked into Jack Yates Senior High School in the fall of 1989 as a lanky fifteen-year-old with a middling academic record. After leaving Waynel Sexton's second-grade class academically on par, he fell behind as he attended a series of underfunded schools in Houston's segregated inner city. Still, the Yates teachers appreciated that he was a polite, respectful student who showed up for class on time. In the morning before school, he would often ask his teachers for hugs, charming them with his habit of adding "ma'am" to the end of each sentence.

A quiet student, Floyd would only occasionally display his mischievous side in the classroom. During one of his classes, Floyd and some of his teammates joked around so much that the teacher struck a deal with the players in an attempt to regain control of the class.

"Hey, you football players," he said one day when Floyd and his friends walked in. "If you guys just be quiet and sit in the back, I'll pass you."

They picked up their desks and moved them to the back of the class, hardly believing their luck. At the end of the semester, they had all received passing grades. It was a privilege that came with being an athlete at Yates, and one of the numerous incentives encouraging Floyd and his friends to prioritize sports over school.

While many of the Yates teachers—overwhelmed by the flood of students with significant economic and academic challenges—were content to let quiet athletes like Floyd do the minimum to skate by, Bertha Dinkins was determined to deliver hard truths about the dangers of an overreliance on sports.

"All of you will not be successful in going to pro teams," Dinkins, who taught government at Yates, told Floyd and her other students. She cited the minuscule statistical chances of any particular student making it to the NFL or NBA.

Dinkins took a special interest in Floyd, in part because he didn't fit the stereotype of an unruly athlete and in part because she, too, had once lived in Cuney Homes. She saw in Floyd a smart kid who struggled with testing and did not always see the long-term value of education. She encouraged him to think beyond the walls of Yates High and the lines of its sports fields. She had attended Booker T. Washington High School in the 1950s, so she appreciated what it was like to go to an all-Black school with a dominant tradition in athletics.

"I want to read about you in the newspaper," she told Floyd and the other students in her class. "I'll probably be old then. But I want to read about you in the newspaper that you have made history and done something to contribute to society."

Floyd listened in silence as she spoke. Dinkins's argument, while persuasive, stood in contrast to the overwhelming message he was receiving while in high school: that his most effective way to contribute to society was by conditioning his body rather than his brain.

It was an easy message to internalize in a school where few students achieved passing scores on standardized exams and many of the most celebrated recent alumni were excelling in arenas, not boardrooms. The college recruiters who came to visit Yates were usually men from athletic departments scouting for their next prospect, not professors or admissions officers seeking out bright minds.

During Floyd's time in high school, there were numerous Yates alumni in the NFL, including three players on the forty-five-man roster of the 1990 Chicago Bears, an achievement that not many high schools in the country could claim.

Floyd told friends that he would soon join their ranks.

While he had excelled as a basketball player in junior high school, it did not take him long to realize that football was the more popular sport at Yates, so he decided to try that out as well.

When he was pulled up to the varsity football squad during his freshman year, he was ecstatic, considering it to be a sign that he had a decent chance to make good on his boasts about joining the other Yates alumni in the NFL one day. Just a few years earlier, they, too, had gotten the call up to varsity as freshmen.

More than anything happening inside the classroom, the action on the football field had become the focal point for Yates students and the surrounding community. For years, Floyd had been a spectator on Friday evenings as the Yates marching band led parades from the school to the Lions' stadium. Now, he would be among the players who the entire neighborhood rallied behind with a kind of raw pride that had been rare in the Bricks. He would be at center stage during the school's most dynamic moments of the week, the nights when a group of Black boys from one of Houston's poorest neighborhoods could compete on a level playing field with their wealthier peers from across the city. And on the nights when the Yates Lions dominated their opponents, as they often did, he would soak in the adoration of thousands of Black fans from his community as they chanted, "Third Ward High!"

Named after a formerly enslaved minister, Jack Yates Senior High School opened in 1926 as Houston's second school for colored children—its six hundred Black students separated by race from the city's White pupils. The 1896 Supreme Court decision in *Plessy v. Ferguson* had given racial segregation an official stamp of approval on the grounds that public institutions that were separate but otherwise equal did not run afoul of the Constitution's Fourteenth Amendment. Like other states across the South, Texas enthusiastically enforced the "separate" part while flagrantly flouting the equality mandate. Throughout the state, like in much of America, colored schools were underfunded, their teachers underpaid, and their population of Black students systematically denied opportunities to fulfill their academic potential.

That Yates was still segregated and unequal when Floyd walked through its doors in 1989 was a testament to the enduring power of the racial hierarchy that had taken root throughout the country, and most blatantly in Southern states like Texas.

After the Supreme Court reversed its *Plessy* ruling with its 1954 *Brown v. Board of Education of Topeka* decision, declaring that school segregation violated the Fourteenth Amendment's equal protection clause, officials in Texas spent years resisting. The series of legal schemes and justifications in the decades after *Brown* would keep schools like Yates segregated indefinitely.

In 1955, Texas governor Allan Shivers, a segregationist Democrat, set up a committee to look into ways to reject forced integration. In its final report in 1956, the committee decried the *Brown* decision and hailed "the great counterattack" underway in other states. In legislatures and school boards across the South, officials had responded to *Brown* with several countermanding measures, including ending compulsory education, offering private school vouchers, and threatening to shut down schools rather than integrate. Texas legislators passed a slate of laws in 1957 encouraging school districts to resist the federal government's desegregation push.

In Houston, school administrators and local politicians took up the baton, working over the next fifteen years to undermine mandatory integration. Determined to prevent mandatory busing or other federal interventions, the Houston Independent School District endorsed a series of voluntary integration programs that only perpetuated the problem of separate schooling.

Courts rejected the measures as inadequate—with one judge questioning whether the moves had been purposefully designed to fail. By 1970, when Houston was the largest school district in the country that remained segregated, judges had grown tired of the delay tactics and ordered a more aggressive approach. But by then it was too late for Jack Yates Senior High School.

Yates, which was a couple of blocks away from Cuney Homes, saw its population drop during the ensuing decades as it lost top students to other schools. And with few White parents willing to enroll their children in a resource-starved school in historically Black Third Ward, it never achieved integration, remaining almost 100 percent Black when Floyd attended.

Months before Floyd enrolled, Yates made national headlines when the principal stopped the school newspaper from writing about the 1989 valedictorian, a teenage mother who was pregnant with her second child. In her graduation speech, the valedictorian lamented that more than half the students who arrived as freshmen at Yates four years earlier were not graduating with their class.

"Where did they go?" she asked her fellow graduates. "You and I are special. Special because we didn't give in to drugs, alcohol, or peer pressure."

Her speech reflected a school that had become known for high dropout rates, dilapidated facilities, and a concentration of at-risk students. But as Yates's academic reputation flagged, its status as an athletic juggernaut was as solid as ever when Floyd walked the halls in the early 1990s as a skinny teenager with large hands and quick feet.

Impressed by Floyd's athletic potential, Coach Maurice McGowan had made the decision to call Floyd and a few other freshmen up to the varsity team near the end of the season. But Floyd presented a conundrum—he had good size and speed but lacked the kind of aggression that was key to Yates's physical brand of football.

"He was tall and a string bean," McGowan recalled, describing his struggle to figure out what position to assign to the promising athlete.

Players on opposing teams immediately noticed his height, with some shouting, "Watch out for Tree Branch!" when he took the field.

McGowan settled on tight end, where Floyd's size could be an asset. When coaches yelled at him to be more physical, Floyd would simply bow his head.

Floyd's timidity on the field sometimes made for comical scenes. During one practice, Floyd had just caught a pass when a 250-pound linebacker named Oscar Smallwood bore down on him to inflict a punishing blow. But Floyd, too tall to achieve a lower center of gravity against the densely built defender, was not interested in trying to defy physics. A moment before impact, he stopped in his tracks and tossed the ball toward Smallwood—essentially volunteering a turnover.

If it had been anyone else, the surrender would've been seen as an act of cowardice by a player who lacked the kind of heart needed to compete for the Yates Lions. But it was Floyd, and he was always goofing off on the field, so the crescendo of laughter that ensued was not laden with derision. And if there was any doubt that Floyd was the initiator and not the butt of the joke, it disappeared as he burst out laughing as well.

Floyd's jokes often lightened the mood for his teammates as they battled suffocating heat and grueling conditions. Sometimes he would break into spot-on mimicry of the Yates marching band's dramatic drum majors, tossing his head back while lifting his knees high and driving his cleats into the ground. No matter how tired the players were—they sometimes fell asleep in their uniforms on the porches of Cuney Homes apartments after practice—Floyd's mock high-step never failed to send them into howls of laughter.

These high jinks provided a momentary escape from the poverty, the violence, the police, and the drug trade ravaging their community. But upon leaving the schoolyard and the field for the day, the boys were often jolted back to the cruel reality of growing up Black and poor in Third Ward.

August 8, 1991, was one of those steamy summer days that separated the Yates football devotees from the dilettantes. The Texas heat combined with the voluntary nature of football workouts helped the coaches know which players were truly committed to the program. Floyd had finished his sophomore year of high school and liked the idea of spending the summer playing sports with his friends from school, without having to worry about the schooling part.

Floyd's friend Carl Owens, a stellar athlete who played

quarterback and safety, would usually be one of the last guys in the weight room at the end of the workouts. Owens, whose athletic skills had been honed on the courts and fields of the Cuney Homes housing project, was the team's fastest player and one of the city's most promising recruits. At nineteen, he was preparing for a senior season where he had been tapped as a team captain and was being courted by Division I college programs. He had already become the subject of arguments in the Bricks about just how long it would take for him to make it pro, and whether it would be in basketball or football.

Vaughn Dickerson, however, was typically one of the first to leave the weight room. At five foot eight and just under 165 pounds, the sixteen-year-old wide receiver knew his value to the team came from his speed and litheness on the field, not brute strength.

"Man, fuck them weights," Dickerson would often say as he walked out after a few minutes of lifting.

But on this Thursday, Dickerson stuck around long enough to see most of his teammates leave; Owens was the only other player in the locker room as the afternoon tilted into evening. Some of the older guys in the neighborhood had invited Owens to a party later that night, and a few of the Yates players had been talking about making an appearance too.

Owens had had his eyes on a pair of black Nike sneakers Dickerson recently debuted to great fanfare at the school, and he knew just the outfit to sync them with for the party. Dickerson agreed to lend them out to him, as the teammates often did for one another. Walking out with the pair of sneakers in his hand, Owens, who had planned to go to the party with Dickerson's older brother Van, told Dickerson he should stop by as well.

Over in Cuney Homes, Floyd, PoBoy, and a couple of other friends were making their way on foot to the same event, at the Finish Line Club on Pierce Street. It was just a mile from the neighborhood, and the nondescript two-story building was a gathering spot for Third Ward's hustlers to show off their cars and jewelry against the backdrop of downtown Houston's skyline.

Dickerson and another teammate had gotten dressed at his house and were headed for the front door when a voice stopped them in their tracks.

"Where are y'all going?"

Dickerson's mom was standing behind them, looking determined.

"Mama, we're going to go to the little thing around the corner where the kids—"

"No you ain't," she said, cutting him off. "Get your ass in this house."

Dickerson immediately knew his mother was not to be toyed with, at least not on that night.

"If you leave out this fucking house, you can't never come back in here," she added for good measure.

"Man, Mama's tripping," Dickerson muttered under his breath after she left the room, steaming over all the fun he would no doubt miss.

Less than two hours later, a loud bang on the door snapped him from his self-pitying daze.

"Man, your brother got shot and Carl got killed!" a neighborhood kid shouted.

Dickerson took off running. When he got to Pierce Street, he saw a body lying on the ground with arms splayed out at awkward angles. A sheet covering the corpse's head, torso, and legs left a question about the victim's identity. But as Dickerson's eyes traced down the length of the blanketed mass, the black Nike shoes sticking out from beneath the covering erased any doubt.

Just minutes earlier, Owens and Van had been shooting craps with some older guys when they noticed one of them was using crooked dice. An argument quickly escalated to the point where guns had been drawn.

As shots rang out, Owens and Van, both unarmed, ducked behind a car for cover. Owens raised his head to see where the shots were coming from and immediately jerked as a bullet pierced the side of his body. The shooter then closed in on his injured body and shot at least once more at closer range, rendering him still. Van had also been shot in his lower back while running away and was being treated at the county hospital for a non-life-threatening wound.

Floyd, PoBoy, and the other Cuney Homes kids—who had been in the club when the shots rang out—stepped outside to find Owens's bloodied corpse lying on the pavement.

Floyd and his teammates would shed tears that night both for the loss of their friend and for the stark reminder of their own mortality. Carl Owens had just been in their midst, his vitality on display as he slipped tackles, pushed out reps, and knew just what to say in team huddles. For the folks in Cuney Homes, he was a model for how to transcend the stifling housing project. And just like that, he was gone.

"Carl raised us," PoBoy said decades later, struggling for words as he reminisced about the pathway to stardom that Carl Owens seemed destined for. "We knew Carl was going."

The death weighed heavily on Floyd, who had seen Owens as a big-brother figure and a role model for how he could capitalize on his own athletic skill. It would not be the last time he would shed tears as someone he admired—someone who reminded him of himself, or who he wanted to be—lay dead in front of him.

"YATES ATHLETE'S MURDER STUNS COACHES, FRIENDS COMMUNITY MOURNS SENSELESS TRAGEDY."

The last two words of the headline in the *Houston Chronicle* summed up what was increasingly common in Floyd's neighborhood. The story about Owens's death ran in the newspaper's A section to broad readership that included Houston's business leaders and stay-at-home mothers. It was the latest in a series of news reports that further solidified Third Ward generally and Yates specifically as dangerous and volatile in the eyes of outsiders. As they read the headlines and watched true crime stories on local news programs like *City Under Siege*, Houston's White families went to ever-greater lengths to shelter their offspring from Black neighborhoods and Black students.

Long before Owens's murder, a substantial number of White Houstonians had viewed racial integration in the city's public schools as a dire threat to the physical and social safety of their children. Some were willing to say so publicly, and school board meetings in the early 1970s were packed with angry White parents protesting the district's new integration plan.

Many more spoke with their actions. Their attitudes toward racial mixing in schools—and their willingness to protect their children from it by any means necessary—would be the checkmate play that doomed integration efforts permanently.

In 1970, federal judges ordered Houston's public schools to get serious about ending school segregation and conform with the *Brown* decision after years of delay tactics and bureaucratic resistance. In response, the district instituted a plan that would have sent more White students to schools like Yates and, in turn, allowed more Black students into majority-White classrooms.

Faced with the prospect of allowing their children to learn alongside minority students, many White parents instead chose to either pay for private schools or leave the Houston public school system altogether by moving to Whiter, wealthier suburbs outside the district's lines. The city's school district, which was 53.1 percent White in 1970, saw a precipitous decline in White enrollment in the ensuing years. By 1978, the portion of White students in Houston's public school classrooms had fallen to 30.8 percent. And by the time Floyd entered Yates in 1989, Whites comprised only 15 percent of the district's student population.

Schools that had been almost exclusively White suddenly became undesirable to parents once Black students were allowed to enroll in significant numbers. Between 1970 and 1983, sixteen Houston schools saw their populations go from 90 percent White to 90 percent Black, to the frustration of integration proponents.

"People said, 'Nope, my kids are not going to this school. We are going to move,'" recalled Kelly Frels, an attorney who represented the city schools in prolonged desegregation litigation.

While some went to suburbs, others moved within Houston to areas seen as safe from integration. On the west side of the city, parents from the mostly White Westheimer neighborhood tried to break off and form a new school district. After a legal battle that lasted for most of the 1970s, courts blocked the plan as a deliberate attempt to subvert the *Brown* decision.

But other attempts to perpetuate segregated schooling by capitalizing on existing systemic inequities were more successful, both in Houston and across the country. Like Detroit, Atlanta, St. Louis, Wilmington, and several other cities, Houston had a majority-minority school district at its urban core surrounded by suburbs that were almost all White. Local officials had drawn the district boundaries in a way that allowed the suburbs to benefit from White flight. Under the system, suburban districts—some of which were otherwise indistinguishable from Houston's metropolitan area—cordoned off the wealthiest children and their tax dollars from city schools, thwarting integration efforts.

In 1980, the Justice Department took the rare step of asking a federal judge to force Houston's school system to merge with twenty-two suburban districts. In the first such challenge in U.S. history, Attorney General Benjamin R. Civiletti argued that minority students had been deliberately and systemically concentrated in Houston in a "radical" attempt to create a "racially segregated system." The case also cited government policies at play outside the school system, including housing discrimination. Civil rights groups welcomed the challenge, but the school districts and many suburban parents opposed it.

A federal judge sided with the suburban districts.

By the mid-1980s, after years of litigation and with relatively few White students left in the Houston school system, federal judges determined there was little more that could legally be done to force integration. One declared that

Houston had achieved "unitary status," meaning that the government had done "everything practicable" to stop segregating schools by race. Citing the rapid exodus of White students from the district after previous integration measures, the judge predicted that more aggressive efforts—such as busing—would be both impractical and counterproductive.

"There are not enough White students left in the district to effect greater integration of student bodies without untoward costs on the students themselves," a federal circuit judge ruled in 1983, upholding a district court's findings.

Specifically citing the impact of White flight, the circuit court added that it was not the duty of school districts "to respond to the private actions of those who vote with their feet."

The court rulings helped to uphold a system in which 70 percent of Houston's Black students still attended segregated schools in 1983. Despite federal attempts to enforce *Brown*, the number of predominantly Black schools had almost doubled since 1960.

It was not lost on Floyd and the other Yates football players that many of the wealthier White student athletes they sometimes competed against didn't want to attend their underresourced school in Third Ward. Yates coaches used this inequality to motivate the players, describing their suburban opponents as entitled and arrogant. Coach McGowan would give rousing speeches before games against richer schools, contrasting the gap in living standards and explicitly telling his players that this was their opportunity to legally retaliate against people who looked down their noses at inner-city schools like Yates.

"Hey, guys, it's the rich against the poor," he would say.

Leaning into this construct, Yates players embraced their reputation as aggressive punishers and took pride in their physical style. Coaches told them that the fear that reputation produced in opposing teams was tantamount to a seven-point advantage before the first whistle blew.

While Floyd was content to let others uphold Yates's reputation for pugnacity, by the fall of 1991, his junior year, he had added a few inches to his frame and enough weight to look like a true football player, and not just a basketball player impersonating one.

People across Third Ward were starting to notice.

"Man, who is that dude?"

Robert Fonteno, who had left Yates a few years earlier to take his chances stealing cars and peddling cocaine out of Cuney Homes, had just gotten out of prison when a friend invited him to a football game. Fonteno, who was twenty-four years old, had asked about the angular, agile player who used a combination of size, power, and quickness with head-turning efficiency. Number 88 seemed to be involved in every big play, Fonteno thought. Who was he?

"Man, that's Big Floyd," his friend replied. "He's from the Bricks. He's a monster, man."

A few weeks later, Fonteno was hanging outside the Blue Store when he spotted a tall kid walking in.

"Dude got some size on him, don't he?" he remarked to no one in particular.

"Yeah, that's Floyd."

"That's Big Floyd, number 88?" Fonteno asked. "I saw dude play a couple of weeks ago. Man, he was all over the field."

Fonteno walked into the store and saw Floyd buying a bag of chips and a twenty-five-cent can of soda.

"Big Floyd, right?" he said, walking up to him.

"Yeah, that's me."

Fonteno congratulated him on the impressive game and offered him some advice—the first of several times he would do so over the next twenty-five years.

"Just stay out of trouble, man. Keep your head down, man, and stick to that football field, and you'll go somewhere."

"Yeah, man, that's the plan," Floyd said. "That's what I plan on doing."

Floyd thanked him and walked out of the store, crossing the pockmarked street to go back to the housing project.

When he met up with Vaughn Dickerson later, his friend could tell that the growing weight of expectations—from his family, from his neighborhood, from himself—was pressing on Floyd. Ever since Carl Owens's death, folks in Cuney Homes had started looking at number 88 as the next prospect to make it out and make it big. Financial struggles at home only added to the pressure Floyd felt to succeed on the field.

"You don't owe nobody shit, man. We going to make it, one way," Dickerson said, trying to cheer him up.

"Yeah, I know, V," Floyd said.

If his words had not provided much consolation, Dickerson knew how to get his friend back into a jovial mood. On weekends, Floyd and Dickerson would pick up a few friends and ride around Houston in an older relative's GMC truck, with 2 Live Crew blasting on the radio. The rap group's sexually explicit songs had just the right mix of irreverence and insouciance for teenage boys who felt like society had written them off.

The Supreme Court had recently turned back an effort by local authorities to have 2 Live Crew's album *As Nasty as They*

Wanna Be banned for being too obscene. Floyd would crack open the windows, crank up the volume, and play the prurient lyrics for his friends riding in the truck's cargo bed.

Floyd would also play rapper MC Lyte's 1991 hit "Poor Georgie," a song that described a handsome playboy who saw his life rapidly upended by alcoholism and disease.

"If you love someone you should say it often / You never know when they'll be layin' in a coffin," MC Lyte rapped in the final verse of the song.

It was just the kind of tortured ending that Floyd wanted to avoid.

Floyd's crew, which sometimes grew to as many as five or six guys in a truck designed for no more than three, would usually set out in the evening without a specific plan. They would end up jumping in on a dice game, or hanging out at the Burger King near Yates, where they could split ninety-nine-cent Whoppers. Sometimes, they would grab cheeseburgers at a spot in the Bottoms called Dave's or stop by Guidry's, where Floyd's mom was working the window. On a good evening, she might slip them some fries or a sandwich.

They'd wait until they got away from Guidry's to crack open the forty-ounce beers that they had picked up from friends who were old enough to buy alcohol. Floyd was not much of a drinker, but he'd sip from the bottle just the same, passing it along in this timeless bonding ritual.

One day, a kid from Houston's South Park neighborhood was drinking in Cuney Homes with Floyd and his friends. As they were passing the bottle around, they heard a loud thud. The boy from South Park had fallen over and was out cold.

The boy's inebriation presented a problem because his home was five miles away, and none of them had a car.

"I know what to do," Floyd said, breaking the silence. "We going to put him on a bus and put this hat on him."

They held the boy upright and placed a hat on his head while waiting at the bus stop. When the southbound bus arrived, Floyd picked the boy up and sat him inside, the hat covering his head as he drifted off.

Floyd and the other boys stepped off the bus, laughing, and headed to their homes, figuring their drunk friend would eventually sober up and do the same.

The next day at school, Dickerson was in class when Floyd came up and knocked on the window to get his attention.

"Hey, we in trouble. Coach and them—everybody know."

Floyd said word had spread that a student on the football team had gotten drunk in Cuney Homes.

Other students had started whispering about how the young man had thrown up on the bus where his friends had left him—leading the police to get involved. Unhappy that police had shown up at her door with her intoxicated teenage son, the kid's mother had reported the incident to school administrators.

Coach McGowan, who eventually learned that some of his players had been part of the prank, did not say anything about it that day during practice, where their teammate's absence was conspicuous.

"Everybody, call it up," McGowan said at the end of the practice, gathering the players around him. "Let me tell you a story," he said, before recounting how one of his friends from school had died after getting drunk.

He didn't call out Floyd or Dickerson by name, but he didn't need to.

"You ain't got no goddamn friend if they take you and get

you drunk," he said, his voice rising as he turned toward Floyd and Dickerson. "You're a hoodlum."

On the last day of junior year, a handful of guys Floyd had grown up with walked over to a grassy spot between two hills near the University of Houston's campus. They would sometimes grab snacks from a convenience store after school and head to this secluded location—holding impromptu picnics that allowed them to escape the hardness of the neighborhood and talk about whatever was on their minds.

The sun was high overhead on this late May afternoon in 1992 as the group settled on the grass under a sprawling oak tree. Some lay on their backs and stared up through the branches at the patches of blue sky. Others, including Floyd's teammate Jonathan Veal, sat on the ground and munched on chips and sipped soda. At the precipice of their final year of high school, it dawned on them that their days of playing together were numbered. In twelve months, they would all be responsible for charting their own futures as adults.

Like Floyd, many of the young men had grown up without fathers and were haltingly navigating the transition into manhood. Together, they had wowed packed stadiums with athletic exploits, won and lost fistfights, felt the thrills and troughs of teenage romance, and, tragically, experienced more loss and trauma firsthand than most people would in a lifetime.

The conversation that day shifted away from girls and sports and turned serious as each person told the group how he saw his life playing out in the coming years.

Someone talked about going to college, maybe on a sports scholarship. Someone mentioned signing up for the military. Others mused about going to trade school or getting a job. Unmentioned but understood was the prospect of earning a living through the fast-spreading crack cocaine trade, which most had been able to avoid due to their status as athletes.

When it was Floyd's turn to speak, he stunned the group, first by not taking advantage of a semiserious moment to poke at their earnestness with an inappropriate joke; then by the confidence in his voice as he declared his grand vision.

"I'm going to be big," he said. "I'm going to touch the world."

It was the first day of senior year, a time when the halls of Yates turned into a veritable fashion show, with students competing to flaunt the best outfits and shoes from their back-to-school shopping sessions. But Floyd and a few of his football teammates had all shown up in black jeans and plain white T-shirts.

For Floyd and his friends Vaughn Dickerson, Jonathan Veal, Jerald Moore, and Herbert Mouton, the sartorial statement reflected the zeitgeist of an era influenced by gangster rap and West Coast cholo streetwear. Rap groups Run-DMC and N.W.A had put out black-and-white album covers and embraced the achromatic motif in their fashion.

Floyd's crew appreciated that the jeans-and-T-shirt look was as inexpensive as it was simple—sparing their mothers from having to spend scarce funds on fancy school clothes. They were varsity lettermen at Yates, and their humble outfits—including plain black-and-white Champion tennis shoes—did not stop them from acting like they ran the school.

"We were like gods walking through there," Vaughn Dickerson recalled.

"It was electric," Jerald Moore reminisced about the fall of 1992 at Yates. "We knew it was going to be a special year."

They had all been in fifth grade when the 1985 Yates football team had won the state title against Odessa's Permian High School. Yates beat Permian, later of *Friday Night Lights* fame, 37–0 to complete an undefeated season. Five players from that Yates team were playing professionally in 1992 and one, Santana Dotson, was the NFL's defensive rookie of the year. Almost thirty of the thirty-six seniors on the 1985 squad had received college scholarship offers, a fact that coaches regularly brought up as they primed this 1992 team with the idea of another ring.

The football players did what they needed to do academically to pass their classes, determined to remain eligible to play on game nights. Floyd would sometimes stay at school late after practice to get extra tutoring ahead of a pivotal test—but just as often, he would skip class or neglect his homework assignments until his coaches warned him that he was in danger of losing his eligibility.

Despite the swagger the seniors had showcased on the first day of school, their football season got off to a rocky start. Yates lost its first game to perennial powerhouse Dallas Carter High School, an 18–15 defeat made no easier by the fact that the Cowboys were ranked as one of the top five teams in the state. The Lions barely squeaked out a win in their second game, beating crosstown rivals Madison High School by a less-than-comfortable 26–20 margin.

During Yates's third game—against nearby Ross Shaw Sterling High School—the teams were locked in a 7–7 tie with just over five seconds left to play. Yates had pushed down the field and was on the five-yard line when Coach McGowan called for the field goal unit to go in.

The offensive players could not believe the call. The team's placekicker was a giant defensive lineman who made up in brute power what he lacked in the finesse typical for the position. He had missed his fair share of attempts already during the young season.

Dickerson, who in addition to being wide receiver was the placeholder for special teams, had an intimate view of the kicker's sometimes farcical attempts to steer the football through the uprights.

He had another idea for how to win this game. In the huddle, he whispered to Floyd to get ready.

"Fire! Fire!" Dickerson yelled as the field goal unit lined up. The coaches listening from the sideline knew the audible call meant someone on the team had defied their conservative approach and would try to win the game by scoring a dramatic walk-off touchdown. They had no choice but to watch and hope that the fake field goal play they had designed specifically to take advantage of Floyd's height would work.

As the center snapped the ball backward, Dickerson caught it and, instead of placing it on the ground to be kicked, picked it up and rolled to his left. Floyd, who was lined up at the edge of the formation, faked like he was blocking and then took off in a sprint toward one corner of the end zone. Before the defensive players could figure out what was happening, he was behind them and awaiting the pass from Dickerson. Even if the defense had been aware of what was planned, Floyd was at least four inches taller than any of the defenders, so as long as Dickerson threw the ball high enough, a touchdown was a sure bet.

The ball hung in the air as the clock ran down to zero. It was a play they had practiced dozens of times, and it was the kind of easy catch Floyd could make with his eyes closed. But this time, with the game on the line, his hand-eye coordination tripped for a split second—long enough for the football to slip through his gloves and bounce off his helmet and onto the grass.

The game ended in a 7–7 draw, leaving Yates with a record of one win, one loss, and one draw after three games.

Dickerson and Floyd went to the sidelines deflated and avoided eye contact with their coaches.

Dickerson thought he could hear Coach McGowan berating him to one of the assistant coaches: "Them hoodlums going to do what they want to do."

The following week, the coaches suspended Floyd and Dickerson for the next game.

As they sat on the sidelines unable to suit up, they went back over the doomed trick play, reenacting it second by second.

"How'd you drop the goddamn ball?" Dickerson asked.

"Man, I couldn't see the motherfucker," Floyd said. "The lights were in my eyes."

They both burst out laughing.

But with a middling record and an offense that had scored only a handful of touchdowns in three games, Yates was starting to become the subject of whispers in the Third Ward community. People wondered aloud whether this 1992 squad would be the team that let Yates's legacy fade as one of the best Black football programs in Texas. Maybe the magic that had put Yates in the playoffs for fifteen straight seasons had ended. Maybe the 1985 team that had gone 16–0—considered by some to be the best football team in Texas high school history—was the last one that would bring a championship ring back home to the Tre. Maybe the school that had seen its attendance fall by a third and its test scores drop annually was also losing its last source of pride: its luster as an athletic powerhouse.

"I'm not trying to win a popularity contest. I really don't care whether you like me or not," Bertha Dinkins told her Yates students with the stern familiarity of a mother admonishing her children. "All I want you to do is be the best student you can be in this class, okay?"

Dinkins's tough-love approach to educating was designed to break through to students like Floyd who had academic potential but were reluctant to put in any more effort than was needed to pass. She could not be sure the other teachers at the school knew how to reach these kinds of learners—by the time Floyd entered her classroom, Dinkins was part of a shrinking cohort of experienced Black educators who still lived in the same community where they taught.

In 1970, as federal courts condemned the glacial pace of integration efforts in Houston, the city's school board approved a plan to achieve racial parity among its teaching staffs, even as schools remained largely segregated. Under the plan, two-thirds of Black teachers were transferred to predominantly White schools and a third of White teachers were sent to Black schools. The reassignments were designed to jumpstart the long-delayed integration process—or at least create the illusion that they had—but they were beset by problems from the start. Because the transfers were voluntary, some of the youngest and most inexperienced White teachers ended up going to schools like Yates, while many certified instructors declined to be transferred from more affluent parts of the district.

Yates, however, lost a large portion of its Black educators and decades' worth of cultural and institutional knowledge. Many of the Black teachers who had taught at Yates had remembered the culture of academic achievement that had once governed the school in the 1950s and 1960s. Despite being segregated and starved of funds, there was a sense of camaraderie and pride that students felt as they learned from teachers who could relate to their experiences and shared their desire for equality. Alumni who graduated during the civil rights era included city leaders, broadcasters, and national figures such as the actress Phylicia Rashad and her sister, choreographer Debbie Allen—the latter of whom described 1960s Yates as "the high school of your dreams."

By the 1970s and 1980s, that sense of camaraderie was gone. Many of the White teachers who transferred to Yates were culturally ignorant of their new environment, knowing neither the students nor their parents like the Black teachers had, Dinkins recalled. Some struggled to maintain order and were taken advantage of, operating more like permanent substitute teachers.

Dinkins was one of the few Black teachers who stayed behind, and she felt uniquely positioned to connect with Floyd and his fellow athletes sitting in the back of the class.

In Dinkins's government class, Floyd was required to send his first letters to lawmakers—at least fifteen members of Congress and five U.S. senators. Another assignment required the students to find five people in the community and help them register to vote. Floyd could not afford to take the class field trips to Washington, DC, or to the state capital in Austin, Dinkins recalled, but he did join his classmates on a visit to meet Houston's city councilmembers and tour the Harris County courthouse.

"He knew government," she said. "He knew the basic things he had to, even if he ended up with a C average."

Dinkins had grown up during the height of Jim Crow segregation and had attended colored schools. She would show her Yates students scrapbooks with relics from the 1950s and 1960s—poll tax receipts, pictures of colored-only facilities, news clips of nonviolent protests disrupted by brutal state force.

She also had roots in the community. Though she had lived in Cuney Homes while her husband was attending Texas Southern University on the GI Bill—less than a block away from where Floyd now lived—she did not pretend to know the kind of poverty Floyd and other students faced. Her father and grandfather had owned the largest Black funeral home in Houston. She had used that upper-class status to push for equality during the civil rights movement, demanding to be allowed to shop and eat alongside Whites at establishments in downtown Houston. When the dining room in Foley's department store abruptly increased the cost of hamburgers from twenty cents to $5.50 to discourage Blacks from eating there, she had coolly brought out a $20 bill, sat down, and asked to be served.

As a teacher, a job she had taken in the mid-1960s without asking what the annual salary was (it was $2,495), she witnessed new forms of systemic racism ossify the inequities she had once marched to eliminate. She watched as the lack of funding left Yates with books and facilities that were both falling apart and a shrinking list of vocational programs; as high turnover left the school unmoored as it seemed to change principals every other year; as Yates was whiplashed by a series of reform measures and requirements enacted by faraway judges, legislators, and school board members who rarely, if ever, set foot in Third Ward.

In 1975, working to avoid mandatory busing of students, the city started a magnet program, ostensibly designed to attract students to integrated schools by offering specialized programming. Some students were drawn to the communications magnet established at Yates. But far more, including many from middle-class Black families, left for programs elsewhere in the city.

"We were losing all the cream-of-the crop students," recalled Beverly Ratliff, who was Yates's registrar from 1991 to 2014. "You don't have a lot of people at the top level to balance off those who fall behind."

In 1989, near the end of his NFL career, Dexter Manley testified before the U.S. Senate about how he had graduated from Yates twelve years earlier and gotten through college even though he had been unable to read. He struggled to read his statement.

"The only thing that really made me feel good in schools was athletics," the All-Pro defensive end and Super Bowl champion said. "That built self-esteem and some self-worth in Dexter Manley. Other than that, I had no identity."

When Floyd entered Yates four months later, he faced a similar predicament.

The Astrodome was packed with some thirty thousand fans on December 12, 1992, as the Yates football team was preparing to face San Antonio Holmes High School in the Class 5A semifinals. After the 1-1-1 start, they had turned things around and gone undefeated for the rest of the season, making it deep into the playoffs. They were on the brink of a state championship appearance.

To get this far, they had persevered through a grueling schedule and survived a number of close brushes with elimination. They had been down 22-0 at halftime in the quarterfinals against Katy High School when Floyd exploded into the locker room, shouting at the offense to wake up. Coaches had warned the players not to let the rich kids from Katy—a suburban school that would later spend a record $70 million on its football stadium—end their season. The halftime pep talks appeared to work, as Yates scored thirty-six points in the second half to win 36-22.

Floyd had helped contribute to the winning streak, earning All-City honors as a top tight end in Houston. During the third quarter of the regional final, quarterback Sean Porter had flung a third-down pass to an impossible location on the sideline when Floyd stretched his long frame to pull the football out of the air for a crucial first down. A photographer for the *Houston Chronicle* captured the moment: Floyd's body suspended in the air, halfway out of bounds, as a defender tried in vain to jolt the ball loose from his hands.

"You thought I was going to drop it," Floyd told Dickerson after Yates had won the game, an allusion to the botched fake field goal attempt earlier in the season.

Few things excited Floyd more than seeing himself in the newspaper, and high school playoff football in Texas was a prime opportunity to capture the spotlight. He had built a reputation as an animated player on the field with a love for the flashy parts of the game, but he continued to show little appreciation for mundane tasks like blocking.

Jerald Moore, the team's explosive running back, had been watching film of some of the earlier playoff games when he noticed something strange. On several of Moore's touchdown runs, Floyd could be seen racing ahead of him with his hands in the air. He had been responsible for blocking the defense's strong safety, but he instead headed straight down the field celebrating as he waited for Moore to score.

Moore, who led the team with thirty-three touchdowns through fifteen games that season, confronted Floyd about his lackluster blocking.

"What's going on?" he asked.

"Well, you just scoring touchdowns," Floyd responded. "I want to be in the paper too."

Floyd had figured that he could almost guarantee himself a cameo in the news photos and footage from the game if he was the first player congratulating Moore after a score.

"Okay, I guess that makes sense, but you got to block the strong safety for us to keep scoring touchdowns," Moore told him, laughing.

The Yates players had worked up a remix to Donny Hathaway's 1970 hit "This Christmas," and they were on a bus belting out their off-key version of the holiday classic:

Hey, ho, the whistle blows,
We're going to state, don't you know?
Together . . . This season.

Sean Porter's dropping baaack, and Big Floyd's on the caaatch.
And this season will be, a very special season, for me . . .

School was out, Christmas was just a few days away, and—after defeating San Antonio Holmes High School 41–39 in a shootout—they were headed to Austin for the 1992 state championship game. The mood was joyous as the bus made its way up US-290. Third Ward High had defied the odds and silenced the doubters, and the players were closer than they had ever been to a state championship ring. It was also an optimistic time for Floyd, who had racked up strong stats during the season and could expect college scouts to be watching the televised championship game. Despite all the obstacles he had faced, it seemed like he might finally be turning a corner.

The team arrived in the state capital and checked into a hotel not far from the University of Texas at Austin. Dickerson and some of the other receivers had snuck liquor bottles in their overnight bags, and word quickly spread that their room was the place to be. When Floyd got there, he could see teammates sitting on the bed playing spades, while a few others gathered around a small table where an intense dominoes game was taking place. Marvin Gaye's voice blared from the speakers of a portable CD player.

"They got a store, but Coach says we can't go," Floyd told the players in the wide receivers' room.

Coach McGowan had called a team meeting earlier. He had spoken eloquently about the Yates football tradition and the last championship team—recalling how the 1985 players would go to sleep in their jerseys, wake up at four a.m., and be focused on nothing but football. His message was clear—go to bed on time, no foolishness, stay out of trouble—but he had enacted a mandatory nine p.m. curfew just to be sure.

"Man, I'm going to the store," Dickerson said, and, minutes later, Floyd and about a dozen other boys from the team were breaking curfew as they bought soda and chips from a shop across the street. They snuck back into the hotel, and those who could fell asleep, ahead of the biggest competition of their lives.

"You ready?"

The players had suited up and were about to run into Memorial Stadium when Dickerson paused to gut-check his friend.

"Let's go, man," Dickerson said. "We can't let these White folks kick our ass. Let's go."

"I'm ready, I'm ready, V."

A thick fog had engulfed the field and rain was in the forecast, but the cloudy conditions had not stopped throngs of spectators from showing up for the last high school football game of the year.

Temple's cheerleaders, clad in the team's blue-and-white colors, were on one end of the field holding up a large sign that read, "Blue Front White Back Magic." Four teenage boys up in the bleachers had stripped off their shirts to reveal *C-A-T-S* painted in black letters on their pale torsos. On one side of the stadium, thousands of Temple faithful held small, printed blue-and-white placards bearing the letter *T*.

The Yates side of the stands was full of thousands of Black fans, some of whom held handmade cardboard signs that read, "Yates to State." Faces that would have been familiar to Floyd—aunts, teachers, neighbors, classmates—were shaking maroon-and-yellow pom-poms and cheering for Third Ward High.

Ralph Cooper, who had traveled over from Houston, was one of several journalists on the sidelines. Camera crews were in place to capture the action from multiple angles. As two sports commentators raised their voices to adjust to the blaring sounds of the Yates marching band, the scene could have been mistaken for any of the college football bowl games that were set to take place around the country the following week.

"Temple in white, Yates in red. All set for press time to make this opening kickoff here," television commentator Ed Biles said as the game was about to begin. "Here we go!"

Yates received the kickoff, and its offense took the field. The players seemed nervous, making a number of early mistakes, including giving up an interception on the third play of the game.

Things picked up for Yates later in the first quarter, when Floyd caught a pass from Sean Porter. He snatched the ball out of the air, weaved through the defense, and dived forward for a first down, the team's first of the game.

"Floyd George. He's a six-foot-six, 210-pound senior," Biles told viewers after the play. "He's got good speed."

Temple emerged with an early 10–0 lead, before Yates responded with two touchdowns to go up 14–10 in the second quarter.

But the game slipped away from the Lions in the second half as Temple's duo of running backs ran for more than 250 yards. The runners took advantage of the absence of Oscar Smallwood, Yates's All-State linebacker who had broken his fibula a couple of games earlier.

Floyd managed to make three catches in all, and

Dickerson caught a touchdown—but in the end it wasn't enough. As the final seconds ran off the clock, the Temple players started to rejoice over the 38–20 victory. The Yates players shook hands with the victors, but only some were able to hold back their tears until they got off the field.

Coach McGowan congratulated Temple's coach, accepted the runner-up trophy, and did a few interviews on the field.

"We're real happy to be this far," he told the sideline reporter Craig Way. "Once you get to the state finals, people say you're a winner. We just would've really liked to have won the game."

But when he got to the locker room, he broke down weeping. He hugged the players and let them know how proud he was of what they had accomplished.

"Nobody gave us a chance to get here," he told them. "Nobody believed in us but us."

Floyd was in the locker room crying with the rest of the team. They wept over the sudden realization that they had lost more than just a game. For the seniors on the team, there would be no spring practice to look forward to, no summer workouts, no fresh new season to face together with lofty expectations of winning it all. This was the last time they would be together like this.

"Man, it's over," Jonathan Veal muttered to himself as reality set in.

The mood on the bus ride back to Houston was eerily quiet as the players sat in the dark, grappling with the feeling that they had let Third Ward down by returning as losers.

Floyd pounced, piercing the somber moment with a quip about how they would've won if Porter had just passed the ball to Big Number 88.

"Man, the first goddamn person who cracked a joke was Floyd," Dickerson later remembered. "He was back there cracking just like we ain't even play the game. And everybody just had to laugh because that was him."

The rest of the trip, as the sting of their loss faded, the Yates High Lions partied like they had won the Super Bowl.

The euphoria of football season was long gone, he had played his final high school basketball game, and Floyd was complaining to PoBoy about the academic part of school. It was the spring of 1993, and he was stressed out about the Texas Assessment of Academic Skills test. Earlier in the year, Floyd had failed the math section for the third time. He had been struggling to prepare for his final try before graduation, and he worried about what another failure would mean for his scholarship dreams.

"Bro, this is like a black cat on us," Floyd said. "I got these big old hands; I got my weight up. Man, why it got to be this?"

State officials had introduced the TAAS test in 1990, requiring all high school students in Texas to pass the three-part proficiency exam in order to graduate. Before the Texas Education Agency instituted the test, its own experts warned that its adverse impact on Black students would be drastic—73 percent were expected to fail the math portion, 55 percent were projected to fail the reading section, and 62 percent were likely to fail the writing part. The projected failure rates for White students were 50 percent, 29 percent, and 36 percent, respectively.

In 1999, a suit brought by the Mexican American Legal Defense and Educational Fund asserted that the high-stakes exam was racially biased against Black and Hispanic students. By requiring minority students to pass a test that their underfunded schools had failed to adequately prepare them for, Texas was further entrenching the existing disparities within its education system, the plaintiffs argued. The suit pointed out that minority students had indeed failed the test at disproportionately high rates, a phenomenon that cut across socioeconomic factors.

Despite agreeing with the plaintiffs that "the TAAS test does adversely affect minority students in significant numbers," and asserting that the disparity "must give pause to anyone looking at the numbers," U.S. district judge Edward C. Prado dismissed the suit in deference to Texas's right to set its own education policy.

A national movement toward more standardized testing was underway, led by politicians, corporate titans, and education think tanks. In 1983, a federal education commission released a report titled "A Nation at Risk," which declared that "the educational foundations of our society are presently being eroded by a rising tide of mediocrity that threatens our very future as a Nation and a people." It recommended more rigorous standardized testing, and most states moved swiftly in that direction.

Texas—which at the time ranked fortieth in the nation in per-pupil spending on education—was one of several states that forced students into high-stakes testing while failing to adequately invest in teaching them what they needed to succeed. A 2000 study commissioned by the Civil Rights Project at Harvard University found that Texas's testing policies deepened existing racial and socioeconomic inequalities, requiring instructors in predominantly Black and Hispanic schools to prioritize teaching students how to properly take tests over providing actual academic instruction. The study called on other states—many of which were using the Texas model championed by then governor George W. Bush as a template for education reform—to reconsider using single tests as prerequisites for graduation.

"Damn, V, I can't . . ." Floyd told Dickerson one day while they walked home together from school, the prospect of not graduating if he failed the test looming over him. "Man, I'm trying."

Dickerson, who had watched Floyd study for the exam in vain, suggested that he consider cheating.

"Do something, shit," he said. "You got to do something."

In his home life, Floyd was confronted with the kinds of troubles that most of his peers taking the test would never have to deal with: overcrowded conditions, a lack of healthy food, regular bursts of gunfire at night, the omnipresent trauma of the crack epidemic. His sister Zsa Zsa was in the throes of addiction, and Floyd had taken responsibility for raising her toddler son, Brandon Williams.

The TAAS test did not account for the fact that thousands of poor and minority students like Floyd were dealing with those kinds of stresses outside the classroom, said Lynn Gordon, a teacher at Yates who tried to help Floyd prepare for the exam.

"He was the man of the house," Gordon recalled. "You have to look where they come from. They had to go to school, but did they eat the night before?"

Floyd attended senior prom awaiting the test results and spent much of the night aloof and distant. A week later, he learned he had failed the test again. Floyd was inconsolable.

"He didn't want to be around anybody no more," Dickerson recalled. "He felt like he was an outcast."

On graduation day, Floyd was absent as his best friends

celebrated and smiled for pictures in gowns and square-shaped academic caps. Decades later, friends and family members would debate the point at which Floyd's life journey started to veer off track. PoBoy, who shared a room with Floyd and saw him every day during those harrowing final weeks of the spring in 1993, said the descent likely began much earlier than most knew.

"I think the fight really kind of got out of him when he didn't get that diploma," PoBoy recalled after Floyd's death. "When he ain't get that diploma, it just crushed him."

While Floyd's shaky education kept him from realizing his goals, sports still offered him a lifeline to make it out of the Bricks.

George Walker, who was the head basketball coach at South Florida Community College in Avon Park, had been looking for a power forward to build out his team. Walker had played basketball at the University of Houston and remembered seeing Floyd on the court at Yates. He knew of Floyd's academic problems but believed the young man when Floyd promised that he would be able to pass the necessary exams before the season began.

Just to be sure, Walker had asked around about Floyd, checking with the Yates principal and others in the neighborhood.

"They were all pushing for me to take him down to South Florida," Walker recalled. "It's pretty good when you're recruiting a kid and the whole community is behind him."

The fall after his senior year at Yates, Floyd retook the TAAS test and received a passing score. He quietly obtained his high school diploma a few months later.

Floyd, who had grown up envisioning himself playing for the University of Florida Gators, was initially reluctant to go to a much smaller school with less appeal to professional scouts. But with limited options, Floyd decided to take Walker's offer of a basketball scholarship. His goal was to eventually transfer from there to a four-year Division I school, where he would have a chance at going pro.

Michael Riggs, a friend from Houston who was already playing basketball at South Florida, picked Floyd up from the Greyhound bus stop in Avon Park in the fall of 1993. Riggs took him to his new dorm—a room in the Hotel Jacaranda on Main Street—and then introduced him to the rest of the basketball team.

It didn't take long for Floyd's athleticism to set him apart from his teammates.

"Man, it ain't that bad, Po," Floyd said over the phone to his old roommate. "It shouldn't be hard for me to go D-1 from here. They ain't that good, Po. Ain't no good people down here. Looks like I'm going to be the man."

Despite breaking his foot early in his freshman season, Floyd rebounded and was soon putting up solid stats as a starting forward for the Panthers.

He eventually got attention from some of the colleges that had passed on him due to his academic struggles in high school. A coach from Texas A&M–Kingsville's football program asked Floyd if he would consider playing tight end for the Javelinas. The largely Hispanic Division II school in south Texas had a reputation for recruiting Black players and sending dozens of them to the NFL. Floyd jumped at the opportunity. It didn't hurt that Riggs, a fellow Houstonian, had also been recruited to play basketball there.

"Riggs, I'm just happy to be here," Floyd told his friend as they sat in their apartment near campus. It was the fall of 1995, and Floyd had finally made it to a four-year college, the first in his family to do so.

The red tile–roofed Spanish Mission architecture of the campus, with rustling palm trees lining quiet streets, was a sharp contrast to the hardscrabble landscape of the Bricks, and Floyd felt lucky to be there as a college athlete, Riggs recalled. Now, he just had to get on the field.

"When he got to Kingsville, he was a prop," said Floyd's other roommate at the time, Marcus Williams, using a term for a player who had not yet met the school's requirements for athletic eligibility.

Floyd's academic struggles had again emerged as an obstacle. To remain eligible to play basketball at South Florida, he had taken vocational classes like welding and auto repair, Riggs recalled.

Most of those classes did not transfer to his new school and didn't prepare him for the entrance tests in subjects like math, writing, and reading. He had scored so poorly on those exams that he was assigned a full slate of remedial classes at Kingsville. But developmental classes did not count toward the twenty-four credits required for athletic eligibility, so he was stuck on the sidelines. Floyd seemed to always be treading water at Kingsville, trying to get enough regular credits to become eligible but never moving any closer to getting on the field.

Jonathan Veal, who visited Floyd at Kingsville in the spring of 1996, saw how the situation was weighing on his twenty-two-year-old friend.

"They got these restrictions, man, but I want to play,"

Floyd told Veal as they sat in the stands watching a football game he could not participate in.

Back in Third Ward, his mother was looking after his sister Zsa Zsa's children. Overwhelmed with stress, Miss Cissy had started exhibiting health problems that would vex her for the rest of her years—high blood pressure, hypertension, strokes.

Floyd's pathway to the NFL had all but closed, and he started to survey friends about what they thought he should do; as the months passed, it increasingly looked like he might never see the field at Kingsville.

Floyd made up his mind. In the summer of 1997, he packed up his belongings and asked a couple of friends from Houston to come pick him up. His four-year journey into the world of higher education had come to an end without a degree, without a sports contract, and without an income.

He was going home to Third Ward.

"Look, man. I'm just a ballplayer trying to make some money," Floyd told the two men who had pulled up to the corner at the edge of Cuney Homes.

It was six thirty p.m. on August 2, 1997, and Floyd was trying to upsell the potential buyers on a larger rock of crack cocaine than they had initially requested.

Floyd was wearing a blue T-shirt and white jogging pants, and his low-fade haircut—accented with a middle part—looked no more than a few days old. He was standing just steps away from his mother's apartment, an area where police were known to target young Black men for easy arrests.

Floyd, like everyone in the neighborhood, knew it was risky to be operating at the corner of Winbern and Tierwester

Streets, but the high-traffic intersection was a lucrative place to find customers. And he needed the money. The drug game was a business of calculated risks, so he had set up shop on this corner, instituting a set of safeguards he hoped would reduce his chance of getting arrested.

"Look, in case you the law, I'm going to put the money away first then bring you your stuff and lay it down by the dumpster," Floyd told the men in the car, after convincing them to increase their purchase from $10.

The officers had made sure to use the right slang—asking for "rock," not "crack," for example—but Floyd was suspicious.

"You sure you ain't Five-O?" he asked after accepting $18 from one of the men.

They assured him they were not. But the undercover cops from Squad 23 were among several who had been circling Cuney Homes in unmarked cars that evening, as they had on many previous days. When Floyd walked off to get the drugs they had ordered, they radioed to their uniformed partners stationed around the corner in a police car. They asked their colleagues to pull them over in a simulated traffic stop, the officers would later write in their incident report.

Under the ruse they had developed, they, too, would be victims of overaggressive policing—something they figured might help them build rapport with their suspect and ease his fears that they were cops.

After the fake stop, the police car drove off and the undercover officers pulled back around to where Floyd had been standing. A middle-aged man with a goatee walked over.

"You didn't get your stuff?" asked the man, who lived nearby and had also been dealing drugs, police later said.

"No, you saw the law."

The goateed man asked the undercover cops to wait, promising to make sure they received what they had paid for. He walked over to Floyd, and after a brief conversation, he walked back to the buyers and handed them the rock of crack they had bought. The undercover officers drove away and radioed again to their colleagues nearby to let them know they had made their case.

As Floyd turned to head back toward Cuney Homes, two police cruisers were speeding to the scene from around the corner.

The swift crescendo of the approaching sirens made one thing clear as he stood frozen in his tracks: it was too late to run.

PART II
Big Floyd

CHAPTER 5

The State of Texas vs. George Floyd

W HAT YOU THINK, BIG bro? They came at me with five."
Floyd was fighting back tears as he explained his predicament to his friend Travis Cains over a phone call from jail.

As a bail bondsman, Cains had grown accustomed to receiving collect calls from Floyd during the decade that had passed since his first conviction in 1997. He had lost count of how many times he had bailed Floyd out of jail cells, but now he was trying to convince his friend to get used to the idea of being locked up for the next five years.

Floyd had been charged with aggravated robbery in 2007 for allegedly pointing a pistol at a young woman in front of her children while a group of men ransacked her home. He had told Cains he had not robbed the house, but police had pulled him over months later in the getaway car and the victim had tentatively identified him. He was the only suspect they had been able to track down, and the prosecutors were determined to secure a conviction for the brazen break-in.

Floyd would not be an especially sympathetic defendant at trial, Cains told him. He was not only a young Black man, but a young Black man with a criminal record. He had racked up a series of arrests and convictions for petty drug offenses over the previous decade, and prosecutors would have little trouble defining him to jurors as a habitual criminal who had turned violent. The state had explained to Floyd's court-appointed lawyer that they might seek a forty-year sentence if he were convicted. They likely weren't bluffing, Cains warned.

"You go to trial, they're going to hang your ass," he said. "Man, you better take that goddamn five. Hop on that five so you can go on and come back home, man."

Floyd was torn. His previous stints in jail were mostly monthslong bids for small-time drug deals, but he was now staring at the prospect of doing extended hard time as a convicted violent criminal. That Cains was presenting the prospect of five years in a cell as an opportunity to be jumped at signified for Floyd how far downward his life had spiraled since he had returned from college.

Fifteen years had passed since he told his high school friends that he would be different, that the world would feel his impact. And now, it seemed, he would be just another Black man wasting away in a cage.

Floyd thanked Cains for his advice and hung up the phone, letting his tears drop to the jailhouse floor.

Cains's work in the bail bonding business had familiarized him with the vagaries of the criminal justice system. He had become a kind of de facto legal counsel for the Bricks, as indigent defendants regularly turned to him when their court-appointed lawyers were hard to reach or seemed disinterested in their fate.

Cains had grown up wanting to become a police officer, though a driving-while-intoxicated arrest in 1988 had dashed those dreams before he could make it to the academy. Instead, he had responded to a newspaper ad for a local bail bonding company. His hefty size, profane lexicon, and intimidating visage were seen as assets in an industry that dealt with sometimes-elusive criminal defendants.

Working for $3.35 per hour at first, Cains would help arrange bonds for people desperate to get out of jail while awaiting trial. In exchange for a fee, the bonding company would assume responsibility for the defendant's bail, agreeing to pay it in full if they failed to show up for their court cases. Cains would let his clients know in no uncertain terms that he would personally come find them if they skipped court after he helped bail them out of jail. When that happened, Cains doubled as a bounty hunter, chasing down suspects like the cop he had once aspired to become, only with lower pay and fewer regulations on the use of force.

Throughout Third Ward, Cains had a reputation as someone with access to the resources to get people out of jail, and he would often wake up to phone calls from distraught mothers pleading with him after their sons had been detained. Miss Cissy was occasionally on the other end of those calls, asking him to help free Floyd.

Even as he tracked down men who skipped bail, Cains understood why many of them opted to live as fugitives rather than submit to the whims of the Texas justice system. He had largely avoided serious prison time himself, but it wasn't for lack of trying by the Jump Out Boys of the Houston Police Department.

One night back in 1996, Cains and Floyd had been watching a late basketball game on television. Floyd was on one of his increasingly frequent trips home from college, and

Cains had introduced some weed into the already relaxed atmosphere. After the game ended and the blunts had extinguished, Floyd realized he was hungry.

"Let's go to the store, get us some snacks," he suggested.

It was almost midnight, and Cains was tired, but he also had the post-high munchies. Plus, he figured a trip to the corner store would allow him to get a refill of the Swisher Sweets cigars the two had used up during the game.

They hopped in Cains's Cadillac and headed over to the corner store, where Floyd bought chips, soda, and candy. Cains got the cigars and a pint of ice cream.

They were on their way back to Cains's house when they saw the red-blue flash of police lights in the rearview mirror. Cains cursed under his breath as he pulled over.

"Your license and registration," a stern-looking White officer said after walking up to the driver's-side window. Another officer had approached Floyd on the passenger's side.

"So, what are y'all doing?" the first officer asked after Cains handed over the requested paperwork.

"We ain't doing nothing. We were just going to the store."

The cops asked Cains and Floyd to step out of the car. Confused, both men looked at each other and froze. Within seconds, the officers moved in concert to let them know that the request was, in fact, a demand.

They pulled Cains and Floyd from the car and forced them onto their stomachs. They pushed the men's faces into the ground, hard enough for them to taste the gravel and dirt. After handcuffing them, the officers stood up and placed their boots on the lower backs of their prone suspects—refusing to tell them what they were suspected of.

Another police cruiser pulled up to assist, and two other officers made a beeline for Cains's Cadillac.

"Ain't nothing in there," Cains yelled from the sidewalk as they opened the doors.

The officers rummaged through the car for a few minutes, ignoring the men on the ground.

"We ain't got no drugs!" Cains said as he lifted his head to see different items being tossed out of the vehicle.

The tub of ice cream fell to the ground near Cains's face. He watched its contents melt along the pavement as the officers continued their vigorous search.

When the cops failed to find any incriminating evidence, they pulled Floyd and Cains upright, unshackled them, and let them know they were free to go. The two men returned to the car to find its entire interior disheveled. Cains's radio had been torn out, and his speaker system was dislodged. The snacks they had just purchased had been thrown to the ground alongside the melted ice cream.

"Damn, man," Floyd said, shaking his head as he surveyed the damage.

"These motherfuckers tore up my car," Cains said.

But as they got back in the car and started driving home, their anger turned into relief. They had survived an encounter with Houston's notorious narcotics unit without being badly beaten or hauled off to the county jail.

Floyd breathed a loud sigh before cracking a smile.

"Whew, Lord. Thank you, Jesus!" he said, looking over at Cains. "We ain't got to go to jail. Man, we ain't going tonight!"

The officers had left without apologizing for the aggressive stop-and-search, without explaining why they had targeted

the two men, and without saying whether they had established probable cause to rifle through their vehicle. They had
not presented a search warrant or gotten the car owner's compliance, recalled Cains, who knew enough about the legal
system to understand that otherwise rock-solid criminal cases
could be tossed out for such breaches in constitutionality.

But in communities like Houston's Third Ward, the protections of the Fourth Amendment's search-and-seizure clause
had become little more than window dressing in the aftermath of the 1994 crime bill and the war on drugs that had
preceded it. As Miss Cissy had warned Floyd, his status as a
Black male in America meant he had been born with two
strikes already against him. He had also emerged into the
world at a particularly ill-fated time. The nation's incarceration rate, which had largely held steady for generations,
began to inch up around the time of Floyd's birth in 1973.

President Richard Nixon had declared a war on drugs in
1971, and the nation's prisons swelled over the ensuing decades as each successive president embraced militaristic
language and tactics to combat the spread of illegal sub-
stances. Nixon's assertion that drugs were "public enemy
number one" reflected the sentiment that America's substance-
abuse problem should be tackled with brute government
force, rather than with treatment. The policy approach of the
1970s—when mandatory-minimum sentences, new federal
drug agencies, and the use of aggressive policing tactics like
no-knock warrants were established—helped set the country
on a pathway of criminalization that would endure into the
twenty-first century, with devastating consequences for communities like Houston's Third Ward. A top aide to Nixon
admitted in 2016 that the drug war was launched in part to

target, vilify, and disrupt Black communities—seen at the time as a political threat to the president. By that point, nearly a half century of drug-enforcement policies embraced by a series of Republican and Democratic presidents alike had accomplished Nixon's original goal.

Floyd had just started middle school when President Ronald Reagan spoke to the nation from the White House residence in 1986, describing crack cocaine as an "uncontrolled fire" and calling on the media to "send alarm signals across the nation" about the scourge of this "new epidemic."

A few days after Floyd enrolled as a freshman at Yates in the fall of 1989, President George H. W. Bush brandished a plastic bag filled with crack cocaine during a televised presidential address aimed at shocking the national consciousness.

"All of us agree that the gravest domestic threat facing our nation today is drugs," he asserted from the Oval Office, specifying crack as the nation's "most serious problem."

Both Bush and Reagan touted the rush of federal resources to the issue after Congress passed major drug bills in 1984, 1986, and 1988. Funding for federal drug enforcement tripled, and prosecutors more than doubled their narcotics cases in an unprecedented expansion of the drug war. America's prison population nearly tripled during the back-to-back presidencies of the tough-on-crime Republicans, surpassing 850,000 by the time Bush left office in 1993.

But Democratic politicians, who watched as the GOP turned the crime issue into a winning political message in the 1980s, also aimed to show the country that they were serious about tackling urban drug use. In 1994, President Bill Clinton signed into law the Violent Crime Control and Law Enforcement Act, which had been sponsored by then senator Joe

Biden. The legislation funded a hundred thousand new police officers for America's streets and provided $9.7 billion for prisons, money that incentivized states to pass harsher sentencing laws.

The crime bill's impact disproportionately fell on low-income minority neighborhoods where millions of blue-collar jobs had been shipped overseas while millions of pounds of cocaine, marijuana, and other drugs flowed in the opposite direction. At all levels, the government responded with an aggressive crackdown, ensnaring both the hardened criminals and the downtrodden men and women seeking an escape from impoverished conditions by either using or selling drugs.

The most punitive efforts were targeted in neighborhoods like the one where Floyd grew up. While studies show that Whites and Blacks used drugs at the same rate, Houston's narcotics officers were rarely seen patrolling the fraternity houses of the University of Houston or the well-landscaped subdivisions of the city's west side. By the time Floyd returned from college to Cuney Homes in 1997, the U.S. prison population had soared above 1.2 million, with his demographic cohort fueling most of the increase. Drug offenders made up the vast majority of the new inmates, and young Black men were disproportionately pursued for petty arrests. Between 1986 and 1999, the number of young White Texans imprisoned for drug offenses declined by 9 percent, while the number of Black youths locked up on drug charges grew by 360 percent, according to the Justice Policy Institute.

Texas was on the bleeding edge of the 1990s race to incarcerate, locking up Blacks at a rate seven times higher than Whites. As the state's prison system tripled in size between 1990 and 2000, it overtook California's to become the largest in the country and was second only to Louisiana's on a per capita basis. By the time Floyd began cycling through that system at the age of twenty-three, almost a third of young Black men in Texas were under the supervision of the state's Department of Criminal Justice—in prison or jail, or on probation or parole.

Floyd had managed to avoid jail time as an athlete in high school and college and at first was successful in keeping things that way when he came home. Cains helped him get a job as a bouncer at a nightclub called Wet Spot, but Floyd quickly found that the money was not enough to make ends meet.

The neighborhood around Cuney Homes was bustling with fast money from the drug trade, and Floyd's friends who had been selling for years were more than willing to cut him into the business. But they soon learned that Floyd was not a very good hustler. It seemed he lacked both the drive and the ruthlessness to hold down a corner in the Bricks. But Floyd's friends could also see that he needed money, so they tried to show him how he could make plenty of it without having to venture far from his home.

Floyd's undercover drug bust in 1997 had led to a predictable sequence of events: a trip to the county jail, the assignment of a court-appointed lawyer, and the quick settlement of a plea in exchange for what prosecutors presented as a lenient sentence. The state had said the crack rock that Floyd allegedly sold to the undercover officer for $18 weighed about 0.3 grams. He pled no contest, agreeing to serve six months in jail.

It was Floyd's first criminal conviction, and despite the relatively short sentence, he left jail with the psychological wounds that come from spending day after day locked in a tiny cell. In addition to the bouts of anxiety and claustrophobia that would follow him for the rest of his life, Floyd walked out of jail in 1998 with a label he would never be able to expunge: convicted felon.

Floyd's jail stint also left him with hundreds of dollars in court debt and few ways to pay it off. He complained to friends about how he had served his time but still did not feel fully free from the grip of the Texas Department of Criminal Justice.

One of those friends was Jacob "Fathead" David, who was younger than Floyd and part of the crew of Cuney Homes kids who had looked up to the star athlete. As a teenager, Fathead, who was affectionately given that nickname on account of his round cheeks, would play sandlot games in the oversize basketball jerseys Floyd brought back to the Bricks during breaks from school. Because he had idolized Floyd growing up, he was one of the few people who still entertained the former college athlete's visions of grandeur.

"We're gonna be the biggest dudes in the world," Floyd told him one day in the late 1990s. "Everybody's going to know our name."

They had gotten a glimpse of what it was like to be famous after Floyd struck up a friendship with Stephen Jackson, a professional basketball player to whom he bore an uncanny resemblance. A mutual friend had introduced Floyd to Jackson, who grew up near Houston and was drafted to the Phoenix Suns in 1997. Floyd had brought Jackson to the Bricks, introducing him to Fathead and a few of his other friends, and the group soon figured out ways to benefit from Floyd's famous doppelgänger.

"I got Stephen Jackson with me," Fathead would whisper to bouncers outside nightclubs, pointing to Floyd standing in line.

The Cuney Homes guys would spend the rest of the night relishing VIP treatment as they skipped the line and sipped on free drinks. Afterward, they would go to McDonald's and split a $5 value meal, laughing at the success of the prank.

But then they faced the sobering reality that they were grown men who had to sneak into clubs, scam free liquor, and share Big Macs because they were broke. Sometimes, Floyd would spend the night at Fathead's home because the lights or cable had been cut off in Miss Cissy's house due to unpaid bills.

He confided in his friend about the financial pressures he was facing. Floyd's sister Zsa Zsa had continued to battle drug addiction, and after recently giving birth again, she had checked herself out of the hospital the very same night, leaving Miss Cissy to take custody of the newborn, family members recalled. Floyd's mother turned to him to help ease the financial burden she faced while trying to raise her grandchildren.

Floyd had promised her he would take care of things, even though his criminal record and lack of a college degree made finding a decent job difficult.

Around this time in the late 1990s, Floyd's plans for achieving stardom had shifted from the sports field to the recording studio.

He had befriended Robert Earl Davis Jr., an up-and-coming DJ on Houston's south side who had pioneered the chopped-and-screwed musical style that dominated the city's hip-hop scene at the time. Popularly known as DJ Screw, Davis was beginning to get noticed outside Houston when Floyd returned home from college. Floyd was drawn to the mellow beats of the chopped-and-screwed sound, impressed that the new genre gaining buzz across the South had emanated not only from Houston but from his side of the city.

DJ Screw's technique involved slowing down the tempo of a hip-hop song, giving the music a heavy, languid sound that crawled along in a deep octave. Houston rappers would freestyle over samples of popular soul, R&B, and hip-hop jams that were manipulated to make the singers sound like they had been sedated. Davis released the music in a series of mixtapes, dubbed "Screw Tapes," that flooded Houston and eventually found a national following.

Floyd would boast to friends about the time he was spending with Davis and other members of the Screwed Up Click—a loosely defined collective of aspiring artists who would congregate for all-night sessions at the recording studio known as the "Screw House." Sometimes, Floyd would take his friends from Cuney Homes to the studio, a highly sought-after invitation that let them meet local rappers and watch as DJ Screw turned their freestyles into mixtape tracks.

"That was like going to Michael Jackson's house or Jay-Z's house," Fathead recalled years later.

For Floyd's childhood friend Cal Wayne, the invitation to the Screw House was an opportunity to try to advance his burgeoning career as a rapper. He was a naturally gifted lyricist and had begun rapping about the reality of growing up poor in Cuney Homes, performing under the stage name

Killa Cal Wayne and building a loyal fan base across Third Ward.

Wayne asked Floyd, who had been featured as Big Floyd on several popular Screw Tapes, to appear on his studio album. Floyd agreed but wasn't sure how to go about it. He had played around freestyling for DJ Screw but had never performed a song with written lyrics.

"What you want me to say on it?" Floyd asked Wayne.

"Just tell your truth," Wayne said, seeking to calm his friend's nerves. Wayne promised that he would take care of the musical accoutrements, adding the chopped-and-screwed sound effects to enhance Floyd's deep voice.

While Floyd's freestyles at the Screw House had been carefree boasts about money, cars, and women, the written verse he came up with reflected the more somber reality that he was living:

"Damn, little Wayne, I've been broke for so long / I've been stuck in last place for so long / Loaded (loaded) with potential but I'm still going wrong / Need to get my act together quick, nigga, and start being grown . . ."

In the unreleased song, Floyd went on to complain about being reprimanded by friends for "sitting on my ass" instead of fulfilling his potential.

Floyd had rapped his truth, and the result was a lyrical diary entry that bore little resemblance to the 2 Live Crew party-rap songs he had once relished while joyriding with his high-school buddies. Instead, Floyd had described a tragic set of traits reminiscent of the "Poor Georgie" character that MC Lyte had rapped about in her 1991 cautionary tale.

Wayne could see that his friend was struggling, but he figured the malaise wasn't anything that a little money couldn't fix. Wayne had been hustling since adolescence, after the incarceration of both his parents left him to fend for himself and his siblings in the Bricks. He had made a living peddling weed and cocaine, and new products had brought a fresh path to prosperity in the neighborhood in the late 1990s and early 2000s. The success of chopped-and-screwed music coincided with the rising prominence of "lean," an illegal recreational beverage that mixed codeine-based cough syrup with soda. The drink, which originated in Houston and was also called "purple," "syrup," or "drank," had the effect of slowing down the brain—complementing DJ Screw's trippy, slow-moving tracks.

Wayne saw music as a potential off-ramp from the street life, but until he got a record deal, he planned to keep hustling. He tried to help Floyd to make a little money as well, but as Floyd struggled to find his footing in the booming drug trade, people in the neighborhood began to whisper that he had been using more than selling—breaking a cardinal rule of urban hustlers: never get high on your own supply.

Floyd's petty dealing landed him in the back of a police cruiser for a second time on October 29, 2002. Officers from the Houston Police Department had been watching him as part of an investigation into alleged gang activity inside Cuney Homes. He had been standing in the courtyard of the projects as a steady stream of people approached him, handed him cash, and then waited for him to collect a small object from the ground near the porch of a nearby apartment, the officers went on to write in their arrest report. After seeing this pattern repeat several times within fifteen minutes, the cops approached Floyd and told him he was being detained. One of the officers went to the porch of the apartment and found a plastic bag with four rocks of crack cocaine.

Seconds later, Floyd was in handcuffs. Unlike in his previous interactions with the cops, Floyd was defiant as he rode to the police station. The only reason they had arrested him, Floyd told the two cops as they carted him away, was because he was Black. He said plenty of other people had been selling dope, but the police seemed to be picking on him. He felt the whole world seemed to be conspiring against him in the fall of 2002.

When Floyd got to the station, the intake and triage documents he completed for county health authorities revealed the deep anxiety of a man who, just days after his twenty-ninth birthday, was about to be locked up.

He wrote that he was saddened by the death of his father three weeks earlier. George Perry Floyd Sr. had been found slumped over in his car in North Carolina and was rushed to Cape Fear Valley Medical Center, the same hospital where his son had been born. He was declared dead on October 8, 2002, at the age of fifty-three. The younger Floyd had not really known his father and was dismayed by the reality that he would never have a chance to bond with his namesake.

On the intake form, Floyd checked boxes indicating that he had been suffering from sleeplessness, crying spells, feelings of guilt, and a loss of energy. He wrote that he had been abusing Vicodin pills on a daily basis. He complained that he struggled with being easily distracted, making foolish business investments, and starting projects that he didn't complete.

"When I talk, people listen to me," he wrote, adding that

he had been successful in getting other inmates to follow the jailhouse rules. "I write to myself. I'm pretty smart. I write raps and don't finish it."

During a meeting with his court-appointed attorney, Floyd complained that he was depressed and had been hearing voices. His deceased friends were talking to him, he said. Noting Floyd's erratic behavior, the attorney filed a motion for his client to be given a psychiatric assessment.

A clinical psychiatrist for the county concluded Floyd was likely faking a mental illness. He was sent back to his cell to deal with his issues alone. He later pleaded guilty and was sentenced to eight months in state jail, which he would have to serve without treatment or rehabilitation services.

As Floyd battled his inner demons inside a cramped dormitory filled with hundreds of other men, the state of Texas faced a $10 billion budget shortfall for the 2003 fiscal year, in part due to the ballooning cost of imprisoning more than 160,000 people.

After more than a decade of prison expansions, mandatory minimums, and lock-them-up drug enforcement policies, several other states had decided to reverse course at the turn of the twenty-first century. The war on drugs had proven untenably expensive and, despite falling crime rates, was ineffective in reducing drug dependency. Other nations that prioritized treatment saw both drug abuse and crime decline, strengthening public safety without the massive fiscal and social costs of America's unprecedented program of mass incarceration.

The tough-on-crime policies swept up an entire generation of young Black males into a seemingly never-ending cycle of incarceration and deepening poverty, with legal fees accruing and job opportunities dwindling. Over the course of Floyd's lifetime, the number of incarcerated Americans would jump from about two hundred thousand to more than two million.

By 2002, states were spending almost $40 billion on corrections, even as they faced revenue crunches in the aftermath of 9/11 and the dot-com bust. The circumstances presented lawmakers with difficult decisions over whether to devote scarce tax dollars toward incarcerating nonviolent offenders or educating young children. Many state legislatures began reversing the harshest drug laws and shifted toward treatment and other less expensive alternatives to imprisonment.

But Texas opted to stay the course, with lawmakers determined to find cost savings without letting up on the state's punitive reputation. Rick Perry, the state's Republican governor at the time, directed officials to cut spending on corrections even as they locked up a growing number of Texans in newly built prisons.

As the inmate population continued to increase, Texas prisons cut medical costs by 8 percent between 2001 and 2008, the largest margin in the country. Texas reported reducing per-inmate health-care costs by almost 13 percent during that period, a time when health-care inflation both in the broader economy and in the corrections sector had skyrocketed. The state also set a caloric ceiling on inmate meals, cutting daily totals from 2,700 calories to 2,500 calories in a bid to save money.

Governor Perry was following in the footsteps of George W. Bush, who served as governor from 1995 to 2000. During his term, Bush established his tough-on-crime reputation by leading the nation in executions and overseeing a prison budget that increased from $1.4 billion to $2.4 billion. The rapid increase made imprisonment the fastest-growing part of the state government, dwarfing the growth in spending for education, health care, housing, and other services.

George W. Bush had himself engaged in youthful indiscretions, but the scion of a well-connected political family had found redemption from a life of hard partying and heavy drinking at age forty. He had survived his encounters with police without the kind of future-limiting criminal record that George Floyd had amassed. Instead, Bush's message of "compassionate conservatism" would carry him to the pinnacle of political power in the White House while the other George was locked up in a Texas state jail cell.

Floyd did not have an opportunity to treat his substance issues while he was imprisoned after his 2002 arrest. Instead, he passed the time by exercising, doing five hundred push-ups each morning with an old Third Ward friend named Reginal Smith, who was serving time for unauthorized use of a motor vehicle. Floyd worked in the jail's kitchen, but like hundreds of other inmates he spent his days trying to fight off boredom and watching television in the unair-conditioned facility.

Floyd was released in the summer of 2003, having gained little from his time in prison beyond another entry on his rap sheet. He returned to his old neighborhood, where police officers were still circling the block, looking for people to arrest.

Since adolescence, Floyd had learned that a consequence of living in Third Ward was that the police were a constant and often hostile presence, showing up at all hours prepared to use force first and ask questions later. After being stopped by Houston police at least twelve different times as an adult,

Floyd knew he could be detained for a wide range of activities—driving too slow or speeding, dressing too nicely or looking unkempt, walking with too much purpose or meandering about.

In 2001, shortly after Floyd's mother moved out of her apartment in the Bricks to a house across the street, Floyd was arrested after police saw him walking in the rain through his old neighborhood. In their report, officers said they had stopped Floyd in Cuney Homes because he "did not look like he was going anywhere imparticular [*sic*]." Floyd served thirty days in jail on a failure-to-identify charge.

A few months later, Floyd's teenage brother Rodney was detained after stepping out of the house on Nalle Street, after cops said there was a stolen car nearby. Floyd had been walking back home when he saw Rodney, dressed in church clothes for his grandfather's funeral, being placed on the ground in handcuffs. Floyd rushed over and asked the officers to arrest him instead.

"I'll take it. It's mine," Floyd said, before even knowing why Rodney was being detained. "Let him go. It's me. Let my brother go."

Rodney didn't have a criminal record at that point, and Floyd wanted to spare his brother from the stigma and trauma that came with being arrested.

But when the cops heard they were brothers, they decided to detain them both. At the police station downtown, the arresting officer walked to the holding cell where the brothers were waiting and told them their fate would be determined by the coin in his hand.

"Heads, you stay," he said, looking at Floyd. "Tails, you go." The coin landed on heads.

"All right, little brother, I guess you get to go," the officer told Rodney, before letting him out of the holding cell and shutting the door on his older brother. Floyd was released a few hours later and was never charged.

Police officers and departments were financially incentivized to keep their stats up, which made Third Ward an attractive location for patrols. Millions of dollars in federal grants and overtime hours were linked to arrest statistics, based on the perception that a large number of apprehensions meant police were actively reducing crime.

"You had a lot of crack in Houston and officers that needed hours or numbers," recounted Houston's former police chief C. O. Bradford, who led the department from 1996 to 2003. "They would swoop through the neighborhood and make these low-hanging-fruit arrests to keep numbers up. They picked up the same person over and over again."

A few officers made so many arrests that they became notorious among residents of the Bricks for allegedly filing fake charges or stealing money from suspected drug dealers. The officer who had arrested Floyd in 1997 was decertified by the state in 2002 after he was charged with theft and hampering arrest. Texas cops routinely choose to be decertified instead of facing other possible consequences, including additional misconduct charges.

On February 5, 2004, Floyd was standing on the corner of Winbern and Tierwester Streets—the same intersection where he had been arrested for selling crack to an undercover officer seven years earlier—when another plainclothes cop pulled up and watched him from afar.

The narcotics officer, a Black man named Gerald Goines,

had spent more than fifteen years working the beat for the Houston Police Department, helping to send hundreds of other Black men to jail on petty drug crimes. He had perfected a strategy of using paid informants to buy drugs from dealers around Cuney Homes. He was so ubiquitous and stealthy that residents had given him the nickname "Batman."

Goines radioed for uniformed officers to arrest Floyd, later writing in his arrest report that he had given a confidential informant $10 to buy a "dime rock" of crack from Floyd and watched as his suspect had delivered the drugs.

When Floyd was arrested, he did not have any money on him, and Goines did not reveal the name of the anonymous informant. Goines, the only witness to the alleged sale, would later be accused by the Harris County district attorney of falsifying charges in hundreds of drug cases, including the one involving Floyd. Goines targeted impoverished minority men in part because he knew many of them already had criminal records, the district attorney said. Most could not afford a lawyer, and several accepted plea deals to avoid potentially being sentenced to years-long prison stints.

Goines's attorney, Nicole DeBorde Hochglaube, vigorously denied the accusations, describing her client as a longtime officer commended by his superiors. She said there was no reason to believe Goines targeted people, fabricated evidence, or falsely accused Floyd.

The revelations about Goines's allegedly illegal policing tactics would come long after Floyd faced the consequences of being on the corner while Batman patrolled the Bricks.

*

"Hello, this is a collect call from 'Hey, big bro, this is Floyd,' an inmate in Harris County jail . . ."

Travis Cains had come to expect the incongruent sounds of a high-pitched robotic voice interrupted by the deep, fast-paced drawl of a frantic-sounding Floyd calling collect from behind bars. So, he was not surprised when Floyd called him from jail after he was arrested in the Goines sting.

He pressed 3 to accept the call, bypassing pleasantries to get straight to the point.

"What'd you do?"

"Them Jump Out Boys came through and they got me," Floyd said.

Floyd initially tried to fight the charges, delaying and resetting the case multiple times over the course of five months. Prosecutors offered him a two-year prison sentence in exchange for pleading guilty. He declined. When the state came back with an offer of ten months, Floyd considered how difficult it would be to prove himself innocent in court. For a Black man in Texas, Cains had told him, the presumption-of-innocence legal standard was flipped on its head.

Floyd couldn't afford a private lawyer and realized it would be his word against that of a police officer during a trial. He had prior convictions for drug possession and had been arrested in a location that was recognized by police as a spot for narcotics trafficking. Texas prosecutors were known to disproportionately exclude Black potential jurors during jury selection, and there was a good chance Floyd's fate would be decided by a group of people who did not look like him. Floyd agreed to plead guilty and prepared to spend ten months in prison for the alleged $10 sale.

Throughout his history with the Texas criminal justice system, Floyd never faced a jury of his peers, instead opting to accept plea deals. He ultimately signed his name eight separate times at the bottom of guilty-plea documents that were topped by the words "The State of Texas vs. George Floyd." The lopsided title accurately reflected the odds he faced in the nation's most punitive state.

During the time he was cycling through the criminal justice system, Texas was one of the few states in the country that did not have a public defender system for defendants who could not afford lawyers. Instead, felony court judges appointed private defense attorneys paid by the court to represent low-income clients. In an examination of Harris County, Texas, researchers found judges were more likely to hand cases to lawyers who had donated to their campaigns; in many cases, the clients had adverse outcomes.

In 1999, a Democratic state senator representing Houston's Third Ward convinced the Texas legislature to pass a bill that would have established a statewide independent public defender program. Eight days after launching his presidential bid, then governor Bush vetoed the bill.

Waiting for Floyd when he was released from jail in 2005 was Becky Sue Johnson, a woman he had started dating shortly before his incarceration.

Johnson had gone to Yates High School with Floyd but had since left Third Ward to settle into a professional life in one of Houston's new suburban subdivisions. Her $80,000 salary working as a manager of operations for one of the city's largest health-care systems had allowed her to purchase a brand-new four-bedroom home in southwest Houston. On the weekends, Johnson would invite old friends from the south side over for dinner.

When a mutual friend brought Floyd to one of the get-togethers, he wasted little time sidling up to Johnson. She told him she wasn't interested, but she continued to invite him over. Soon, she was tailoring the menu to suit his tastes—setting aside thin-crust pizzas just for him after he told her that deep-dish pies were too bready.

Still, she resisted his entreaties until one Sunday night when he called her in a panic after he had been pulled over by police near his mother's house. He was riding in a friend's car, and the officer suspected he was under the influence of something, though he did not have any drugs on him.

Johnson drove out to the scene and gave the officer her identification. She had done some petty hustling in Third Ward but had been discreet—always operating behind closed doors—so she had a clean criminal record. She told the officer she worked for Memorial Hermann Health System and would take responsibility for her friend.

"Release him to me and this won't happen again," she said.

The officer agreed to let him go. Johnson took it as a sign that she and Floyd were meant to form a more serious partnership.

She told Floyd that she had to be at work the next morning and that, if he wanted to, he should grab some of his clothes from his mother's house and come stay with her.

"Look, if you want to be with me, you're going to have to have some structure," she said as they drove to her home in her black 1999 Ford Explorer.

From then on, the two spent every day together, easing

into a mutually beneficial coexistence. Floyd offered Johnson a familiar outlet from the stress of the corporate world, and Johnson provided him an escape from the traumas and temptations of Third Ward.

For their first date, they went to an Anthony Hamilton concert, using tickets Johnson had received from an ex-boyfriend who was trying to get back together with her. Hamilton sang his R&B hit "The Truth," and Floyd enjoyed it so much that he started referring to himself as "The Truth" in conversations with his new girlfriend.

Johnson helped him apply for jobs through a temp agency, and soon Floyd was hired to work at a warehouse on Murphy Road, a few minutes away from her house. His first paycheck was less than $500 but, with Johnson agreeing to cosign a car loan, he was able to purchase a silver Pontiac Grand Prix from one of the used-car dealerships on the outskirts of the city that catered to subprime borrowers.

Floyd, Johnson, and a few other friends would sometimes pile into the Pontiac and drive out to Club Reminisce to party in the middle of the week. On quiet nights, Floyd would get behind the bar and make drinks for his friends, and sometimes Johnson would take over the DJ booth for a few minutes.

One Wednesday night, Johnson's nine-year-old daughter, Ashli, got upset that the adults were planning to leave her with the babysitter again. She begged to go out with them.

Johnson planned to dismiss the request out of hand, but Floyd had a different idea.

"I got this," he told Johnson, before instructing Ashli to go get dressed. She rushed to her room and put on a flowing *folklórico* dress.

They left the house around eight p.m., touring some of their neighborhood spots—Club Reminisce, Turning Point, Carrington's Sports Bar. Floyd got Ashli virgin daiquiris, and by ten thirty p.m. she was exhausted and falling asleep. She also thought she was drunk.

"Nope, get up," Floyd told her, laughing as they headed to another bar. "You wanted to go out, right?"

The trio kept barhopping until midnight, when the little girl was practically begging to go to bed.

Ashli had learned her lesson.

"I don't want to go out," she said after they got back to the house.

After nights out on the town, Johnson and Floyd would lie in bed together, and she would read to him from a notebook that contained her diary entries and life goals for the year. For 2005, she had written that she wanted to fix her credit, exercise more, and "get married to the man that God has for me." She had used another page in the book to plan out the wedding, from its music ("All My Life" by the R&B duo K-Ci & JoJo), to its location (Good Hope Missionary Baptist Church in Third Ward), to its color scheme (platinum and metallic gold). But next to "Date," she had left the space blank.

Floyd had introduced Johnson to friends and family as "my wife" but was decidedly less enthusiastic about the prospect of actually getting married and settling into a life as a suburban husband. Over the course of 2005, the relationship hit turbulence as Floyd avoided the topic of long-term commitment to Johnson and to the new lifestyle she had envisioned for him.

Floyd had trouble staying employed, as temp jobs often

remained temporary. And, despite being fifteen miles away from Third Ward, he struggled to put distance between himself and his old hardships. Often, he would find his way back to familiar territory, driving the Grand Prix through his old neighborhood.

Johnson also suspected Floyd was using drugs and grew frustrated as he sometimes disappeared until the wee hours of the night. She responded by giving Floyd the silent treatment, ignoring him when he tried to talk to her. After a nasty argument in 2006, she took her blanket from the master bedroom and started sleeping on the couch. She was fully committed to the silent strategy, essentially pretending as if Floyd was not in the house.

When she went to work the next morning, Floyd grabbed her diary, figuring if she wouldn't talk to him, he could communicate with her there. He crafted a note that was part apology and part love letter.

"God thank you for all the blessings you gave me," he wrote. "Thank you for a great family, most of all a great future wife. Becky-Sue you are the definition of a real woman. You are my life, my joy, my breath. I thank God for you because if it wasn't for him there would be no you. Please forgive me for the time I hurt you."

When Johnson got home and saw Floyd's handwriting in her diary, she let out a laugh, unable to maintain her steel-faced silence.

She grew quiet again as she read Floyd's words: "We were married before we saw each other ... You are my heart, forever."

Floyd had never been so expressive during their time together as he had been in the one-page diary letter. They made up, and Johnson told Floyd he should consider writing more often. Taking Johnson's advice to heart, he started putting his internal trauma down on paper in her diary. He wrote letters to Johnson, letters to himself, and letters to God, describing the battles he faced and the trials of his faith.

"Sometimes we have to go through things to get to where we are going," he wrote in one undated entry. "I shouldn't worry knowing I put everything in God's hand but I'm only human."

In other entries, he pleaded for absolution, telling God he was sorry for his growing list of sins and shortcomings. He encouraged himself to fight the dark temptations of his past. He prayed for help navigating the court system, where he had pending drug cases.

"Oh heavenly father we are tore down, please help to build us back up," he wrote in another entry. "Please forgive me . . . I'm sorry for turning my back on you."

Floyd was battling a range of vices—"the devil tries to get next to me," he wrote—that he feared were becoming too strong to resist.

Some of those vices came in the form of old friends from Third Ward who started visiting Floyd at Johnson's house, occasionally floating dangerous ideas for how to solve the problem of their shared poverty.

During the summer of 2007, a rumor was spreading among Floyd's old crew about "the Mexican," a man who was believed to have a massive stash of money in his house on the north side of the city. Cuney Homes had once had a reputation for producing prolific armed robbers, and a group of guys who had come up in the Bricks during that era saw a lucrative opportunity to revive the tradition.

On August 9, 2007, Floyd had asked Johnson if he could use her SUV for the day, adding that he would drive her to work and pick her up in the evening. Johnson wondered why Floyd needed her car when he had the Grand Prix but decided not to press the point.

As they headed to her office at the medical center, she pleaded with her notoriously tardy partner not to be late picking her up. As a salaried employee, she did not have a set closing time, but she often left the office around five p.m. and would continue working on her laptop at home if she hadn't completed her tasks for the day.

There are conflicting recollections about exactly what happened after Floyd dropped off Johnson that morning, but there is little dispute that he was inside the Ford Explorer right around five p.m. when it pulled up to the driveway of a three-bedroom home on a cul-de-sac on Houston's north side.

Inside, Aracely Henriquez, a twenty-seven-year-old mother of two, had been cooking and talking on the phone with her father in El Salvador when she heard a knock on the door. She walked through the living room, looked through the blinds, and saw a Black man dressed in a blue uniform carrying a clipboard full of papers.

"Who is it?" she asked through the closed front door.

The man replied that he was from the water utility. Henriquez remembered that she had called the water department a couple of weeks earlier and thought the man may have been on a belated service call. When she opened the door, the first thing she noticed was the folder the man was carrying. It bore the logo of Aflac, an insurance company that had nothing to do with water issues. She tried to close the door, but the man stepped forward, using his body to hold it ajar. Within seconds, a group of between three and five men exited the SUV and rushed into the house while the driver stayed behind the wheel.

The largest of the men held a pistol to Henriquez's abdomen and shouted at her.

"Where are the drugs? Where is the money?" yelled the man, who had a short Afro and was wearing a black hat, black pants, and a red shirt.

Henriquez, whose English was limited, told him she had no idea what he was talking about.

The other men ransacked the house, tearing through cupboards, cabinets, and closets in search of something they could not find.

A second, shorter man wearing all black pushed Henriquez's phone out of her hand and pinned her face-first against the sofa next to her crying seven-year-old son. He presided over them with a pistol as Henriquez's ten-month-old daughter stood in her walker, screaming as the robbery took place. When Henriquez tried to scream as well, he hit her with the pistol.

Soon, it became clear the men had the wrong house. They did not find money or drugs, instead making off with some jewelry and a cell phone. The men piled back into the Ford Explorer, where the driver was still waiting inside, then sped away. Unbeknownst to them, a fifty-two-year-old Black woman who lived two houses away on the same cul-de-sac had a clear view of the scene. She had immediately become suspicious when she saw the men enter the home of her neighbor. As they ran out of the house, she jotted down 284CYS—the license plate number for the black SUV.

When the police arrived at Henriquez's house, the neighbor was able to provide them with the license plate number. The cops turned to Henriquez, asking her to describe the men who had robbed her.

She said she could not properly describe the robbers but knew the largest of them had a "lunar" face with a protruding chin and large lips. The other assailants were shorter, but they all appeared to be Black men between the ages of twenty-five and thirty, she told the cops. She said she had not gotten a good look at the man who stayed in the car.

Meanwhile, Johnson was wondering where Floyd had gone with her SUV as she waited on a bench outside the medical center. She couldn't reach him and grew annoyed as the summer's late sunset began to dim the sky. A little after eight p.m., the Explorer finally pulled up next to her.

In the driver's seat was Floyd's childhood friend PoBoy. Johnson had let PoBoy stay at her house for a short stint after he had been released from jail in 2006—Floyd had insisted that his friend had nowhere else to go—but she was surprised to see him driving her car.

"Where's Perry?" she said after getting in.

"I'll tell you when you get home."

"Is he all right?"

As they drove, Johnson kept asking about Floyd, and PoBoy told her what had happened.

Within days, police were leaving messages for Johnson at her office and at her mother's house. Johnson did not respond, knowing the reason why they wanted to talk to her.

Floyd had told her about the robbery but insisted that he had not gotten out of the car and did not know that guns would be involved.

She believed him. She had also done her own research, asking contacts back in Third Ward what they had heard. Word had spread that the gunman was an acquaintance of Floyd's who also happened to be tall and dark-skinned.

None of those rumors had reached the authorities who were looking for the robbers, a result of the neighborhood's rock-solid "no snitching" policy. But detectives on the case got a break on November 15, 2007, when narcotics police pulled Floyd over near his mother's house on Nalle Street. The drug-enforcement squad had been posted up in Floyd's neighborhood, trailing a man they suspected was involved with cocaine trafficking.

As police watched the man, Floyd drove over and picked him up in Johnson's black Ford Explorer before heading out. The officers pulled them over a few minutes later. Not finding drugs on either man, they took down their identification and let them go. When police later checked the vehicle's license plates against HPD records, they made the connection to the August robbery.

Officer Javier Tapia, the lead detective on the Henriquez robbery, had moved on to other matters when he received a voice mail alerting him to a potential suspect in the dormant investigation. Frustrated by his repeated attempts to reach Johnson without success—the address officers had visited was her mother's house, and the two were estranged at the time—Tapia had shifted the case to "inactive" status on October 17. But he had marked the black Explorer as a "wanted" vehicle and had called on any Houston police who pulled the car over to contact the robbery division if any occupants matched the description of the suspects.

The November 15 traffic stop had located the getaway car,

and one of the occupants matched the description. Tapia re-activated the case with a potential new suspect: George Perry Floyd Jr.

A few days after Thanksgiving, Tapia came back to Henriquez's house with an array of photos of twelve Black men for her to review.

With the images spread between her and Tapia, Henriquez pointed to Floyd's mugshot. The picture resembled the large man who had held a gun against her abdomen, she said in Spanish. But she wasn't certain.

Tapia gave her three options to describe her level of confidence: positive, tentative, and negative.

She chose tentative. None of the assailants had worn masks but, in the chaos, Henriquez had only vaguely remembered their faces, she said in a September 2020 interview.

"It was really difficult to distinguish between them," she recalled, describing her assailant as a "big guy with thick lips, young and strong."

She had selected Floyd out of the photo lineup because he was the one who looked most like the *grandotote*, or "giant" of a man, who had those features, she said.

"But I wasn't sure it was him," Henriquez recalled. Her seven-year-old son had also identified Floyd, but she discounted his account, saying his eyes had been "bathed in tears" during the robbery.

Still, the officers had what they needed to establish probable cause. They put out a warrant for Floyd's arrest, charging him with aggravated robbery with a deadly weapon.

It took the authorities almost six months to track down Floyd, but when they did, they threatened to throw the book at him. It was a standard negotiating tactic for prosecutors, especially in cases with weak evidence. Investigators had not found any fingerprints or DNA linking Floyd to the robbery, and they had no confession, no weapon, and no cooperating codefendants.

The case largely relied on Floyd's connection to the SUV and the photo lineup, which had not been videotaped or audiotaped. The Houston Police Department later upgraded its photo lineup standards to include a "double-blind" technique. To follow best practices, officials said, pictures should be presented by officers who were not tied to the case and did not know the suspect, to avoid bias and steering witnesses to a particular person. The process should also be recorded. None of that happened in Floyd's case.

Prosecutors had another problem: a "tentative" ID from a victim who spoke limited English would likely fall short of the beyond-a-reasonable-doubt legal standard needed to ensure a guilty verdict at trial.

Soon, attorneys for the state were reaching out to Floyd's court-appointed defense lawyer to negotiate a plea deal. To open the negotiations, they presented the risks Floyd would face at a jury trial, pledging to pursue a sentence of up to forty years if they succeeded in convicting him.

They offered to accept a guilty plea in exchange for a twenty-year sentence. Floyd immediately rejected the prospect of staying in jail until he was fifty-five years old. After Floyd turned down additional plea deals and prepared to take his chances in court, the state proposed five years, describing it as a final offer. Floyd realized he would have to make one of the most important decisions of his life. He started calling friends to ask for advice.

After consulting with Cains, who told him to take the

deal, he dialed his high school teammate Vaughn Dickerson, who had faced a similar choice a few years earlier.

"They offered five years, man," Floyd said, fighting back tears and repeating that he was not the gunman. "I don't know."

Dickerson and his brother Van had been offered a plea deal in a 1999 aggravated-robbery charge that resembled Floyd's case. Police had accused them and two other men of knocking on a victim's door, forcing their way inside when it opened, and brandishing guns as they demanded money and ransacked the residence.

The brothers had been identified in photo lineups by the homeowners but insisted they were innocent. They had rejected the state's offer of a plea deal, and, at their three-day trial, they suspected that their lawyer had been getting drunk before coming into the courtroom.

"I don't know if the defense is even going to put on a case," the prosecutor told the jury during opening arguments.

The brothers were found guilty in 2000 and sentenced to ten years in prison. Dickerson had gotten out early on parole in 2005, just as Texas was attempting to rein in its soaring prison budget.

Realizing that Floyd would have to rely on a court-appointed lawyer, Dickerson told him to think carefully about the options before him: he could risk a trial, where his prior criminal history might be unfurled before jurors, and prosecutors could make an example out of him by putting him away for decades, or he could take the surefire plea deal. The idea of snitching on the man Floyd and many people in the neighborhood claimed in private was the actual gunman was never even considered as a possibility.

People who knew Floyd and spoke candidly about his criminal history—including the friends and family he was closest to at the time—adamantly insisted that he was not a robber. Dickerson also couldn't believe that Floyd, who avoided aggression even on the football field, would ever pull a pistol on a terrified mother. Still, he encouraged his friend to plead guilty.

"Take the five," Dickerson advised, trying to put a positive spin on his friend's predicament. "You're going to see parole in two years, and in two and a half years, you'll be home."

Floyd listened quietly, weighing the heavy choice that lay before him.

He hung up the phone and made peace with his decision: he would call his lawyer and sign his name to a plea document, confessing to a crime he claimed he had not committed. He prepared to spend the next five years as Inmate No. 01566124.

Three months after the first Black president was inaugurated, a thirty-five-year-old Floyd rode prison transport from Houston up to the tiny town of Bartlett, Texas, just north of Austin. By some combination of fate and statistical probability, he was seated next to his childhood friend and rapper Cal Wayne, who had also been recently convicted—in his case, on forgery and drug charges.

As Houston's urban landscape gave way to wide swaths of ranchlands and cotton fields, Floyd looked down at the shackles that bound his legs and wrapped around his waist, restricting his movement and linking him with the other inmates. He observed the prisoners packed tightly in the vehicle, which had a ceiling so low that Floyd's head brushed against it when he sat straight up. Hunched over, he began to tremble with anxiety.

"Wayne, you can lift your head up, you a little bitty dude," Floyd complained, stuttering and sweating. "Wa-Wayne, I'm . . . I'm claustrophobic."

"Calm down, man," Wayne said. "Damn."

"How long is the ride?" Floyd asked, unable to suppress his nerves. "How long is it going to take us to get there?"

Wayne told his friend to relax, but every few minutes Floyd complained about his claustrophobia.

After about three hours, to both men's relief, they arrived at Bartlett State Jail, a minimum-security facility designed to hold more than a thousand inmates. During initial processing, Floyd was handed a copy of the Texas Department of Criminal Justice's *Offender Orientation Handbook*. The 111-page book consisted of rules, restrictions, and penalties designed to create an orderly, safe, and rehabilitative environment in each of the state's 105 penal facilities.

Like many prisons across the country, the privately run Bartlett State Jail had a historical link to the profit models of slavery and convict leasing that had preceded the era of mass incarceration. In 1967, a thirty-two-year-old farmer's son named Terrell Don Hutto became the warden of the Ramsey plantation prison in east Texas, where 1,500 mostly Black inmates picked cotton from dawn to dusk for no pay. Slavery had been abolished a century earlier, but the Manhattan-size plantation had all its hallmarks, from the ruthless overseers on horseback to the stately Big House, where Hutto lived with his family and was catered to by unpaid "houseboys." Texas's plantation prisons were a financial boon to the state, bringing in $1.7 million annually in the 1960s (more than $13 million in today's currency).

The brutal efficiency with which Hutto ran Ramsey got the attention of officials outside Texas. Hutto spent the 1970s helping state governments in Texas, Arkansas, and Virginia turn incarceration into a lucrative enterprise. The timeless concept of limiting expenses and increasing revenue seemed simple enough, so he decided to go into the business for himself. In 1983, Hutto cofounded Corrections Corporation of America, which would become the country's largest operator of for-profit prisons.

Its ascendancy ran parallel to America's ballooning incarceration rate in the 1980s and 1990s, a period during which spending on prisons quadrupled. When CCA was awarded a contract to run Bartlett State Jail—after a competitive bidding process that was open to other for-profit prison operators—it told Texas officials that it could save them money by doing so at a daily rate of less than $30 per inmate.

While inside, Wayne and Floyd quickly learned how to fend for themselves. They slept on the same bunk in the cavernous dormitory room they shared with more than fifty other men.

Wayne often did the talking, negotiating for prison comforts and privileges while Floyd stood in the background as the muscle. Floyd's tall, imposing frame—which he honed by working out while locked up—was enough to shield both men from the worst of the violence inside. Floyd did not join any of the various prison gangs at Bartlett, having little use for the protection they promised. He was one of the biggest men in the facility, and few were willing to test whether the nickname some of the inmates had given him, "Jolly Green Giant," was a misnomer.

But in quiet moments away from the other men, Floyd

confided that he remained uncomfortable with the fact that his mere presence instilled fear in people.

"Why you be acting like that?" Wayne asked him one day, questioning why Floyd was reluctant to exploit his size advantage over other inmates.

"I never like to get into it with nobody because it'd look like I'm bullying them," Floyd said. He just wanted to do his time and go home, he told Wayne.

Floyd was more comfortable acting as a consoler than a brawler, his bunkmate learned. When Wayne received a letter from his wife ending their relationship, Floyd spent the next few days trying to comfort his heartbroken friend. He encouraged Wayne to listen to Jay-Z's "Song Cry," a soulful tune in which the rapper laments the loss of a long-term love by pledging to express his sorrow through music rather than tears.

He encouraged Wayne to turn his own pain into lyrics, and Wayne fantasized about pursuing a music career on the outside, with Floyd working as his bodyguard and occasionally appearing on tracks.

While they dreamed of freedom, there were multiple stakeholders outside the prison walls benefitting from the men's confinement.

During the time Floyd was at Bartlett, Texas was undergoing a broader privatization initiative that helped the state's Department of Criminal Justice deliver some of the $95 million in savings that Governor Perry had requested for 2010 and 2011. The state faced a projected budget shortfall of more than $20 billion in the aftermath of the Great Recession and sought to rein in its prison budget by slashing health-care costs, selling more than $160 million worth of furniture, clothes, and other products made by unpaid inmates, and privatizing a larger share of its operations.

The Bartlett contract also held promise for the economic fortunes of the fading, predominantly White town where the jail was located. While Floyd was at Bartlett, the former cotton-shipping town's economy was heavily dependent on the jail. CCA hired locals to help guard a population of mostly minority men, eventually becoming Bartlett's largest employer and a major source of tax revenue for the town of 1,623, accounting for a third of its entire budget.

Local officials came to rely on CCA to keep residents employed and to stave off the economic decline that had taken hold in a small town left behind by the fast-moving pace of globalization, recalled James Grant, who was Bartlett's mayor at the time Floyd was incarcerated.

"They did pump a fair amount of money into the economy," Grant said.

The city had wooed the prison, spending $100,000 to buy the needed land and passing a $1.9 million bond referendum to help pay for the water, sewage, electrical, and street improvements around the property, Grant said.

The benefits accrued quickly: CCA touted the fact that the state jail had hired more than two hundred people, paid $868,000 to the city's water utility every year, and spent another $166,000 supporting local businesses. For residents, water bills plateaued, and the city began replacing antiquated clay pipes with more durable metal ones. Even with the upgrades, Bartlett residents had some of the lowest utility costs in the state.

The economic benefit was so great that when the state of

Texas later weighed whether to close the jail, Grant and other city leaders pleaded with prison officials to keep it open. The jail, Grant wrote, "has been tightly woven into the fabric of the community. The prison is now a critical financial component of the City and its loss would have a significant impact on our budget."

While Floyd was locked up, CCA had average occupancy rates across the company's facilities exceeding 90 percent. Its investors, which included public pension funds and university endowments, were rewarded as the company's performance helped push its stock price up more than 30 percent in 2010, a year in which CCA took in nearly $1.7 billion in revenue and reported almost $1.4 billion in expenses.

CCA, which changed its name to CoreCivic in 2016, said it tried to focus on providing programs and other assistance to help inmates like Floyd successfully rejoin their communities.

"During our tenure as the operator of the Bartlett State Jail, the individuals in our care were provided a wide range of programmatic opportunities in adherence with our management contract and geared toward preparing individuals to successfully rejoin their communities and families," CoreCivic spokeswoman Amanda Gilchrist said in a statement. "We are proud to have helped many student inmates at Bartlett earn their GEDs and industry recognized certificates, which help reduce their likelihood of returning to prison and increase their chances of earning gainful employment."

Floyd told friends he languished while locked up. He worked as a porter, carrying items and supplies between the prison's dorms. Like most prisoners in the state, he received no pay for his labor but hoped the work would aid him in his desire to make parole and get out early.

He read *The Purpose Driven Life* by evangelical pastor Rick Warren after Johnson mailed him a copy. The motivational book aimed to help readers answer questions like "Does my life matter?" and "What area of my life am I holding back from God?"

It was a "definite game changer," Floyd told Johnson.

But the book was designed to be read in forty days, a fraction of his 1,826-day sentence. And during his second year in prison, Floyd learned that he would be doing the rest of those days without Cal Wayne, after his friend made parole.

Floyd occasionally got to speak by phone to friends back in Third Ward, when they could afford the costs of collect calls from jail. He exchanged letters with his nephew Brandon, who had recently won the state championship with the Yates High basketball team. The snippets of news from home reminded him about how much he was missing as the months slipped past.

Because of Bartlett's remote location 165 miles away from Houston, few people came to visit Floyd while he was there. And when Floyd was transferred in 2011 to Diboll Correctional Center, another privately run facility in a remote location, his childhood friend Adarryl Hunter could sense his loneliness had only worsened as he was confined to a small cell. In the letters they exchanged, Hunter promised to come see his friend every few months. Floyd had listed Hunter as his half brother, allowing the two men to have contact visits rather than having to speak across a plexiglass divider.

They would talk about sports, relationships, and Third Ward gossip during the two-hour sessions. Floyd, who grew frustrated as the years passed that he still hadn't made parole, rarely wanted to discuss what was happening in the prison.

But he was happy to hear life updates and receive advice from his garrulous friend. Hunter's career as a pharmacist was advancing, and he told Floyd he was hoping to open his own pharmacy in Houston.

They also discussed Floyd's postincarceration plans, strategizing ways for him to earn a living without risking getting locked up again. Floyd said he wanted to get into truck driving, hitting the open road after years of being constricted to tiny spaces.

Hunter wasn't so sure about that, knowing that his friend was not a very good driver and had been pulled over countless times by the cops. He suggested Floyd consider opening a smoke shop instead, where he could sell legal products.

"It's the same principle," Hunter said, comparing the legit business to street hustling. "You got a wholesaler—somebody you buying it from for cheap—and you retail it to people for a marked-up price. All you got to do is build a customer base."

Keying in on their shared love of movies, Hunter would sometimes deliver life lessons by quoting films they had watched together. During one visit near the end of Floyd's bid, Hunter referred to a scene in the 1993 drama *A Bronx Tale* in which a 1960s bus driver played by Robert De Niro erupts at his son for idolizing gangsters rather than the working man.

"The tough guy is the one who pays bills, the one who goes to work every day, takes care of his business—that's the tough guy," Hunter said, paraphrasing De Niro's character. "The guy on the corner, that's not the tough guy."

Nearing his fortieth birthday after more than four years locked up, Floyd prepared to leave jail determined to never return to a cramped cell. But his stint had done little to show him how to be the responsible, bill-paying kind of tough guy his friend had described. In fact, most of the people who walked out of Texas state jails would soon be arrested again, state statistics revealed. After spending almost a third of his adult life behind bars, all Floyd had to show for his time were intensified claustrophobia, nightmarish anxiety, and emotional demons that would follow him out of the prison gates and trail him back to Miss Cissy's house in Third Ward.

CHAPTER 6

The Use of Restraint

O N SEPTEMBER 9, 2010, in a city more than a thousand miles north from where George Floyd withered in a prison cell, two Minneapolis police officers confronted a twenty-eight-year-old Black man named David Cornelius Smith. Smith, who had a mental illness, had gone to the YMCA downtown to play basketball. Officers soon received reports he was acting strangely and disturbing teenagers on the court. Upon arriving at the scene, the officers fought Smith and Tasered him five times. They wrestled him to the ground, handcuffed him, and forced him to lie on his stomach. Then, one of the officers, Timothy Callahan, sat on Smith's legs. His partner, Timothy Gorman, pressed his knee between Smith's shoulders, where it remained for four minutes and thirty seconds.

Smith cried for help, then fell silent. When officers checked for a pulse, he had none. They administered CPR to revive his heart, but the relief wasn't lasting: Smith died eight days later. The medical examiner ruled that Smith would have been alive if some external force had not interfered with his breathing. Smith's cause of death was mechanical asphyxiation.

The officers were cleared of any misconduct; the internal affairs unit concluded they had followed protocol. The city settled a civil suit with the Smith family for $3 million in May 2013. The department also committed to retrain officers on how and when to employ the series of maneuvers that could lead to asphyxiation. Those use-of-force techniques included the neck restraint, in which an officer uses their body to apply pressure to the neck; the prone restraint, which involves laying a suspect down on their stomach and putting their hands behind their back; and the maximal-restraint technique, which combines both maneuvers.

Top brass in the department did not want to ban officers from utilizing those holds—they saw them as additional tools that officers could use before resorting to fatal force. Instead, the department decided to conduct trainings on how to employ the tactics safely. In 2014, a defensive-tactic training session opened with a discussion about neck restraints. Instructors were told to talk about "unbalancing the suspect, body positioning (chest to back), taking the suspect to the ground." The hold was intended to be used only if the suspect was resisting—and never with deadly pressure. When they stopped resisting, the officer was supposed to place the subject on their side.

After the discussion, trainees had to practice using the prone-restraint technique three times. The fulfillment of the department's promise to the bereaved family of David Smith was a lesson intended to take twenty minutes.

There were some indications that the training was effective, but not always in the way the department had intended. On February 25, a veteran street cop from the Third Precinct attended the session and soon began to use the technique with atypical frequency. The officer's name was Derek Chauvin.

The American journey of Chauvin's German family traces back to 1855, two years before Floyd's great-great-grandfather Hillery Thomas Stewart was born enslaved. Chauvin's great-great-great-grandparents Anton and Regina Neideck freely boarded the *Antarctic* to make the voyage to a country that promised them a better life.

Unlike George Floyd's family, the Neidecks had a chance to ride the crest of American opportunity. They settled in Detroit's immigrant neighborhoods, where they lived among the city's population of German, Belgian, French, and English transplants, taking on work as carpenters, painters, machinists, and soldiers. Anton was employed as a stonecutter and had settled into a middle-class lifestyle with Regina, a housekeeper, and their children.

Anton's granddaughter Veronica married Richard Chauvin in 1907. The Chauvins had traced a similar pattern of European migration followed by manual labor and upward mobility, settling in Detroit in the early 1700s. While Richard's French ancestors had worked as farmers, he had learned the bookbinding trade and found a job in the city. By 1925, he had amassed enough capital and expertise to start Cadillac Book Binding Co., a name that sought to benefit from the cachet around Detroit's growing auto industry. Richard's son Arthur—Derek Chauvin's grandfather—joined the family business located on the Detroit River shortly after finishing high school.

The company grew alongside Detroit, as the Motor City's population tripled between 1910 and 1930. By the 1960s, when Arthur's son Robert was entering high school, White Michiganders had begun to leave Detroit en masse. Yet, at the cusp of the Motown era, the city's Black population was soaring.

In 1972, Robert Chauvin, an accountant, married Carolyn Runge, who was described as "silent" and "good natured" in her yearbook from the predominantly White Simley High School in the suburbs of St. Paul, where she was listed as being in the school choir and a member of the Future Homemakers of America. They settled near her hometown in Ramsey County, Minnesota.

On March 19, 1976, Carolyn gave birth to a son, Derek Michael. But her marriage didn't last, and she soon took the surname of her new husband, Leroy Jerome Pawlenty. Carolyn and Robert shared custody of their son, who attended four different elementary schools as his parents settled into their new lives. Those who knew Derek at the time said he was a quiet, well-adjusted boy who played with friends in his mother's backyard, drew a set of projects in art class for each of his parents, and loved watching cop shows.

As a teenager, Chauvin was a largely unremarkable student at the almost exclusively White Park High School in Cottage Grove—he was not known to have been deeply involved in any major clubs, sports teams, ROTC, or honor societies. After graduating high school in 1994, Chauvin tried his hand at the culinary arts. He enrolled at Dakota County Technical College, where he took classes in baking, table service, shellfish identification, and stocks, soups, and sauces. He also worked as a prep cook at Tinucci's, a locally owned Italian buffet, making ribs and chicken and salads.

But after 1995, Chauvin's academic interests shifted

toward something else. He enrolled at Inver Hills Community College and then got an associate degree in law enforcement at Metropolitan State University, where he took classes in criminal justice, constitutional law, and ethics. After years of being uncertain about his life purpose, Chauvin seemed to find a calling in putting on a uniform and enforcing the law.

He joined the U.S. Army, serving at posts in Rochester, Minnesota, and various parts of Alabama. In the autumn of 1999, Chauvin was told that he would be going overseas as part of a military police unit. Sergeant Jerry Obieglo was set to lead the Seventy-Ninth Military Police Company, a group of about a dozen officers and a handful of other commanders.

After talk that they would be deployed to Bosnia or Kosovo, they were instead sent to the base in Hohenfels, Germany, a tiny municipality in Bavaria, in September 1999. East of Nuremburg, nestled in the country's rural bluffs, was an American training center, best known for drills in which members acted as if they were "bad guys" conspiring against soldiers during tactical training. The base itself wasn't built much differently from those in the United States, with grocery stores, bars, clothing stores, and schools. The team's mission was to guard military equipment, set up roadblocks and checkpoints, monitor traffic, and process prisoners of war.

The cases they encountered in Germany were typically for minor indiscretions, but Obieglo instilled a strict policing philosophy for his charges: Do not be lenient, just do the job. Don't compromise or make deals. If someone is speeding, write the ticket.

"People started telling us that we made a difference, that

people really started slowing down," Obieglo said. "Chauvin wrote a lot of tickets."

Chauvin was also one of the officers that Obieglo worried about the least. Many were fresh from high school and had never been out of the United States before, much less in a country where they could legally go to bars and drink. He reminded them that their conduct was important, that they needed to set an example. Chauvin was a good example, Obieglo said. At twenty-three, he was one of Obieglo's oldest troops. He had focus. He did not drink and didn't mind serving as a designated driver.

Chauvin was roommates with Matthew Peppersack, a twenty-year-old from rural Minnesota. Their room was small and spare—two twin beds side by side, bare white walls. Conversations between them were also spare. When they were off-duty, Peppersack wanted to hang out with his friends at clubs and bars. Chauvin preferred watching 1970s television shows, his favorite being *Starsky & Hutch*, the buddy action series of two police officers committing acts of derring-do. Soon, Chauvin developed a new, singular focus: he wanted to become a civilian cop when he went home.

"He wanted to talk about this procedural stuff," Peppersack said. "I didn't want to talk about that kind of stuff. I wanted to relax."

After six months, Chauvin asked Sergeant Obieglo if he could list him as a reference for police jobs when he returned to Minnesota. Obieglo was happy to oblige and said he would have told any employer that he was diligent, dedicated, and punctual.

Upon returning home, Chauvin entered training to become a Minneapolis police officer. His records show that he received three oral reprimands related to one incident in which he used unspecified "demeaning" or "derogatory language." Nonetheless, in January 2001, Chauvin stood before the American and Minnesota state flags to take an oath to join the Minneapolis Police Department. His mother pinned his badge onto his uniform. "Don't stick me with it," he whispered.

He was assigned to the Third Precinct, a racially diverse area that comprises Little Earth, a housing project that has long been the centerpiece of the Native American community in the city, and the Powderhorn neighborhood, which has struggled with gang violence for decades. One of the most notorious hangouts was the corner of Thirty-Eighth and Chicago, near a corner store known as CUP Foods.

Early in his tenure, Chauvin was walking with a field training officer when he was introduced to Sergeant Gwen Gunter, one of the few Black women officers in the city.

"Hey, what's up?" Gunter said as she extended her hand to greet him.

Instead of reciprocating the greeting, Gunter recalled, Chauvin left her hanging and walked away. She was stunned.

"That was weird," she said.

The field training officer, who was White, tried to explain the rookie cop's behavior.

"Well, Gwen," he said, "either he's heard something about you, or he's an asshole."

As one of about a half-dozen Black women on the entire force, Gunter had grown used to officers ignoring her, looking at her differently, or spreading rumors that she was aggressive or did not like White people. When she joined the department in 1992, two other Black women officers reached out to her to prepare her for its culture.

"First of all, shut up," they warned her, fearing that officers would target her if she was too outspoken. It was better for Gunter to fly under the radar and help the community. Those who spoke up found themselves passed over for promotions, taunted with racist or sexist language by their peers, or stranded in dangerous situations without being able to get backup. Some of those allegations were made by Janeé Harteau, who is Native American, and Medaria Arradondo, who is Black—both of whom would later be appointed by mayors to become police chiefs.

Gunter, like Harteau and Arradondo, knew that a toxic culture within the department would inevitably permeate to the outside, impacting how officers treated people of color on the job. She would spend twenty years in the department trying to distinguish whether some of her colleagues treated African Americans differently because of racism, or because of some systemic bias in how they were trained, or because they were just "assholes."

But she also struggled with how to best change an institution in which racism had been embedded from the very beginning. In the United States, the roots of modern policing in the South started with patrols monitoring and capturing the enslaved. In the North, the idea of a centralized municipal police force originated largely to tamp down labor organizing in Irish Catholic neighborhoods.

According to Malcolm Dwight Holmes, a professor at the University of Wyoming whose work focuses on policing, "This new system developed in no small part to control populations that were seen as a threat."

And as long as there have been police officers, there have been calls from minority residents to find gentler and more respectful ways to deal with their neighborhoods. The modern Minneapolis police, founded in 1867, was not immune to that history. As early as 1922, the local chapter of the NAACP called for police reform in Minneapolis after officers beat and arrested four Black men who had allegedly invited a group of White women to a party. With a marginal Black population that had no political power, the calls were ignored.

Appeals for reform reemerged in 1967, against the backdrop of the civil rights movement. On July 15 of that year, Black residents had traveled downtown to participate in the annual Aquatennial parades celebrating their city. But any sense of civic pride and unity faded quickly when Black people were denied entry onto city buses that would take them back to North Minneapolis. White people harassed the Black revelers, throwing bottles at them, and many Black attendees had no choice but to walk five or six miles home. Police did not intervene.

Later that day, police watched four White boys beat up a Black boy along Plymouth Avenue. When the boy asked for a ride to the hospital, an officer replied, "Nigger, go home." The final straw came that same week after a White bar owner shot and wounded a Black patron. Riots broke out across the Black community, and businesses with a reputation for discriminating against African Americans were torched. In response, Mayor Art Naftalin pledged to expand civil rights ordinances and hire more minority officers, solutions similar to those that would later appear in the federal Kerner Report on race relations that President Lyndon B. Johnson commissioned in response to rioting in major American cities.

But these solutions didn't last, and by the 1980s, officers began to take even more aggressive tactics to root out drugs and crime. On January 25, 1989, police tossed a stun grenade through the window of an apartment during a "no-knock" drug bust. The grenade hit a chair in a living room, and the apartment soon caught fire. Lloyd Smalley, seventy-one, and his wife, Lillian Weiss, sixty-five, had been cuddling in their bedroom on twin mattresses they had pushed together, watching *True Grit* on a small television. Smalley and Weiss did not make it out of the building. The police had acted on a bad tip, and an elderly African American couple died of smoke inhalation. Still, a grand jury decided not to indict the officers involved in the incident, causing many residents to again question if the city valued Black life.

A student at the University of Minnesota Law School, known for his op-eds defending the Nation of Islam under the pen name Keith Hakim, organized protests in response to the jury's decision. Born and raised in Detroit, the twenty-five-year-old student's given name was Keith Ellison. On the day before one of those rallies, police were called to the Embassy Suites downtown to respond to noise complaints about college students partying in a hotel room. There were two parties happening on the same floor: a kegger hosted by White students and a low-key party hosted by African Americans. Police raided the party with the less-boisterous Black students, beating them up so badly that some walked out with broken noses and bruised ribs.

A few days later, a bandana-wearing Ellison barged into a city council meeting with seventy-five protesters, demanding a state investigation and "public justice." They were successful. Out of that protest came a renewed call for civilian oversight of the police department, building upon the idea that the community would be able to better assess officers who threatened their neighborhoods. The council eventually agreed to a civilian review authority in 1990, but the board lacked the enforcement capability that the community had desired. Its powers were limited to "fact-finding investigations." They could make recommendations but could not discipline officers and had no subpoena power. No matter what the crime, the decision to get rid of bad cops was left to the institution that supported them.

When Gunter joined the department, she felt as if she had to straddle both worlds. She had decided to go into law enforcement to be the type of empathetic police officer she had not seen growing up in Chicago and its suburbs. But crime in 1990s Minneapolis was so out of control that Gunter felt she and other officers needed the latitude to tackle it aggressively. Housing projects were so overrun with drugs that children were warned not to go outside to play. Police would find victims pistol-whipped or locked in closets by gang members. Residents began referring to the city as "Murderapolis."

"We had Detroit Boys here, they were taking people hostage and holding them up in their own houses while they sold drugs," Gunter said, referencing a Michigan gang that would expand its turf as far away as North Carolina. "And you start to think, the criminals are way ahead of us—how are we going to take the area back for our citizens?"

The funding for cops and resources through the 1994 crime bill helped to send a lot of the "bad guys" to prison, Gunter said. From a policing perspective, the push had worked: crime was down, streets were safer. But many in the community had a different view of the bill, which ushered in an era of mass incarceration marked by police officers beating up residents, stealing their money, and harassing them during daily activities. They saw a beloved community center that served Black kids in North Minneapolis repurposed as the location of the Fourth Precinct. Gunter had hoped that once they had cleaned up neighborhoods, officers would be able to spend more time doing community-building exercises. But supervisors, she said, still expected officers to keep arrests high. The feeling that the community needed aggressive policing, even if it was for petty crimes, never went away.

"Instead of saying, 'We achieved what we wanted to achieve, so now we can enjoy the community,' we started to overpolice," Gunter said. "And when we started to overpolice, then *we* became the problem."

That issue was particularly true in the Third Precinct, where officers had a reputation for being rough and "using more force than they needed to," according to Lucy Gerold, who served as a deputy chief for the department. Internally, the officers of the Third Precinct were known as "the thumpers." Across the city, other precincts referred to them as the "cowboy district." When Gerold began to oversee the precinct in 2006, she found it to be undisciplined and unregulated. Some sergeants and officers had been tenured within the department for more than a decade, which ran contrary to the prevailing wisdom among managers that officers should transfer beats and precincts to maintain fresh perspectives and avoid resentment from a single community. She wanted to shake up the staff, but union-negotiated contracts prohibited such movements except for in the most extreme cases.

So Gerold found a precinct in which officers felt

untouchable, leading to indiscretions like parking in handicapped spots to more serious allegations that officers were taking young people to the Mississippi River and assaulting them.

"People kind of did what they want, and there wasn't direction," Gerold said. "People weren't in touch with—and this is probably true in other precincts—what the mission for the city was or the vision and mission for the department."

Early in his career, Chauvin received some praise for carrying out the mission. Two women wrote letters to the department lauding Chauvin's and his partner's empathy and patience in handling domestic violence cases.

"They did everything possible to make me feel comfortable and not ashamed," one victim wrote. Another person commended them "for the steady and thorough manner" in which they handled a domestic crisis nearby.

Between 2006 and 2009, Chauvin received two medals of valor and two medals of commendation for fatally shooting a man who pointed a sawed-off shotgun at officers, demonstrating "devotion to duty to the highest degree" by tackling and disarming a man with a gun, shooting and wounding a man who was accused of beating up his girlfriend, and intervening in an altercation between gang members.

But in 2007, Chauvin received a letter of reprimand after a woman complained about his irrational and aggressive approach when she was pulled over for speeding while driving back from the grocery store. He reached into her open window, unlocked her door, and began dragging her out. The woman, a breastfeeding mother, told *The New York Times* that either Chauvin or his partner made a comment about her chest.

"Be advised that any additional violations of Department Rules and Regulations may result in more severe disciplinary action up to and including discharge from employment," the letter stated.

Over six years as the precinct inspector, Gerold tried to change the department's culture by soliciting feedback from other officers and from the community, as well as by training supervisors to look for warning signs for officers who were pushing the envelope of acceptable behavior. Complaints about policing are difficult to assess, Gerold said; given the nature of law enforcement, members of the public can sometimes overstate a problem when an officer is doing routine police work.

Complicating matters is the methodical way in which internal affairs or civilian research agencies typically investigate a case—for example, it took more than a year to research the 2007 traffic stop. The complaint process in the city is also convoluted: A staffer decides if the complaint meets basic requirements and can funnel it to a civilian investigator or a police investigator. The investigator writes up a report for a group of supervisors. That group of supervisors then decides whether it should be sent to the civilian oversight review board or directly to the police chief. If the supervisors send it to the review panel, they make a recommendation to the chief. The chief dismisses the complaint or recommends a consequence for an officer—either coaching, in which a supervisor instructs an officer on how to avoid repeating the mistake, or disciplinary measures, which range from a letter of reprimand to a suspension, demotion, or termination. By the time the investigation has concluded, an officer might have forgotten the incident in the first place.

Inside the department, Chauvin's record didn't draw much attention. His colleagues saw him as a lanky, cocky officer with a boyish face, a cop who was defined by his career. Off duty, he had driven a Crown Victoria his mother gave him that resembled an old police vehicle. He took on the night shift regularly, working ten-hour days four days a week. And then, he moonlighted as a security guard at restaurants, nightclubs, and grocery stores in the same district in which he worked. Many in the department did not even realize that he was married to a woman named Kellie, a Hmong refugee who had previously left an abusive marriage. She was working as a radiology technician at the local hospital when Chauvin asked her out.

Kellie Chauvin was known to open their home to other Hmong women fleeing abusive relationships. Her husband would be by her side when she was eventually named the first Hmong Mrs. Minnesota.

"Under all that uniform, he's just a softie," Kellie Chauvin said to the *Pioneer Press*, describing a doting husband in 2018. "He's such a gentleman. He still opens the doors for me, still puts my coat on for me."

But when the uniform was on, Chauvin acted like a thumper. Over time, a certain pattern of behavior emerged in his civilian complaints. He didn't receive more than the average officer, according to Michelle Gross, president of Communities United Against Police Brutality, a Minneapolis-based watchdog group that tracks such complaints. But residents in the Third Precinct consistently reported that Chauvin was impulsive, abrasive, and violent.

In 2009, Luz Maria Gonzalez received a call from her eleven-year-old son, Armoni, after he was caught stealing chips from the Cub Foods grocery store on Lake Street. She became furious when she arrived at the juvenile detention center downtown and saw the dark ring around his left eye.

Examining her son's bruised face, she asked what had happened.

"It was Derek," he said. "That cop, Derek, slapped me around."

Gonzalez wondered what kind of cop would beat up a kid over petty theft, but then she remembered the aggressive tactics that she had observed Chauvin use when he moonlighted at a Latin nightclub she sometimes attended called El Nuevo Rodeo. Her friend Maria Isa occasionally performed there, and the two observed him with trepidation. He seemed robotic, blunt, and disinterested in de-escalating problems.

Most off-duty officers would concentrate on the most serious issues at the club, such as uncovering drugs or weapons, leaving the rest to the security team. But Isa and other patrons noticed that Chauvin often took it upon himself to play a more active role in strictly enforcing the club's rules. As soon as two a.m. hit and performers had to stop playing live music, Chauvin would appear with a can of pepper spray to start dispersing the crowd. If attendees lingered, he'd spray them with Mace.

That aggression was particularly true during "urban nights," when the crowd was mostly Black, according to Maya Santamaria, who was the club's owner at the time. When Santamaria asked Chauvin to take a gentler approach, he dismissed her with two words: "It's protocol."

Glimpsing her son's battered face, Gonzalez hoped someone would hold Chauvin accountable for assaulting a child. She said she filed a complaint, but "nothing happened about it," she recalled years later.

The incidents piled up. On a cold December day in 2012, Adrienne Kleinman's Eurovan broke down on a busy street and she called police for assistance. But instead of helping her, she reported that, upon arriving at the scene, Chauvin yelled at her and demanded she move the immobile car. At every turn, Kleinman noted, he seemed dismissive and aggressive.

"He talked to me like I was a joke," said Kleinman, who uses a wheelchair. "I recommended he take sensitivity training."

The department did not take her recommendation; in fact, they did not discipline him at all. The next year, over Thanksgiving in 2013, Chauvin used an approach during a traffic stop that was similar to the one he was reprimanded for in 2007. LaSean Braddock had just finished a sixteen-hour shift working in the mental health unit at the county hospital when he jumped in his Buick LeSabre and headed home.

When Chauvin pulled him over, Braddock figured he knew what this was about; someone had stolen his identity months before and he had been stopped often enough that he kept paperwork from the police department explaining the situation. But Chauvin didn't wait for his explanation, Braddock recalled. Braddock said Chauvin slammed his flashlight on his window so hard that he almost broke it.

"He tried to pull me out of the car," Braddock said. "I was still in my seat belt."

Braddock eventually stepped out of the vehicle, and Chauvin and his partner asked him to lie on the ground. When he was down, the two officers "jumped on my head and my neck. They put my cuffs on extremely tight and my wrists were scarred."

It was not until they sent him to a detention center that Braddock learned he had been charged with resisting arrest and failure to obey an officer—charges that would eventually be thrown out. He also complained to the civil rights division about what had occurred, but Braddock said no one followed up.

Gross's organization has been able to track down at least twenty-nine complaints involving Chauvin; the internal affairs department lists eighteen of them. Although the events were traumatizing for the complainants, they did not seem to strike internal affairs as being particularly problematic. And that was the scary part of policing, according to Janeé Harteau. There can be so many officers who "do just enough to fly under the radar [because they] haven't killed anybody. You never know about them. They are the ones who put the handcuffs on a little too tight."

After the 2007 reprimand, Chauvin would never again receive disciplinary action for any of the subsequent complaints against him.

The scenario was not unusual. After Harteau became chief in 2012, she asked the Department of Justice to review the police department's process for investigating complaints. They found that 47 percent of complaints were immediately thrown out, and only 21 percent of complaints were investigated. And among the 570 complaints that were investigated between 2008 and 2013, 418 of them were resolved through "sustained coaching," a practice for which there are minimal standards and supervisors receive little training. Furthermore, Gross's group had tracked 3,434 complaints between 2012, when the civilian review board was folded into the human rights division of the police department, and May 2020. Of those complaints, only 12 resulted in any type of discipline for the officers—a rate of 0.35 percent. On a national level, while there is a dearth of research around officer discipline, a 2006 federal study estimated that 8 percent of civilian complaints about use of force resulted in a ruling that the officer should be disciplined.

There are innate dangers in a force in which officers are not disciplined for malfeasance. The lack of accountability might embolden cops to make riskier or more aggressive decisions, choices that disproportionately impact people of color. In Minneapolis, publicly available data from 2021 show that Black people represent close to 64 percent of cases in which police used force, while comprising only 19 percent of the city's population.

Harteau said she tried to help change the culture of systemic racism in policing. She introduced training for implicit bias, which Chauvin took in 2015, and "procedural justice," which Chauvin attended the following year. But she found herself frustrated that she could not uproot the long-standing beliefs and biases within the department, and then mayor Betsy Hodges asked her to resign in 2017 amid concerns about police shootings and officer training.

"The culture that's been built over decades was primarily White men who served in these positions," Harteau said. "When I look back, I was a little naive on my part, I think, to believe that I could make the change I really wanted to ... It was like turning the *Titanic*."

The tendency to use greater force against people of color, of course, was not a phenomenon in Minneapolis alone; it hearkened to stereotypes that have existed since chattel slavery about the need to subdue Black bodies.

Those stereotypes often showed up in pseudoscience. During the period of slavery, the scientist Samuel Cartwright coined the phrase "drapetomania," a mental illness rooted in Black "rascality" that would prompt an enslaved African American to desire freedom, a disease that needed immediate treatment. It was a type of junk science, based more on supposition and confirmation bias than on research, that had been used to reify the social order of the day—often through criminalization. Other research during the time suggested African Americans needed to be strictly monitored and handled more violently because of primitive nervous systems, thick skins, and hard heads. None of these studies would meet scientific standards today and, in some cases, included research that was falsified.

But those tropes never fully went away. Ayana Jordan, a New York University professor who has studied the history of addiction and medical racism, noted they endured into 1914, when physicians posited that the "cocaine-crazed negro brain" could be resistant to fatal wounds, as a means of justifying the passage of the Harrison Narcotics Act, which made cocaine illegal. They were on display again during the debates over the 1994 crime bill, when lawmakers used the term "superpredators" to describe savage teenagers who would kill without conscience.

And after David Smith's death in 2013, another term surfaced around the maximal-restraint technique that relied upon similar stereotypes. That term was "excited delirium," and it was described as "the main culprit" in arrest-related deaths in a PowerPoint presentation used to train Minneapolis police.

"Excited delirium is a condition that manifests as a combination of delirium, psychomotor agitation, anxiety, hallucinations, speech disturbances, disorientation, violent and bizarre behavior, insensitivity to pain, elevated body temperature, and superhuman strength," the PowerPoint presentation read.

But the training did not cite the controversy around whether the condition even exists: excited delirium is not listed as a medical condition in the *Diagnostic and Statistical Manual of Mental Disorders*, nor is it recognized by the World Health Organization or the American Psychiatric Association.

"We were told it exists, so we trained people on it," Harteau said.

And even though the term was first applied to explain the sudden death of White cocaine users in 1985, it had since been consistently and disproportionately ascribed to the conditions of Black men. One study of the period found that medical examiners in Miami-Dade County, where the phrase had originated, were three times more likely to use "excited delirium" as a cause of death for Black male cocaine users than White ones. A 2017 article in *American Emergency Medicine* found similar disparities from larger national studies.

Critics were also disturbed that much of the research about the condition's pathophysiology came from scientists who were paid consultants for Taser. And because these studies centered their discussions about excited delirium in the context of law enforcement, there were questions about whether the term was primarily invented to excuse officers who might otherwise be accused of using excessive force—from Tasering, to the use of ketamine as a sedative, to neck restraints.

Minneapolis police were taught to look for warning signs. Another PowerPoint presentation from 2019 opened with an image of three White officers chasing a Black man who was removing his clothes. It described a person experiencing delirium as seeming "tough and unstoppable," requiring multiple officers to get the subject on the ground. Another slide explained what to do when the subject is finally handcuffed. The picture showed officers holding down arms and legs, while a third officer places their knee on the subject's neck.

"Place the subject in the recovery position to alleviate positional asphyxia," it read.

Abigail Cerra, who serves as a commissioner on the city's police conduct oversight commission, criticized the training on neck restraints for being insufficient. For example, the PowerPoint presentation described excited delirium in detail, but only one bullet point in a forty-one-slide presentation addressed asphyxia, the condition that killed David Smith. The Department of Justice had warned about the dangers of the prone restraint and asphyxia since the 1990s, but there was no discussion beyond the single bullet point about the medical risks listed in the training guide. To lawyers like Cerra, the department had essentially given officers reasons why they should use neck restraints without equipping them with enough information about the risks.

Neck restraints represented about 2 percent of use-of-force cases in Minneapolis between 2008 and 2020. Sixty percent of those who received neck restraints were Black. And even though it was rarely used, there were some officers who began to rely on the technique more than others.

Derek Chauvin's first known use of the neck restraint came just eighteen days after his training. He had been trying to escort a drunken man out of the Midtown Global Market, but Chauvin reported that the subject, who was in his sixties, kept trying to pull away from him, eventually spinning himself around and falling on the sidewalk. Chauvin lodged his knee into the subject's neck while he handcuffed him. He then sat him up as he waited for an ambulance. It was deemed an appropriate use of the restraint—Chauvin used it until the suspect stopped resisting, then placed him in a position in which it would be easier to breathe while they waited for emergency medical technicians.

Almost a year later, on February 15, 2015, Chauvin wrapped his hands around the neck of a drunken patron named Julian Hernandez at El Nuevo Rodeo, after the two argued about which door to use to exit the club. Chauvin said he attempted to handcuff the suspect, but Hernandez resisted, so he applied the neck restraint to push him near a wall. Chauvin, who is five foot nine, said he used the restraint because of their difference in size. Hernandez, he wrote, "seemed to be of a muscular type of build." After wrapping his arm around his neck, Chauvin pulled Hernandez to the ground and lodged his knee into his back while he waited for a squad car.

By September 4, 2017, Chauvin had used the restraint at least five times. His sixth reported incident happened that evening, when he and his partner were called to a home after a mother reported that her fourteen-year-old son, John Pope, had assaulted her. According to the arrest report, the mother told the officers that her son had grabbed her arms after she unplugged his phone charger. She complained that her children lacked discipline and directed the officers to the bedroom, in an apparent attempt to scare them straight.

When they got to the bedroom, they saw the fourteen-year-old boy lying on the floor. Again, Chauvin noticed his build, sizing him up to be six foot two, 240 pounds. The child refused to get up, so Chauvin grabbed him and pushed him against a wall. Chauvin then thrashed the boy with a flashlight multiple times, hard enough to make his ear bleed. He asked his partner to use a Taser, but he did not have one, so Chauvin put his arms around the child's neck, causing him to fall to the ground. He then placed his knee on the boy's back. The boy's mother begged Chauvin to remove it. He refused.

"He's a big guy," Chauvin said.

The boy, who was African American, asked to be placed on his back, but Chauvin refused. The mother implored Chauvin to remove his knee from her son's upper back four times, but he persisted. He kept it there for seventeen minutes until an ambulance arrived. Body cam footage captured the entire incident, but Chauvin's report does not mention the multiple strikes with the flashlight, the mother's pleas, nor the length of time for which his knee remained on the boy's neck. The family did not file a complaint; there is no public documentation of any investigation into how the officer could beat a child unconscious.

"His behavior continued to get worse," Cerra observed. "And there was no one in the department who stopped him."

Chauvin's seventh reported use of the neck restraint happened on March 12, 2019, after he and another officer responded to a call from Monroe Skinaway, a man who had just recovered his stolen car and was following up with police. While the officers were discussing the incident at a gas station, Skinaway said a mentally ill man interrupted them to ask the police officers for a ride. Chauvin pushed the man to try to get him away from the scene. The man shoved him back.

"They get into it, they're wrestling around, and one of the

officers used Mace," Skinaway recalled. "But it was windy, so the Mace blew back in their face. That part was hilarious."

Any humor quickly vanished. The officers managed to handcuff the man and then laid his face down in a puddle of water. The man tried to lift his head above the puddle, telling the officers he could not breathe. The officers then put a hood over his head before driving his face back down into the water. Chauvin kept him in that position for a couple of minutes, until paramedics arrived, according to the police report.

"I kept wondering: When is the danger point? When do I jump in?" Skinaway said. "But this was such a normal thing to see the police act this way, I did not think much of it. And if you jump in, the next thing you know, you're a target. But no matter what, it was wrong to put that man's face in the water. It seemed excessive. He could have drowned."

Four months later, Chauvin used the technique for the eighth reported time. He responded to a call from an elderly woman who told dispatchers that her son was trying to burn down the house. The woman pointed out her son to Chauvin, who drew his gun on him. Chauvin wrote in his report that the man briefly raised his hands in surrender. But when the man set them down, Chauvin kicked him in the stomach because he "had observed a side table near a chair . . . that contained many scissors and sharp objects. I wasn't going to allow [him] the opportunity to grab for one of these items."

When the man fell, Chauvin applied a neck restraint. He was on the suspect's neck long enough to render him unconscious. The report does not note whether Chauvin rendered aid before EMS arrived at the scene.

Between the time the Minneapolis Police Department started tracking them in 2014 and May 2020, there were at least 295 uses of the neck restraint by its officers—nine of which were employed by Chauvin. Not one of Chauvin's incidents resulted in a reprimand or a public investigation, and Chauvin continued to walk the beat, even training officers on proper policing. At least three of his subjects were Black, one was Latino, and one was Native American. In a department that was typically staffed with well over eight hundred officers, Chauvin alone accounted for the use of 3 percent of all neck restraints.

Eight of his subjects survived. His ninth was George Floyd.

CHAPTER 7

You're on Your Own

T HERE GOES MY BABY."
Miss Cissy had not been expecting to see her firstborn son when he walked into the house on Nalle Street on a
chilly January day in 2013.

Brandon Williams and Philonise (pronounced "fa-LOAN-
us") had gone to pick Floyd up from a prerelease facility in
Huntsville, Texas, without telling her that he would finally be
coming home after the longest prison stint of his life.

Floyd had been calm and relaxed on the drive to Third
Ward, silently taking in the changes that had occurred in the
neighborhood while he had been incarcerated, but he lit up
when he saw his mother. After walking in the door, he immediately rushed over to envelop her in a hug.

As they embraced for the first time in more than four
years, the changes in their respective physiques were stark.
Floyd's body had hardened and the muscles around his shoulders and chest were chiseled, the result of countless hours
working out to pass the time in the penitentiary.

By contrast, Miss Cissy had grown frail and now used a
wheelchair, having suffered another stroke while her son was
locked up. Her hair had gone fully white, and it was styled in

a closely cropped Afro that formed a halo around her aging face. She was now sixty-five, and the last few years had taken an intense physical toll on her.

Still, the deep connection she had with her oldest son was one thing that had not changed.

As a parolee, Floyd was required to remain at home in the evenings and on weekends. An ankle monitor tracked his whereabouts, and if he was not at home to answer the phone when a parole officer called to enforce his house arrest, he risked being sent back to jail.

When Floyd's friend Adarryl Hunter learned of the conditions of his release, he immediately thought of a way to help. He had been to Miss Cissy's house a few times to check on her while Floyd was locked up and had seen new faces during each visit—grandchildren, family friends, neighborhood hangers-on who had needed a place to sleep. Hunter knew that his friend would be vexed by the crowded conditions, restricted movement, and lack of privacy—all of which would have conjured memories of the penitentiary he just left.

Hunter went to the Micro Center electronics store and bought a hundred-foot telephone cord. That way, he figured, Floyd would be able to abide by his parole restrictions without having to stay cooped up inside. He pictured Floyd roaming around the front yard, talking on the landline as the cord snaked its way back into the packed house.

Before heading to go see Floyd, Hunter remembered a conversation they had had back in the 1990s when they were still teenagers.

"Let me in on the secret: How do you get everyone to like you?" Hunter had asked his friend.

Floyd told him he always tried to greet someone with a

compliment, pointing out a nice haircut or a new pair of shoes. Recognize a person for who they were trying to be, he advised. Following Floyd's philosophy, when meeting his friend for the first time since his release, Hunter dressed up in a white blazer and a pair of aviator sunglasses. Floyd didn't have much—he wore a baseball cap, blue sweatpants, and black T-shirt. Still, Hunter greeted Floyd as the person he wanted to be, referencing a line from one of their favorite movies, *Face/Off*, as they tried to one-up each other in a game of escalating compliments.

"Oooh-weee!" Hunter yelled. "You're so pretty."

"All right, baller," Floyd replied.

"All right, taller," Hunter said back.

"All right, smaller."

Hunter's professional career as a pharmacist had advanced while Floyd was locked up. He had worked for a couple of local pharmacies before opening his own outfit in 2012. Determined to give Floyd a fitting welcome-home experience, he hopped in his black Mercedes E 350 and headed to Miss Cissy's house with the telephone cord in tow.

Since Floyd was allowed to leave the house during the day, Hunter decided to take him out to a nice lunch. They picked up a third friend and headed to the Grand Lux Cafe at the Galleria Mall. The restaurant's swanky exterior featured four Roman-style columns and three arched entryways. Inside, gaudy chandeliers hung from dark coffered ceilings. Wood panels and marble floors and tabletops gave it the look of an upscale Cheesecake Factory.

Floyd ordered a sirloin steak with shrimp and a lemon-drop martini. As they dined, Floyd told his friends he never wanted to see the inside of a jail cell again. After spending the second half of his thirties behind bars, he insisted to Hunter that he was done with that lifestyle. He was going to start anew, find himself a good job, and take care of his family, he said.

Hunter was glad to see his friend determined to make a change. At thirty-nine years old, Floyd had goals that were admittedly less ambitious than they had been before he started cycling through the criminal justice system. But staying out of prison would itself be an odds-defying feat in a state where more than 60 percent of prisoners released from state jail were rearrested within three years.

As he paid for the meal and prepared to take Floyd home, Hunter could tell his friend was determined to beat those odds.

A few weeks later, Floyd had the chance to catch up with old friends at the Jack Yates High class of 1993's twenty-year reunion. Jonathan Veal, Floyd's old football teammate, was one of the first people to greet him during a picnic the class had organized.

"Hey, man, what's going on?" Veal said, embracing him for the first time in nearly two decades.

"Man, I just got out," Floyd responded.

Veal was shocked to hear that his friend—the team jokester and on-the-field gentle giant—had been incarcerated with murderers and rapists. He decided not to ask Floyd what he had been imprisoned for, instead giving an update on his own life.

Veal had moved to Oklahoma City and worked for Chick-fil-A's corporate office. He had a wife, four sons, and one daughter—a family of seven that included a pair of twins. He told Floyd that he was glad to see him and wished him well before moving on to swap stories with his other classmates.

Over the course of the afternoon, Floyd had a chance to reconnect with other old friends he had lost touch with. He told them about his imprisonment, and they told him about the mostly stable lives they had settled into as middle-aged men on the cusp of forty.

His teammate Herbert Mouton had gotten a bachelor's degree in computer information systems from McMurry University in Abilene, Texas, and taken an IT job before realizing that working behind a desk was not for him. He eventually obtained his commercial driver's license and earned a decent salary driving tractor trailers.

Jerald Moore, the star running back, had played four seasons in the National Football League, with the St. Louis Rams and New Orleans Saints. His NFL pension ensured he would be comfortable for years to come.

Many of Floyd's classmates had not been able to attend the reunion, because they had fallen through one of Third Ward's battery of trapdoors—prison, early death, addiction. Still, Floyd left the gathering acutely aware of how far his life had trailed behind those of his peers and fallen short of his own dreams.

After the event, he told Hunter he was fully committed to getting his life back on track. While he had completed a post-conviction vocational training program, he was having a hard time finding a job. He complained that prospective employers stopped communicating with him after seeing his long responses on applications that asked questions like: "Have you ever been convicted of a crime? If yes, please explain ... Use additional paper if necessary."

His answers to the sections asking about his employment history were considerably shorter.

Floyd was headed to a job interview one day in 2013 when his old classmate Vaughn Dickerson saw him waiting by the bus stop. Dickerson was surprised to see his friend dressed up in slacks and a dress shirt with a necktie. He pulled up and got out of his car.

Dickerson, like Floyd, had struggled to make ends meet after his incarceration, but he eventually found work in construction. Seeing Floyd at the bus stop, he remembered how his friend was one of the first people to come visit him after he was released.

"I love you, man," Floyd had told him at the time, slipping him a handful of cash.

Dickerson was happy to see that Floyd had taken his advice about the plea bargain, survived prison, and come out seemingly in good shape.

"You home?" he asked, walking up to Floyd.

"Yeah, yeah," Floyd said.

"Boy, you done blew up," Dickerson observed, scanning the former tight end's physique. "You must've been the biggest dude on the damn compound."

"Yeah." Floyd cracked an uneasy smile.

"You look good, chump," Dickerson said, tossing a combination of fake punches into his torso. "Where you fixin' to go? Man, you need a ride?"

Floyd said he was on his way to a job interview across town and that he was fine taking the bus.

"You need something?" Dickerson asked.

"Nah, I'm cool."

Dickerson looked at him again, more seriously now, as if

offended that his friend of more than twenty-five years was putting up a front.

"You need something?" he repeated.

"Nah, V."

Dickerson insisted that he take a hundred dollars, pulling the cash out of his wallet and handing it to Floyd. "Here, man."

A few hours later, Dickerson ran into Floyd again, near the same bus stop. He wanted to ask how the job interview went but figured by Floyd's downcast expression that things probably had not panned out.

"They talking about my felony, man," Floyd volunteered.

Dickerson understood what Floyd was going through and offered the only advice he knew would be useful to a Black ex-convict trying to find a job in Texas.

"You can't stop, though."

"I ain't going to stop, man," Floyd responded. "I just got to do it on my own."

As a former felon in Texas, Floyd had little choice but to commit to rebuilding his life on his own. At the time of his release, the Lone Star State had some of the harshest laws in the country restricting rights, opportunities, and support systems for the previously incarcerated. Former felons were barred from getting a variety of state trade licenses, keeping them from finding work as barbers, real-estate brokers, locksmiths, plumbers, and dozens of other positions. Each year, the state rejected applications from thousands of people trying to obtain licenses that would allow them to earn a living legally—often because of long-ago convictions for minor offenses. With about a third of all jobs in Texas requiring licenses, those with a criminal past found themselves automatically excluded from millions of positions they may have otherwise been qualified for. Desperate to earn an income, some of the rejected applicants returned to criminal activity.

The state also had a lifetime ban on food assistance for ex-felons, barring them from accessing food stamps designed to aid people in poverty. The ban extended to other welfare benefits as well, complicating the path for prisoners to transition to stability once released. The state's housing regulations also made it easy for landlords to discriminate against potential tenants who had served time in prison. Some public housing authorities blocked all applicants with an offense in the previous twenty-five years, despite federal recommendations that those with no new felonies in the last five to seven years should not face additional barriers.

And Texans with criminal records were largely banned from taking any of the more than three hundred thousand state government jobs, excluding them from a sector that was otherwise disproportionately favored by Black residents.

The same year that Floyd was released from prison, Texas attorney general Greg Abbott sued the federal government to ensure that the state could continue excluding former felons from the hiring process for these positions. Guidelines issued by the Obama administration's Equal Employment Opportunity Commission in 2012 had warned Texas and other states that instituting blanket bans on hiring people with criminal records violated civil rights laws and had a "disparate impact" on Black and Hispanic applicants. Abbott, who was running for governor at the time, touted the lawsuit during his campaign as he sought to bolster his tough-on-crime image.

Floyd's friend Travis Cains, who worked with hundreds

of felons and reoffenders as a bail bondsman in Houston, said Texas's unforgiving attitude toward people who had left prison was part of the reason for the state's stubbornly high recidivism rate.

"In Texas, they don't believe in repentance," he said. "You come home, you're really on your own. You can't stay in most places because you're a felon. You can't get a job. Most guys that come out resort to doing the same thing you done before because you can't get no help."

Floyd, one of almost five million Texans with a criminal record in 2013, felt the pressure of a state that locked up so many of its residents and then released them into almost impossible circumstances.

Convinced that his limited education and criminal record were obstacles to employment, Floyd took classes and became certified in weld inspection. Some friends who were familiar with his academic struggles in high school were surprised when Floyd told them he had passed his exam and gotten certified.

He eventually did get a job at a testing and inspection company in northwest Houston, but he lost it after only about two months. The company later accused him and a few colleagues of stealing X-ray equipment worth more than $150,000. Floyd told friends he had not been involved in the plot and that he would not have taken the risk of being sent back to jail. He was never arrested or charged. Still, he was out of a job, and the stigma of his criminal record made it difficult to find a new one—the familiar catch-22 that helped fuel Texas's recidivism rates.

In the months after his release from prison, there was at least one thing in his life that Floyd did feel was going right:

he had a budding relationship with a woman he had met weeks after leaving the penitentiary. Roxie Danielle Washington lived a few minutes away from his mother's house on Nalle Street and did not mind that he had a record. She had one of her own, with charges stretching back to the early 2000s.

She was attracted to Floyd's large, muscular frame, his size dwarfing her body. Their romance was instant and intense. Weeks into their relationship, he had moved into her unit in the Calumet Court Apartments near Riverside Park.

It was not long before the thirty-one-year-old Washington informed Floyd that they would soon become a family of three. Though the pregnancy was unexpected, Floyd was excited about the prospect of welcoming a new child. He told friends that he now had even more motivation to get his life together and that he was happy to be part of his child's life from conception.

By that point, two women who claimed Floyd fathered their children had sued him for child support. But, given the brevity of the relationships that led to their births, he was unsure if he was the actual father. His interactions with his exes had devolved into legal skirmishes, handled through lawyers and process servers.

His relationship with Washington was different, at least at first. Their daughter was born in the middle of December. Floyd held her and stared at her plump face and full head of hair, staying at the hospital each night until they all went home.

Floyd had wanted to name his daughter Georgianna after himself, but the couple settled on Gianna as a compromise. They chose a colorful middle name that added some showbiz flourish. But it didn't take long before Floyd came up with a special pet name for Gianna Pink Floyd: *Buttercup*.

"When she got there, oh man, it was kind of like Floyd totally just lit up," recalled Floyd's friend Nikki Smith, whose husband, Reginal, had been Floyd's cellmate a decade earlier. "That was his baby. He was very dedicated to changing his life for his daughter."

In the months after Gianna was born, Floyd began to reconnect with his faith, telling friends of the peace he found while reading the Bible and spending quiet time in prayer.

He was attending "Hope for the Tre," a concert at Good Hope Missionary Baptist Church in Third Ward, one day in 2013 when he heard two Christian rappers perform songs about Jesus with the same streetwise swagger typical of Houston hip-hop tracks about codeine and cars. Intrigued, he decided to walk over and introduce himself to the performers after the concert.

Ronnie Lillard, who performed under the stage name Reconcile, and Corey Paul Davis told Floyd that they were looking to bring the ministry deeper into Third Ward, with plans to shoot a video and hold a Bible study in the coming days. Neither was from the neighborhood, so Floyd told them he would help introduce them to the right people.

"I love what y'all out here doing," Floyd said. "If y'all about God's business, then that's my business. If y'all need anything, tell 'em Big Floyd said you good."

Patrick Ngwolo, a youth minister at Good Hope and an organizer of the concert, was also seeking the kind of Third Ward connections Floyd could provide. He was planning to start a new church called Resurrection Houston and wanted to hold occasional services in the middle of the city's largest housing project. Ngwolo, who had studied law at the University of Texas at Austin, told Floyd he felt called to bring the gospel to the Bricks.

The services would take place on the Cuney Homes outdoor basketball courts, part of a slate of activities aimed at leading some of the city's poorest residents to Christ. Ngwolo also planned to host basketball tournaments and barbecues and help residents out with basic needs like groceries and hospital visits. Floyd leaned into his role of liaison between the upstart ministry and the Cuney Homes residents, some of whom had become leery of outsiders promising hope and relief.

Floyd's stamp of approval helped Ngwolo fill dozens of chairs on the basketball court, as people in Cuney Homes felt comfortable attending the outdoor services once they saw a Third Ward "OG" participating.

Floyd also helped Resurrection Houston set up for the "Church in the Bricks" services, bringing out the chairs, electronic equipment, instruments, and tables that transformed the blacktop court into a sanctuary. On days when Ngwolo planned to baptize new converts, Floyd would help drag a massive horse trough to the middle of the court and fill it with water.

He would watch from the sideline as people wearing white robes settled into the trough after a crowd of believers had laid hands on their shoulders and prayed for them. These new Christians would cross their hands over their chests as ministers on either side of the trough dipped them backward into the water until their entire bodies were submerged. After a couple of seconds, they would be lifted from the trough, exultant and renewed as water cascaded from their smiling faces and the crowd around the courts erupted with applause.

Floyd did not get baptized himself but became more deeply involved with his faith while trying to put his turbulent past behind him. He had included the phrase "bigfloyd4god" in his Instagram handle and told friends he found purpose encouraging young people in the neighborhood to reject the twin vices of guns and drugs.

"I just want to say, man, I've got my shortcomings and my flaws and I ain't better than nobody else," Floyd said in one video. "But, man, the shootings that's going on, man, I don't care what 'hood you're from, man, where you're at, man. I love you and God love you, man. Put them guns down, man. That ain't what it is. God bless, man, and y'all hold y'all head up."

The 2015 school year had just started, and Tiffany Cofield was already having problems with her students at Hope Academy, a charter school in Third Ward. The school had taken in several students who had been kicked out of traditional public high schools like Yates, and from the beginning of the semester it seemed like a fight would take place every day. As the violence escalated, Cofield became worried that a student would show up to the school with a gun.

Cofield was Black like all her students, but she had grown up in a stable household in southwest Houston and, like her parents, had attended college. She wasn't privy to the turf battles and neighborhood dynamics of Third Ward and struggled to understand why there was so much tension in the school. She ended some school days quietly sobbing in her Cadillac SRX SUV as she questioned whether breaking up fights was the best use of her Howard University degree.

Sensing her frustration, a couple of her students who lived in the Bricks suggested she reach out to a man who was well known throughout Third Ward.

"Miss Cofield, you got to talk to Big Floyd," one of them said.

"Who the hell is Big Floyd?" she responded, wondering how a man with a street nickname could be useful to her.

"Nah, Miss Cofield," the other student said. "Big Floyd can help."

She dismissed the teenagers with a curt "Whatever" and went back to preparing for her next class.

Two weeks later, the students came back, letting Cofield know they were serious about brokering the conversation.

She took down Floyd's number while still looking at her students skeptically.

Floyd was at the Wendy's near Yates when his phone rang.

"Hello? Yeahhh . . . What's up, girl?"

Hearing his raspy voice and cool-cat affect, Cofield immediately questioned the wisdom of making the call. She gathered her bearings and introduced herself, sprinkling in the word "sir" a couple of times to show due respect to someone she believed was a senior citizen.

"Hold on right quick," Floyd said, still drawing out his words like a Blaxploitation film star. "Let me place my order right quick."

Cofield contemplated hanging up the phone.

"How in the hell is this old-ass man going to help me with my problem?" she thought as she waited for Floyd to finish ordering a double cheeseburger and fries.

"How can I help you?" Floyd said after picking up his meal.

"Look, sir. The kids at my school told me that I need to reach out to you because we keep having these fights every day. I don't know what to do to help."

"You in Third Ward?" he asked.

"Yeah, I'm in the Third Ward."

"Pull up on me," he said.

Cofield hopped in her Cadillac and drove over to the Blue Store, where Floyd had said he would be waiting. She saw a man seated outside, but thinking she should be looking for someone much older, she pulled out her phone and dialed Floyd's number. When the muscular forty-two-year-old man she had been looking at picked up his phone, she quickly apologized under her breath before walking over to meet him in person.

"You feel like taking me somewhere?" Floyd asked after they had talked for a few minutes.

"Let's go," she said.

As they drove around the neighborhood in her car, Floyd explained the history and culture of Third Ward.

He knew most of the students in her class and could rattle off many of their struggles by memory. Over the course of an hour, he told Cofield about the kids who had to take care of their siblings because their parents were in jail, the ones who suffered from the trauma of seeing a family member killed by gun violence, the one being raised by a grandmother who was on dialysis and didn't have a car, and the students who, like him, didn't see the value of an education in an environment that prioritized day-to-day survival. He told her about Cuney Homes and how the students who lived there felt a kinship even more binding than their relationship to Third Ward, the south side, or Houston as a whole.

"One roof, one family," he said, repeating the neighborhood mantra.

Cofield let Floyd know she appreciated his insight. He told her to come by his mother's house anytime she needed more help.

Before long, the two were spending almost every day together, forming an intimate bond as Floyd's relationship with Washington began to dissolve. After leaving the school, Cofield would pick up Floyd and they would ride around the city, talking for hours. Floyd would engage in what Cofield called "hood diplomacy," visiting different parts of Houston attempting to squash beefs between rival gangs. Cofield had connections to local rappers and entertainers and would get Floyd backstage at events around town. Floyd introduced her to his family, and she would spend Sunday evenings giving Miss Cissy pedicures. Since Floyd's sister Zsa Zsa was still largely out of her children's lives, Floyd and Cofield would attend parent-teacher meetings at the schools of his younger nieces.

Sometimes, Floyd and Cofield would take spontaneous road trips out of state, paying visits to Floyd's friend Fathead in Louisiana, where Floyd would do landscaping work to make a little money. Other times, they would go see one of Cofield's friends who was incarcerated in Tennessee.

Cofield was part of the entourage when Floyd worked security for his friend Cal Wayne, who released new music and performed across Texas in 2015. But when Wayne wasn't earning money from rapping, Cofield noticed, Floyd's income also dried up. And the carefree hours they spent together opened the door to vices they both struggled to keep at bay. Floyd's addiction to Percocet worsened and Cofield was hooked on codeine and Tylenol, and they repeatedly succumbed to their cravings in a city where those products could so easily be obtained.

They fell behind on bills as they sought refuge in self-medication. Floyd's light-brown GMC Yukon XL was repossessed, and Cofield had to leave her job at the school after being injured in a car accident.

Some nights, Cofield would sit with Floyd in front of Miss Cissy's house, talking until they fell asleep in her SUV. Floyd's mother's house was crowded, and Cofield had not been able to save enough rent money for a deposit, so she bounced between friends' homes and hotels. Effectively homeless on many nights, the duo had tried to make themselves comfortable sleeping inside Cofield's Cadillac.

They were fortunate to not be in the car one evening when a tree branch fell onto the windshield, smashing it. Cofield was too afraid to drive the car in that condition, and from then on, Floyd drove her everywhere she needed to go, craning his neck out of the driver's-side window while wearing a pair of clear construction goggles.

"He would literally drive borderline Ace Ventura–like, with his head halfway out the window," Cofield recalled.

At the same time, Floyd was also reconnecting with old friends, struggling to resist the pull of his past life.

He would spend long nights in the smoke-filled recording studio of De'Kori Lawson, a popular Houston DJ known as DJ.D. They would reminisce about their glory days as players in Houston's hip-hop scene, focusing on the period almost two decades earlier when the city's trademark chopped-and-screwed sound had gained national prominence.

Floyd had first met Lawson back in the late 1990s, when

the Texas Southern University student was working as a DJ and beginning to make a name for himself on Houston's south side. Lawson had adopted DJ Screw's signature style, and after DJ Screw died of a codeine overdose in 2000, he was brought on to help complete a posthumous mixtape. That album, *DJ Screw The Legend*, was released in 2001 and became one of Floyd's favorites. He would play from its twenty-seven tracks while joyriding around Houston's south side, a pastime he referred to as "sailing the south."

Floyd was in Lawson's studio in early February 2016 when he found himself recalling those heady days of Houston's ascendancy in a hip-hop culture that had largely been shaped by New York, Los Angeles, and Atlanta. Surrounded by sound mixers and television screens, Floyd, Lawson, and another friend sat on comfortable chairs with a spread of snacks, alcohol, and cigarettes laid out across a coffee table. A blunt passed from hand to hand as the third man recorded the hazy scene with a cell phone.

Floyd was slurring his words as he reminisced about his high school football exploits, telling Lawson about a mutual friend who had dabbled in the music industry.

"Ishmael's big brother was in the tenth grade when I was in the twelfth," Floyd said. "His brother threw me a touchdown. It was a game winner, against Beaumont Central."

Lawson interrupted Floyd's boast by bringing up an embarrassing memory from his Yates football days.

"Hey, fool, remember when you dropped that touchdown?" he said, referring to the failed trick play in 1992.

"Yeah, whatever, man," Floyd said, looking down at the floor, before trying to steer the conversation back to the previous topic.

But Lawson, who was bald, big-bellied, and about five years younger than Floyd, wasn't finished teasing his friend. "Hey, you want to make that nigga mad?" he said to the other man in the studio. "Just tell that nigga he dropped the touchdown, bro."

Floyd sat silently, shaking his head instead of shooting back with a retort. Lawson took the cue and eased up on the taunting. But Lawson's bluntness occasionally reminded Floyd that his dreams of making it big in sports or music hadn't materialized and, given his age, likely never would.

"The ball dream is over, bro," Lawson said to him on another occasion.

Still, those close to him sensed his disappointment.

One day, while they were driving home, Hunter tried to get Floyd to open up about it. He asked Floyd if he was disappointed that he never made it to the pros.

Floyd squinted, letting the silence hang between them.

"I'ma let you answer that question," he said.

Floyd felt as if his life was unraveling: his relationship with Washington was falling apart, he couldn't find steady work, and he still regularly found himself sleeping in Cofield's car outside his mother's overcrowded house. Among the friends Floyd confided in during this period was Travis Cains.

"Big bro, I got to holler at you," Floyd told Cains.

"What's up?" Cains said, looking up at his friend.

The bashful expression on Floyd's face let Cains know that whatever he was about to unveil would not be good news.

"Aw, man, what the fuck you done done now?" Cains said, his voice escalating as Floyd hesitated to say what was on his mind.

"Man, I feel bad," Floyd finally let out.

"You feel bad about what?"

Floyd pulled his phone out and handed it to Cains.

"Man, I done this porn," he said.

Floyd was feeling a sense of regret over a decision he had made to chase some quick money, and perhaps some measure of fame, by agreeing to appear in an amateur pornographic video. He had been approached by adult filmmakers while working out at the gym one day and had decided to take them up on their offer.

"What?" Cains said, averting his eyes and pushing back against the phone. "Man, I don't want to see this shit."

But Cains then grabbed the phone, which was opened to an adult website that hosted amateur videos. The scene on display began with Floyd walking into a low-budget hotel room wearing a T-shirt that read "Young Risk Takers." A man behind the camera complimented Floyd on his height and size.

A young Black woman was seated on a couch, in full makeup, exchanging awkward glances with the tall stranger who had just walked into the room.

Adarryl Hunter noticed that Floyd was sinking. The pharmacist wasn't fully aware of Floyd's drug use, but he knew something was not right.

"I really think something is bothering you," he told Floyd one day as they sat in a car, riffing on a line from Richard Pryor's character in one of their favorite movies, *The Mack*. "Man, I really feel like something is deeply rooted in you that you yourself can't figure out. It's like a void that you don't know is there."

Floyd listened in silence, realizing that his friend was just getting warmed up.

Hunter thought that Floyd needed to go back to his origins. He suggested that Floyd drive to North Carolina with his mother to see where his people came from.

"Even if you just drive down there and turn around and drive back. Even if y'all don't get out of the car. Just go home, go to where your roots is from," he said. "I think that experience will give you some type of clarity or closure."

A few months later, Floyd learned that his father's relatives would be getting together in North Carolina and New York, two places where George Floyd Sr. had lived. Floyd's father had died in 2002, but the younger man had never connected with most of his paternal relatives, a group that included two younger half siblings.

After driving out to Tennessee with Cofield, Floyd decided to take a Greyhound bus farther east to meet some of his relatives for the first time. LaTonya Floyd, who had met her paternal relatives as a child and remained connected with many of them, helped Floyd spot their half brother, Terrence.

"I know that's not him," Floyd announced, smiling as he looked at the back of his half brother's bald head. "Bro!"

Terrence Floyd, who had no reason to expect that his older brother might show up, was perplexed when he heard the familiar voice bellowing in his direction.

Seeing Floyd, he was immediately overwhelmed with emotion. He ran over and embraced the man who looked and sounded just like their father, letting his head sink into Floyd's chest. The resemblance was not only physical—they both had large hands and tall, fit frames—but also visible in the confident way he carried himself.

The emotional meeting gave the brothers an opportunity to process the almost forty years they had spent living separately despite having the same blood. Floyd put his hands on his little brother's shoulders and smiled down at him. He immediately began peppering Terrence and his sister, Bridgett, with questions about George Floyd Sr., curious about the man whose absence had left him with a lingering sense of longing.

"Man, it fits," Floyd said, after Terrence described their father.

"What you mean?" Terrence said.

"Certain things I'm thinking, certain things I want to do, now I know why," Floyd said, without elaborating. "It fits."

Floyd seemed to be at ease as he played with Bridgett's two sons and caught up with his paternal relatives.

"That really, really brightened up his soul," Bridgett recalled of Floyd's visit. "He was making his rounds as he hadn't done before."

It was a joyful occasion, but, like the high school reunion three years earlier, the family gathering reminded Floyd how far behind he had fallen from his goals: He was the older brother, but he was the one in the most precarious financial situation. He was the one with the lengthy criminal record, the Percocet cravings, the child-support lawsuits. He had gone back to his roots like Hunter had advised, but the kind of clarity he found was not what his friend had envisioned.

As he got on the bus to head back to Houston, just weeks shy of his forty-third birthday, he had to deal with the reality that he had become something he had so desperately wanted to avoid: an unemployed man who lived with his mother and spent his days hanging out on the corner.

*

Floyd was sitting outside the Blue Store in December 2016 when Aubrey Rhodes, an old friend of his from Yates, drove up in a shiny rented SUV. Rhodes was rounder in the belly and had more vibrant skin than the last time anyone in Third Ward had seen him. Before leaving Houston for Minneapolis a couple of years earlier, Rhodes had cycled in and out of jail, and substance abuse had robbed him of the spark of life that friends who called him "Tutu" had grown accustomed to.

He was back in town visiting family, but the trip also gave him an opportunity to evangelize about the kind of transformation that was possible in the state of Minnesota.

"I got my life together," he told the men outside the Blue Store, before inviting them to join him there.

Most of the men chuckled.

"Nah, that's not for me," one of them said.

But Floyd was not so quick to dispel the idea, curious about his friend's transformation since he left the corner. Floyd and Rhodes had bonded as teenagers and trusted each other. As a trainer for the Yates football team back in the early 1990s, Rhodes had been an honorary member of Floyd's crew despite being a couple of years younger and less athletically inclined.

Floyd pulled him aside, away from the other men, for a one-on-one conversation. He confided that he was "struggling" and asked Rhodes if he could help him get to the Twin Cities.

Rhodes gave him the number of Pastor Johnnie Riles III, a man who had built up a reputation for taking struggling Houstonians and sending them far away for rehabilitation.

Before calling Riles, Floyd checked in with some of his friends about the idea of leaving Houston.

"Man, I think I'm going to go up to Minnesota," he told Vaughn Dickerson over the phone.

"What, with Tutu and them?"

"Yeah."

In asking around about Minnesota, Floyd had learned that it might be easier for someone with a criminal record to obtain a commercial driver's license there.

"Yeah, man, I think I'm going to go up there, man, get into truck driving and stuff," Floyd said.

"Man, if this is going to make you get better, go for it," Dickerson responded. "If you need me, call me."

The two old friends hung up the phone, and Floyd decided he was ready to pay a visit to the Church on Holman Street.

Pastor Johnnie Riles III was known around Third Ward as a minister to lost souls. His church was in the middle of the neighborhood, and its doors were open to the drug dealers and homeless addicts who populated Holman Street and the surrounding area.

He had moved with his wife to the neighborhood from the Houston suburbs in 1999, buying an old building that hardly looked habitable at the time.

"The best thing to do to that building was to take a bulldozer to it," one of his pastor friends had told him after he bought it. Instead, Riles renovated the space and gave it a simple name: the Church on Holman Street.

Its mission was simple as well: ministering to "the least of these"—the poor, hungry, imprisoned, sick, and destitute souls Jesus had instructed his disciples to protect in Matthew 25. A sign in front of the building read: "Your changing station."

But soon after he settled in Third Ward, Riles realized

that many of the downtrodden residents he wanted to help would only achieve the kind of change they needed at new stations far away.

In 1995, Texas had stalled funding for its "therapeutic communities," which were designed to help convicts get clean and reintegrate into society—programs that would have disproportionately helped Black men. Originally the state was supposed to earmark fourteen thousand prison beds for such services. A decade later, it had set aside only five thousand, according to news reports at the time.

Texas had declined to expand Medicaid under the Affordable Care Act, denying more than 1.4 million low-income residents access to free health care and drug treatment. By contrast, states like Minnesota had accepted the federal funding to expand Medicaid under President Barack Obama's signature health law and had kicked in their own state dollars to bolster a robust and well-integrated apparatus of recovery and aftercare programs.

Realizing the limitations of trying to heal people struggling with addiction and mental anguish in a state that had deliberately limited public funding for health care, Riles began partnering with other religious and charitable organizations hundreds of miles away. He would take people who were battling drug and alcohol dependency and put them on buses to places like Minneapolis and Chicago, where they could get clean and find adequate care in well-funded programs.

Before sending them off, Riles would tell them the story of the man rescued by the Good Samaritan and the parable of the prodigal son. Those two biblical figures, he would say, had to leave the locations where they had reached rock bottom to find rehabilitation.

"Sometimes you just need to take a break, and go on vacation," he would say. "Go on vacation from your neighborhood, from people, places, things, and events that you're involved in, and go rethink. Get quiet and still and try to compose yourself."

When Floyd went to see Pastor Riles in late 2016, he knew he needed a change, but he was not yet sure what that might look like.

Riles sat down with Floyd and asked him about his criminal record, his employment history, and whether he had been using drugs. Reviewing Floyd's background, Riles could see that a typical thirty- or sixty-day rehab program would not be sufficient to reset Floyd's life. He recommended that Floyd leave Houston and go to a six-month program at the Salvation Army in Minneapolis. The all-encompassing program would teach work skills and life practices, in addition to offering rehabilitation services.

"We're going to stay with you until you win," Riles said. "And we know that along the way, you're going to stumble and fall, because relapse is common. But we're going to stand with you until you win."

The pastor had watched several people he had sent away from Third Ward return to Houston seemingly recovered, only to fall again in a matter of weeks. Recalling the amount of time Jesus spent training his disciples, Riles believed it could take three years or longer to truly break an addiction and change a life. Houston had nothing even close to that kind of long-term support for poor and uninsured men like Floyd.

Floyd was still on the fence after speaking to Riles. When

he called Nikki Smith to talk through his decision, she could tell he was struggling with the idea of leaving behind his family, friends, and neighborhood. She had grappled with similar doubts before departing Houston with Reginal Smith in 2008 in an attempt to break a debilitating drug addiction that had consumed the couple.

"If that's what you need to do, just go," she told Floyd, pressing the benefits of relocating. "Maybe everybody doesn't need to, but I did, and it worked for me."

Floyd listened as she continued to explain how she had benefitted from her move to Minneapolis, where she and Reginal had spent five years before returning to Houston sober.

"It's a well-funded state," she said. "There are so many resources."

Floyd had been to her four-bedroom, three-and-a-half-bath home in Katy and seen how much her life had changed since the days when she could be found passed out in Third Ward crack dens. In Minneapolis, she had gotten into nursing and Reginal was driving trucks, bringing in the kind of steady income that afforded a suburban lifestyle.

"Yeah, Nicknack," Floyd said. "You and Reg, y'all did it big."

"We left with a backpack. We came back to Houston with a huge U-Haul, two cars," she told him. "We literally sky-rocketed."

While Floyd outwardly resolved to go to Minneapolis, he was a no-show after Riles sent him a bus ticket shortly after their talk. As Floyd equivocated, his friend Adarryl Hunter decided to pull the trigger on resetting his own life. Hunter had lost his pharmacy license after being arrested for driving under the influence and possession of illegal pills. His wife had asked him for a divorce, his driver's license was suspended, and child-support bills for his six kids were beginning to pile up. He had told Pastor Riles about his predicament in early January 2017, and within days he was headed up to Minneapolis in search of a fresh start.

After his friend went through with the move, Floyd became more serious about leaving Houston.

He called Robert Fonteno, who back in 1991 had encouraged him as an eighteen-year-old to stay focused on sports and out of trouble, to see if he could help. Fonteno had also relocated to Minneapolis, and word had spread back in Houston that he had been sending money down to help more people make the journey.

Before relocating, Fonteno had slipped from selling drugs to abusing them and was at his nadir when he decided to visit Riles as a last resort in 2009. Upon arriving in Minneapolis with Riles's help, Fonteno enrolled in a ninety-day treatment program. Within months, he had gotten clean and found a job driving trucks. Soon he was making more than $2,000 a week, and he decided to send some of his earnings back to Riles's church—both as a way of showing gratitude and as a lifeline to others facing the same desperation he once felt.

As the news of Fonteno's generosity had spread in Third Ward, some struggling men began contacting him directly, seeking a bus ticket or money to make the trip. In January 2017, Floyd made one of those calls.

"I'm in the dark, bro," Floyd said. "I don't see my situation getting no better, man. I need your help."

Fonteno, who had been taking classes to become a

rehabilitation counselor, immediately realized that Floyd was using a euphemism for the kind of all-consuming addiction that made it difficult to function.

"Okay, what is it you need?" Fonteno asked.

"If I stay here, bro, I'm going to either die in the streets or I'm going back to prison."

"Damn," Fonteno said, taken aback by the gravity of Floyd's tone.

"I need a light," Floyd said. "I need a hand, man, to get to the light."

Fonteno was moved by Floyd's earnestness, but he knew addicts could be both convincing and capricious, especially when money was involved.

"Bro, just give me a couple of days, man, to pray on the situation, and I'm going to get back to you," he said.

Floyd agreed, and they were both about to hang up when Fonteno offered some parting advice to let his friend know that achieving true change involved more than just geography.

"Wherever you go, bro, you take yourself with you," he said.

"What you mean?"

"Well, the same thing you doing there, you could be doing up here if you don't watch it. But if you really want to change, man, you can change. But just keep in mind that you going to have to want it from the inside out, man."

"I feel you," Floyd said. "Okay, man, I got you."

Fonteno put down the phone and sighed. He appreciated that Floyd was still the same humble, respectful guy he had met at the Blue Store in the early 1990s but knew from experience that the grip of addiction could bend even the most levelheaded of men. He had already spent thousands of dollars trying to help friends and strangers alike, with mixed success, and knew that Houston could be a pit for his hard-earned income. He asked God to tell him what he should do.

When Fonteno called back a few days later, the peace he felt about his decision was strengthened when he learned Floyd had been praying as well.

"Hey, man. You still want to come up here?" he asked Floyd.

"Yeah, man. I've been waiting on your call," Floyd said. "I've been praying, man, asking God to touch your heart to send me a ticket."

Fonteno told him he would book the bus ticket for the following week—the last week of January 2017—and that it was nonrefundable. He reiterated that he was sending a ticket and not money because he wanted to make sure Floyd was really committed.

"If you need something when you get up here, I got you, bro. But I'm not going to send you no cash. All right?"

"Cool, man, that's all I need is a ticket."

They hung up the phone, and Fonteno went online to book the Greyhound bus ticket, spending $225 for the 1,200-mile journey.

A few days before the scheduled trip, Fonteno began to question Floyd's conviction when his calls to him repeatedly went to voice mail. He dialed Riles to see if he had heard from him and learned that Floyd had missed the trip a few weeks earlier after Riles had bought him a ticket.

"Hopefully, it won't be the same situation with you," Riles told him.

Fonteno kept dialing Floyd until he finally picked up, a couple of days before his scheduled trip. Fonteno told him he had been trying to contact him to make sure everything was still on track for the upcoming trip. Floyd's response was noncommittal.

"Well, you know, man . . ."

"Oh, here it comes," Fonteno thought to himself, certain he was going to hear yet another excuse from someone he had gone out on a limb to try to help.

But Floyd said that he was going to pay a $10 change fee to reschedule the ticket for a few days later so that he could have a proper send-off before leaving town. The Super Bowl was set to take place in a few days, with Houston as the host city, and he said it didn't feel right to leave his hometown before such a big event.

"Cal Wayne's throwing a Super Bowl party in the 'hood, and everybody's supposed to be there," he said.

"Okay, cool," Fonteno said. "But I'm going to tell you like this, bro: if you don't take this ticket, you know you can't ask me to do this again?"

"I know," he said, assuring Fonteno that he was still committed. "I'm going to do it."

Tiffany Cofield was also skeptical that Floyd would go through with the move to Minnesota. He had been openly contemplating the trip for weeks but never seemed to do much more than talk about it. She had been with him before when he had claimed he was on the cusp of departing for Minneapolis, and each time he had stayed put.

"You aren't fixing to leave Texas," she had told him. "Shut up. There's no way you're fixing to leave Third Ward."

"I'm for real, Stiff," Floyd said, using the nickname he had given her. "I got to go. Tutu and them said if I come up there, they can help me get on my feet. I can take this program. I can get custody of Butt Butt."

She knew that Floyd would do anything for his daughter, no matter how extreme it seemed. And she knew how dysfunctional the situation had been since Floyd and Washington had broken up, their flame extinguished almost as quickly as it had been ignited.

Floyd had told friends he wanted to get full custody of Gianna. His bond with his daughter had deepened during three years of diaper changes, laughter-filled teeth-brushing sessions, Halloween trick-or-treating, and Chuck E. Cheese birthdays. Getting sober in Minnesota and earning his commercial driver's license would be the first steps to becoming a more present father, he figured.

Still, Cofield didn't believe Floyd would leave the only hometown he had truly known.

And then there was the matter of Miss Cissy, who needed more help moving around to care for her grandchildren as her health declined. During his time at home, Floyd would lift her body up from her wheelchair for spontaneous dance sessions. Sometimes, he would wheel her over to the Blue Store to play the electronic slot machines stationed by the entrance. His departure, scheduled for just three weeks before Miss Cissy's seventieth birthday, would hit his mother especially hard, Cofield thought.

"But, Floyd, you going to leave Mama?" Cofield asked him one day in January. Left unstated were the implications for Cofield's relationship with Floyd.

Floyd insisted that the journey would be temporary—just long enough for him to get himself together.

After the new year, Floyd still was not behaving like someone about to uproot his life and relocate to a new city. Floyd had rebooked his ticket for February 6, the day after the Super

Bowl, but spent the weekend hanging with Cofield like he always had.

They attended an awards event at the Galleria honoring Houston figures like Mayor Sylvester Turner and rapper Trae tha Truth, whom Cofield had worked with. Floyd wore a black button-up shirt, dark-framed glasses, and khaki pants to the event, which was also attended by rapper T.I.

Professional photographers had captured Floyd and Cofield on the red carpet of the Porsche-sponsored program, one of the dozens of see-and-be-seen events taking place across the city in advance of the Super Bowl.

The pair had booked a hotel room for Super Bowl weekend in Baytown, a suburb twenty-six miles east of Houston. They had watched the game with Cal Wayne and his entourage, an epic comeback in which the New England Patriots overcame a twenty-five-point deficit in the second half to beat the Atlanta Falcons in overtime. The game ended with announcers mentioning that the 2018 Super Bowl would be held in Minneapolis, which Floyd considered to be a sign.

The watch party did not end until well past midnight and, as they pulled into the hotel parking lot, Cofield was certain that Floyd wouldn't make the six a.m. bus.

As she prepared to go to bed, she was surprised to hear Floyd say he had one more thing to do before leaving Houston in the morning.

"Tiff, before I go, I got to go see Butt Butt," he said, eager to visit his daughter one last time.

She considered arguing with him about the late hour, but she was tired enough that she just passed him the keys to her red Ford Escape rental and settled into bed, not even bothering to set a predawn alarm to get Floyd to the bus terminal.

She woke up to the sound of Floyd returning to the room shortly after four a.m.

"Let's go," he said, calculating that it would take at least an hour for them to drive from Baytown to the Houston bus station downtown.

"Where's your stuff?" Cofield, still half-asleep, asked him.

"This is all I'm taking with me," he said, shaking the large duffel bag that was draped over his shoulder.

They got in the car and started the westward drive on I-10, surrounded by darkness.

As they approached downtown Houston, Cofield suddenly had to grapple with the reality that her best friend, the man she had spent nearly every day with for the past two years, was actually leaving.

"Man, you ain't never coming back," she blurted out.

"Tiff, I am coming back," he said. "Quit saying that."

CHAPTER 8

Turning Point

GEORGE FLOYD STEPPED OFF the Greyhound bus in Min-neapolis on a frigid winter day. From his pocket, he pulled a scrap of paper with the phone number of a man Pastor Riles said to contact for a ride.

"Can I speak to Byron?" he asked formally, unsure of the identity of the man on the other end of the line.

"Big Floyd," the voice said, chuckling. "It's me!"

The man turned out to be Byron Jeffrey, an old friend from Houston. Floyd smiled widely when he saw Li'l B pull up in a gold Grand Marquis. Floyd walked outside to meet him, confidently striding through the front doors, ready to take his first steps in a new city. And then, as soon as he stepped out of the depot, he slipped.

"People here be ice skating," said Floyd, dusting himself off.

"Walk slow," Jeffrey told him. "You have to get used to it."

The two gave each other a handshake and a hug. Floyd was thinner than Jeffrey remembered, which he attributed to his drug use. Still, he couldn't recall the last time he had seen Big Floyd with this energy, this bounce. Jeffrey imagined Floyd would do great things in this city. In Minneapolis,

Jeffrey had found a way to completely change his life. He was sober, faithful, working—he had started cutting hair at a barbershop. He had developed a passion for helping others and enrolled in classes to become an addiction counselor.

If Jeffrey could get his life together, he was certain Floyd—with his smarts and charisma—could do even more. Within minutes, Floyd was joined by Tutu and Robert Fonteno and some of the other corner boys from Cuney Homes.

Even though they all had the same nicknames and still listened to the same DJ Screw tapes, the men at the bus depot told Floyd they had changed since the time they used to hang outside the Blue Store together. Because they wanted to stay clean, they avoided being around drugs and alcohol. They had picked up trades and worked jobs as security guards and truck drivers. But one thing remained the same: they were committed to looking out for one another. Like Floyd, they had left behind their families and children, resolved that, as Pastor Riles would say, "Houston could take care of itself."

"You ready for this?" Aubrey Rhodes asked Floyd. "Here you can change your life. You can find a way to live."

Floyd said he was ready. He talked about his baby girl and his desire to find a good job and send money back home. After about an hour of catching up, Floyd hopped into Jeffrey's car and they drove to an imposing brown building next to a Salvation Army thrift store that housed the agency's rehabilitation program.

Floyd, in his eagerness to get a fresh start, didn't fully realize what he had signed up for. As Jeffrey drove him to the site, he told Floyd about all its programs—life skills, job training, group therapy, church services. But there would be no cell phones or connection to the outside world. He'd spend his days volunteering at the thrift store and in counseling. Clients were given about a dollar per week to learn how to save money. All it took was six months, Jeffrey told him.

"I don't know I can do six months, man," Floyd said, realizing just how long this journey would be.

Jeffrey encouraged him to stay optimistic. During Jeffrey's first few weeks at the Salvation Army, he had been mischievous and rebellious and refused to participate in group sessions. But he found a mentor there who vowed not to give up on him. And over time, he began to enjoy his experience. Floyd considered these words before nodding his head. Then he walked through the doors of the Salvation Army, ready to start a new life.

About a week later, Jeffrey returned to see how he was doing. Floyd was sitting by himself, slumped on a chair in a common area, watching sports. Jeffrey sat down to join him. Something seemed off. Floyd confessed that he was ready to leave the program.

"I'm not feeling it," he said. "It's too much like jail. I don't know why I got to wait. I want to get out of here and go to work."

"You've got to give yourself time," Jeffrey said. He pointed out how nice the television was and that there was a weight room where Floyd could get his size back. "Be chill, be chill."

Floyd's duffel bag was already packed. He wanted to go through the same program that Tutu had been through, and that Adarryl Hunter had just started. They seemed to be doing well for themselves, and they were confident Floyd could find his footing too. And that program was only three months long.

"It's done," Floyd told Jeffrey. "Tutu is on his way."

Jeffrey realized there was no use in arguing. The men from Third Ward wanted to find a way to help Floyd heal. They wanted it for him because they had admired him back in Third Ward, when he was the person who could do great things if he only got the chance. And they also wanted his success for so many other men back home, who might be inspired to get clean if they followed Big Floyd's example. They were confident he would succeed—the only question was figuring out the best path.

Although Floyd was focused on the length of his rehab program, Rhodes and his other friends were making a different calculation, taking Floyd to a place whose name invoked a type of optimism: Our Turning Point. The program was unlike anything they had ever seen before—a recovery center owned and operated by Black people, specializing in improving the health and well-being of Black people.

The recovery philosophy at Turning Point, as it is commonly known, stemmed from director Peter Hayden's experiences as the only Black man in his Alcoholics Anonymous group in 1973—the year Floyd was born. Hayden remembered shaking his head in disbelief when a White man told the group he felt like drinking because he didn't want to give his wife $50. Hayden's friends drank because they didn't have $50. It wasn't simply addiction that was a problem for Hayden and his cohort: It was access to jobs. It was resources. It was finding a way to cope in a prejudiced world in which they were taught that any misstep might lead to a prison cell or a coffin.

Hayden theorized that African Americans might heal differently because they were treated differently. But in a country aiming to move toward colorblindness, Hayden's theory could be controversial. Emerging social science research, though, was beginning to support his hunch. At the time, a wave of public health experts had become interested in the effects of "high-effort coping"—how attempts to overcome tense situations could result in increased rates of high blood pressure.

Sherman James, then an epidemiologist at the University of North Carolina in Chapel Hill, noted that the existing research had centered around the lives of middle-class White men. James, who is Black, set out to the farms of eastern North Carolina, the same fields that Floyd's forebears tilled. There, he met a Black man named John Henry Martin, who had grown up under the oppressive sharecropping system. Martin had worked tirelessly to pay off a forty-year mortgage in five years. He was in his early seventies when James met him, but he had developed a host of conditions that made him appear much older—bad legs, osteoporosis, stomach ulcers, and high blood pressure.

"His own diagnosis was that he pushed himself too hard," James recalled. "It reminded me of my dad's story, my uncle's story, my granddad's story, my mom's story. It was emblematic of the story of Black Americans."

It was also emblematic of the legend of John Henry, the hammer-wielding African American folk hero who died of a heart attack trying to prove his worth by single-handedly building a railroad. So, in the 1980s, James coined a term that described the coping mechanism of going to great lengths to combat racism—the old belief that Black people had to work twice as hard to get half as far. He called the phenomenon "John Henry–ism."

James cautioned that the outcomes of John Henry–ism

could be positive; John Henry Martin was able to rapidly pay off his mortgage, after all. But without societal support and awareness, the health consequences could be dire. A future colleague of his at the University of Michigan, a behavioral researcher named Arline Geronimus, took the thinking even further in the 1990s. She hypothesized that the young Black mothers she had been following were consistently in worse shape than young White mothers because their bodies were responding to a distinct type of stress. Even when controlling for income levels, age, geography, and educational status, experts across the country were finding Black people were often sicker than their White counterparts.

Those sicknesses manifested themselves when researchers started to compare hormones that can produce inflammation, such as cortisol. In their studies, African Americans tended to have elevated levels of those hormones, which typically rise as a response to stress. While those rises can be helpful in limited spurts—providing focus to pull an all-nighter or increasing heart rates to accomplish a strenuous physical challenge—they also strain the immune system. That's why students get sick after finals week or athletes get so sore after big games. If those cortisol levels remain high over a prolonged period, as has been found in African Americans, the strain makes people more susceptible to sickness. These discoveries called into question the thinking that bad diets and a lack of exercise caused African Americans to have higher rates of hypertension, diabetes, and heart disease. It turned out that the stress of everything, from everyday slights to fears of a deadly interaction with the police, was altering human physiology. Being Black in America is its own preexisting condition.

"There's nothing different about how people respond to

stress across race," according to Darrell Hudson, a public health professor at Washington University in St. Louis. "The context that people live in *is* racialized, however. It's about the chronicity of it and your relationship with it: Do you feel you have some control over what stresses you, without a herculean effort and a lot of luck? If not, everything piles up."

Because so little research was being conducted on how to best treat these phenomena, Hayden relied on his charm and his passion to persuade local governments and foundations to provide him grants and funding. He used to dress in the flashiest clothes—colorful suits, alligator shoes—to convey a sense of confidence that his program might work. He eventually secured enough grants from the county government and foundations to start Turning Point in 1976.

In addition to partnering with clinics that provided chemical treatment, staffers taught Black history to instill a sense of self-worth and prepared soul food dinners on Sundays to foster community. They mixed the traditional twelve-step program with the principles of Kwanzaa—a standard step such as "come to believe that a power greater than myself could return me to sanity" was turned into "come to believe that a power within myself could return me to a lifestyle that would not hurt me." The change spoke both to affirming a Black person's sense of agency and the deliberate avoidance of the word "sanity."

"African Americans don't like to talk about being crazy," Hayden said, which he believed was a product of a long history of distrust and dismissal between Black patients and White doctors. It was that distrust that had complicated Hayden's mission, while also demonstrating the need for it.

A 2019 analysis of federal data showed that one in ten

African Americans said they had an unmet need for mental health treatment—twice the rate of the general population. And those who did find help were more likely to end treatment early, citing factors such as cost, stigma, and a sense that their provider didn't understand them.

These feelings are particularly damaging when it comes to substance abuse and mental health. Ayana Jordan, the psychiatry professor at New York University who studies race and addiction, noted that clients must trust that their providers take their concerns seriously and are treating them as individuals, not as stereotypes. But Jordan said there is a reason to believe health-care professionals aren't conscientious enough, citing statistics that show that Black people are underdiagnosed with mood disorders such as depression while being overdiagnosed with issues such as schizophrenia—a disorder associated with aggressive behavior.

The persistence of those stereotypes influenced practically every institution that could have helped George Floyd as he came of age. When drug crises ripped through Black communities, they resulted in the Rockefeller Drug Laws in the 1970s and the 1986 Anti-Drug Abuse Act that stiffened sentences, as well as the spending spree for prisons that came with the 1994 crime bill. But studies have shown those laws neglected to fund the job trainings, drug treatments, and education programs they promised. For example, the 1994 law promised $2.7 billion to the Department of Housing and Urban Development over three years for such programs, but a federal review shows lawmakers never sent the agency the money. By contrast, lawmakers have steadily increased funding for those same types of programs since the opioid epidemic hit White suburban communities. At least $2.5

billion was spent between 2016 and 2019 on treatment, through the 21st Century Cures Act and the Comprehensive Addiction and Recovery Act.

Those stereotypes also had a direct impact on Floyd's well-being. His fear of being arrested and his dissatisfaction with the Salvation Army approach could not be divorced from his experience as a Black man in America. The continued and aggressive police presence in his neighborhoods not only increased the risk of arrest, but research from professors at the University of Minnesota shows that Black people who have negative interactions with law enforcement have a heightened distrust of institutions. Even more, a 2017 study conducted by professors at the University of Michigan conducted over eighteen years found that Black boys who said they experienced discrimination were more likely to experience depression and anxiety as adults.

On the national level, the tilt toward criminalizing Black men—rather than treating them—also meant there was little interest in finding ways to address these specific mental health issues. A 2013 review published through the American Psychological Association found that there had been only nineteen empirical studies examining depression in Black men in the previous quarter century and stated that "depression among African American men needs to be at the forefront of our research, practice, and outreach agendas." But change was slow to follow. Six years later, *Science Advances* magazine estimated that White scientists were twice as likely to receive research dollars as Black scientists, whose proposals were more inclined to examine disparities and inequality. The result is a medical system with twin problems stemming from institutionally racist practices. It had caused a particular form of stress among Black Americans that it was not fully equipped to quell.

Programs such as Turning Point hoped to address the issue. Over the next half century, Hayden and his staff fought to find ways to expand its programming. Instead of flaunting fashion, Hayden began to flaunt success—the program expanded from one tiny house on the city's majority-Black north side to a series of connecting homes. They even had a clean-living apartment building called Ms. Bea's House, which could allow clients to transition more easily to life on their own.

And the stories of its success started drawing clients from Illinois and Missouri and Texas—Black men from all over the country who were like Floyd, modern-day John Henrys who were willing to uproot their lives for one last chance at healing.

The first day Floyd walked into his life-skills class at Turning Point, he realized it would not be a typical talking circle. The room was instead set up like a classroom, and the course, which was called "Blacks in Recovery," felt like another chance at college.

The class was led by Woodrow Jefferson, a diminutive former math whiz whose life had been overtaken by substance use. He had believed that Black men might respond differently to a setting in which they were treated as intellectuals—particularly because so many had been criminalized and stereotyped as uncontrollable, impulsive, and stupid.

Jefferson would pace around the class giving examples about Mr. Cool and Mr. Slick—two types of neighborhood hustlers, one enviable and assured, the other manipulative and subversive. He then added two other examples of how Black people operate in the world, bringing up Muhammad Ali and Uncle Tom—one braggadocious and bold, the other obsequious and deferential. Jefferson did not try to cast aspersions on any of them. He told the class all four men were trying to figure out a way to survive in a world that provided them with limited options. All four men, in some way, were broken by racism, searching for a way to find dignity.

Over the next few weeks, Jefferson told the group that their sense of dignity could not be realized in fancy phrases or affirmations—even though he certainly knew his share of those. Rather, Jefferson wanted them to find hope by tapping into their full potential as Black men willing to take on the systems of racism that hobbled them. The challenge was to be in control of their life before someone else—a judge, a bad boss, a police officer—could even try.

And then he would discuss the attempts to demean and dehumanize Black bodies, using topics such as enslavement, breeding, the prison system, and medical experimentation.

"Look at history," Jefferson often said. "Have you noticed how people are always trying to profit off of us, own us? . . . But what about you? How can you find you again? How can you love yourselves again? . . . It's about finding your purpose."

Jefferson's talks empowered clients to open up about their own histories. Some grew up in households of addicts, while some didn't know anyone else who took drugs. Some talked about the impact of growing up fatherless, and others shouldered guilt about disappointing their dads. Many of them had been incarcerated, traumatized by the isolation and the violence they had seen in prison. One day, Jefferson recalled, he saw a hand go up in the back. It was Floyd's.

Floyd finally felt comfortable expressing his personal struggles in ways he had not been willing to say plainly to his friend Hunter back in Houston. He talked about how disappointed he was that he never went pro. So much of his identity, his self-worth, hinged on the expectation that one day he would be able to play ball. And now his body was a mark of pride and a constant reminder of his failures—the physique of an athlete who tried but didn't measure up. The thing that people most admired and feared.

Jefferson dismissed that kind of talk.

"You are lovable," Jefferson would tell the class. "You are important. You are valuable. You are empowered."

Sometimes during classes, Jefferson asked the group to stand up. Together, Floyd and the men repeated the mantra: "I am lovable! I am important! I am valuable! I am empowered!"

After forty-five days of sobriety, Floyd was allowed to leave the property under curfew, finally able to explore his new home.

To celebrate, Rhodes and Jeffrey drove Floyd to the Mall of America, eager to show him the largest indoor mall in the Western Hemisphere. Floyd marveled at the cavernous place, at 5.6 million square feet, with four floors of stores and an amusement park running through its center. The group bought him a new pair of sneakers and a cell phone. They ate wings at Hooters and discussed Floyd's next steps. Now that he was able, there was one thing he wanted more than anything else: a job.

Rhodes thought that Floyd's background in security would make him a perfect fit at the homeless shelter where he worked, which was also run by the Salvation Army. Rhodes knew exactly who to call.

"Floyd wants a job here?" Darlene Phillips shouted. Phillips was a tall and boisterous woman who had grown up with Floyd's sisters, Zsa Zsa and LaTonya. She had moved to Minneapolis in 2014 to overcome her addiction to crack cocaine. She was now clean and helping to manage the homeless shelter in one of the most crime-ridden corners of the city, on the western edge of downtown. Outside the shelter, in the shadows of the interstate and the baseball stadium, was an open-air drug market for crack, PCP, and pills. Inside the shelter were vulnerable men and women who were easily agitated and prone to fight. She thought Big Floyd's intimidating stature would help.

"He's exactly what we need," Phillips told Rhodes.

By mid-April 2017, Floyd had his first job in Minneapolis. They paired him with Sylvia Jackson, a second-generation security officer who herself had moved to the city from Chicago in hopes of finding better-paying work. Floyd was trained on how to give CPR and administer Narcan, a nasal spray that can rapidly reverse the impact of an opioid overdose. He had to learn the smaller things as well: the right keys to use, how to work the security cameras, and how to transfer calls on the telephone. But Phillips told Floyd to remember that what mattered most was how he treated others. Around six o'clock each night, the tired, the weary, the abused, and the addicted would walk into the shelter's cafeteria for dinner. They were a different crowd than the shelter residents and would come in carrying their most precious belongings and their frustrations with the world. Phillips encouraged Floyd to be conscientious, courteous, and kind.

"Put yourself in their footprints," Phillips said. "And if they tell you to pray for them, don't just say you will. Stop and pray with them."

Because of her connection with Floyd's sisters, Phillips did not see herself as just his boss. She vowed to be an enforcer, to speak truth to Floyd if he began to fall into temptation. Floyd let her know he had no intention of even looking like he was going to slip, so much so that he declined an invitation to go to a Harlem Globetrotters game with Phillips and her daughter because he did not want to be seen cavorting with a married woman.

"It won't look right," Floyd said.

On shift, Floyd would observe the young clients to make sure they weren't being bullied and accompany groups on trips to the movies. At dinnertime, he'd fold his arms and keep watch over patrons in the cafeteria, looking out for trouble. Floyd had a patented way of handling people who were acting up. He'd tap them on the shoulder and say, "Take a walk with me." Then, he'd try to escort them past the white lights and linoleum floor in the lobby and back outside.

"You can't come back in here today," Floyd would say, "but you could try tomorrow."

A few months into the job, a client came back to the shelter after having had too much to drink. He was boisterous and vulgar and continued to mouth off as Floyd moved him across the slick floor. Floyd marched on, paying no mind to the fact that the client had stiffened his body enough that he needed to be dragged out.

"You got to go," Floyd said. But then the client tripped over his feet and fell, hurting himself. Floyd recoiled and started heaving at the sight of the man's blood. As other staff tended to the man, Floyd retreated to an empty room, where a pastor found him crying.

"I was too hard on that guy," Floyd told him. He didn't want to be the type of enforcer who hurt people; he'd seen enough aggression in the name of law and order, and he knew there were other ways to enforce rules.

The pastor prayed with Floyd, reminding him to forgive himself.

Later that summer, around August 2017, a woman with long brown hair and square-rimmed glasses entered the lobby of the shelter. Courteney Ross was looking for the estranged father of her two sons, hoping that he had been staying there. As she waited, her mind took a dark turn and she started weeping, nervous that her older son's birthday would be tainted by the disappearance of his father.

Floyd was making his rounds when he saw the crying woman in the lobby. Sensing her anguish, he attempted to use one of the tactics that Phillips had taught him, but with his own spin on it.

"Sis," Floyd said, "can I pray with you?"

The woman was startled but agreed. They held hands as he prayed for calm. Afterward, Ross got word that her son's father was okay. As she turned to leave, Floyd put his hand on her shoulder and walked her outside. Something about the woman intrigued Floyd. He dropped his voice even deeper to ask: "Can I get your number?"

She stopped to look at the large security guard she had just met. She did not typically go for men his type, but she wondered if there was some sort of divine reasoning for all this.

She divulged her digits.

"My name is Courteney."

"They call me Big Floyd."

Under the glow of night, they kissed.

*

Floyd was starting to fall in love with the city. After ninety days of sobriety, he had transitioned to Ms. Bea's House. He'd express his enthusiasm at group check-ins. Sitting on plush chairs and couches in the common area, the men discussed how they were going about finding their purpose.

"God's been blessing me," Floyd told them. He was clean. He was going on dates. He had health insurance and could finally make doctor's appointments to treat his aching knees and his high blood pressure. He had the Salvation Army job and then found another weekend gig as a security guard at a Latin nightclub called Conga. He started lifting weights again, and his muscles swelled from hundred-pound biceps curls. He loved calling his daughter Gianna on the phone. He had saved enough money to buy a green Pontiac Bonneville, which he called the Green Machine, and enough to send some money back home to his ailing mother.

He was making his family proud. And the hopes of his friends in Third Ward also began to materialize. The more Floyd posted on Facebook about his success in Minneapolis, the more his friends back home expressed an interest in heading up north to get clean. Together with Hunter, who was now working a job in construction while he took steps to regain his license to practice pharmacy, Floyd would visit the many lakes around the state and play basketball at local parks. They were often joined at those games by one of the elders at Ms. Bea's House, a six-foot-four man with a big stomach and a warm smile named Eric Cornley. Everyone called him Big E. He and Big Floyd bonded over their similar backgrounds: They were both college athletes—Cornley had played basketball for Illinois State—who had come from out of town. And they were both self-conscious about their size. In the "Blacks in Recovery" class, both Big E and Big Floyd chose to sit in the back row to ensure they would not block anyone's view.

At Ms. Bea's House, Big E earned a reputation for being responsible and respectable. He was one of the older residents, eight years Floyd's senior. He coordinated the list of chores assigned to each resident and enforced unpopular duties like collecting and taking out the trash. Floyd, like everyone else at Ms. Bea's, took to his optimism and drive.

Though he'd lost a step since his college days, Big E gave everything he had on the basketball court at their pickup games around town. During breaks, Cornley would often talk about his plans. He had wanted to own his own business—maybe putting hand sanitizer in bus stops or running a bathroom butler service at nightclubs. To gain experience in the industry, Floyd helped Cornley get a security job at Conga too.

It wasn't unusual for residents to stay longer than three months at Ms. Bea's, given the difficulty of obtaining housing with a criminal record. Floyd was no exception: he had handed in applications for apartments across the city but found himself repeatedly rejected and was still trying to find his own housing in September 2017. He told his friends that he refused to be despondent.

"God is going to see me through," he said.

One night, while he was working security at Conga, his housing fortunes changed. Floyd overheard some bartenders chatting; it turned out the club's owner, Jovanni Thunstrom, rented properties to workers across the Twin Cities, and there happened to be an opening at a townhome on a tony block in the White suburb of St. Louis Park. That night, after Floyd escorted the last lingerers from the club, he found Thunstrom.

Thunstrom was a little nervous about renting the

property to Floyd—he didn't presume that Floyd had references or good credit. But Thunstrom had taken a liking to Floyd ever since the day of his interview. He was sympathetic to Floyd's assessment of where he was in his life, and Thunstrom soon found Floyd to be a responsible worker who showed up to the club on time.

Thunstrom agreed to rent him the apartment, provided he could find a roommate. Floyd asked Hunter, but he declined because he was on a waiting list for his own place. He asked Fonteno, but he was traveling so much that he could not fully commit. Tutu and Li'l B already had accommodations. And so, he asked his new friend.

"Big E, you want to do this?"

Big E said yes.

Courteney Ross was nervous as she got ready for her first date with the deep-voiced man she had met at the Salvation Army. She put on a short green dress and a pair of brown high heels with big gemstones on them and made her way to a restaurant named Ray J's. She showed up right on time that evening, perched at a high-top, ready to meet Floyd. Five minutes passed, then ten, then fifteen. She called Floyd to make sure he was still coming, and he assured her that he was taking care of some business with his boss at Conga, the club across the street.

"This is when I first realized Floyd runs late everywhere he goes," Ross recalled.

Eventually, Floyd showed up. Ross had been nervously drinking gin and tonics on an empty stomach and ended up getting drunk. As the evening wore on, Floyd took her to a bathroom and pulled her hair back while she braced the toilet.

The next few dates went better. Ross told him that she was a mother of two: James, a sweet and curious seven-year-old, and Gavin, a funny and smart high school chess champion who did great impressions. Floyd told her about Gianna and the big family he had left behind in Houston to start afresh. Ross, too, was reassessing her life. She was burning out disciplining children as an administrator at Edison High School.

At first, Floyd did not mention his criminal record or that he was finishing up rehab. But he did casually mention that he might have made an adult film. "Baby, baby, baby, how would you feel if I told you that?" Floyd said.

It depended, Ross said. It was one thing if the reasons for making the film were about empowering oneself through sex. It would be another thing if the film played into stereotypes or made him uncomfortable. But Ross said she understood him. She had been a cocktail waitress at a local strip club.

"Everyone's got a past," Ross told him.

They went on more dates. They shared a love for silly movies and hip-hop. Floyd introduced her to the Houston sound, and she introduced him to the stylings of Minneapolis rapper Brother Ali. They ate fruit pancakes at Maria's and ambled around the Sculpture Garden. Over time, she pieced together Floyd's past. She eventually learned he was living in rehab and that he had spent time in prison. She sympathized with him. She had done drugs since high school. And after she had Gavin, doctors had given her oxycodone to deal with lingering neck pain. The pain never subsided, and doctors continued to prescribe the medication for years before finally telling her to stop.

It took many more years for Ross to shake her dependency. But as she was a White woman, doctors were willing to help her without criminal consequence. Walking around the city with Floyd, she knew the world treated him differently because he was a Black man. She'd notice how others stared at him. Ross picked up on how uncomfortable the attention made him, even though he tried to ignore it.

"It is what it is," Floyd said.

Ross always insisted to Floyd that she liked him despite his body, not because of it. It was her way of trying to avoid objectifying him.

In the beginning, they were hanging out so much that Ross's mother, with whom she was living during that period, grew concerned she was neglecting her responsibilities as a single mom. At the same time, momentum was building in Floyd's life. About a month into dating Ross, Floyd was set to move with Big E to their boss's property.

The two-floor townhouse with red shingles was a far cry from the crowded corridors of Ms. Bea's House. It stood at the corner of a street with wide single-family homes, near a day spa and a bistro selling $35 sea bass. Overlooking the sparkling waters of Bde Maka Ska lake, the home provided a sense of tranquility and peace Floyd had never before known.

Even the police seemed to be different there. They smiled and waved, seemingly undisturbed by the sight of two large Black men. It was nice and a little weird. The two friends set up a television in the living room and a weight room in their shared basement. And even though the townhome had three bedrooms, Floyd and Big E put their mattresses in the dining room so they could sleep in the same place. After living in Miss Cissy's house, then going to prison, then to rehab, Floyd did not feel comfortable sleeping in a room alone. Plus, this way they could look out for each other.

Floyd had completed back-to-back shifts at his security jobs on October 1 when he came home at around four a.m. to an unusual sight: the front door was slightly open. "Big E," he called, but no one responded. Floyd headed toward the basement steps. "Big E?" he called again. Still nothing. When he walked downstairs, he found Big E slumped on a couch, naked and unconscious.

"Big E!" Floyd yelled. Floyd touched Cornley's skin, which had gone cold. He held his arm and felt no pulse. Floyd shook him, but Big E did not move. Floyd's mind drifted to his observations that Cornley had seemed a little bit more fidgety in recent days. Had he been using again?

He grabbed a black T-shirt and covered his friend's chest, then covered his lower half with an olive-colored blanket. Through tears, Floyd called 911.

A medical examiner confirmed what Floyd had presumed: Big E was gone. Cocaine overdose.

As the news spread about Big E's death, the men at Turning Point tried getting in touch with Floyd, but he did not answer their phone calls or text messages. Ross wondered if her new man had ghosted her. Big Floyd had disappeared.

"Bro reach out to me," Jeffrey texted. The next day, he tried again: "Talk to me, bro."

Several days after the incident, Jeffrey was at a gas station when he noticed a green Bonneville pull in. Jeffrey thanked God for the chance encounter.

"Big Floyd!" Jeffrey called out to him. "You all right?"

Floyd said he was doing fine but did not elaborate. He kept changing the subject back to Jeffrey, avoiding the recent tragedy in his life. Floyd gave Jeffrey words of encouragement for trying to become a counselor, telling him that he had the skills and the drive to be successful. Jeffrey appreciated the support, but what he really wanted was to make sure that his friend was still staying on his new path. They stared at each other awkwardly. And then, Floyd lowered his head to show Jeffrey his raggedy hairline.

"I need a cut," he said.

Floyd filled up his tank, and the men traveled back to the townhome in St. Louis Park. It was Jeffrey's first time visiting his place. He marveled at how Floyd was able to secure a spot in such a nice neighborhood. Jeffrey toured the common space and the kitchen and then made his way to the basement. He could hear Floyd's footsteps behind him.

"Damn, bro, this is nice, you know what I'm saying?" Jeffrey said as he walked past the weight equipment. Floyd didn't respond. Jeffrey turned around to see him standing at the base of the steps, staring off distantly.

"This is where it happened," Floyd told him. He began to describe what he had seen the early morning when Cornley died. Jeffrey thought about the skills he learned in his classes on counseling. He lifted his head and tried to make eye contact to demonstrate active listening. He prepared to ask follow-up questions and mirror back Floyd's responses.

"It must have been hard, bro," Jeffrey said. "How's your mental health?"

"To be honest, man, I feel fucked up," Floyd replied. "I had to see my partner slumped over. I had to figure out what to do. That took me to a dark place. I'm in a dark place."

Floyd had a request for Jeffrey.

"We all have to look out for each other," Floyd said. "We have to stick together if we are going to make it."

They walked up two flights of stairs to get to Floyd's

bedroom, so Jeffrey could cut his hair. Floyd's mattress had been moved back up there. The room was messy, with shoes and clothes piled on the floor. There wasn't anywhere for Floyd to sit, so he asked Jeffrey to bring up a chair from the dining room.

As Jeffrey made his way through the townhome, he reflected on just how easy it seemed for his friend to articulate his feelings. Of course, Floyd would joke around to keep things light, but he could be so expressive and vulnerable when he was serious. It was this attitude and Floyd's love for community that convinced Jeffrey that Floyd would not end up like Big E.

Jeffrey picked up the chair and walked back to Floyd's room.

Floyd was startled when Jeffrey entered. He was standing over a mirror placed on his mattress, next to a small jar of pills. In his anguish, Floyd had returned to a familiar comfort.

"Li'l B," he said, his eyes welling with tears, "I'm sorry."

CHAPTER 9

The Real Comes In

Had 2 see it to believe it,

Seen it, still didn't believe it,

*Close friend in addiction, he surrounded by dem
leaches and got da nerve to smile.*

—GEORGE FLOYD, undated writings

BIG E WASN'T SUPPOSED to die like this—not now, and not here in Minneapolis. Floyd mourned his friend in self-imposed isolation, trying to process what Big E meant to him and struggling with the implications of his death. They were two men with the same unfulfilled dreams, the same body type, the same challenges, and the same solution: a new life in a new state. But if Minnesota, the state of opportunity, was not enough to save Big E, how could it be enough to save Floyd? He realized that his time in Minneapolis would present a new test of his fortitude, that the risks that threatened his existence would never fully go away.

A little more than a week after Big E's death, Floyd reached out to the woman he had swept off her feet, Courteney Ross. He wanted to pick things up where they had left off.

He apologized for not keeping in touch and revealed what had happened with Big E.

"I needed time to clear my head," Floyd said.

Ross told Floyd that he did not need to retreat from her; she would be there to help him. It was the kind of love that she had seen growing up, as her mother tried to help mend her father, a veteran who suffered from post-traumatic stress and alcoholism after he returned from Korea. She came over more often to the house in St. Louis Park, where Floyd would eventually get two new roommates, a friend from Conga named Alvin Manago and his girlfriend, Theresa Scott. Manago was in many ways the opposite of Big E; he was thin and lanky, quiet and reflective. Scott, all five-foot-three of her, became the drill sergeant of the house, regularly commanding Floyd to dine with them. They hung African art on the walls and vowed to keep the home drug-free.

To add some warmth to Floyd's room, Ross gave him two of her sister's old orange chairs and brought him a bed frame, which quickly collapsed under his weight. She also carried in a twin bed for her son James and placed it by Floyd's closet, so they could all sleep in the same room together, like a family, whenever they came over. Gavin usually stayed home.

They added a tan couch to the living room, where sometimes Manago and Ross would watch sports with Floyd when they weren't all working. Floyd dazzled them with his ability to describe a football play or analyze a strategy on the basketball court seconds before the commentators stated the same thought. They'd marvel at his ability to remember percentages and statistics, making calculations in real time.

Floyd often visited Ross at the Coffee Shop Northeast, where she worked full-time after quitting her job at the school. Some days, as he waited for Ross to finish her shift, he'd sit down with a group of elderly White people, charming them with his repartee. Ross's heart melted as she watched his ease with others and observed his magnetism.

"My six-foot-six baby," Ross called him.

But there was another side of Floyd that she had begun to see. Although he had been an athlete, Floyd seemed uncomfortable in his massive body. He resisted taking elevators or sitting in the back seats of cars because of intense claustrophobia. He'd break his glasses by holding them too tightly and had a bad habit of dropping his cell phone. Like so many in his life, she was both fascinated and charmed by his knack for getting involved in bizarre situations.

"It couldn't just be a normal day with Floyd," she recalled. "It has to be somewhat fantastical."

Aware of his reputation for sometimes being hapless and clumsy, he'd knowingly express a mixture of humor and shame at such situations. "Old Floyd's done it again," he'd say.

In time, between the residual trauma from his stints in prison and his ongoing grief over Big E, it became clear to Ross what was really driving Floyd to be successful. She also knew it would not be easy. Growing up, she had been bused from her predominantly White neighborhood in northeast Minneapolis to the predominantly Black schools across town, and she saw firsthand just how dismissive White people could be toward the concerns of Black Minnesotans. And she understood that her city, with all its progressive bravado and "Minnesota nice" courtesies, possessed a prejudice that could sometimes seem hidden under its snowy shroud.

"These people come to Minneapolis with big dreams;

they think it's a place where every culture will get along," Ross recalled. "But then the real comes in."

The promise of progress in Minnesota can be a cruel mirage. Its history of integration started early: the state university system enrolled Negroes in the 1800s, and the governor was willing to start an all-Black state battalion at the request of African Americans who wanted to serve their country during World War I. But there were also lynchings outside Duluth in the early 1900s, and restrictive racial covenants prohibited homeownership in parts of Minneapolis and St. Paul. For close to forty years, the state's tax code was a model of liberal aspiration because it evenly distributed school funding between urban and rural areas, a legislative achievement known as the "Minnesota miracle." Even so, this longtime egalitarianist state still had some of the most glaring disparities between Blacks and Whites in the country, a phenomenon that would come to be known as the "Minnesota paradox."

For example, in the realm of public health, Minnesota is known for being one of the healthiest states—the home of the Mayo Clinic and the headquarters of top medical companies like UnitedHealth Group. Yet researchers and doctors found themselves flummoxed that Black mothers are twice as likely to die giving birth as their White counterparts, and wide gaps also exist in access to care for diabetes, heart disease, and depression.

Minneapolis is a prosperous city, but one in every four Black households lives in poverty—five times the poverty rate for White households. Census Bureau data shows that the median Black family income in Minneapolis was $36,000 in 2018. That's better off than the median income for Black families in many metropolitan areas across the country, but it's still significantly less than the $83,000 median income of White families. Of the nation's hundred largest metropolitan areas, only Milwaukee in neighboring Wisconsin had a larger gap between Black and White earnings.

Minnesota is likewise known for its excellent education system, but a 2019 report from the Federal Reserve Bank of Minneapolis found that only four states have a bigger chasm between Black and White students when it comes to meeting benchmarks for college readiness in reading, with only Wisconsin again having a larger disparity in math. Overall, Minnesota boasts the highest percentage of students who meet the reading benchmark and the third highest for math—driven by the high marks of White students—which can obfuscate these racial disparities.

Samuel Myers, a professor at the University of Minnesota who coined the term "Minnesota paradox," notes that the state's history with race has always been unusual. Because the state economy had not been driven by industrial work as it was in Pittsburgh, Detroit, or Chicago, African Americans who came to the Twin Cities in the late nineteenth century and early twentieth century were more likely to be skilled laborers or professionals seeking opportunities in a state that would allow them to practice as doctors, pharmacists, porters, and shopkeepers. Even as they established their own businesses, churches, and thriving neighborhoods, their small numbers limited their political influence. As happened across the country, lawmakers were unrepentant in the mid-twentieth century when they ripped through thriving Black neighborhoods to build highways, which notably decimated the Rondo neighborhood, a well-to-do Black enclave in St. Paul.

In his research, Myers learned that Interstate 94 could have been built more efficiently through White neighborhoods, but lawmakers were sensitive to those residents' concerns about traffic and disruption. Legislators did not make grand proclamations about the importance of segregation or cast a negative light on Black residents when making the decision. Instead, they said they were operating under a philosophy they thought was fair: majority wins.

The legislature seemed less concerned about what would be lost. More than six hundred Black families surrendered their homes and three hundred businesses vanished. A similar dynamic played out in Black communities across the country: near Lambert International Airport in St. Louis, along the Cypress Freeway in Oakland, along interstates in Miami and Wilmington, in Nashville, Detroit, Buffalo, New Orleans, and elsewhere. In each of these communities, the infrastructure projects only reiterated Black residents' lack of political power and the disregard American decisionmakers had for their lives. Their sense of civic pride dwindled as slabs of concrete sliced through their old neighborhoods, bringing traffic and air pollution that raised rates of asthma and other lung problems for those whose homes were spared.

"You can have racially disparate effects without having racists," Myers said. "But because [White lawmakers] believed that they were not racists and they were not bigots, no one was doing the analysis on race."

Over time, the demographics within the Black community changed. Economic decline in industrial cities and the aftermath of the 1967 riots sparked influxes of poor and working-class Black residents from other cities who were eager to seize on the promise of Minnesota's liberalism. And in the 1990s, thousands of Somali refugees were resettled there, coming with their distinct language, culture, and traditions. Of the 395,000 Black people residing in the state, close to 70,000 were estimated in 2019 to be Somali—with the vast majority living in the Twin Cities. These population shifts complicated the portrait of the Black community, as the new residents also brought different professions and levels of education. Often, African Americans and Somalians found themselves lumped together because of the color of their skin, as lawmakers and businesses lagged in recognizing and addressing the unique needs of these groups.

When former local NAACP president Nekima Levy Armstrong was first wooed to the state as a law professor at the University of St. Thomas in 2003, she, too, was pitched about the wonders of Minneapolis. Faculty told her about the Minnesota miracle and the affordability of housing; that the conditions of poverty that afflicted so many Black communities around the country were not so bad there.

For her first few months in the city, she had believed it. Because of the disproportionate number of Fortune 500 companies in Minneapolis, it was relatively easy to run into educated, prosperous Black people who had moved there like she had. But as she spent more time away from elite circles and more fully established herself in the larger community, the racial inequities became apparent.

The most obvious issue was policing. When police killed twenty-two-year-old Terrance Franklin in his home in May 2013, Levy Armstrong noticed the skepticism within Black neighborhoods regarding the official police narrative around his death. Police said that Franklin had entered someone's house after a chase and then grabbed an officer's gun when he was confronted. There were no body cameras back then to verify their story—but the family pointed to a video shot by a neighbor across the street that captures Franklin saying, "Let me go!" to the officers, as well as someone shouting racial epithets at him. County Attorney Mike Freeman gave the case to a grand jury, which cleared the officers of wrongdoing.

Then, after the Black Lives Matter movement blossomed following the shooting of eighteen-year-old Michael Brown in Ferguson, Missouri, there was another incident that captured local attention. In November 2015, Minneapolis police shot and killed Jamar Clark outside of a friend's birthday party. Police said that Clark, twenty-four, had fought with officers, resisted arrest, and grabbed one of their guns. But several witnesses maintained that Clark was not resisting. Some said he was handcuffed or had his hands tied behind his back. Again, Levy Armstrong was disturbed by a troubling divergence of accounts between the police and the community.

The wave of activism emerging across the country inspired Levy Armstrong to organize protests outside the Fourth Precinct, where the officers involved in Clark's death were based. The activists demonstrated there for eighteen days, demanding more transparency in the court process rather than leaving decisions to anonymous grand juries in which the evidence never becomes public. Levy Armstrong encountered the state's progressive mirage: In March 2016, Freeman agreed to no longer rely on grand juries. But he would use this shift in policy to justify not charging the officers who shot Jamar Clark.

"His DNA is all over that gun and he had no business having his hand on that gun, which is why they shot him [and] which is why I didn't prosecute them," Freeman said in an interview with a local news station.

Then, in July 2016, the world would learn the name of Philando Castile, a thirty-two-year-old Black man and beloved elementary school cafeteria worker, after an officer shot and killed him during a traffic stop in the St. Paul suburbs. Upon being pulled over, Castile told Officer Jeronimo Yanez that he had a licensed firearm in the car. Even though Castile told Yanez he would not pull out the weapon, the officer became nervous and shot him. Castile's distraught girlfriend, Diamond Reynolds, jumped to Facebook Live to record the aftermath, crying as blood seeped through Castile's shirt. Her four-year-old daughter was in the back seat.

Castile's mother, Valerie, was surprised when the Ramsey County attorney charged the officer with second-degree manslaughter and dangerous discharge of a firearm—there was little precedent for families of victims receiving any measure of justice. Nonetheless, a jury acquitted Yanez in June 2017, swayed by his insistence that he feared Philando Castile was going to shoot him. Valerie Castile was outraged and began meeting with public officials, including Tim Walz, a Democratic congressman who would soon run for governor.

"You have to do something to control the police," she told him. "If you don't, one day, they are going to tear this motherfucker down."

In late 2017, as a tribute to her cafeteria-worker son, Castile volunteered at an event to feed the homeless. There, she met a large security guard who had moved to Minneapolis from Houston. When he learned who Castile was, he wrapped his arms around her and pulled her in close.

"I want to give you my condolences," George Floyd told her. "It wasn't right."

Floyd wasn't a person who followed the ins and outs of

the daily news cycle. When he'd talk about President Obama, he referred to him as a history-making man who had great taste in women, referring to the first lady. He'd get exasperated with discussions about President Donald J. Trump. ("I'm not saying that man doesn't have angels watching over him," he would say to Adarryl Hunter, "but if he does, they must be high.") He did not pay much attention to the Black Lives Matter movement; the murders back in Third Ward were often enough to think about.

But there was something about the Castile case that affected him. Maybe it was the girl in the back seat, who was a little older than Gianna. Maybe it was the feeling that Castile had done everything right but still lost his life. Maybe it was just that he lived so close to where the incident happened. Whatever it was, Castile's death spooked Floyd. One day, he was hanging with a friend when Castile's death came up. Floyd looked at the friend and said, "I know these cops just waiting to kill a big Black nigga like me."

After Big E's death, Floyd tried to accelerate his hustle, digging into a new plan to become a truck driver. But the first time he took the test to get a learner's permit for his commercial driver's license, he failed. He recruited Adarryl Hunter, the most academically inclined friend in his orbit, for his help.

Hunter told him that the key to test-taking was not that different from Floyd's philosophy on endearing himself to people: it required brains and memorization, but also a bit of empathy.

"You have to think about what the people making the test would want you to know," Hunter told him. "Don't think about the answer you want to give them."

Floyd promised to take the advice. And in November 2017, he sent a message on Instagram to his sister Zsa Zsa, showing off his new learner's permit.

Floyd's plate was full: He loved his job working at the Salvation Army with so many of his friends. He became a staple at Conga, where regulars christened the "Big Floyd" dance move in his honor, in which they would stiffen their hips and roll their shoulders. And then, in the morning, after working double shifts, he ventured to the YWCA in St. Paul to enroll in a course for his commercial driver's license. He passed a drug test and started learning the ins and outs of maneuvering the large vehicle.

This positive stretch started to slow sometime in 2018. Floyd's schedule proved to be too demanding, and he dropped out of the course. He also stopped working at the Salvation Army—he told friends he was fired after messing around with a woman who lived at the shelter. His wandering eye and indiscretions would become a perpetual issue in his relationship with Ross, who tried to forgive him each time he stepped out on her.

Ross rationalized Floyd's behavior as an attention-seeking defense mechanism from a broken man. Still, it angered her. Sometimes, she asked herself why she was so willing to forgive him, why she didn't just walk away. The more intimate she got with Floyd, the more she realized how many people had already walked out on him, and how few chances he had been given by society. Ross told herself that what he needed most was unconditional love.

"When you're still damaged, and you're still hurting, and you still kind of cling on to that idea that you can get someone—even if it's just for that moment—to get that attention, to get that little filler-upper," Ross said.

Together, they applied for jobs, but most rejected him on account of his criminal record. The only work he was able to secure relied on his strength: Manual labor. Bodyguard. Security.

"The jobs that would want a big Black man," Ross said.

He jotted down his feelings on scraps of paper and old records, sometimes reciting them to Ross. These lyrics revealed a level of introspection and conscientiousness, as he wrote about the people who did not see the deeper truth of his experience—and the barriers caused by their ignorance:

> *For them people can't name 1 person I robbed*
> *Make sure they get the memo all I do is love . . .*
> *You can say what you want*
> *Make sure you say what you know*
> *It's levels to this life + erbody don't go*

But the jobs weren't coming, and he worried that his past, no matter how hard he tried, would prove to be an insurmountable obstacle. Hunter ventured to Floyd's home to try to get him to refocus. He insisted they write out a list of long- and short-term goals, so Floyd could feel like he was moving forward. The list included daily tasks like reading the Bible, staying clean, working out. Then, more practical items: get new tires for the car, fill out job applications. And, lastly, longer-term goals like getting a commercial driver's license and supporting his family. Hunter suggested he tape the paper on a wall, as a reminder both of what he had accomplished and of his next steps. Each goal was more complicated than he expected. And so was maintaining a backbone of support.

Robert Fonteno recalled one day when Floyd was again insisting that the friends from Houston needed to find more ways to get together. Everyone agreed, in theory. But Fonteno tried to be real with him: all of them had their own obligations, their own dramas, their own time-consuming set of goals that could make it difficult. There was little time to dawdle.

"You have to remember that everyone has a schedule," Fonteno told him.

In early 2018, Floyd started to hang out more often with Maurice Hall, a friend from Houston who had recently been released from prison after serving time on burglary charges. Hall had come to Minneapolis with the help of Pastor Riles for the same reasons as most of Floyd's friends, but they largely avoided him. He had a reputation for pressing pills and a penchant for getting in trouble.

After his experience working with the homeless at the Salvation Army, Floyd wanted to give Hall a chance when other friends looked away. When Hall did not have a place to stay, Floyd would invite him to his home to use the shower. He let him sleep in his garage and told him how much he loved him.

They would talk about mutual friends while listening to music. What Hall loved most about Floyd was that he kept his ear to the ground, always trying to predict the next big thing—the next great basketball player, or the latest sound in hip-hop that would soon take the country by storm—something that was happening a little under the radar.

"We just lost track of time every time we'd be together," Hall recalled. "Like when we was together in Minnesota, it felt like we was in the streets of Houston."

And then, perhaps, it began to feel a little too much like Houston. Few around Third Ward knew it at the time, but they were coming of age in the epicenter of an emerging drug crisis that researchers are still trying to grasp. As prescription pills flooded suburban communities, the usage of codeine was skyrocketing in cities, remaining largely unseen and unregulated. In Houston, where the phenomenon started, Black residents sipped drank, lean, sizzurp, or syrup; its ability to depress the nervous system, which allowed for a sleepy, trancelike high, was a welcome distraction from the stresses of living in a poor Black neighborhood. What started as a trend among the associates of DJ Screw, and was then popularized by artists from Lil Wayne to Justin Bieber, ended up becoming a drug of national concern.

One night, Hall brought out a cup of green drank that hearkened back to their days using down South. Floyd, who had been trying to keep clean, snuck in a taste. And then another. Before they knew it, getting high became a part of their hang-out plans. But living in the Midwest, where syrup was hard to come by, Hall said the two found themselves following a common path to chasing a similar high, one that led to synthetic opioids like fentanyl, which was disproportionately taking root in Minnesota's Black community.

"We used to once drink syrup," Hall said. "So once you used to drink syrup and you're not getting syrup, you take a pill ... and now—bam—you're struggling with your addiction again. You do as the Romans do, so they do pills up here. They do a bunch of opiates and fentanyl and heroin."

Public health officials were starting to notice the same trend in the state, as well as its dangerous repercussions. In 2002, the rate of fatal overdose from synthetic opioids such as fentanyl for African Americans was 0.043 per 100,000, compared with 0.026 per 100,000 for Whites. Some fifteen years later, the rate for African Americans was 10.43 per 100,000 compared with 3.23 per 100,000 for Whites.

This disparity was yet another example of the Minnesota mirage: though the state ranked eighth lowest in overall drug mortality rates, its own health department said those numbers "mask the problem"—Minnesota had the second-highest gap in drug deaths between Blacks and Whites of anywhere in the country. In 2019, only nine other states, as well as the District of Columbia, had rates in which Black residents were more likely to die from opioids than White ones. By 2020, the federal government issued a report noting the alarming rise of opioid misuse and death in Black communities.

Floyd was slipping by the time the Super Bowl arrived in Minneapolis in 2018. A group of friends had come up from Houston to party with Floyd during the big game, to mark his one-year anniversary in this new city. Floyd had to juggle these distinct worlds—a group of men who had come here to get sober, and people from Hall's crew, who were involved in the drug game. According to Hall, Floyd didn't want to be left out of the hustle, so he went along with it.

Within weeks, Hall's friends grew concerned that Floyd might have been using the pills they intended for him to sell. And so, Hall said, they cut Floyd out.

"They cut him off out of love," Hall reflected. "They knew he was supposed to be here to make himself better. It just wasn't working for him. He was supposed to be growing."

His Minneapolis friends started to notice a shift in Floyd's behavior too. At their home, Manago and Scott heard him complaining that he needed to take medication to deal with back problems. Some days, he didn't want to leave his room. Scott wouldn't take kindly to his isolation. She'd come with her Bible and suggest they read a verse, or she'd tell him he needed to come enjoy some of her cooking.

Over time, Floyd became bolder about his substance use. Ross, who had her own issues with drug dependency, did not stop him. She had recently had neck surgery, and pounding out espresso shots all day at work didn't help matters. One morning, she noticed a five-milligram pill of Percocet on one of Floyd's tables. When Floyd jumped in the shower, she took it.

"That's when it started for me," Ross said. They soon began taking pills together.

"I'm really hurting, can I get those?" evolved into his asking, "Baby, are you feeling okay?" And when Ross would say that she was in pain, Floyd would vow to find some way to stop the hurt.

"It turned to, 'Who's got some? Where are we going today? We got to find some today,'" Ross recalled. "Every day. It became a pattern: I would get off work, go see him, we'd get some dope, get fucked up ... and start the next day again."

Meanwhile, Floyd's family continued to encourage Perry to come home. Miss Cissy did not have much longer to live, and she wanted to see her eldest son. Floyd kept promising he'd get around to making the trip, but the truth was that he had not shared the full extent of his struggles with his family. His absence had surprised family members; he had such a special connection with Miss Cissy. Some figured he may have been in denial about the state of his mother's health, convinced that the woman who had survived several strokes would eventually pull through. Others surmised that he wanted to keep the image of a lively and energetic woman with that same thousand-watt smile as his lasting memory.

Miss Cissy had spent spring of 2018 at Ben Taub Hospital and in a local hospice, slowly fading away. Toward the end, her children made calls across the country to let relatives know it was time to say their goodbyes.

On May 30, 2018, she spoke to Perry for the last time. "I love you," he told her.

Later that day, surrounded by family at Philonise's home, Miss Cissy looked at the people gathered around her bedside and said, "I'm ready to go now." Minutes later, she was gone.

The funeral was held on June 9, 2018, at the Mabrie Memorial Mortuary in Houston's Museum District. Following the color scheme of the service, Floyd showed up in a bright yellow dress shirt, black pants, and a black bowtie. As friends and family eulogized the resident mother of Cuney Homes, Floyd sat next to Tiffany Cofield, saying little. Zsa Zsa and his other siblings had never seen him so withdrawn. He walked up to the casket and kissed his mother's cheek.

His cousin Shareeduh Tate walked over and gave him a hug, but he could not stop staring at the casket. When he finally returned to his seat, his aunt Angela Harrelson sidled up to him and tried to console him.

"Everything's going to be okay," she said. "You know, I'm here. We have each other."

But Floyd could not take his eyes off the body. He refused to leave the hall after others had gone to the repast. Zsa Zsa went to check on him. Hours after the service was over, he kept muttering to himself, "Mama, Mama."

Later that night, Cofield and Travis Cains ran into him not far from the Blue Store. Surrounded by concerned former neighbors, Floyd could barely walk or talk. Cofield figured someone had given him some bad pills. Cains offered one of his patented pep talks.

"Get your shit together," Cains said. "You need to go back to work on your treatment. You were doing well. We ain't going to let you just fall off like that."

Floyd was so disoriented that Cains wasn't sure if his message was sinking in.

Cofield helped Floyd into her car and took him to her house, where she put him in a wheelchair before settling him onto her couch. He soon fell asleep.

The next morning, he woke up acting more like himself, casually going to the kitchen to fix a bowl of oatmeal with peanut butter. Floyd spent the next few days recuperating on Cofield's couch, listening to old DJ Screw mixtapes that he had appeared on. He would soon share another dream.

> *The streets a lifestyle*
> *Either you in or u not*
> *Jail time might come with it*
> *Either u in or you not*
> *Could leave yo ass 4 dead*
> *Either u live or u not*
>   —*George Floyd*, undated song lyrics

Back in Minneapolis, Floyd told Adarryl Hunter of his new scheme to make it big. After his mother's passing, he felt particular urgency to send money back to Houston, to support his nephew Brandon.

"I got some good lyrics," Floyd told Hunter one day. "Maybe now is my time."

Hunter was skeptical that the music world was ready to be introduced to a new fortysomething rapper. He encouraged Floyd to stop looking for quick fixes and instead find a steady job in which he could develop some lasting skills. He tried to use a sports metaphor to get the idea to sink in.

"Every time you come up to the plate, you try to hit a home run," Hunter said. "But sometimes, you just need to make sure you can get to first base, you know what I'm saying?"

Given Floyd's people skills, Hunter suggested he find a service job, perhaps working at FedEx or UPS. He tried to encourage Floyd to believe that something good would happen if he just stuck to the plan—any plan—to make an honest living. Hunter was a Christian, and he recalled a church sermon about Jesus healing a man whose hand had withered. Before the Lord performed the miracle, he asked the man to take some initiative and stretch out his hand.

"It's in the stretch," Hunter told him. "That's where the power is."

After Miss Cissy's death, Floyd's roommates became even more concerned about him. Manago and Scott didn't see him on the couch catching up on sports anymore. Sometimes, they could hear him praying in his own room. And other times, they could hear him crying.

When he was with Ross, he would just want to be held, resting his head along her chest, his legs dangling off the mattress. He became needier, less assured. Their drug dependency deepened from Percocet to oxycodone, Valium, codeine—whatever would make them feel lighter.

Even when they recognized that they had gone too far, it now became physically painful to stop. If they did not use, Ross recalled, they would experience gut-wrenching stomach pain. They would tell themselves to take it day by day, to try to make it to two weeks without a relapse.

"It was the dumbest thing," Ross said. "So many times we would do that, and then we would reward ourselves by getting high."

Floyd tried to stay on track by leaning into his body, doing pull-ups by the hundreds to keep his mind off drugs. For his friends, Floyd's body became the tell: If he was pumped up, he had been sober. If he looked more gaunt, he had been using. Floyd at some point started taking Suboxone to quell his opioid cravings, but he did not take the medication consistently.

Meanwhile, his body continued to allow him to find security gigs around the city. In October 2018, a local DJ asked him if he was interested in working the security detail for a rapper named Big Freedia, who had been gaining mainstream popularity after being sampled on Beyoncé's "Formation" and Drake's "Nice for What." Big Freedia was one of the biggest purveyors of New Orleans bounce sound. While the Houston brand of hip-hop that Floyd loved was heavy and slow, suited for chilling, bounce was energetic, horn-heavy, and ideal for twerking.

Ross wondered how the two would get along. Floyd still had some reservations about gay culture, and Big Freedia was a queer, gender-defying performer who was designated male at birth but often appeared onstage in wigs and dresses.

It turned out that Floyd and Big Freedia became fast friends. They met up at First Avenue, the club where she was performing, and Big Freedia was struck by his kindness as much as by his size. After the show, Big Floyd joined Big Freedia's entourage as they hung outside a nearby club called the Gay 90's. They smoked weed and entertained themselves watching drunken revelers on a Thursday evening.

That night, Floyd asked Big Freedia something that had been on his mind.

"What should I call you?" he asked. "Man? Woman? Are you a him or a her?"

"Well, George, it doesn't matter, because I answer to both," Big Freedia said. "Growing up in my era of the gay world, it was either you are gay or you're straight, or it was either trans or butch queen. And so we didn't have a lot of options like we do now."

Big Freedia gave Floyd her cell phone number, and they promised to keep in touch. Floyd had mentioned he used to be a performer but demurred when she invited him to spit off a track. He had a different aspiration with Big Freedia's crew: he wanted to be her go-to security detail.

"When you're ready," Floyd told her, "I'd love to go on the road with you."

Floyd returned home that night with a new feeling of possibility. After the experience, Ross noticed something different about Floyd: he would no longer turn away if he saw a gay couple on television and became conscious of his earlier biases. In Minneapolis, he learned a lesson about tolerance.

Big Freedia did not think her national profile was growing quickly enough to warrant a dedicated security staff, so she never ended up taking Floyd on the road. Meanwhile, Floyd kept trying to find a path forward, picking up more security gigs and hoping that full-time work would materialize.

As the months passed, Ross and Floyd drew closer. She delighted in making meals for him, even though he would occasionally complain that they lacked the rich flavor of his mother's Southern cooking. They'd run around the city listening to hip-hop, then come home and watch movies. Floyd loved the film *Rudy*, a story about a White kid from a rough neighborhood who overcomes a learning disability, poverty, and his diminutive physical stature to become a football player at Notre Dame.

"Why do you like this movie?" Ross asked him one day.

"It's about an underdog who wins," Floyd told her.

She began to think of Floyd as a part of the family, and they'd talk about what it would be like for Gianna to gain two brothers. Floyd would hang out at the park with James and brag to friends about Gavin, who ranked fifth in the state in chess. In the last months of 2018, Gavin, whose father is Black, was hard at work rehearsing the role of Seaweed Stubbs, a teenager who helps integrate a television dance show, in a high school production of *Hairspray*. Despite promising to attend, Floyd ended up missing the show. Ross was furious.

When she saw Floyd the next morning, Ross yelled at him for disappointing her son in that way. She told him he needed to take responsibility for how his actions could hurt people. Ross wasn't asking for marriage; she didn't really believe in that. But she at least wanted Floyd to be there.

"I should have known you wouldn't show up," Ross yelled. "You can't even show up for your own daughter."

Afterward, they did not talk for days.

"I went right to his heart," Ross recalled. "It was mean."

*

Like those of anyone else, Floyd's actions were informed by his circumstances. His environment had been such a vital part of his identity when he was growing up, but as he got older, he learned that his status as a poor Black man meant he could not pick up an entirely new lifestyle by osmosis. Right before him in suburban St. Louis Park, Floyd encountered so many White neighbors who were his age and thriving—nice homes, pets, kids who were not terrified of the police. He could never fully enter this new world. And he could never fully leave the old one behind.

And in that world, men around Floyd's age were beginning to die. Friends were dying by suicide, succumbing to cancer, having heart attacks. They were overdosing and dying in their sleep. They were being shot and killed. Back in Houston, the names of those lost friends and acquaintances were scribbled in marker and spray paint on the wall outside the Blue Store; their photos were screened on clothing so often that Floyd would tell his friends he did not want to join the T-shirt Society.

This wave of death was not unusual—in the United States, Black men are twice as likely as White men to die of a cocaine overdose, at least twice as likely to be killed by police, and, in Floyd's age group, ten times as likely to die of a homicide. Hearing about death was so common that Hunter and Floyd developed a macabre way of absorbing the pain.

"AD, just say you're glad that it wasn't me," Floyd would tell him.

Hunter would laugh and concede, "Yes, I'm glad it wasn't you."

Floyd's encounters with police would fuel even more anxiety. In May 2019, Floyd burst into tears after being pulled over in a traffic stop. As officers approached the vehicle, one observed him swallowing a white substance.

The officers drew a service weapon and a Taser when attempting to pull Floyd out of the vehicle.

"Don't shoot me, man, please!" he begged.

The situation de-escalated quickly. After getting him in handcuffs, the officers called for paramedics. His blood pressure was rising to dangerous levels—216 over 160. He told them he had taken seven Percocet pills that day. Police and emergency workers asked Floyd to allow them to bring him to the hospital. He began to shake, fearing that this was some scheme to take him back to prison.

"We do this all the time, we know we can take care of you," one officer said. "This might be the time that you get to feeling better."

After hesitating, Floyd relented. During the encounter, an officer asked Floyd if he dealt drugs.

"No," Floyd replied. "Well, the reason why I don't get involved with that [is] because Minneapolis has been good to me."

Floyd did not complain about Minnesota to his friends or family—even in the throes of his struggles, it felt to him like a place that offered the best chance of success. Yet the path to recovery remained elusive, especially since so little attention had been paid to the drug issue that was impeding him. In a 2021 survey of literature about African Americans and opioid use, NYU professor Ayana Jordan found that there were few studies broad enough to measure the nature of treatment and the root causes of addiction in Black people specifically. But some of the studies in the survey did show promise in identifying traits that likely drew Black men to opioids, several of which applied to Floyd. They included finding higher rates of opioid use among Black men who had been incarcerated, and especially those who were distant from their parents.

Still, the nature of how chemical dependency operates in the brain does not change across race—the physiology of a craving works the same way under the skin. What does change, scholars like Jordan note, is how a person is treated and perceived when they have an addiction.

These differences became clear to Ross when Floyd described his interaction with police that spring. Even though they mostly lived together and took the same drugs, she never felt like a suspect. She told him stories about being pulled over by police while high, with Percocet pills visible in the car, and getting away without so much as a speeding ticket. She vowed that she would take the hit if they were ever caught using together.

"I've done drugs. I've sold drugs," Ross recalled. "I can get a job—people try to make me happy. The reason he has a record is that he's a Black man and the reason I don't is because I'm a White woman, and that's as real as it gets."

It wasn't long before Ross had a chance to test her theory. Though he no longer worked there, in August 2019, Floyd and Ross were hanging out in the Salvation Army parking lot to catch up with Maurice Hall and his girlfriend. As soon as she pulled out some drank from a cooler, four Chevrolet Suburbans pulled up. The officers immediately went for Floyd, the biggest member of the group. Police demanded Floyd put his hands against the wall and searched him for contraband.

In Floyd's fragile state, he expected the worst.

"He got so scared," Ross said. "I knew he wouldn't be able to breathe. He was screaming and crying and sweating."

After police ran his name through the system, Floyd was told he was free to go. Ross was flabbergasted.

"They did that to you for no reason," she said to Floyd on the way home. "This system is so shitty."

"Be thankful," Floyd said, squinting. "I'm so glad they didn't take me to jail."

That summer, Floyd became more elusive, disappearing for weeks at a time. A friend told Ross that Floyd had been hanging out with some other woman who lived near downtown.

"No one is going to take a man away from Courteney Ross," she said, so she would hang out downtown, hoping to run into them. One day, she saw his car outside an apartment building and slashed his tires. Eventually, after about a month, Floyd resurfaced and apologized to Ross for stepping out on her.

As 2020 rolled around, he finally accomplished his long-standing goal of getting a job driving trucks. While he still did not have a CDL, he could drive a truck shorter than twenty-six feet, carrying loads below twenty-six thousand pounds. He began making deliveries across the Midwest, from North Dakota to Montana. Occasionally, he'd call his brother Philonise, who also spent time on the road.

The brothers talked about how the open highways gave them a sense of freedom that they could not get in their daily lives. Floyd soon felt more secure. Ross did too. She moved out of her mother's house and into a two-bedroom basement apartment nearby, giving one of the bedrooms to a pregnant seventeen-year-old who needed a place to stay; she and James slept in the primary bedroom. Gavin, now out of high school, was living on his own. Floyd was still paying rent in St. Louis Park, but he kept coming back to Ross's place each night. The couple felt good about the future, and both resolved again to give up drugs. The year 2020 was going to be their best one yet.

Then, one day in January, Floyd and Ross were lying in bed when the phone started to ring.

"Floyd," she asked. "Who is Shawanda?"

Shawanda Hill lived in an efficiency apartment on the outer edges of downtown. Hill had moved to Minneapolis from Georgia in the 1990s, following her mother, and had seen her share of hardship. She had recently given up cocaine after being brutally assaulted while under the influence, which resulted in her having surgery on both feet. She couldn't fully extend her fingers, the consequence of an abusive boyfriend.

Hill and Floyd first met in the summer of 2019, around the time Floyd and Ross had become distant, after a friend introduced them. Despite Hill brushing him off at first, Floyd was persistent, and they ended up connecting over music. Hill loved a good slow jam—Mary J. Blige, the Isley Brothers, Monica, Jodeci—and Floyd looked at her wistfully as the soft sounds filled the room.

"This is the music I used to dance to with my mama," Floyd told her.

Floyd stayed the night, then the week, then the month. Hill loved cooking for her new man. In the morning, she'd put together breakfast burritos with bacon, eggs, cheese, and onions, slathered in her own homemade gravy. For dinner, she'd prepare big pork steaks with all the fixings, just like his mama used to make.

Hill doesn't recall them ever going out together or meeting any of his friends. But staying inside with Floyd was more than enough for her. She loved watching him play with her granddaughter, who would climb his body like he was a human jungle gym. The two lovers smoked weed together, but she said they never did more than that when it came to drugs. And she loved being alone with him, believing that she had finally found herself a decent, sexy man.

But there was one peculiar hang-up about living with Floyd: he always needed to keep the bathroom door open. Hill's bathroom was small and had a door that would sometimes jam if it wasn't closed the right way. One time, Floyd accidentally locked himself inside. His breathing became heavy as he tried to break down the door from within.

"That boy almost died in there," Hill recalled. "He got real bad anxiety, claustrophobia. He was a big ol' man crying like a little baby."

Their love affair lasted for about a month in the summer of 2019, until Floyd accused Hill of cheating on him with another man in her building. Hill was offended by the accusation, and Floyd told her he could no longer live in such a cramped space with a person he could not trust.

"Your lifestyle and my lifestyle are just different," he told her. "I'm gonna go."

Their relationship was over, though the two would occasionally still talk over social media.

But by mid-January 2020, after Ross saw Hill's name pop up on Floyd's phone, he found himself back at her apartment. For her part, Hill didn't inquire much about Ross—she already knew that she was a woman capable of slashing tires—because she felt that that was Floyd's business to handle. What mattered to her was what was right in front of her. And she began to believe that fate had placed Floyd there for a special reason.

That became apparent on January 20, 2020, when Hill got a call that a man who she helped to raise—the rapper known as Mr. Blue Ghost—was found dead in an alley with a single gunshot to the head. Lemandre Ingram was forty. A man Hill called his "cousin," Jeffrey McRaven, was accused of being his killer. McRaven would eventually be convicted on second-degree murder charges.

Hill was heartbroken, angry, and confused. Not only did she have to grapple with Ingram's death, she also had to deal with relatives who wanted to seek retribution on McRaven. Floyd tried to comfort Hill, conveying his experience of what to do when a life was lost to the streets.

"Let God handle it," Floyd suggested telling them. "It ain't worth it because God would not want us to hurt the same family all over again. You can't fuck up a family twice."

"He let me cry, let me snap," Hill recalled. "He was there for me."

Their reunion was brief. Despite their chemistry, Floyd did not seek Hill's emotional support or talk about his own inner struggles. When Floyd lost his job days later after falling asleep at the wheel of his truck, he called Ross with a familiar refrain.

"Old Floyd's done it again," he said. And Ross welcomed him back into her life.

One day the following month, in February 2020, Floyd happened to run into his old instructor Woodrow Jefferson, who had taught the life-skills class at Turning Point when he first arrived in Minneapolis.

"I need to come see you," Floyd told him.

Floyd didn't have to elaborate; his desire to return was not unusual. Jefferson said many clients went through the program two or three times.

"We're here for you when you are ready," he replied. Floyd still wanted to try leaning into himself, searching for an inner strength so many believed he had. He wrote more raps and read scriptures from the book of Psalms. He drew up new goals, looking both inward and to God for help.

"Let this be the day I claim victory over this dark situation through the Holy Spirit," he wrote. "No matter the time you can always grab you some word . . . Follow that with your workout."

Having also crashed his car, Floyd relied on Ross to drive him to and from work at Conga, the place he referred to as his "honey hole"—his main, consistent source of income. One day during the first week of March 2020, she came over to pick him up, only to find him doubled over in pain. Floyd didn't need to tell her; he had swung back again, and this time it looked like he may have gone too far.

"We're going to go to the hospital," said Ross, and he was admitted right away. She told medical workers that she was Floyd's wife and followed him to the hospital room.

"My stomach hurts!" he told doctors, who asked him if he had taken anything that might have caused this pain.

"And that's the first time I had heard him say that he used heroin," Ross recalled. "And I was in shock, I guess."

Doctors checked his levels and determined that Floyd needed to be intubated and placed in a coma. In a relationship filled with wake-up calls, Ross swore to herself that this would be the last one. She asked for some gauze and

Vaseline to soothe his dry lips. She bent over his body and kissed him.

Ross paced around the hospital and felt she should do what she thought Floyd would have wanted her to do: make an appeal to the Lord for his healing. So she walked to the prayer room, closed her eyes, and clutched a string of beads. Then she wrote out a prayer for something good to come out of this moment, for Big Floyd to become healthy and their relationship to stabilize, that the pendulum between addiction and sobriety would settle in the right place. After two days, Floyd was revived and back to his old self. When she was finally able to talk to him, he asked if she could find him some lunch.

As they made their way back to his home in St. Louis Park, she thought more seriously about their commitment to each other. She knew neither of them was fond of marriage, but she thought about just how important it was that she had been able to tell doctors she was his wife. She imagined having a small wedding ceremony at the courthouse. But then, with the promise of spring quickly approaching, the world conspired against that idea. A pandemic was afoot, and courthouses and government institutions would soon be locked down as Americans were encouraged to self-isolate to prevent the spread of the novel coronavirus.

The virus was disproportionately infecting Black Americans, and it soon entered Floyd's home. Both his roommates got sick, and Floyd developed an asymptomatic case. But the economic impact was devastating. Conga had shut down, and his security guard jobs dried up. Floyd found himself unemployed, as did nearly one of every two Black residents in Minnesota. The racial disparities lurking underneath Minnesota's prosperous veneer revealed themselves anew.

He scribbled another poem, acknowledging the situation but promising he would not give up:

> *Man at dat low point again*
>
> *Back stuck all up in my addiction*
> *It get worse got corona + 300 bucks*
> *Man life suck*
> *But life never ever suck*

Ross felt consumed by the amount of work she had to do to keep her home afloat. Her hours had been cut at the coffee shop, so she tried picking up jobs cleaning houses while making sure her son James stayed on track at middle school.

Feeling restless, Floyd spent more time with Sylvia Jackson, one of his old security guard partners. Occasionally, Ross would join them and hang out together with Jackson's three girls during the daytime. But she noticed that Floyd started acting a little differently. He was clumsier, more erratic, irritable.

He had started to hang out with Maurice Hall again, and Ross suspected they were using. She admitted to being jealous of all the time Floyd was spending with Jackson but was more nervous about what might occur to Floyd if he kept hanging out with Hall—it had been little more than two months since he had overdosed.

"Look what happened," Ross said. "Everybody's telling you he is bad. Everyone's saying don't hang around with him. Stay away from him."

"That's my boy," Floyd said. "You can't tell me who I can hang out with."

On the last Sunday in May, the two were talking on the phone when Ross gave him the ultimatum, hoping some tough love might knock some sense into him.

"Me or Reese," she said.

Floyd got defensive, thinking that Ross was becoming overbearing. He told her that Hall had been a good friend who was always there for him, even when his other friends were too busy.

Ross started to cry. "If you go hang out with him," she warned, "I'm going to have to step back, then."

"Step back?" Floyd said. "What do you mean, step back?" Floyd hung up the phone, and Ross blocked his number.

The next day was Memorial Day.

CHAPTER 10

Memorial Day

CUP FOODS, WHICH STANDS for "Chicago Unbeatable Prices" and was a play on the established chain of local grocery stores called Cub Foods, had become a staple in the community as it expanded its services over three decades. A wraparound awning above the entrance documented its diverse array of offerings in bold white lettering: *Stamps—Keys—Phones & Accessories—Bus Cards—Organic Milk—T-Shirts—Mexican Food—Halal Meat*. The store buzzed from morning to evening with people coming in to buy snacks, grab a quick meal of wings or sandwiches, get checks cashed, send money via Western Union, pay bills. The city had largely restricted the sale of menthol cigarettes in 2017, but they were still available for purchase there—which neighbors contended could attract an unscrupulous crowd.

A Palestinian immigrant named Samir Abumayyaleh had opened the store in 1989. A growing number of relatives had worked there over the years, learning the family business as children. The location in a diverse and bustling neighborhood and at the intersection of two busy thoroughfares made it a wise investment. Initially favored by Swedish immigrants and other newly arriving Europeans in the early twentieth century, the area around Thirty-Eighth and Chicago later developed as a cultural hot spot for Black residents on the city's south side. In the decades after World War II, the practice of redlining, White flight, and interstate construction facilitated the neighborhood's decline, with economic disinvestment taking hold as Blacks began to make up a larger share of the population. Still, by the early twenty-first century, the minority-majority neighborhood was home to almost twenty-five thousand residents and remained one of the most dynamic commercial zones in the city.

The neighborhood had also become familiar territory for cops from the Minneapolis Police Department's Third Precinct. Some officers had marked the store as a known hot spot for gang activity and crime, while members of the community accused the police of targeting CUP's customers for harassment.

On Memorial Day of 2020, after cashier Christopher Martin came back into CUP Foods without Floyd or proper payment for a pack of menthol cigarettes, his manager told another employee to call the police—hoping to teach a lesson about responsibility. The teenage employee who dialed 911 had recently moved to Minneapolis from West Africa, and English was his second language. He was almost as tall as Floyd and dark-skinned, but, as he would later tell a reporter from *Slate*, did not fully understand the long history of police brutality against Black Americans. He had no idea how a call to 911 to report a petty crime could escalate.

"Um someone comes our store and give us fake bills and we realize it before he left the store, and we ran back outside, they was sitting on their car," the new employee said during the call, adding that the alleged counterfeiter was "awfully drunk" and "not in control of himself."

The dispatcher told him the authorities would be there shortly.

At 8:04 p.m., the two police officers that Shawanda Hill observed from the car walked into CUP Foods. Thomas Lane and J. Alexander Kueng were both rookie cops. Kueng (pronounced "king"), twenty-six, was only in his third shift as a police officer. The son of a White single mother and a Nigerian father, he had signed up to join the Minneapolis Police Department in February 2019 and felt he was uniquely positioned to help address some of the lingering racial tension between law enforcement and minorities, his mother told *The New York Times*. Kueng had a shaved head, narrow eyes, and a rusty beard.

Lane, thirty-seven, was five days out of field training. He stood at six foot seven, slender with salt-and-pepper hair and a serious countenance that made him look older than his years. The two officers consulted with the store's owners, who led them through the back entrance to point out the group of people who had just used the questionable $20 bill.

Lane tapped his flashlight against the driver's side window. "Let me see your hands," he said, lifting his own two palms as an example.

Floyd leaned forward in his seat, his head coming within inches of the steering wheel. He began to open the car door.

"I'm sorry, I'm sorry, I'm sorry, I'm sorry, I'm sorry," he said. He raised one of his hands. Lane was trained to be concerned about the positioning of both hands, in case a suspect was trying to hide something or reach for an object under the seat. But he could only see the left one as Floyd tried to step out of the car.

"Stay in the car. Let me see your other hand," Lane said,

his voice rising as it intersected with Floyd's rapid flow of apologies. "Let me see your other hand!"

Now, Lane tried to use the flashlight to block the door from swinging open. He placed his free hand on his gun.

"Please, please, Mr. Officer," Floyd said.

"Both hands!" Lane shouted as he unholstered his gun, a SIG Sauer P320, and pointed it toward Floyd.

Floyd's eyes bulged in horror. It was as if the prophecy that his mother told him about what happens to Black men who get into trouble with the law was about to come true.

"Put your fucking hands up right now!" Lane shouted, holding the firearm sideways. "Let me see your other hand."

"Let him see your other hand!" Hill yelled from the back seat.

"All right, what'd I do, though?" Floyd asked Hill, turning his body briefly to face her.

Hill could not believe how quickly Floyd panicked. It reminded her of the day he got locked in her bathroom—the crying, the stuttering, the abject fear. She knew Floyd was claustrophobic. But she figured that a man of his stature, with his time in prison—and a Black man at that—would have been accustomed to being confronted by police.

"It was only about a twenty-dollar bill," Hill recalled. "So, in my head, I'm like, 'This ain't no big deal. Do you do this every time police come around your ass?'"

By the time Floyd turned back around from talking to Hill, the barrel of Lane's pistol was closing in.

"Goddang," Floyd said.

"Jesus Christ!" Lane said, his voice a mix of relief and aggression as Floyd raised his right hand. "Keep your fucking hands on the wheel."

Floyd now began to employ the lessons he had learned from childhood about how to interact with police.

"Yes, sir," he responded, rocking his body back and forth between the steering wheel and his seat. "I'm sorry, so sorry."

Lane lectured Floyd about the importance of complying and then launched into the string of verbal commands he had learned at the academy and during field officer training.

"Hands on top of your head. Hands on top of your head," he said. "Step out of the vehicle and face away from me, all right? Step out and face away. Step out and face away."

Floyd leaned forward and put his forearms on the steering wheel, rested his head in his palms, and started to cry.

"I'll look at you eye-to-eye, man," Floyd said. "Please don't shoot me, man."

"I'm not shooting you, man," Lane said. He placed his gun back into its holster and moved to continue his arrest of Floyd, who was now sobbing and doubled over. Floyd mentioned that his mother had recently passed away.

"320, we're taking one out," Lane said into his radio, letting the dispatcher know he was about to eject a suspect from the vehicle.

Kueng heard the commotion from the passenger side of the car, where he had been questioning Hall. He told Hall to stay put, and then walked over to aid Lane in pinning Floyd's arms behind his back.

After a brief struggle, the two men placed handcuffs on Floyd. He fell to his knees.

"Please, please, man," he cried. "I don't want to go back. I don't want to go back, man."

Kueng and Lane decided to switch positions. Lane went to question Floyd's companions.

"What's his deal?" Lane asked them.

"I don't know," Hall said. "He's a good guy." Standing on the sidewalk, Hall was still nervous that the police would discover that he was a wanted man.

"I was trying to get out of there as fast as I can," he recalled.

Meanwhile, Kueng tried to finish Floyd's arrest.

"Come on, walk with me," Kueng said after lifting Floyd from the ground. He spun Floyd around at the wall of the building across the street from CUP Foods and asked him to sit down.

With his hands clasped behind him, Floyd began to slide down the wall. Conversing with a police officer of color, Floyd tried to see if he might be able to reason with him.

"Thank you, man," he said, looking up through tears as he settled into a seated position, before returning to a more formal address. "Thank you, Mr. Officer."

Kueng explained to Floyd that the officers had come after him because he had been accused of using a fake bill. He added that the officers pulled him from the car because he had not been listening to their orders.

"Right, but I didn't know what was going on!" Floyd replied.

Kueng told Floyd he was about to be placed in the squad car, and Floyd grew nervous again. He was stuttering, trying to find the right words to make an appeal.

"Mr. Officer, ca-ca-can I talk to you, wo-wo-wo-one second, please?"

"Are you on something right now?" Lane asked, joining the conversation.

Kueng finished his thought: "'Cause you acting real erratic."

They thought they saw something foam from his mouth.

Floyd denied being under the influence. He told them he had been "hooping," and that he was "scared."

"All right, let me calm down now," he said as he shuffled across Thirty-Eighth Street toward the police car. He took a deep breath. "I feel a little better now."

But as he neared the cruiser, trapped between two policemen and staring at the prospect of yet another trip in a cramped squad car to a cramped jail cell, Floyd broke down again. He stumbled, speaking of his condition.

"I'm claustrophobic, man!" he cried. "I'm claustrophobic."

Kueng yelled at Floyd to stay on his feet and pushed him against the police cruiser. Floyd continued to try to explain his claustrophobia, but the officers told him they weren't interested in talking. They searched his pants for weapons— finding none—and opened the car door.

"I'm not that kind of guy, Mr. Officer," he said.

He looked at Kueng and asked: "Why y'all don't believe me, Mr. Officer?"

Kueng pushed down on Floyd's collarbone to force him inside the vehicle while Floyd continued to try to plead with them. He explained that he had recently had COVID-19. Lane promised to roll the windows down or turn on the air-conditioning if he just went into the police car. Floyd was inconsolable.

"Y'all, I'm going to die in here!" he said. "I'm going to die, man!"

It was 8:16 p.m. The interaction had been going on for eight minutes.

Those who lived around CUP Foods were used to hearing odd police encounters, so few paid attention at first. But Charles McMillian, a balding sixty-one-year-old and self-described nosy neighbor, was driving by when he stopped his vehicle to see what was going on. He was wearing a pair of khaki cargo shorts, a black T-shirt, and white sandals over his dark-colored socks. He had grown up in rural Mississippi and moved to Minneapolis with a third-grade education. He'd had his own struggles with the police and had overcome his own demons—he was just over two decades free of a crack cocaine addiction. McMillian knew the dangers Black men faced during encounters with police.

"You can't win," McMillian told Floyd after walking over to the scene.

"I don't want to try to win, I don't want to try to win," Floyd replied. "I'm scared as fuck, man."

Meanwhile, the two rookie cops had called for reinforcement. Two other officers left the police station, hopped in a cruiser, and started driving toward CUP Foods. One, a Minneapolis police officer named Tou Thao, later said he felt an urgency to provide backup because the dwellers on that corner had a history of being "hostile" to the police. The other was a man who'd been walking the beat in the Third Precinct for years, a veteran who had trained Kueng. His name was Derek Chauvin.

The two officers were still trying to get Floyd to settle into the police car when Thao and Chauvin arrived. Floyd's body thrashed as he refused to go inside. When Kueng shoved him into the car, he gasped for air. His upper body began to jerk and wiggle out of the police car from the other side.

"Slide your butt over here, I'm going to pull you in," Lane said flatly.

Chauvin, wearing black gloves, jumped in to help them. He grabbed Floyd's neck and tried to force him inside.

"I can't breathe!" Floyd cried. It was 8:18 p.m.

McMillian, who had walked from the sidewalk to the street as the action moved to the passenger's side, warned Floyd that he might soon add "heart attack" to his list of medical troubles if he didn't give in.

The officers' plan of getting him in the vehicle was just not working. Lane suggested a different approach.

"Let's just take him out and just MRE," he said, using the wrong acronym for "maximal-restraint technique."

Kueng and Chauvin pulled Floyd out of the vehicle, allowing his body to fall to the pavement.

Floyd thanked the officers, grateful to be outside the confines of the police car. But his predicament was about to get worse.

The officers pushed Floyd down to the ground on his stomach. Chauvin lifted his left knee and placed it on Floyd's upper back. Then he shifted his knee to the back of Floyd's neck.

"I can't breathe!" Floyd shouted again.

Kueng and Lane stepped in. Lane held Floyd's legs. Kueng shifted his weight on Floyd's lower back and pushed away Floyd's hands. Chauvin then pulled Floyd's fingers upward and forced his wrist into an unnatural angle, causing him to writhe in pain.

"You're under arrest, guy," Chauvin said, and then Floyd begged for help to someone beyond the earthly realm.

"Mama!" he shouted from beneath Chauvin's knee, with his neck cranked sideways. "Mama! Mama! Mama! Mama! Mama! Mama!"

Chauvin continued to dig his knee into him. Floyd pressed his knuckles on the pavement and slightly raised the right side of his torso off the ground, trying to gasp for more air. He begged for mercy.

"I can't breathe for nothing, man. This is cold-blooded, man," Floyd cried. "My face is gone."

Chauvin looked down and dismissed his suspect's concerns: "All right, you're doing a lot of talking."

Lane showed concern about one aspect of his health. He noticed Floyd's bloody lip, which prompted him to ask the dispatch to send an ambulance. He used a low-priority "Code 2" to indicate that the matter was not particularly urgent.

Meanwhile, Floyd continued begging for his life. Chauvin dug his knee into Floyd even more, a half smirk on his face.

The other officers continued to talk among themselves casually. They assumed Floyd was "on something" and called his behavior erratic. Lane speculated about whether Floyd could be one of those cases they had learned about in training, in which a person under the influence supposedly gains superhuman strength and poses a threat to officers and the community.

"Should we roll him on his side?" Lane asked Chauvin, who said no.

"I just worry about excited delirium or whatever," Lane said.

"Well, that's why we have the ambulance coming," Chauvin replied.

Thao tried to manage the small crowd of witnesses that was starting to form along Chicago Avenue. Around the corner on Thirty-Eighth Street—more than 150 feet away from Floyd and with their view obscured by the police cruiser—Hall and Hill could hear their friend's cries. A parks officer, who had been tasked with watching them and the blue Mercedes, stood between Floyd's friends and the action. They asked him what was going on, but they were told not to move because they were being detained. When the parks officer asked Hall for his name, he simply made one up: William Ricardo. Hill's mind turned toward her granddaughter and her daughter, the latter of whom was trying to get to work. She figured that the police were just "roughing Floyd up," as they were known to do. Then she stopped hearing him. Hill figured he had calmed down.

Floyd was not calming down; he was dying. His cries grew more strained as he expended the last of his energy.

"Please, I can't breathe. Please, man. Please."

"I'm through."

"Oh my God."

"You're doing a lot of talking, a lot of yelling," Chauvin said. "Takes a heck of a lot of oxygen to say that."

Floyd's voice had lowered by this point, his cries growing faint.

"I cannot breathe. I cannot breathe."

"They're going to kill me. They're going to kill me. I can't breathe."

"Please, sir. Please."

"Somebody help me."

"I'm claustrophobic. My stomach hurts. My neck hurts. Everything hurts."

"They're going to kill me. They're going to kill me, man."

George Floyd had always believed that God was watching over him.

Back in Texas, after his mother died in 2018, Floyd was on

one of the spontaneous road trips he liked to take with his friend Tiffany Cofield. They had picked up Cofield's sixty-seven-year-old uncle and headed east on I-10 toward Orange, Texas.

It was already dark when the trio left on what was supposed to be a two-hour drive to see a friend near the Louisiana border in a place Floyd referred to as "Fruit City."

As they passed cow pastures and timber farms, Floyd turned up the volume on DJ Screw's 1998 mixtape *Tre World*, in which he had featured as a host. He was nodding to the crawling beat when the car started to sputter. He looked down to see the gas light beaming a bright orange and the needle settling confidently below the letter *E*.

"We ran out of gas, man," he said matter-of-factly as the car slowed to a stop. They were in a rural stretch of east Texas, the kind of place where freeways slice through farmland and forest, with several miles of bleakness between each exit. It was pitch black.

Cofield was incredulous.

"How are you driving and you don't check the damn gas?" she said, trying to contain her disbelief.

Floyd looked across the car, unbothered.

"Stiff, it's going to be okay, shug," he said, speaking just above a whisper, as if trying not to upset the eerie quiet of this forsaken stretch of highway. "God's got us."

"Don't you bring God into this!" Cofield interjected.

"Stiff, I'm telling you, God got us," he said. "For real, just calm down. Just calm down, I'm going to go ahead and push the car a little bit up the way and then—"

Cofield cut him off again: "You can't push this motherfucker by yourself!"

She looked back at her uncle, who had bad knees and a frail frame, and grew even more incensed as she realized what was about to happen.

Floyd, still betraying no sign of stress, got out of the car while the elderly man took his place behind the wheel to help steer.

"Shug, don't worry," Floyd said as he and Cofield got behind the car and prepared to push. "God's got us."

Just then, a loud truck pulled over in front of them.

The door creaked open, and out came "the most redneck-looking White guy I have ever seen in my life," Cofield later recalled. Her mind flashed to images of James Byrd's body being dragged behind a rusty Ford truck not far away, near Jasper, Texas, twenty years earlier. Three white supremacists were convicted of murdering the forty-nine-year-old Black victim and dumping his body in front of an African American church.

"Hi, how are y'all doing?" the man said in a deep drawl.

He was barefoot and looked far too excited for the hour and circumstances.

"Oh my God, please don't let this be my end," Cofield thought to herself.

Floyd walked over with an outstretched hand and told the man what had happened.

"Well, you're in luck because I pull people off the beach in the sand dunes, and I'm just getting back from Galveston," the man said. "Let me hook you up."

Floyd stepped into the cab of the wrecker while Cofield and her uncle got back into the car as the man hitched it up for a tow.

They rode for five miles until they reached a gas station.

The truck driver put $15 of gas in their car, told them to be safe, and then drove off into the darkness.

Floyd got back in the car and turned to Cofield.

"See, I told you," he said, his grin breaking through his best efforts to hold back for the punch line. "God got us."

But God did not appear to be intervening with the law as Floyd began to deliver his final words.

"Please."

"Mama, I love you."

"Reese, I love you."

"Tell my kids I love them."

"I can't breathe for nothing, man."

"This is cold-blooded."

"I'm dead."

A growing group of bystanders tried to intervene. Around 8:20 p.m., Hill and Hall saw a White woman in leggings and a gray T-shirt walking past them. They could see that she had turned on her camera and started to film.

Genevieve Hansen had recently moved to the area and worked as an emergency medical technician at a fire station nearby. Hansen recalled being stuck at home all day, so she stepped out of her house about a mile away and went on a walk. She took pictures of flowers and then sat in a neighborhood park, eating a vanilla ice cream cone from Dairy Queen and listening to a murder mystery podcast. Then she saw the flashing lights in the distance.

Hansen had figured the commotion was coming from CUP Foods, so she wandered over to see if any of her colleagues had come to the scene. But by the time she got there, a group of onlookers were watching a murder.

She walked up to Thao and identified herself as a Minneapolis firefighter. Chauvin and the other officers warned her not to come any closer to them. Thao motioned for her to back away.

"Does he have a pulse?" she asked.

Thao ignored her question and shouted at her to move from the street and onto the sidewalk.

"Check for a pulse, please," she said after joining the group on the curb, growing more agitated.

"A lot of things were running through my head," Hansen recalled. "I wondered if I was one of my colleagues—a built, White, middle-aged man—would they have said I could step in? I would have stepped in, taken a knee, and checked his vitals. But they wouldn't let me. I just got more and more upset."

"Check for a pulse!" she exhorted.

Moments later, Kueng reached up and grabbed Floyd's right arm, feeling for a sign of life.

"You got one?" Lane asked.

"I can't find one," he said.

Hansen stood near Alyssa Funari, a seventeen-year-old high school junior who had been headed to CUP Foods to buy an auxiliary car stereo cord. She stopped about twenty-five feet behind the squad car and pulled out a phone to record.

"What the fuck?" she could be heard saying in the shaky video, which captured Floyd's face being pressed into the pavement by Chauvin's knee. "He's not moving!" she shouted at the officers. Her red acrylic nails could be seen in the frame as she pointed to the police and told them she hoped they would rot in hell for their treatment of the man on the ground.

Her schoolmate, Darnella Frazier, had spent Memorial Day afternoon posting dozens of memes on her Facebook page about topics ranging from relationships to racism.

She lived just a short walk from CUP Foods, and her nine-year-old cousin, Judeah Reynolds, was in the mood for a snack before bedtime. Frazier had given her $3 earlier in the day, and she was eager to use it. Frazier initially denied the little girl's request to stroll to the store, but she gave in when Judeah's persistence turned into unabashed begging. Wearing a dark-gray hoodie over shoulder-length hair, Frazier walked to CUP and told her cousin to go inside.

She then turned around and went back to the part of the sidewalk where she had just seen three police officers subduing a man who was on the street begging for his life.

She walked toward the curb and pulled out her phone. She initially kept her distance, filming from behind the bus stop about forty feet away. But as the situation grew more dire, she got closer.

"Look how they doing people out here," she said.

Speaking to another person in the crowd, she gave a succinct explanation for why the officers had shown such little concern for the handcuffed man's well-being.

"He's Black," she said. "They don't care."

Donald Williams II, a thirty-two-year-old mixed-martial-arts fighter, had decided to drive to CUP Foods that evening to get some fresh air after taking a holiday fishing expedition with his son. He had a patchy beard and wore a black hooded sweatshirt with the words "Northside Boxing Club" printed on the front.

As he approached the store, he saw Floyd's head poking out from the ground behind the police cruiser, as well as

Chauvin's body pressing him into submission. He looked at Chauvin and noticed the "blood choke" technique he had learned years earlier, used for stanching the flow of blood at a man's neck.

Williams would later recall that he saw Floyd's "eyes slowly pale out and begin slowly rolling to the back of his eyes," like the bass he had caught earlier that day.

"You're trapping his breathing right there, bro," he said to Chauvin. "You don't think nobody understands that shit right there, bro? I trained at the academy, bro . . . That's bullshit."

Thao, attempting to keep the crowd back, dismissed the complaints. He tried to make it seem as if Floyd and his suspected drug use had been the problem.

"This is why you don't do drugs, kids," he told the group.

Williams became more animated as Chauvin dug deeper into Floyd's neck with his kneecap.

"You're enjoying it," he said, addressing Chauvin directly. "Look at you, your body language explains it, you fucking bum."

Williams took out his phone and said he was going to note down Chauvin's badge number. When he stepped off the sidewalk, Chauvin swiftly reached into his duty belt, grabbed a canister of Mace, and shook it. The move sent the crowd into a collective backpedal toward the store.

"First thing you want to grab is your Mace, because you're scared, bro—scared of fucking minorities," Williams said. "Bro, he's not even fucking moving! Get off of his fucking neck, bro! Get off of his neck!"

He turned to Chauvin and delivered a somber prediction: "You about to have dreams at night, bro. You're going to fuck around and shoot yourself, that's what you're going to do. That man's going to haunt you for the rest of your life."

As Hill heard Williams yelling at Chauvin, she said, "I started tripping."

"Did they beat him up or something?" she recalled thinking. "Because I couldn't see nothing."

And then she saw an ambulance drive up to the scene.

On one side of the street, bystanders had watched a heinous, traumatizing crime. Around the corner, the sounds and the police activity that Floyd's friends heard seemed like an unfortunate but not uncommon example of a Black person in America dealing with law enforcement: Small problems become big problems. Police might detain you for no reason. There's a big hullabaloo that eventually quiets down.

Hill and Hall hoped for the best. Hill figured the ambulance came because it was customary for an ambulance to come. She figured that once the commotion was over, Floyd would get checked out, fingerprinted, receive a ticket for the counterfeit money, and be on his way.

Still, the flashing sirens of the ambulance worried her.

"Can I just see what y'all did to him?" she said, walking past the parks officer to try to get a better vantage point. She got as far as the edge of the sidewalk before the officer told her to come back.

"Why is he going to the hospital?" she shouted across the intersection.

There was no response.

Hill thought about her granddaughter, who she still needed to pick up. After the parks officer said she was free to leave, Hill called her daughter and asked her to meet her at CUP Foods. Hall overheard her and asked for a ride. He had tried unsuccessfully to get the officer to tell him what was happening with Floyd and decided it was best to take off and catch up with his friend later.

Hill's daughter dropped Hall off on Lake Street. Hall ran into an alley to call a friend who was staying at the hotel in Bloomington. After the adrenaline subsided, he called a mutual friend from Houston to tell him the tale of Floyd breaking down in tears because he was stopped by the police. It didn't seem like a tragedy to him at the time, just a run-in that could happen to a person as calamitous as Floyd tended to be.

"That's Big Floyd," the friend said, laughing.

He had no idea that by the time the Hennepin County ambulance arrived, Floyd's body had gone limp; that Kueng had already searched in vain for a pulse. The officers stayed on top of Floyd as a paramedic walked over and pointed a flash-light at his dilated pupils. They didn't move as a man in medical gloves reached his hand under Floyd's pinned neck to search for a pulse. They held steady as the emergency responders unloaded the stretcher and unfolded the gurney on the ground.

Not until the paramedics asked the officers to "get out of the way" did Chauvin take the pressure off Floyd's neck, mak-ing room for the gurney to be placed next to Floyd. It was 8:29 p.m.

McMillian, the man who had arrived first, walked to Chauvin's police car to tell him he did not like the way the arrest had gone down. He was upset that Floyd had not com-plied but also distressed that the officers kept him pinned down for so long, even after he had stopped moving.

"Maggot," McMillian called him.

"That's one person's opinion," Chauvin said from the car. "We got to control this guy because he's a sizable guy, and it looks like he's on something."

It was all supposed to be a fun, freewheeling day. An afternoon barbecue, a trip to Wendy's with a friend, a rendezvous with an old flame. And yet it ended with Floyd's face on the warm asphalt on a muggy late-spring evening, begging an agent of the state to believe that he wasn't a bad guy. He told officers he could not breathe at least twenty-seven times, and each time he was ignored. The last conversation Floyd had was under duress, with an elderly Black man he did not know, who told him that in this country, he could not win.

But what was winning exactly?

One of Floyd's last aspirations was to create a place called Convict Kitchen. He had been fixated on the idea of opening a restaurant that would model its menu after prison delicacies made from commissary food.

The idea came about one day as he and Courteney Ross were talking about his time in prison, and some of the culinary wizardry he had perfected using the bland ingredients available in the penitentiary.

"Wait, how the fuck do you make pizza in prison?" she had asked him. "Hold on, break this down for me."

"Oh, baby, we take the ramen, we smash it up a little bit into a crust," he'd said. "Then we take the ketchup packets and get the sauce going. We cut up the sausage and put the sausage on it and then we put it on the grate."

"The grate? What the fuck do you mean—like a heating grate?"

"Yeah, yeah."

When they stopped laughing, Floyd explained how inmates would also make chocolate cake. It was a complex formula that involved separating the wafers from the icing in Oreo cookies and mashing up the ingredients before putting them all back together with a level of care and precision that bordered on artistry. The final product, at least to the prisoners, would rival the best pastries they'd had on the outside.

Floyd had mused about hiring a staff of only ex-felons, making it easier for people with records to get their lives back on track. They had joked that the job application would have only one question: "Have you served time in the penitentiary: Yes or no?"

He had planned to cover the restaurant's walls with large black-and-white photos depicting life inside real prisons. There would be mental health services for ex-inmates and resources for people transitioning back to life on the outside.

It was one of the many things that he wanted to do when he got his life back together. He would not get the chance. By the time paramedics arrived at the hospital, he was already a corpse. George Perry Floyd Jr., Miss Cissy's oldest son, was officially pronounced dead at 9:25 p.m.

At around 12:30 a.m., blue-and-red police lights were flashing through Darnella Frazier's upstairs window. The bright screen of her phone offered the only other source of light in the room as she peered out into the distance, where a handful of police cars were buzzing around the intersection of Thirty-Eighth Street and Chicago Avenue.

She held her phone up to the window, focusing its camera on the police cars several hundred feet away as she turned on Facebook Live.

"Y'all, it is so freaking crazy, bro," she said, narrating the scene from behind the camera. "They really killed somebody at CUP. I got the whole video."

Her hands shaking, she ended the livestream, promising to post the video of the incident when she woke up in the morning.

But she couldn't wait. Fifteen minutes later, she typed out a message to introduce the ten minutes and nine seconds of footage she had recorded.

"They killed him right in front of cup foods over south on 38th and Chicago!! No type of sympathy," she wrote, adding two emojis with broken hearts. She ended the message with "#POLICEBRUTALITY" and hit post.

Maurice Hall woke up the next morning to a slew of missed calls and texts from folks in Houston telling him that the police had killed Floyd. Suddenly, the incident he had laughed about with his friend was not funny anymore. He could not comprehend how much he had missed on the other side of the street. His friend had been dying, and he had run away. A group of bystanders had seen it, but Hall had left without checking in.

"I had emotions," Hall said. "The devil tried to make me feel . . . guilty. Like, what the fuck, I let him down, you know what I'm saying? The reality was that the world is turning him into something huge. It's like, God, was he the sacrifice?"

Hall picked up his phone, called back the friend he had just spoken with hours before. His response was ominous.

"You know what that means," his friend said. "Bro, they coming for you next."

Hall thought about the warrants, the pills, the kids. He

ran. He got in a truck and drove to Houston right away. But before he left, Hall returned to Thirty-Eighth and Chicago, where a collection of teddy bears and candles was starting to form as a memorial.

Hall found a piece of poster board and a black Sharpie. He scratched out the letters "W-A-R-D" and then drew a box around them with three vertical lines—a logo for the community from which they came. Hall had no doubt that people would associate Floyd with this corner in Minneapolis. But to understand Floyd, to truly understand Floyd, Hall felt the world needed to know the place where he came from: Third Ward.

Shawanda Hill had been up all night after taking her granddaughter to her small efficiency apartment near downtown Minneapolis. The four-year-old turned on the television and watched at the edge of her mattress while she sat on the windowsill, waiting to hear Floyd yell out one of his nicknames for her from the back alley. *Baby. Chocolate Drop. Queen.*

Her granddaughter fell asleep with the television on, and Hill sat there, waiting. "I felt God wanted us to be together that day, so I knew he'd come back to me," she said. The early-morning news started playing. They reported that police killed a man near Thirty-Eighth and Chicago, and Hill fell to the floor.

"It ain't true, it ain't true!" Hill screamed.

And in the tiny brown house on the north side, Sylvia Jackson woke up wondering where Floyd was with her car. She heard a knock on the door; it was another one of their friends, his eyes red with tears.

"The police killed Floyd," he told her. "There's a video."

*

Before Frazier's video circulated widely, the machinery of the Minneapolis Police Department whirred into action to defend its officers and cast Floyd as the instigator of his own death. The department's initial press release, full of inaccuracies and obfuscations, only added to the feeling of agitation that was beginning to spread across the city:

MAN DIES AFTER MEDICAL INCIDENT
DURING POLICE INTERACTION

May 25, 2020 (MINNEAPOLIS) On Monday evening, shortly after 8:00 pm, officers from the Minneapolis Police Department responded to the 3700 block of Chicago Avenue South on a report of a forgery in progress. Officers were advised that the suspect was sitting on top of a blue car and appeared to be under the influence.

Two officers arrived and located the suspect, a male believed to be in his 40s, in his car. He was ordered to step from his car. After he got out, he physically resisted officers. Officers were able to get the suspect into handcuffs and noted he appeared to be suffering medical distress. Officers called for an ambulance. He was transported to Hennepin County Medical Center by ambulance where he died a short time later.

At no time were weapons of any type used by anyone involved in this incident.

The Minnesota Bureau of Criminal Apprehension has been called in to investigate this incident at the request of the Minneapolis Police Department.

No officers were injured in the incident.

Body worn cameras were on and activated during this incident.

The GO number associated with this case is 20-140629.

PART III

Say His Name

CHAPTER 11

We Have Nothing to Lose but Our Chains

A FEW MINUTES AFTER MIDNIGHT on May 26, Minneapolis police chief Medaria Arradondo received a text message from a concerned resident.

"Chief," he recalled it saying, "have you seen the video of your officer choking and killing that man at 38th and Chicago?"

Arradondo was confused. He had seen a video from Thirty-Eighth and Chicago—it was from a street camera without audio that showed officers huddled around a man. No choking, no apparent killing. But then the resident forwarded the video from Darnella Frazier, which had started circulating on social media. Frazier's video was closer, shakier. You could see Floyd's eyes bulging and hear his cries for his mother as one of Arradondo's officers kneeled on top of him. A fifth-generation Minnesotan who had grown up a block away from CUP Foods, Arradondo knew the explosive potential of this recording.

He called Mayor Jacob Frey with a startling admission: the video circulating online showed something far more egregious than their press statement let on. Frey couldn't believe what he was seeing. First, there were the passionate cries of a human being pleading for his life. But he also knew there was an administrative problem—it appeared his own government had obscured the truth of the matter, and his city was about to find out.

Frey, a thirty-nine-year-old former distance runner with a square jaw, left his pregnant wife and put on a gray suit, light-blue shirt, and dark-blue tie. In the middle of a muggy night, he walked to city hall. He spent the night thinking about what he should say to an angry public who'd look to their leader for answers in the morning.

His police department had taken pride in trying to be a progressive, transparent organization. The last two police chiefs were people of color. The police force did antibias training, required two-year degrees, and worked to diversify its ranks. And still, the first public accounting of events they had published was so different from what he had seen in the video.

The suspect "appeared to be suffering medical distress," the statement had read.

No mention of Floyd being subdued by four officers. No indication that the policemen declined to roll him on his side after he stopped resisting. In declaring that no weapons had been used, it glazed over the fact that Lane had pulled a gun on Floyd seconds after knocking on his window.

The press release felt like the opening statement to the usual choreography when something tragic and controversial happens under a city's watch. Afterward, civic leaders usually express sympathy to the family and withhold judgment until an investigation is complete; they urge calm and proclaim faith in the justice system. But, in the middle of the night, Frey wrestled with following that pattern.

Pacing around his office, Frey gave himself a pep talk to establish some guiding principles for the next few days: Tell the truth. Try to do the right thing. Keep one foot in front of the other.

He called the city's attorneys to prepare them to abandon the usual script, even if the police's version of events had not yet been reconciled with what Frazier had shown on her video.

"I'm going to tell the truth about what I feel about this," Frey remembered telling his staff. "And we're not going to shove it under the rug."

Before the sun rose, Frey called a press conference. Around seven thirty a.m., he walked to the press room in city hall, frazzled and wearing the same suit. Chief Arradondo was next to him.

"For the better part of the night, I've been trying to find the words to describe what happened," he said, his voice breaking. "And all I can keep coming back to is he should not have died. What we saw was horrible—completely and utterly messed up. When you hear someone calling for help, you are supposed to help."

Arradondo informed the journalists that he had called the FBI to investigate whether the officer had violated the victim's civil rights. According to a video posted by Libor Jany at the *Star Tribune*, the conference ran for about eleven minutes. It was so early, and the specifics were still so murky, that Frey didn't share many details about the man who died. The mayor tried to convey some sense of his humanity—that this man's life mattered because he was flesh and blood, that he had friends, a family, a community. He had a name. But, at that point in the morning, Frey did not say it.

Later that morning, Donald Hooker Jr., an ebullient twenty-six-year-old chess coach and library staffer with an unkempt flat top and goatee who everyone knows as DJ, learned that the man's name was George Floyd. DJ had never met Floyd, but he was one person in the untold swells of those around the globe whose lives were about to be changed by his death. When Hooker woke up in his basement apartment and checked his phone, everyone was talking about Floyd. DJ's friends partied with him at Conga. They saw him play on the basketball court. They dated him. And they were all texting, encouraging Hooker to watch a video of his death.

At first Hooker felt like he could not stomach another real-life horror film of a soul being squeezed out of a Black body. But the text messages kept coming in, so Hooker logged on to Facebook. As he stared at Floyd's neck cranked under the weight of Derek Chauvin's knee, he burst into tears. He stopped watching after forty seconds.

Hooker was familiar with America's race problem. Growing up, he had watched his chess-master father struggle to get meaningful help for his crack cocaine addiction. When his father got clean, the two attended a multigenerational Black men's reading group to absorb lessons from the past. The proof of an unequal society came into polished view each time he observed the fancy auditoriums and up-to-date technology in the White suburban schools where he'd take his students to play chess, as opposed to the predominantly Black and Hispanic schools in which he taught in the city.

He was now trying to make it through the pandemic

isolated from the community that embraced him, living in an apartment littered with chessboards and Rubik's cubes and old Black history books. He took to his rainbow-colored keyboard, scribbled some notes, and turned on the camera to his computer. At 12:35 p.m., into the anonymous ether of Facebook Live, he delivered a profane message to anyone who might be online at the same time.

"What kind of fucked-up shit is this?" he said. "I would just assume, and I feel like the logical conclusion is, that fucked-up shit like this wouldn't happen during the pandemic. Most people are wearing masks. They are trying to keep themselves contained. And they're still out there killing Black people. I guess the coronavirus isn't doing enough, so the cops gotta jump in now?"

Hooker didn't envision who he was talking to on the other side; he just needed to exhale. Suddenly, two hundred people were watching.

"I don't know necessarily how I should feel," he continued. "I'm not even going to lie. I feel kind of hopeless."

But the truth was that a part of Hooker also felt guilt. As a rep for his union at the library, he had intersected with organizers in racial justice groups who wanted to draw attention to how unfair it was that the cops who killed Jamar Clark and Philando Castile went unpunished. He rarely accepted invitations to those protests; yelling "Black Lives Matter" to change years of institutional bias felt like shouting into the wind.

Hooker wondered if his going to more protests back then would have changed anything for George Floyd. Maybe one more overwhelmed and angry person like him could have tipped the scales of justice and led to a fairer future. Instead, he walked past his friends who were protesting in front of a police station for weeks after Clark died and trying to move discussions about the revolution away from being an academic exercise.

His friends were now spreading word on Facebook about a protest outside CUP Foods being planned for that evening. The community account was radically different—and more accurate—than the city's initial press release.

"Yesterday in broad daylight, Minneapolis Police Officers snuffed out the life of a Black man, George Floyd, in the presence of numerous witnesses," it read. "Mr. Floyd gasped, cried out for help, and said 'I can't breathe' several times until he no longer appeared to be breathing."

Hooker found a mask, put it on, and walked out of his apartment. He was ready to become part of the crowd.

At the same time, others around the world were finding Darnella Frazier's video and experiencing a similar stew of emotions to what Hooker was feeling. And they began to share a hope that maybe the death of this man could change something in the world. Maybe this time, a group of committed people could dismantle the racist system that killed him.

Shareeduh Tate had already started her morning routine. An early riser, Floyd's cousin turned on *CBS This Morning* around five a.m. Gayle King had been broadcasting from her home with a sadly familiar tale.

"This morning the FBI is looking into the death of a Black man after he was stopped by police in Minneapolis," King said.

"Oh my God, this family is going to be devastated when they find out," Tate thought to herself.

A few minutes later, during the same broadcast, there was a story about a White woman calling 911 on a Black bird-watcher in New York's Central Park after he insisted that she obey park rules to keep her cocker spaniel on a leash. The woman reported the incident with theatrical flourish, crying breathlessly as she tried to persuade cops that the man calmly recording her was a threat. Delivering the news, sitting in front of photos of her children, King stepped out of her role as a neutral observer to express a greater feeling.

"As the daughter of a Black man and as the mother of a Black man, this is really too much for me today," she told viewers. "I am speechless. I am really, really speechless about what we're seeing on television this morning. It feels to me like open season, and that it's just not sometimes a safe place to be in this country for Black men."

Tate looked at her phone. Keeta, Philonise's wife, was calling.

"The police in Minneapolis killed Perry!" Keeta said. Philonise was too distraught to talk.

The phone tree continued. Tate called her sister, Tera Brown, who dialed Zsa Zsa, who happened to have slept over at LaTonya's house.

"Zsa, have you heard?" Brown said.

"Heard what?" she replied as she got out of bed.

"There's no easy way to tell you, cuz."

And when Brown told her what happened, Zsa Zsa dropped the phone, unable to speak. Brown shouted so loudly to get Zsa Zsa's attention that it stirred LaTonya, who was still in bed with her wife, Jewel.

"What's wrong, what are you yelling for?" LaTonya said. And when LaTonya heard, she ran out of the house, still in her pajamas, and started pacing on the street, unable to process how this tragedy could possibly be real.

Zsa Zsa's oldest son, Brandon Williams, was getting ready for his shift at the chemical plant where he worked as word spread from the old neighborhood that Perry had died. Brandon, now twenty-nine, recalled feeling a tightness in his chest. He held to a stubborn hope that all these people from Cuney Homes got their facts wrong. He called Philonise.

"Is it true?" Brandon asked.

Philonise tried to compose himself. "It's true," he said.

A lifetime of memories rushed to Brandon. He could see his uncle drilling him to make better layups, pushing him around for skipping class. He saw the laughter, the silly dances, the hugs. Immediately, Brandon tried to latch on to something to keep him from descending into inconsolable grief. Brandon couldn't go to work. Instead, he jumped in his truck and drove back to Third Ward. He figured it would be easier to share information and mourn with the old crew from there.

Brandon knew how many people around Houston would crumble with Perry's loss, even in a community well acquainted with Black men suddenly dying. So many people had always supported Perry, looked out for Perry, wanted to be Perry. He figured someone from the family should be there in the old neighborhood.

Inside Tate's home, a two-story bungalow in a Houston suburb that had long symbolized a sense of middle-class achievement, other members of the family were trying to figure out what to do next. They resolved to extract a measure of justice for Perry. Black death at the hands of police had become so familiar that there was a go-to lawyer they knew they should retain: Ben Crump.

Crump, a North Carolina–born, Florida-based lawyer with a genteel Southern drawl, had become the most visible attorney in the country associated with the Black Lives Matter movement. Crump had barely stepped out of the shower in his Tallahassee home when he saw five messages from his paralegal stating that the family of George Floyd was seeking his counsel.

Attaining Crump's counsel was no guarantee. During the pandemic, with limited travel, Crump was already loaded up. He had recently taken on the case of Breonna Taylor, an EMT in Louisville, Kentucky, who police shot and killed in March 2020 after barging into her apartment using a no-knock warrant. Taylor hadn't been a suspect, and the officers had pushed themselves into her apartment, looking for her ex-boyfriend. The investigation into the death was moving slowly.

Crump was also working on another case in Brunswick, Georgia, involving a man named Ahmaud Arbery, who had been killed that winter while going on his daily jog. A neighbor thought Arbery looked suspicious. The case hadn't begun to gain traction until video of the incident was released in May.

The two cases were already time-consuming. But then the paralegal sent Frazier's video.

"Torture" is the way Crump first thought to describe it. He heard Floyd's cry, and Crump knew that he had a case that could connect with anyone who'd ever called out for a parent, or any mother who wanted to protect their child. He immediately saw the symbolic significance of what it meant to the country: the physical manifestation of how Black life can be overwhelmed by an agent of the state. In this case, he saw change.

"I'm a Thurgood Marshall disciple, and oftentimes, I try to follow the trail he blazed," Crump said. "And one thing I knew, Thurgood Marshall wouldn't take the case just because it was going to impact the individual or the families. He'd take the case that would have the greatest impact on society."

Crump took the case. He then contacted Antonio Romanucci, a Chicago-born-and-bred attorney who was known for aggressive litigation on police brutality cases. Romanucci immediately began to assemble a small investigative team to put up a civil lawsuit against the City of Minneapolis. Usually, Romanucci's firm takes six months to do fact-finding for such a suit. Romanucci told his investigators that he wanted the work done in two weeks. According to staff who were on the call with him, he told them, "We are going to choke the shit out of the City of Minneapolis in the same way they choked George Floyd."

Crump soon asked the Floyd family to gather over Zoom. There were about twenty people on the call—cousins, nephews, aunts, uncles, his siblings. Most of them had collected at Tate's home; others joined from North Carolina and New York. They discovered Crump and Floyd's father were from the same county in the South. They connected with Crump's big laugh and warm spirit but also appreciated when things got serious. There was no question that the incident was horrifying. But then Crump told them what he felt was the truth about the justice system, confirming a fear they had long had.

He urged them not to take faith in criminal cases run by White prosecutors with White juries. It was rare for state attorney's offices to indict and even rarer for a jury to convict. The reason why, according to Crump, was racism—the jury, the lawyers, and the judges were often more interested in upholding the reputation of the government and its agencies than they were in upholding the value of Black life.

In his practice, Crump decided to craft a different type of strategy: the best way to try to get justice for a Black person was to draw as much attention to the crime as possible. It was a skill he had tried to master with Reverend Al Sharpton, an activist who leveraged his bombast and outspokenness to draw attention to police brutality.

This approach was an attempt to try to control the narrative, to amplify the victim's humanity and raise public consciousness of what went wrong. Those efforts only escalated with the advent of social media, which could make a Black victim a household name with the use of a hashtag. That strategy made the cases of Trayvon Martin, Eric Garner, Michael Brown, and Tamir Rice so well known, even though state prosecutors did not convict the killer in any of those examples.

"About thirty years, forty years ago, Black people would get killed by police constantly and nobody would go to jail and no one would get a chance for civil justice," Crump recalled. "If we didn't start doing what we were doing, making this a public health crisis, they would continue to kill Black people with no consequence. I'm making it financially unsustainable for them to keep killing us."

Crump worked through the civil courts system, in which he had won more than two hundred police violence cases. The burden of proof was lower—the "beyond a reasonable doubt" standard in criminal cases was more stringent than the civil court's standard of "more likely than not"—and thus allowed more debate within the jury. Also, many cities would rather settle than go through an expensive, drawn-out trial about potential wrongdoing.

"We are gonna fight to get to the truth of what happened," Crump recalled telling the Floyd family. "Because there's a chance for justice. That's all I can promise, because there's no guarantee that you will get justice. All you have is a chance."

By eleven a.m. on May 26, less than twelve hours since her post, Frazier's video had become the dominant topic of conversation on social media. Back in Minneapolis, Hennepin County attorney Mike Freeman released a statement promising a "thorough, expedited review consistent with our ongoing commitment to justice. Every person is entitled to fairness; no person stands above the law."

Mayor Frey recognized that kind of language—it was the type he had tried to avoid during his press conference earlier that morning. Shortly thereafter, the police chief began calling civil rights leaders for an emergency meeting at city hall.

Around twenty leaders—from the pastors of the city's oldest Black churches to the local heads of the Urban League and the NAACP—showed up. They sat at a circular table in a room near where Frey held the press conference. They told him how upset they were that their complaints about the police department's treatment of Black residents were consistently ignored; the implicit-bias training instituted in 2014 had clearly not done enough.

"I can't even be enraged," said Leslie Redmond, a former NAACP president. "I'm so tired."

The mayor soon joined the meeting. He told them he wanted their advice and their indulgence.

"I am so sorry," Frey recalled telling the group. But the leaders insisted they wanted more than apologies; they wanted action. They asked Frey to allow the community to grieve publicly and find a sense of peace in this mess. They asked for his commitment to make this incident different, so that the lessons wouldn't fade with the news cycle.

They demanded that officials take four steps right away: The first was an immediate release of the body cam videos to ensure that the tapes would not be tampered with. They also asked that the officers involved be publicly named and then insisted they be fired. Last, and most important to them, the leaders told Frey that they wanted an independent investigation.

"The history that we have with the county attorney, which is Mike Freeman currently, is that we get no justice," said Steven Belton, the CEO of the local Urban League, during a press conference following the meeting. "Ask the family of Jamar Clark. So we have no confidence in these institutions."

"The same old okie-doke isn't good enough for us anymore," added Nekima Levy Armstrong, a former leader of the local chapter of the NAACP. "We demand justice for Floyd."

After the meeting, Frey and the police chief fulfilled one of the goals: by three p.m., Chauvin and the three other officers were fired and stripped of their badges.

As Frazier's video continued to spread, momentum started building on the streets. Hooker, the chess coach, arrived at Thirty-Eighth and Chicago around five p.m. The crowd stretched for blocks. It was bigger, more diverse, and angrier than he could have imagined. There were White women on corners, tears soaking their masks. There were strangers debating whether to hug each other or to maintain social distance. They used sidewalk chalk to draw outlines of bodies on the street, honked horns, and yelled, "Black Lives Matter!"

A microphone and podium were placed on the corner where Floyd died, and the civic leaders who had met with the mayor began to speak to the crowd. They each applauded the chief's swift firing of the officers. But Pastor Carmen Means, a recognizable community leader, urged the crowd not to be satisfied by that action. She told them that the struggle for racial justice would continue to be a long, arduous battle that required commitment from people in the crowd, people like Hooker.

"There's a longevity of this fight that should keep you up at night so that you don't have to worry about your grown-man brother, your grown father, screaming out, 'Mama, help me,'" she said. "My prayer is that those words would wake you up to be in such a place that you won't be here just when the action is going down. But you will vote and wake up city hall and whoever needs to be woken up so that laws change!"

Marcia Howard, a high school English teacher who lived two hundred steps away, started distributing masks and hand sanitizer on the corner. It was her way of feeling more useful; Frazier had been one of her students at Roosevelt High School, and Howard was looking for a way to cope with the fact that her pupils had endured such trauma. Even more so, she had felt she could play a part in healing her community. She had known most of the young people in the neighborhood as high schoolers. She had spent years in the Marines, so she understood organization and leadership, which she figured might come in handy if the protests went awry.

David Embaye, thirty-one, cried all the way as he biked over to Thirty-Eighth and Chicago from his home a couple of blocks away. He had already been feeling low. It had only been four months since he had been released from prison after serving eight years following his conviction on aggravated assault charges. At first, Embaye felt confident his life would change after incarceration. He found a job at Jimmy John's and could finally afford an apartment of his own. Then, he was laid off during the COVID-19 lockdown. That morning, he woke up to a message from a friend with a link to Frazier's video. The friend also had a question about the officer: Don't you know him?

In November 2012, Embaye had been pulled over by Minneapolis police while riding in a car they deemed suspicious after a neighborhood shooting, according to the police report. He got out of the Cadillac and ran. The stories then diverge—police claimed he started to shoot at them, and Embaye says the officers fired first and he felt the need to defend himself. Officers had already shot him several times when he put his hands up to surrender. He fell onto his stomach as officers handcuffed him.

He was charged with three counts of first-degree felony assault and felony possession of a firearm. Following his attorney's advice, Embaye agreed to a plea deal of eight years. When Embaye watched Frazier's video that morning, he recognized Chauvin as one of the officers who had harassed him growing up. And he recognized the street corner on which Chauvin's knee pressed on the neck of the victim. It was the same street corner where Embaye had been handcuffed, on his stomach, bleeding and begging for his life.

"I just seen where they were at, where they were located," Embaye recalled. "And I'm like, they're right there in front of the store. That's where I was laid at. Right there. I was handcuffed right there, just like him. They beat my ass. They had their knee in my back, just like how they were on his back.

There were people out there saying, 'Stop beating him up. It's over with.'"

When he flashed back to the scene, he said, "I just started crying. I ain't never cried, but that made me cry, bro."

He ran to his bathroom and vomited, then looked at himself in the mirror.

"This can't be real," he kept saying, wondering what the point was in trying to live a better life if a police officer could so easily snatch it away. His first instinct was to search his apartment for a gun. He ran back to the bathroom and stuck the barrel in his mouth. It wasn't until he saw his reflection in the mirror that he calmed down. "I'm tripping," he said to himself, thinking it would be better to protest, which was why he decided to head to Thirty-Eighth and Chicago.

Gazing out at the masses of people, crowding in the same place where he had been shot, he fainted. He could not handle being at the corner. He came to after someone doused him with water; then he got on his bike and headed back home.

There were thousands of stories on the street, and their reasons for being out there were shaped by their distinct life experiences and the universal horror of watching George Floyd die. Some, like Howard, felt compelled to help. Others, like Embaye, thought it was the only way they would be able to process what they had seen. And some were searching for a purpose. As Hooker walked through the crowd, he saw pockets of different protests, each with a bullhorn calling for their own brand of justice. There were the White anarchists, Black Socialists, and biker gangs. High school students and parents with babies. They reiterated the same messages: "Black Lives Matter!" "All Cops Are Bastards!" "I Can't Breathe!"

Soon, Hooker wound up with a megaphone in his hands.

Hooker didn't know what to say, so he pulled up a playlist on YouTube. He keyed up N.W.A's "Fuck Tha Police" and played it through the megaphone. People around him began to shimmy and dance. At around six p.m., the crowd marched toward the Third Precinct, where Chauvin and the other officers were based. Some did not realize where they were going; they just followed the angry throng. Some banged drums. Others blasted fireworks. They walked past colorful box-shaped condos and sprawling single-family homes. And as Hooker glimpsed the outline of the police department, he wondered what might transpire when thousands of protesters got there.

As dusk descended, the crowd listened to a group of local leaders give speeches about solidarity and maintaining calm. Rain started to fall, and most went home. Hooker stayed and absorbed the increasingly volatile situation. Even with fewer people, the energy became more electric. It also became more aggressive. A group of protesters scaled the fence of the police station. They picked up trash cans and started throwing them at police cars. They spray-painted the cars with the phrase "Fuck 12"—the number being a shorthand for law enforcement.

Hooker made his way to the parking lot of a nearby Arby's. Soon, one of his fellow union members—a White woman named Jayne Mikulay, who worked at a local library—spotted him in the crowd. She had brought along her twelve-year-old son, Raphael, who had a Black father, hoping to show him the potential of racial justice demonstrations to make a better world. Raphael was thrilled to see DJ, whom he knew as the fun, excitable chess teacher.

Now standing together, they observed a troop of police

officers emerge in helmets and bulletproof vests, carrying guns. Mikulay offered Hooker a ride home as the situation grew tense, but the threat of violence no longer intimidated him. Around nine p.m., they saw a man fall to the ground, struck in the face with a rubber bullet.

People threw plastic bottles at the officers. They climbed atop the roof of the Third Precinct, jumping and yelling Floyd's name.

In the near distance, they saw police fire off a flash-bang, and then a plume of smoke rose in the crowd. Witnessing her son's disbelief at the sight of officers shooting at them, Mikulay, too, felt compelled to stay. She wanted Raphael to understand how aggressive police could be toward members of their community—that the stories that Black people told were not fairy tales. And as a White woman, she felt like she did not want to run away at a time when so many of her Black neighbors felt they could not. And then, a cloud of smoke enveloped them. "Tear gas!" someone yelled, although it was unclear what irritant was used. As they coughed and their eyes watered, Hooker looked down and noticed the canister had been set right by Raphael's feet.

"Right in front of a child!" Hooker said. "They don't care about us!"

The two sides continued their standoff until past midnight. Hooker resolved that this would not be the final encounter; he would return to protest the next day, or until they saw some change.

More disturbing images were now racing across the Internet, this time of the nighttime standoff. Arradondo, the police chief, had encouraged his officers to practice restraint, but more drastic measures needed to be taken after protesters breached the police station. Arradondo told the mayor that things could get worse. There were reports that caravans of concerned citizens were driving into the city—and he figured not all of them would be peaceful.

"This can't be happening," Philonise Floyd thought the following morning, May 27, in Houston. As the next eldest male among Miss Cissy's children, he saw himself as the family's de facto patriarch. He appreciated that so many were speaking out, but he was nervous that his brother's death would be defined more by the violent aftermath than by the crime done against him.

He called Crump to ask the best way to keep protesters on message. Philonise was a grieving sibling and a soft-spoken truck driver—what protester would listen to him? Crump knew one person who might have some sway. He asked Philonise to stay on the line as he called Sharpton.

"Rev, did you see this tape out of Minneapolis?" Crump asked. "The family would like you involved. And I'm taking the case."

The path from Crump to Sharpton to bereaved family had become routine because police violence cases were so routine. The men had developed a choreography of their own: they knew what to say to families, how to solicit celebrity support, how to create media spectacles at funerals. Sharpton's initial reaction was more muted than the public outcry; he'd encountered so many horrifying videos over the years. Still, the country was on lockdown—no restaurants, no sports, no movie theaters. It would allow people to focus on the issue at hand, with less distraction. Sharpton pledged to help in any way he could.

Philonise wasn't thinking of asking Sharpton to do anything extraordinary. He simply wanted him to go to Minneapolis and set a peaceful tone.

"I can do that for you," Sharpton said, and he began to craft a strategy. There was another relatively new activist whom he thought might be able to serve as a mentor. He got off the phone with Crump and called Gwen Carr, whose son Eric Garner had been killed after an officer wrapped his forearm around Garner's neck while he was selling cigarettes outside a corner store on Staten Island.

"Have you seen this video?" Sharpton asked Carr, but by this point, the question was rhetorical. Sharpton invited her to join the family in Minneapolis, and she agreed to make the trip. There was one problem: How would they get there?

Because of the pandemic, Sharpton had not left New York in months—and he was nervous about flying commercial. He made more phone calls.

He reached out to boxer Floyd Mayweather, Hollywood magnate Tyler Perry, and Robert F. Smith, the billionaire investor known to be the richest Black person in the United States, and told them he needed their support for this grieving family. Perry loaned a private plane. Sharpton and Carr would fly out in the next twenty-four hours.

Amid this tragedy, the Floyd family was being connected to an unusual network that linked grieving Black families in this situation with some of the most influential African Americans on the planet. Frazier's video was getting picked up by the local and national news, being discussed on talk shows, and broadcast over and over again. Online, celebrities from the Rock to Demi Lovato to Beyoncé to Kim Kardashian West were expressing their outrage about the killing. Memes recommending that White people start reading more books and watch more movies discussing the impact of systemic racism went viral. And in Minneapolis, Mayor Frey again felt like he needed to step out of the typical bureaucratic patterns to move things along.

Frey held another press conference, this time admonishing the county attorney for not yet arresting Chauvin and the other officers.

"If you had done it or I had done it, we would be behind bars," Frey said. "We cannot turn a blind eye. It is on us as leaders to see this for what it is and call it what it is."

Hooker put on his mask and headed back to Thirty-Eighth and Chicago around five p.m. on the second night of protests. Howard was out distributing hand sanitizer again. Embaye was there as well. Activists were becoming even more provocative. Someone had cut loose a city parks and recreation sign and planted it at the corner in front of CUP Foods, pasting on letters that read, "GEORGE FLOYD SQUARE." Concrete barriers were placed at nearby intersections to block traffic, with protesters declaring the area a sacred space that should not be interrupted by cars, public transportation, or police.

Demonstrators laid teddy bears, flowers, and candles outside CUP Foods. Poets spoke of their rage, and singers delivered meditations of hope. Anticipating an even more aggressive police response than the night before, activists carried water and milk to treat the expected chemical munitions.

The protests started peacefully, with more chants and bullhorns. But as they marched again toward the Third Precinct on Lake Street, a man wearing a black mask and carrying an umbrella broke through the glass at a local AutoZone and set it aflame. Someone used a crowbar to break into a Target; among the items demonstrators stole were provisions like eggs and milk and butter. Hooker saw one person grab a television but remembered thinking, "These corporations have insurance. It will be okay."

As the looting near the Target continued, Chief Arradondo begged Mayor Frey for the deployment of the National Guard. Frey in turn reached out to the governor's office around six thirty p.m., but Governor Tim Walz was unsure if it was necessary. Sending the National Guard had its own risks—especially when the protests had largely been peaceful and the situation so volatile.

The governor's office continued to mull it over while the area surrounding Lake Street erupted in flames. Buildings smoldered, and firefighters could not keep up with the spread across sixteen locations.

At 2:25 a.m., the heat from the flames could be felt a block away. The air smelled like burned rubber. Hooker didn't mind; he felt the actions were the natural consequence of a legal system dragging its feet on arresting Chauvin.

He opened Facebook on his phone and began to narrate the action.

"We tried peaceful protest when they killed Jamar Clark," he said. "We tried peaceful protest when they killed Philando Castile. Tonight, we are trying something new. This is what happens when Minnesota nice is pushed too far. Black Lives Matter, and I stand in solidarity."

Friends and family members were blowing up his phone again, asking if he was okay. When he came home in the early-morning hours, he turned on his camera and explained what he had seen that day.

"I hope there can be solidarity among White liberals and others in the community," Hooker said in another Facebook recap. "Open a history book. Tell me how many fucking things have been done with peaceful protests? I can tell you: not many."

Reverend Sharpton arrived with Carr in Minneapolis the next morning, May 28. He set up a meeting with local pastors to prepare for a vigil at what was now widely being called George Floyd Square. They compiled a list of speakers that included state senator Jeff Hayden and city councilwoman Andrea Jenkins, but Sharpton knew these rallies often benefitted from having someone close to the victim speak out. He looked around and asked if Philonise or another family member was available.

It was only then that Sharpton learned that most of the Floyd family was based in Houston and North Carolina, not Minneapolis. He realized how little he knew about the man whose name they had been shouting.

By now, the rough contours of Floyd's life were emerging in public. When Mayor Frey learned that Floyd worked at Conga, a club located a mere block away from his apartment, something clicked: Floyd was not just a resident in his city; he was someone Frey had nodded to and waved at on his way home. Amid a crisis that was reverberating internationally, the realization only reiterated to Frey how personal Floyd's death was for his city. He tried to keep this in mind when he spoke with the Floyd family.

"I knew him," Frey told them. "George was somebody who had a calm and enduring aura . . . Nothing I can say can make it better."

Frey also figured that his city was about to be overrun by protesters who might not share Floyd's aura. He still hoped he could persuade the governor to deploy the National Guard, insisting that the city's officers could not handle protecting city property from angry mobs while also safeguarding peaceful protesters and dousing fires. Neighbors were taking matters into their own hands. They carried mops and brooms to Lake Street to clean up the debris. The smell of ash still hung in the air. Around four p.m., Governor Walz agreed to mobilize the National Guard. But guardsmen had to receive orders, prepare, and make it to Minneapolis. It would take some time.

In the interim, the vigil was underway at George Floyd Square. A pastor asked White onlookers to move to the back of the crowd in order to keep focus on the pain and plight of Black Americans. Sharpton told the crowd that Freeman had been derelict in not yet indicting the four officers. He encouraged them to continue pushing for change until it came about.

"There's a difference between peace and quiet," Sharpton told the crowd. "Some people just want quiet. The price for peace is justice. Don't just tell people to shut up and be quiet and keep suffering. Give them peace. Let them know the value of their life. Let them know the law works for them, and you won't have to quiet them down. They'll be glad about it. We want justice. No justice, no peace!"

That evening, Hooker was shouting that same refrain as he headed back to the Third Precinct. Once again, the mood that day had started out relatively jovial; demonstrators barbecued and held dance parties. But the festive mood started to change after dark. "They're breaching the gates. They are throwing stuff at cops," someone reported on the police scanner at 8:49 p.m.

The protesters pounded on the door until it burst open. Officers worried that someone might throw an explosive inside, so they put on gas masks and started to flee. More activists ran through the front doors after officers had evacuated.

"No justice! No peace!"

A dispatcher reported that demonstrators were running outside with police jackets and riot gear. The police station erupted in flames. The fire department headed toward the building, but protesters blocked their way, refusing to leave.

"I cannot believe what I'm watching," Hooker said as he observed the flames from a distance. "This isn't stopping until we get systemic change."

The previous night, there had been sixteen reported fires. On this night, there were twenty-three. By the time the National Guard arrived in Minneapolis, it was too late. Derek Chauvin's police station was little more than charred walls and ashes.

Around the country that night, the protests had begun to spread. In Columbus, Ohio, demonstrators broke into the statehouse and smashed windows at local bus stops and businesses. In New York, a protester threw a garbage can at a police officer. There were protests unfolding across the country, in St. Paul, Memphis, Denver, Phoenix, and Louisville, where activists saw a surge of interest in people wanting to stand up and shout support for Breonna Taylor. Six hundred showed up there in a city that hadn't seen a protest of that scale since the assassination of Reverend Dr. Martin Luther King Jr.

The protesters were marching through downtown Louisville when, suddenly, around eleven thirty p.m., they heard a spray of bullets. *Pop, pop, pop.* Demonstrators fanned out to look for cover. Seven people were shot, but no one was sure who did the shooting. News shows and livestreams were filled with images of fires and rubber bullets and gunshot victims, and the White House grew concerned that the country was descending into uncontrollable violence. President Trump demanded that state lawmakers take a more aggressive response. He had promised law and order as president, but he felt like he was seeing none. Around midnight, he began tweeting incendiary language.

"These THUGS are dishonoring the memory of George Floyd, and I won't let that happen," he wrote. He was happy to hear that Minnesota's governor had called in the National Guard and suggested he would deploy the military if needed to suppress violence. "Any difficulty and we will assume control, but when the looting starts, the shooting starts."

Trump claimed to not have known the phrase's racial history; it had long been seen as a dog whistle for police chiefs who employed aggressive tactics against Black residents. Twitter flagged the statement as a violation of its rules for "glorifying violence," and public officials accused the president of encouraging racists who were eager to shoot Black people.

By May 29, the third day of demonstrations, Hooker questioned if the protests were becoming too dangerous to attend. The president was talking about shooting; the governor was deploying the National Guard. On the other hand, Hooker was starting to believe that the protests—both peaceful and otherwise—were making a difference. Around noon, he read that the county attorney announced that Chauvin had finally been arrested on charges of third-degree murder and second-degree manslaughter, saying the officer kept his knee on Floyd's neck for eight minutes and forty-six seconds. His office had also named the other officers involved: Tou Thao, Thomas Lane, and J. Alexander Kueng.

But were these charges worth setting a city on fire? Although he did not participate in the looting (he did start marching in a pair of sneakers someone else had stolen), he did not mind it at first. But then protesters started to do things he felt hurt the community, like scorching post offices and breaking windows of gas stations and Black-owned supermarkets. What kind of protester would want to tear down a mom-and-pop store that helped build up the neighborhood?

Rumors swirled around activist circles, later verified by law enforcement, that white supremacists were embedding in crowds, provoking even more violence and anarchy. The man with the umbrella who broke into the AutoZone turned out to be associated with the Aryan Brotherhood, according to police. Federal agents said a man who had fired thirteen rounds at the Third Precinct was a member of the far-right extremist group known as the Boogaloo Bois. Along the predominantly Black north side, Leslie Redmond, the former president of the local NAACP, said she observed White men shooting from unmarked cars. And near George Floyd Square, neighbors complained that groups of White men would punch out side mirrors and destroy parked vehicles while riding through the neighborhood. The occurrences became so frequent that the phrase "White boys on bikes!" became a warning for those who lived in South Minneapolis to be more aware of their surroundings.

Hooker's internal conflict moved into sharper focus after Mayor Frey announced an eight p.m. curfew across the city. Dismissing the order seemed risky. Friends had been listening to the police scanners and kept telling one another they overheard the term "lethal force." The prospect of death, especially at the hands of law enforcement, was scary, no matter how noble.

His friends figured these pronouncements were scare tactics to ward off the protesters. And why should Mayor Frey be able to dictate the terms of protesting? Hooker believed there might be something good in remaining out on the streets to illustrate unnecessarily aggressive law enforcement, if it came to that. These protests were not for George Floyd alone—the protesters were fighting for a broader movement. They were fighting for themselves.

He deliberated over his choice until he felt he had no choice at all. His solution was on the chessboard hanging on his wall: he thought about an opening chess attack known as the King's Indian. Unlike many other chess openings, the King's Indian does not rely on a practiced back-and-forth between the two sides. It is an aggressive play to try to compromise the opponent's king.

Hooker found that the best counter was a style of play unofficially known as the Caveman. It is a risky, all-in approach that can have dangerous consequences. But when facing a more powerful opponent, it might be the only way to protect the kingdom.

The attacking pieces using the King's Indian were like

police, Hooker concluded. The best defense he knew was an aggressive counterattack.

Around 4:25 p.m., he jumped on Facebook Live.

"I decided I'm going to downtown," he said. "I've decided the logical conclusion, the best-case scenario, is I get arrested. I'm going to write down the phone number of police assistance across my arms. But I'm ... I'm really scared. I don't think the chances are in the majority that I'll die, but I do think it's fifty-fifty that I'll go to jail or die. I really hope that I can go home and give my nightly recap of what the riot was."

As he concluded his video, a twenty-one-year-old White college student at the University of Minnesota whom Hooker knew from chess and video game tournaments reached out to him. Sabastian Moore lived in a house with fourteen other White Christian men who were debating some of the fundamental assumptions of the incident: Do you really think police brutality like this happens on a regular basis? And should we assume that it's all racially motivated? What should we do about it?

He reached out to Hooker for his opinion. Hooker told him police brutality was real and that he should be standing in solidarity with activists. To Hooker's surprise, Moore agreed that he needed to make his voice known. He also wanted to make his own assessment of whether the protests were as peaceful as his more liberal friends were saying, or as violent as his conservative friends implied.

"I'm coming to the protest tonight," Moore told him.

"Wait, what?" Hooker said. "Do you realize the risk? They're saying they can use deadly force."

"Something needs to change," Moore said.

And that evening, the two men set out to see what the protests were like. Joining a group marching toward downtown Minneapolis, they saw police in front of the Gay 90's. Protesters threw things at the officers, and the officers advanced toward them, but the situation didn't escalate further. They kept walking past a pizza shop, and things grew tense when they encountered officers on horseback. As protesters approached, the horses raised their hooves, and one protester was knocked over. The protesters continued advancing, and according to Hooker, some dozen people were Maced.

Around them shadows were setting more buildings aflame. More mailboxes were getting blown up. There were more cops at the gas stations, and Hooker and his group decided to kneel for eight minutes and forty-six seconds, the amount of time that Chauvin's knee was believed to have been on Floyd's neck. The group blockaded the highway and marched down I-35. And finally, they returned to Lake Street.

"I don't even recognize it," Hooker recapped on his Facebook feed, after getting home safely.

Businesses were still on fire. The police precinct still smoldered. Another person started a fire and set off fireworks. There were people still looting the Target, getting Gatorade and snacks.

The Caveman attack appeared to be working. The National Guard could hardly keep up with hordes of protesters downtown, near George Floyd Square, near city hall, near the police precinct.

"We outnumber them right now," he told his viewers. "All we have to do is maintain the same number of people and the same distance we have, because they can't keep up . . . They are spread too thin. They are just trying to protect fire trucks and ambulances."

On this, the fourth night of protests, the city fire department responded to thirty buildings on fire.

Governor Walz was even more aggrieved when he spoke to reporters the following morning, on May 30. He agreed with Hooker's assessment: law enforcement was spread too thin. The National Guard needed to be fully mobilized.

"So, let's be very clear," Walz said. "The situation in Minneapolis is no longer in any way about the murder of George Floyd. It is about attacking civil society, instilling fear, and disrupting our great cities."

The unrest continued across the country. In Atlanta, Mayor Keisha Lance Bottoms pleaded for looters to go home after they tossed firecrackers at CNN's headquarters and set fires in Olympic Park. Protesters blocked Highway 101 in San Jose. Demonstrators threw rocks in Charlotte. Around the country, protests now extended from Bakersfield to Boston, Des Moines to Detroit, Indianapolis, Chicago, Cincinnati, and Charlotte.

"This is chaos," Bottoms told reporters at a press conference.

The chaos on the streets was coinciding with a deeper examination from all corners, as organizations and individuals alike castigated themselves for not doing enough to take down a culture in which a White person could kill a Black man so brazenly.

The Black Lives Matter movement was going mainstream— and while Floyd was the catalyst for change, his death wasn't the only reason.

Since Michael Brown's death in 2014, activists and scholars had been working diligently to break the phrase "Black Lives Matter" into the culture. Community activists Patrisse Khan-Cullors, Alicia Garza, and Opal Tometi had started the viral hashtag after the 2012 killing of Trayvon Martin, and Brown's death served to further galvanize the movement. In the years that followed, a new generation of activists joined the push to protest police brutality, seizing on high-profile killings of Black people including Laquan McDonald, Tamir Rice, Walter Scott, and Alton Sterling. They became regulars on cable television and tended to large flocks of Twitter and Instagram followers. They joined academia and made speeches on college campuses, helping shape the discourse on how the next generation of movers and shakers perceived the issue.

These steps helped to foster a new era of negritude, an "unapologetically Black" aesthetic that blended Black history and civil rights causes with fashion and art. That aesthetic seeped into shows like *Black-ish* and movies such as Ava DuVernay's *When They See Us*, helping set the foundation for Americans to understand and interact with the culture. They made the concept of Black Lives Matter more palatable than ever before. And then, there was the heightened sensitivity about race and racism since the 2016 election of President Trump, who infamously referred to white supremacists marching in Charlottesville as "very fine people," made disparaging remarks about Mexicans and Muslims, maligned a majority-Black congressional district in Baltimore as a "disgusting, rat- and rodent-infested mess," and feuded with a civil rights hero, Representative John Lewis of Georgia. Now in the throes of a pandemic, with sporting events canceled and schools closed and edicts to stay inside, the country could not look away from this videotaped incident of police brutality as easily as it had from others.

Floyd's death consumed the country. A study from the Brookings Institution stated that 13 percent of all posts and 15 percent of all engagements on Twitter included the phrase "Black Lives Matter" in the first week of protest. Local chapters of organizations such as SURJ, or Showing Up for Racial Justice, which helps to train White people how to be better allies to Black Americans, saw exponential increases in workshop attendance.

When Hooker came out to march that weekend, there were even more people, including families, who joined to support. On Sunday, May 31, six days after Floyd died, protesters descended upon midtown Minneapolis and George Floyd Square. They chanted outside the city government center and the state capitol in St. Paul. And still, there could never be an assumption of safety. Around five thirty p.m., Hooker was on his way to a march along the I-35 Mississippi River Bridge when he got a message that an orange truck had barreled through protesters.

The police said the driver came across the bridge by accident, but protesters did not believe them—after all, law enforcement had misled the public about how George Floyd died just six days before.

Hooker continued to remind himself of a version of a chant that was created by Assata Shakur, a famed member of the Black Liberation Army. She had found asylum in Cuba after being convicted of killing a police officer, but her words had become dissociated from her controversial past. It was a mix of Marxist philosophy and Black pride, an encouragement for when the fight for justice seemed dicey:

> *It is our duty to fight for our freedom!*
> *It is our duty to win!*
> *We will love and support one another!*
> *We have nothing to lose but our chains!*

The protests were shaping up to be the largest in a generation. Before the end of the weekend, 4,100 protesters had been handcuffed and detained across the country. Shots were fired in Louisville, and cops were concussed in New York. And in the nation's capital, cars were burned and "Amerikkka" was spray-painted on bathroom stalls just blocks away from the White House. A fire was lit in the basement of historic St. John's Episcopal Church, briefly setting it aflame. As the protests intensified, law enforcement placed temporary barricades around the White House grounds. A group of protesters hopped over them and hit dozens of Secret Service agents with bricks and bottles.

The crowds got as close as 350 feet away from the executive mansion, and President Trump, who had previously told governors to do everything they could to "dominate" the streets, was squirreled away to an underground bunker. Soon, Trump was being mocked for cowardly hiding while sending out tough-guy tweets.

On the seventh day after George Floyd died, June 1, the Trump administration planned an extreme response for enforcing the city's seven p.m. curfew. Downtown Washington, DC, continued to rattle with the voices of protesters chanting in Lafayette Square, steps away from the White House. The perimeter was all camouflage and plywood as officers patrolled in front of boarded-up buildings.

Through the afternoon, protests remained peaceful. People danced and chanted. One person brought out an easel and started painting. At about six p.m., officers with the Park Police, the DC National Guard, and the Secret Service formed a barricade around the White House. Behind them, dismayed protesters observed Joint Chiefs of Staff chairman Mark Milley and Attorney General William P. Barr.

As more officers came to the scene, the protesters asked officers to join them in solidarity and take a knee. To the crowd's surprise, the officers did. Some protesters applauded.

It turned out the National Guard members were not taking a knee to pay homage to Floyd. They were putting on gas masks.

Suddenly, officers thrust into the crowd, pushing down protesters. Authorities fired rubber bullets directly at them, released chemical irritants, and set off flash-bangs. They fired pepper balls and sting-ball grenades. Then tear gas. Protesters ran, many with their hands up, shouting, "Don't shoot! Don't shoot!"

The guard had cleared Lafayette Square more than ten minutes before the city was supposed to be under curfew. At first, the action seemed inexplicable in a city already on edge. But the country would soon understand why.

While the square was being cleared, President Trump stepped into the Rose Garden at the White House to restate his insistence on quelling the riots.

"What happened last night in our city was a total disgrace," he said. "As we speak, I am dispatching thousands and thousands of heavily armed soldiers, military personnel, and law enforcement officers to stop the rioting, looting, vandalism, assaults, and the wanton destruction of property."

As the thick, toxic yellow cloud dissipated at Lafayette Square, Trump concluded his speech: "And now I'm going to pay my respects to a very, very special place."

He started walking toward St. John's Episcopal Church. Behind him were more than a dozen aides, including Barr, Milley, his chief of staff Mark Meadows, and members of his communications team, as well as his daughter and son-in-law, Ivanka Trump and Jared Kushner, who served as his senior advisors. By the time he got to the church, he saw only quiet and peaceful sidewalks—a departure from the chaos that occurred moments earlier. He stood in front of a church sign that stated, "ALL ARE WELCOME." In front of news cameras, he raised his right hand, holding a Bible.

CHAPTER 12

Hear My Cry

DAYS BEFORE PRESIDENT TRUMP stunned a distressed nation in front of St. John's Episcopal Church, he managed to infuriate a mourning brother. Philonise Floyd was surprised when the president, whose remarks had so often inflamed and emboldened racists, called to offer his condolences. Nevertheless, Philonise was eager to take the opportunity to share his pain. Trump called his brother's killing a senseless tragedy, and Philonise hoped to find some common ground.

"I can't believe they committed a modern-day lynching in broad daylight, and I can't stand for that," Philonise Floyd told him. He wanted to implore the president to do everything he could to prevent more deaths like Perry's; to join him in the pursuit of justice. But Trump didn't seem interested in hearing Philonise's thoughts. The president continued talking, as if he was in a rush to end the phone call. And then, he did.

"It hurt me," Philonise recalled. "It was like he didn't want to hear what I was saying."

The family would receive personal calls from an assortment of influential political figures. Senator Amy Klobuchar told them she would push for a federal investigation into the city police department. Barack Obama, the first Black president, took the opposite approach from his successor. He told the family the moment was about them, not him, and that he wanted to know how they were feeling. Joe Biden, Obama's vice president, who had all but formally secured the Democratic nomination to challenge Trump in the upcoming election, also reached out. Biden tried to connect with them by discussing the hardship of losing loved ones so publicly— his own wife and daughter died in a tragic car crash in 1972, weeks before he joined the U.S. Senate, and he was vice president when his son Beau passed away from cancer.

"I know what it means to grieve, but I also know my losses are not the same as the losses felt by the Floyd family and too many others," Biden recalled thinking before talking to the family. "At the same time, I know what it is to feel like you cannot go on. I know what it means to have a black hole of grief sucking at your chest."

There were six or so members of Floyd's family on the line when Biden called. He made sure each of them got a chance to speak about the relative they lost. Biden prayed with them and asked for wisdom and strength and encouraged them to "turn all that anger and anguish into purpose." Biden told the family he wanted to visit them in person.

"My brother is more than just a video," Philonise told Biden. "We want to make sure people know who he is."

"If I'm elected president, I'm going to do everything I can," Biden told them. "Even if I'm not elected president, I'm still going to do everything I can to make sure that the world does not forget George's name and the man that he was."

The family had taken to the sentiment. Before George Floyd belonged to the world, Perry was theirs. While they appreciated well wishes, what Philonise and the Floyd family wanted more than anything was justice for their brother. In the courts. In government. In society at large. They also had to figure out what "justice" might look like.

"I don't want to see him just be a name on a T-shirt, somebody sitting and hollering, 'George Floyd, George Floyd,'" Philonise said. "I don't want that. When I look at him, I want to know that officers are going to fear what they do to others."

Philonise had spent his adult life trying to practice the lessons his mother taught about dealing with racism after generations of plunder and pain: keep your head down, make the best with what you have, provide for your family. But now, Philonise realized he couldn't be passive any longer. If hundreds of thousands of people around the country were speaking boldly about justice for his brother, Philonise felt he needed to do the same. His public advocates had a built-in platform: Reverend Al Sharpton had a talk show on MSNBC. Five days after Perry's death, Philonise and Brandon Williams sat in front of a computer screen and explained to Sharpton and his audience how desperate they were to see something change.

"I never had to beg a man before," Philonise said of his interactions with Biden. "I asked him could he please, please get justice for my brother because I need it. I *need* it . . ."

And then he bowed his head and wept, thinking about how his brother had become the latest hashtag.

"Black folks don't deserve that," Philonise said. "We all dying. Black Lives Matter."

He was learning not to be ashamed of his tears. He would use every tool to apply pressure to the many politicians now in his orbit. And it started to feel like the strategy was working.

When Minnesota governor Tim Walz called to express his sympathy, Philonise and his family were clear about wanting Hennepin County attorney Mike Freeman off the Chauvin case. The Floyds were discouraged by Freeman's track record, and his early actions caused even more concern that he would go soft on cops. Freeman had charged Chauvin with third-degree murder and second-degree manslaughter, though the family had hoped for a far more serious first-degree murder charge. And despite two other police officers having held down their brother, Freeman had charged only Chauvin.

The Floyds had also learned that Keith Ellison, the outspoken former University of Minnesota Law School student and Minnesota's first African American congressman, was now the state's attorney general. They trusted that his history and background would mean he would pursue the case with the righteous rigor it deserved.

The Floyds' request reminded Walz of his many conversations with Valerie Castile. She would tell him how she often felt that prosecutors did not listen to her concerns, and how many African Americans had lost faith in the justice system. Walz admitted to her that he had a lot to learn, and the two would go on to form an unlikely friendship in the aftermath of her son's death.

A former world history teacher who grew up in rural Nebraska and cut his political teeth in a state that is only 7 percent Black, Walz acknowledged his blind spots about racism, listening to podcasts like *Floodlines* from *The Atlantic*, which told stories about how the Black community was ignored during Hurricane Katrina. He felt he needed to use his power to avoid similar mistakes, thinking about something Castile had impressed upon him: when Black people share their pain, not only do you have to listen—you must hear them.

On the afternoon of Sunday, May 31, Ellison got a phone call from the governor. The Floyd family's lobbying had succeeded; Ellison was on the case.

Ellison had no illusions about how difficult it could be to persuade a jury to send a police officer to prison. The *Star Tribune* had calculated that more than two hundred people in Minnesota had been killed by police officers since 2000. Only one of those officers—a Somali American named Mohamed Noor, who killed a White woman—had ever been convicted. Energetic and unusually straightforward for a public official, Ellison also understood the risks for his own reputation among the state's Black residents—and the Floyd family—if he did not go further than Mike Freeman in pursuing charges against the police.

"What if we read all the evidence and read all the law, and we can't add any charges, or we can't charge the other three?" Ellison remembered thinking. "Because one thing I wasn't going to do is be unfair to anyone, including the officers."

So he tried to assemble his dream team. Since Ellison had only a few lawyers with experience prosecuting police cases, he started looking outside for high-profile attorneys. One of the first names that had come up was Steve Schleicher, a former federal prosecutor with a warm smile and a strong Minnesota accent who occasionally did legal commentary on local TV. He and Ellison had not known each other, but Schleicher was eager to get back into the courtroom.

Then Ellison reached out to Jerry Blackwell, who was a founding member of the Minnesota Association of Black Lawyers. Blackwell, with gray hair and an assured, steady voice, had experience representing corporations such as ExxonMobil, so he knew how to get juries to see past potential prejudices. Blackwell felt the call of history and took the case right away—he knew that the team had only one African American junior lawyer in a case that needed Black perspectives.

Next, Ellison picked the brains of former attorney general Eric Holder and Tom Perez, a former assistant U.S. attorney general for civil rights who was leading the Democratic National Committee at the time, for more names. One that came up was Neal Katyal, the former solicitor general under Obama. Katyal agreed.

Then Ellison called Lola Velazquez-Aguilu, a former prosecutor who had expressed concerns to him about how the case was progressing. Velazquez-Aguilu, who was working as in-house counsel at a technology firm, had a reputation in the legal community as a tireless researcher and an adept courtroom strategist, so he asked her to join his team.

Knowing the time commitment and mental toll that a high-stakes case could take on her family, Velazquez-Aguilu was reluctant to agree. But her ten-year-old son overheard the conversation and told her that she needed to defend the man who had died asking for his own mother's help. "I'll be okay," he told her.

"And I immediately thought of these women I had seen during the protests who were carrying these signs that said, 'When George Floyd called out to his mom, he activated all moms;" Velazquez-Aguilu said. "And, of course, the context of my son asking me to do this case, knowing that George Floyd had in his last moments called out for his mother, it just gripped me in a way nothing else could."

Ellison had assembled an uncommonly diverse team of fourteen, including two other Black Americans, two Latinas, and two Asian Americans. None had ever been in the same room or even on the same Zoom call before, but they were all bound by a greater mission than winning one case. They wanted to reimagine how the government prosecuted police.

One of the earliest goals was to ensure that the Floyd family got the kind of respect that Valerie Castile thought she had not received. At the urging of the state's victim witness advocate, Veronica Boswell, Ellison flew down to Houston to pledge he would keep the family involved. As a Black man with roots in Louisiana, he appreciated the Floyds' hospitality and love for Southern cooking. Ellison told them that unless Chauvin displayed complete and total contrition, he was not interested in pursuing "a discount," or a plea bargain.

"This is what an attorney general should be," Brandon Williams remembered thinking.

In Minneapolis, the team considered whether there was enough evidence to go beyond Freeman's original charges. They examined the videos and considered how each officer factored into Floyd's death. As they reviewed the footage, Velazquez-Aguilu noted that Floyd tried lifting his shoulders up to gather more breath but could not because the officers were holding him.

A lightbulb went off for Ellison. The group concluded that the three other officers who held Floyd should at the very least face third-degree murder charges, which allege that the defendants acted without regard to the life of the victim. A conviction is punishable by up to twenty-five years in prison.

The team then explored whether they should strengthen the charges against Chauvin. If his actions were premeditated, they would be allowed to add a first-degree murder charge— what the Floyd family had desired. After all, rumors had spread through the city that Floyd and Chauvin had beef with each other after working security on the same nights at a club called El Nuevo Rodeo. Additionally, a woman from Missouri claiming to be Floyd's old drug counselor told attorneys that he had complained about Chauvin for years.

The woman's story could not be corroborated by any account, and the coworker at El Nuevo Rodeo who had made the claims about Chauvin and Floyd's tense relationship recanted under oath. The club's owner, Maya Santamaria, said she did not think the two men had ever interacted because they worked in two different parts of the club. And she could not even provide receipts to show they worked together at the same time. They could not prove his killing was something personal.

The team also investigated Chauvin's previous police encounters, his life story, his career history, whether he had ties to white supremacist groups. The search yielded nothing for them to go on. Despite the family's wishes, Ellison concluded that they could not prove that Chauvin's actions had been premeditated.

The research into Chauvin did incidentally yield that he was not fully reporting income for his side jobs. Neighboring Washington County then charged Chauvin and his estranged wife, Kellie, for evading taxes and underreporting their joint income between 2014 and 2019 to the tune of $464,433. The unrelated charges, to which the Chauvins pleaded not guilty, would come with a penalty of up to five years in prison.

"We spent long periods of time trying to figure out Derek Chauvin until we just quit trying to figure out Derek Chauvin," Ellison recalled. "We tried because we were just trying to come up with a theory of the case."

Over time, Ellison's team figured they had enough to add another charge of murder in the second degree, for which they had to prove Chauvin killed Floyd while committing another felony. In this case, the other felony would be Chauvin's excessive use of force.

The other three officers would be charged with aiding and abetting that second-degree murder and were scheduled to be tried separately.

One part of the case remained a mystery: the counterfeit $20 bill. Ellison found no evidence Floyd knew the bill was fake. He had recently paid his rent in $20 bills and Sylvia Jackson insisted that the money she gave Floyd for barbecue supplies was real. The two people in the car with him, Maurice Hall and Shawanda Hill, both maintained they had not given him money. It was another potential complication that prosecutors decided to avoid.

To Ellison's mind, the theory of the case was simple: "When you look at [Chauvin's] face, you look at his gestures, and you look at the comments that he made—and he didn't make many—it all added up to, 'I think George Floyd is a piece of shit and I don't really care about his life.' I think he put pride, his own ego, and his own need to dominate in front of everything."

The legal advancements could sometimes obscure that the Floyds were still a mourning family, trying to navigate the death of a loved one. Against the backdrop of a raging pandemic, the Floyd family still had to figure out how to make funeral arrangements. That became more complicated as multiple people they had not really known as being particularly close to Floyd emerged from the woodwork, including several women who falsely claimed Floyd had fathered their children.

And in Minneapolis, they were stunned to see a White woman appear on television who referred to herself as "Floyd's other half." Rumors spread online that she was Floyd's fiancée, his wife, or a crisis actress. Most of the family hadn't even heard of Courteney Ross, and they grew more incensed when she told a local reporter that Floyd would "give grace" to the police officers who killed him—a statement they felt was far too charitable toward the police, an overreach from a White woman who was not even family. At the same time, pieces of Floyd's arrest history became public, and stories spread about his drug dependency, many of which were based in truth, if somewhat cooked up. In conservative circles, Floyd was being vilified as a drug-addicted porn actor who had once hit a pregnant woman and held a gun to her stomach, a reference to Floyd's 2007 aggravated robbery conviction. It mattered little that the victim was not pregnant at the time, could not identify with certainty that Floyd was the one who came to her house, and had alleged that the man who had hit her was five foot six. Nor would critics have sympathy for Floyd's economic desperation, low self-esteem, or efforts to break free of drug dependency.

Amid this turbulent backdrop, Rodney Floyd knew what he wanted to do for a memorial service.

"We want to bring our brother home," he thought.

With a large extended family spread across the country, they agreed on two services. The first would be in Raeford, North Carolina, returning Floyd's body to the land where his ancestors had toiled. They wanted that service to be private and away from all the publicity, to give them a chance to grieve. And then in Texas, they wanted to honor Floyd around his friends and his family, together with his Third Ward community. They would bury him next to his mother.

Philonise asked Sharpton for his advice about holding a third service in Minneapolis, as some were urging. Sharpton's calculation had to do with the larger narrative of social justice and building a movement around Floyd.

"I think you should go to Minneapolis," Sharpton said. "That's the scene of the crime. That's where it happened."

The family would make the city where Perry had taken his last breaths their first stop.

Floyd's death had also allowed for so many other tragic stories around policing in Minnesota to reemerge. Hours before the president stood in front of St. John's, Toshira Garraway, a thirty-four-year-old woman with light-blond highlights and a raspy voice, arrived outside the gates of the governor's residence in St. Paul. If the governor was serious about hearing the voices of Black families, Garraway had newfound hope that he might hear her own.

For more than a decade, she had been trying to find a public official who would take her story seriously. In 2009,

Justin Teigen, the father of her child, was found dead and disfigured in a recycling center. Police maintained they were chasing Teigen when he jumped inside a dumpster, which was then picked up by a truck and compacted, crushing his body. This play-by-play always seemed conveniently fantastical to Garraway. But in an age before body cameras or ubiquitous cell phone videos on social media, Garraway had little recourse. She was a young Black woman with a working-class job and no political influence, no powerful connections, no social media platform—someone on the margins of Minnesota society.

She utilized the skills she learned as a mental health worker to form a support group for others who had lost loved ones to police killings. Most of them were coping with the loss of a person of color. And they understood a sad truth about America: that most families have little success when questioning police officers' versions of events. For every George Floyd, Eric Garner, and Sandra Bland who became a hashtag, there were hundreds of families who comprised a murky middle, whose cases might have been too old or too complicated for the likes of Ben Crump or Al Sharpton to amplify. And without that public pressure, they found law enforcement agencies did not care.

Sensing an opportunity to increase public pressure after Floyd's death, Garraway organized a rally outside the governor's mansion. Hundreds showed up. Unicorn Riot, a guerrilla journalism outfit, was on hand to film the protest. On a bright, sunny day, Garraway stood in front of the camera and hoped the governor would hear her recount what happened to Teigen.

"He was brutally beaten and thrown inside a dumpster,"

Garraway said. "Justin had dog bites all over his body; his skull was cracked in half, a 2009 Emmett Till."

Another woman, Paulette Quinn, described calling the suicide hotline for help with her son Philip, only to have police arrive with their guns drawn and shoot him.

"They say he was running forward, but that's not what happened," she said.

Del Shea Perry spoke about her son, Hardel Sherrell, who suffered a medical episode in jail that left him paralyzed. Police officers didn't intervene as he lost control of his body functions and suffocated. His slow death was captured over nearly a week of camera footage.

"If you think the George Floyd video is bad," Perry said, "brace yourself for this one."

And then the crowd took a knee on the street and raised their fists as Floyd's final words played over a speaker system.

"What we've seen with George is the face of hundreds and hundreds [of deaths by police] who've been covered up," Garraway said, grateful for this moment in which people were taking these issues seriously.

Her voice quavered as she described writing to every lawyer and public official she could. After three years, one lawyer finally agreed to take the case—but by then the statute of limitations for investigating officers had expired. She remembered falling to the floor in shock.

"They didn't throw him in the river! They didn't throw him in the woods! They threw him in the trash! That's what they think of our people."

She then endured a campaign of harassment at the hands of police.

"They followed me; they harassed me with my three-year-old in the car after they threw his dad in the garbage," Garraway said. "They did everything to keep me quiet and I stayed quiet, but it was killing me."

Inside his home, Walz could hear Garraway's bellows. He stepped outside and asked to speak to the person who had organized the rally. Around the time Garraway walked over to greet him, the crowd was chanting, "The whole damn system is guilty as hell!"

"I want you to meet with our families," Garraway said.

Walz agreed. He gave her his cell phone number and pledged to work with her to find ways to improve the Black experience in his state.

"This is a great state if you're White," Walz recalled thinking. "Not so much if you're not."

The next time Garraway and Walz would cross paths, the chants of angry protesters had been replaced by the voices of a gospel choir as they each walked through the doors at Floyd's memorial service in Minneapolis. It was held on Thursday, June 4, in the chapel of North Central University, a small Christian college. COVID-19 restrictions meant that in-person attendance was limited, and thousands returned to George Floyd Square to mourn communally. That morning, after putting on a black suit and a pair of wing-tipped black shoes that hurt his feet, Adarryl Hunter stepped out of his apartment building and encountered Big Floyd's silhouette, which had been spray-painted on a wall across the street. "Sometimes, it feels like he's watching me," Hunter thought.

Hunter made his way to the church, hoping that he could find some solace, but the service would not be the balm he hoped it would be. As Hunter approached the building, he ran into Aubrey Rhodes. The two men joined the line to enter, but neither of them was on the list of approved guests at the door. Hunter figured there must be some misunderstanding and asked the security guard to check again—to no avail. Then, they were asked to step out of the line. Hunter thought about protesting, explaining that they were some of Floyd's closest homeboys. But what good would that do? It felt to him that half the world was claiming they had known Big Floyd.

Rhodes thought about sneaking into the church—he knew no one in the family would object once they got inside the building. Hunter texted Philonise to see if he could sort out the situation but left the church after he didn't get an immediate response.

The family had been so overwhelmed during this trip to Minneapolis that there was not much time to check their cell phones. The night before the funeral, Sharpton had met with the Floyd family at a local hotel ballroom. It was their first time seeing one another in person.

Sharpton was taken by the family's humility—he found them to be loving and polite, but understandably dazed. Sharpton noted how important it was for the public to see their mourning and pain, even when it was uncomfortable. He explained that they always needed to speak plainly because the public appreciated authenticity. He also delivered a truthful message: that this was still America, a place that had long been uncomfortable reckoning with race. He wanted them to expect the journey to get harder.

"We're going to go through some stuff," Sharpton said. "I'm going to tell you right now: They're going to try to discredit your brother. They'll smear the victim, and they'll smear y'all."

Behind closed doors, to allow Sharpton to get ahead of any rumors, he asked them to be transparent about any family drama that might be used to impugn Floyd's character, which could create an opportunity for doubters to excuse the actions of the cop who killed him.

"They'll get so busy beating on me, they'll spare y'all," Sharpton told them. "That's part of the job of activists."

Gwen Carr had also returned to Minneapolis to try to provide comfort to the family. Given her son's lack of justice, though, this meant telling them to not have much faith in the legal system.

"You may think that since you have a video, and you have all the supporters right now, that it's going to be cut and dry," Carr recalled telling them. "I can tell you from experience, it's not a slam dunk ... It's just going to be awful before it's over."

The Floyd family was also being introduced to VIPs like the comedians Tiffany Haddish and Kevin Hart. Unlike other celebrity encounters he'd witnessed, Sharpton noticed that the family wasn't particularly star-struck. Philonise would politely end conversations with the same plea: "Please, help me get justice for my brother." Even when former president Obama called to ask if he could do anything to help, Philonise's only request was that he send better food to Minnesota.

Pallbearers brought Floyd out in a closed golden casket. As Mayor Frey approached the coffin, he took a knee and was overcome by feelings of guilt and sorrow. Reverend Jesse Jackson and Martin Luther King III, Senators Amy Klobuchar and

Tina Smith, and Governor Tim Walz all made their way to their seats near the front of the chapel. They sat behind rappers Ludacris and T.I., as well as boxer Floyd Mayweather and the visiting comedians.

Courteney Ross and her two sons entered the chapel dressed in black, together with her niece, Josie Tucker. Since making those comments about forgiving the officers, Ross had shied away from the press. She had come to the funeral with a sliver of hope that she might be able to clear up some of the tension between her and the Floyd family. She carried a little notebook with a speech that she hoped she'd be allowed to make about her relationship with Floyd, to explain why she had variously referred to herself as his wife and fiancée.

"Language limits the ability of humans being able to define the connections we form with one another," she wrote. "The closest I can come to define our relationship is 'soul mates.' Floyd used his voice and his presence to bring peace and calm in tumultuous situations. He was fun, playful, silly, caring, loving, thankful and spiritual."

She tried to make her way to the front of the church, but a pastor yelled at her and sent her to the back, citing social-distancing protocol—the front was reserved for the family and dignitaries.

She wondered if she would have been dismissed so summarily if she were Black. She thought this must be what it felt like to move to the back of the bus in the pre–civil rights era—and then she questioned if she even had the right to think such things. From her perch at the rear of the room, Ross surveyed the attendees. She noted there were so few of Floyd's friends in Minneapolis at the funeral—no Alvin and

Theresa, no Adarryl, no Sylvia. Yet somehow there was space for Haddish and Hart and Ludacris. She then realized that this service was not a tribute to Floyd's time in the city—it was instead a seminal moment for a social justice movement, a collective exhale for Black people around the nation.

When a boom microphone appeared in front of Ross, obscuring her view, it finally all became too much. She fell to the floor, crying for her man and for her lost connection to him. She then felt a pair of hands on her shoulders, and a woman with blond highlights and a raspy voice whispered in her ear: "Give her strength, Lord. We pray for healing, Lord."

It was Toshira Garraway. She explained to Ross what had happened to her own fiancé, and that the women next to her were all members of her support group. Garraway said that they were there for Ross, to do anything to help her feel better. Garraway's arms and prayers helped calm Ross down. They sat through the ceremony together, holding each other's hand. Ross hoped one day she might have the strength and composure that Garraway had in that moment, but the pain was too fresh.

Unable to enter the church, Hunter figured he'd connect with the family at the memorial service in Houston a few days later and stopped to pick up barbecue. When he arrived at Smoke in the Pit, a restaurant that happened to be steps away from Thirty-Eighth and Chicago, the corner where Floyd had died, a large crowd had already gathered at the square. Hunter was shocked to see so many strangers in the street, praying, crying, overcome by what had happened. He could hardly fathom the unexpected impact of Floyd's legacy.

"They didn't even know him," Hunter recalled thinking. "They're feeling the whole thing, this whole moment or whatever. I'm not feeling that way. I'm just really thinking about the loss of my friend. It was a weird position to be in."

Back at the church, Sharpton began his eulogy. Without naming Trump, he referenced his photo op outside St. John's in Washington.

"Since he had a Bible that day," Sharpton said, "I'd like him to open that Bible and read Ecclesiastes 3."

The third chapter of Ecclesiastes is the famous biblical passage that notes, "There is a time for everything." Sharpton told the attendees that the country was ready to enter a new time in which Black people could have the freedom and responsibility to pursue their dreams without being suffocated by systemic racism, a threat that persisted despite some political, legal, and economic progress.

"What happened to Floyd happens every day in this country—in education, in health services, and in every area of American life. It's time for us to stand up in George's name and say, get your knee off our necks."

The message was similar to calls that Sharpton had made over the years, but he noted a key difference to the audience: "I'm more hopeful today than ever. There is a time and a season—when I look at this time, I saw marches where in some cases, young Whites outnumbered the Blacks marching."

And then Sharpton made a surprise announcement for the next major public gathering for activism on August 28, the anniversary of the March on Washington.

"We're going back to restore and recommit that dream," he said, catching King III, the Floyd family, Crump, and even the National Park Service off guard.

At the end of the service, after the attendees had departed, Ross felt like she still could not leave. Tucker grabbed her hand, and the two walked to the stage. Ross pulled out the note she had written and read it to the empty room, hoping her boyfriend on the other side would hear the words. She had to accept she might not be welcomed in the social justice movement happening around her. She would have to find a way to mourn Floyd on her own.

Even amid a pandemic, the following weekend produced the largest, most diverse protests in American history, as people marched for both Floyd and Breonna Taylor. There had been protests in all fifty states, from small towns like Fairmont, West Virginia, and Havre, Montana, to events that clogged the Brooklyn Bridge in New York. In Santa Monica, California, two hundred surfers held a "paddle out" in the ocean, in which they yelled, "Say his name" nine times, one for each minute Chauvin's knee was on Floyd's neck, and sang happy birthday to Breonna Taylor. Protesters in Louisville released balloons to celebrate.

Around the world, oppressed groups were connecting Floyd's death with their own struggles for justice. Floyd's face was painted in Syria, Pakistan, and the West Bank. Activists in Europe called on their governments to address the legacy of colonialism, leading Germany to agree to return looted treasures to Nigeria. In Britain, crowds pulled down the bronze sculpture of a slave trader named Edward Colston in Bristol, and activists called into question the disproportionate use of stop-and-search powers on Black residents. Floyd's name was spoken alongside Christopher Alder's, Sarah Reed's, and Sheku Bayoh's, Black people who lost their lives in British police custody. In Kenya, protesters connected the treatment of Floyd to the unusually violent enforcement of curfews during the pandemic, resulting in officers killing at least a half-dozen people.

More than ten thousand people showed up at Sydney Town Hall in Australia, to draw parallels to the oppression of Aboriginals. There had been more than four hundred Aboriginal deaths in police custody since 1991—none of which had resulted in charges against officers—and in New Zealand, police were eight times more likely to use violence in interactions with the Maori people.

Back in Washington, the justice movement began to manifest in the nation's politics. Amy Klobuchar, Minnesota's senior senator, following the advice that her friend, the late Arizona senator John McCain, gave to her on his deathbed—to remember that the good of the country should always be placed before ambition—concluded that she needed to remove her name from consideration to become Biden's running mate, instead throwing her support behind the idea of a woman of color in that role. And on the same street in which federal agents had run over protesters, Mayor Muriel Bowser authorized painting "Black Lives Matter" in forty-eight-foot-tall, bold yellow letters in front of the White House—an unmistakable call-out of the Trump administration.

Even some Republicans were beginning to embrace the sentiment. Mitt Romney joined a march in Washington the weekend following the funeral, invoking his father, George Romney, a former Michigan governor, who had said, "Force alone will not eliminate riots. We must eliminate the problems from which they stem."

Biden carried all those feelings when he met the family in person four days after the memorial service in Minneapolis, the night before they buried Floyd's body in Houston. Biden had decided against attending the service—aides were concerned about his presence in the middle of the pandemic, and he said he did not want to be a distraction—so he met them at a restaurant outside Houston. Biden looked in their eyes and hugged each of them, apologizing for the pain they must feel. He asked to hear stories about Perry, and the family shared memories of their fun-loving, gentle, and athletic relative.

The family soon shifted to a discussion of how to prevent such instances of brutality from happening again. Crump discussed the importance of federal laws that would punish police officers who kill so recklessly, as well as banning choke holds and no-knock warrants.

Biden's campaign had already tried to make discussion of race and racism a central plank of the campaign, describing Trump's reference to the "very fine people" who had marched in Charlottesville as Biden's inspiration to get back into politics. He had originally intended to focus his racial justice platform on issues such as homeownership, redlining, and education funding. But after Floyd's death, Biden committed to putting police reform at the forefront of his agenda.

As they discussed these issues, Biden could not stop paying attention to Gianna, who was wide-eyed as she bounced around the former vice president. He had seen an interview with her mother, Roxie Washington, in which she mentioned that her daughter did not know the specifics of what happened to her father. Instead, her mother told Gianna that her father died because he had trouble breathing.

"You're so brave," Biden told Gianna. "Your daddy is looking down and is proud of you."

She turned to him and smiled. "My daddy changed the world."

Her words became a guiding light for the Democratic nominee.

"The first thing going through my head was just how brave and courageous Gianna Floyd was in that moment and is today," Biden recalled in an interview. "And her words stuck with me and they stuck with the world because they are true. But also because they make us see the world through her eyes and the eyes of too many children who have to ask, 'Why? Why is Daddy not coming home?' . . . That question 'Why?' has left an indelible legacy."

Despite that budding legacy, tensions were starting to emerge. To some activists, justice involved another three-word phrase that was being popularized by those who embraced the diffuse, decentralized Black Lives Matter movement: defund the police. The slogan's meaning varied. Some invoked the phrase as shorthand for encouraging city governments to reallocate money slated for police departments to social workers, mental health services, and community programs—and civic leaders were beginning to agree to the principle. In Los Angeles, Mayor Eric Garcetti planned on redirecting $250 million from across the city's budget toward programs for health care, jobs, and "peace centers." In Portland, Oregon, the mayor and the superintendent worked out a deal to remove police from schools, instead allocating $1 million to community programs. And in New York, Mayor Bill de Blasio stated his government was interested in doing something similar.

But the police-funding question also cleaved what had been a broadly united movement. It became a wedge issue on the left, and on the right, it was a sign that liberals were taking things too far. With his poll numbers lagging and close to two hundred thousand dead because of coronavirus, Trump used the slogan to suggest that Democrats would be soft on crime. "More money for law enforcement!" Trump tweeted.

There was also a more radical version of the defund the police movement, which called for the literal abolition of police departments. With growing momentum, activists were trying to get lawmakers to commit to completely reimagining public safety. DJ Hooker, the emerging activist, witnessed more aggressive tactics firsthand when he attended a protest a few days after the memorial in Minneapolis. It started with the usual chants and speeches about dismantling the system, and then the crowd began walking toward Conga, the Latin club where Floyd used to work. But the leaders of the rally took the protest to the mayor's nearby condo building, in an attempt to pressure him directly.

At least one part was working—the chants were so loud that Frey decided to go out and speak to the crowd.

There were cheers when Frey emerged from his building in a baseball T-shirt and a black mask. The leaders of the rally asked the mostly White crowd to make way for Black protesters, so they could be closer to the mayor. Hooker watched as Frey made his way to Kandace Montgomery, a leader of a group known as Black Visions Collective, who was standing on a platform. She asked him to clearly state his position on defunding the police department. Ever since Floyd's death, Frey had earned plaudits for his earnest way of governing that spoke to the emotions around the tragedy. He had vowed to tell the truth. But when he was placed on the spot, Hooker noticed he had defaulted to what had now become a standard way of speaking about this moment.

"I've been coming to grips with my own brokenness in

this situation, my own failures, my own shortcomings," Frey said. "And I know there has to be deep, structural reform in terms of how the department operates."

As Frey started speaking about arbitration and police union contracts, the speaker cut him off.

"Yes or no: Will you commit to defunding the Minneapolis Police Department?" she asked.

The speaker pleaded with the crowd to quiet down so they could hear Frey's answer clearly. She reminded them that he had an election coming up and they could organize efforts to boot him out of office if he said the wrong thing. When Frey asked her to clarify if she was asking about full abolition, she said to him, "We don't want no mo' police. Is that clear? Do you have an answer? It is a yes or no."

There was no more room for ambiguity. Frey stared up at her and shook his head.

"I do not support the full abolition of the police," he said.

The crowd broke out in boos.

"Get the fuck out of here!" the activist said, before leading a chant that quickly spread through the crowd. "Go home, Jacob, go home! Go home, Jacob, go home!"

Frey hung his head as activists continued to heckle while he walked back through the crowd.

"I just kept praying that no one would punch him in the face," Hooker recalled. "Things got that hot."

Frey lingered in the crowd for forty-five minutes, partly to answer questions from reporters but also to make sure no one followed him home. He was emotionally exhausted when he went back in. Between the pandemic and the protests, Frey and his wife, Sarah, began to question whether being mayor was even worth all the turmoil. Other mayors in protest hot spots, including Jenny Durkan in Seattle and Keisha Lance Bottoms in Atlanta, would eventually decide they would not seek reelection. Frey felt an obligation to see his city through the crisis. If the protesters could dig in their heels, so could he.

Defund the police was not the only solution. On Capitol Hill, there was an emerging nexus in the so-called great racial reckoning: New Jersey senator Cory Booker, and Senator Kamala Harris and Representative Karen Bass of California—three of the most prominent Black legislators—were meeting to discuss the framework for a new bill that would address police violence. They wanted to create a national police misconduct database to track problematic officers who changed departments after allegations of wrongdoing. They'd provide money for racial bias training, give incentives for states that banned no-knock warrants like the one that led to the death of Breonna Taylor, and bar the use of choke holds and "airway-restrictive holds" like the one that killed Floyd.

The act had the potential to be the most groundbreaking civil rights legislation in more than a generation, helping to fulfill the long-standing dream of activists who had been marching for change for more than a half century.

"The chants and the marches and the songs are about the same issue that we were marching for back when my parents did it in the sixties and when we did after Rodney King, thirty years ago," Harris said. "So now is the time to act."

Even in a perennially divided Congress, in the middle of an election year, there was optimism that the two parties would come together to pass some form of legislation. Four Senate Republicans renewed an effort to require states to track data related to police shootings, including the race of the person shot. South Carolina senator Lindsey Graham, one of Trump's closest allies, said he was ready to come to the table. He recalled a recent discussion in which Black pastors back in South Carolina told him about the need to educate their younger churchgoers about how to act if they got pulled over by police.

"That doesn't happen in my church," Graham told reporters. "So there's a problem here and we've got to get to the bottom of it."

There was one Republican senator who insisted on taking the lead on the police reform issue. As the lone Black Republican in the Senate, South Carolina's Tim Scott was drafting legislation on his own, hoping he could be a bridge between Democrats, Black voters, and a party that had largely ignored systemic issues on race.

"The actual problem is not what is being offered, it is who is offering it," Scott said. "As a Black man, I get the 'who' being the problem. It's one of the reasons why I went to Senator [Mitch] McConnell and said, 'I want to lead this conversation. I am the person in our conference who has experienced firsthand racial discrimination, racial profiling by law enforcement, and I'm still a fan because I believe that most law enforcement officers are good. But I'm the guy. I am your guy, Mitch, because this is my issue.'"

While big ideas on addressing racism swirled around practically every major institution in America, Ellison and his team decided their best chance of legal success would be to focus on a single incident by a single police officer. In handling a case that was suddenly at the center of delicate national conversations around race and policing, they would not try to make broader points about either subject.

"I believe that being successful in that case is going to be what sparks the broader discussion—the policy, the things that people would want us to talk about," recalled Schleicher, who led the legal team's subcommittee focused on the excessive-use-of-force question. "Being unsuccessful in the case would [be] heartbreaking to the same people who want to have these conversations."

His group tried to comfort the witnesses and help them overcome the trauma they had endured. For example, Genevieve Hansen, the EMT who urged officers to check Floyd's pulse, told prosecutors she would be unwilling to watch the video of him dying. When they insisted and played it for her one day, Hansen plugged her ears with her fingers and closed her eyes and started to scream. Recognizing the mistake, attorneys did not make that request again. They brought nine-year-old Judeah Reynolds a big bag of snacks to keep her calm as she practiced her testimony. They also got Police Chief Medaria Arradondo to agree to say on the stand that Chauvin's actions violated department policy, a potentially groundbreaking moment in which a police chief might break the "blue wall of silence" around police misbehavior.

Schleicher figured a potential jury would be more moved by what they saw than what they heard. There were high-quality video recordings from bystanders, the body cameras of the officers, and videos taken from a street lamppost. The multiple angles would allow jurors to see the killing from up close and far away, views they referred to as "the goldfish" and "the fishbowl."

Prosecutors hoped that the brutality displayed in the videos would show the egregiousness of the officers' actions, muting any arguments from the defense that Floyd's size, strength, or his troubled past could have justified such violence. And the video would allow Floyd himself to be one of the state's best witnesses. Schleicher would be able to slow down and amplify the times when Floyd says "please" and his attempts to calm down before entering the police car, helping to strike down the idea that Floyd was in a state of "excited delirium." In the end, they would introduce at least a half-dozen videos as evidence, guaranteeing the jury would have to watch Floyd die dozens of times during the trial.

"I felt genuinely bad for the jurors having to watch that, sit through that," Schleicher said. "Unfortunately, it was necessary and critical."

While they deliberately wanted to downplay discussions of race during the trial, the legal team thought about how race impacts the court system and the law. These conversations became some of their most contentious internal arguments. Blackwell had been charged with leading the team looking at the medical question—whether Chauvin's knee was responsible for asphyxiating Floyd. But he worried that the typical way that prosecutors address these questions—namely, trusting the opinion of the county medical examiner—was fundamentally biased because of the symbiotic working relationship between police, prosecutors, and medical examiners.

"One pitches, the other catches" is how Blackwell described it.

Blackwell had been suspicious of how often medical examiners provide escape hatches for cops in shootings, and that tendency was already evident in Freeman's original charging document for Chauvin. For example, Freeman had included that Dr. Andrew Baker, the county medical examiner, could not find "evidence of asphyxia or strangulation," even though it is rare to find evidence of strangulation in autopsies. Blackwell also questioned the assertion that "underlying health conditions including coronary artery disease and hypertensive heart disease" as well as "potential intoxicants in his system" likely contributed to Floyd's death. And then there was a statement to investigators from Baker that said, "If [Floyd] were found dead at home alone and no other apparent cause, this could be acceptable to call an overdose."

"Well, what is that supposed to mean?" Blackwell asked incredulously. Based on the charging document, Blackwell thought the "pitch" was a theory that Floyd's fentanyl use meant Chauvin's knee might not be the main cause of his death. Blackwell feared that whoever would be defending Derek Chauvin would make the "catch," leading to his acquittal.

Some of his colleagues argued that they should just build the case around whatever the medical examiner had to say, given that is how they traditionally construct cases. Freeman maintained that his office is "not influenced by external law enforcement agencies," but Blackwell insisted on putting other medical experts on the stand who might have a different assessment.

"I just know, given the undercurrents in this case—of prosecuting the police and the race undercurrents also—I don't trust any of the things that you would typically rely on," Blackwell said.

It was unsurprising to Blackwell that the Black medical examiner they hired to review pictures of the autopsy, as well as the medical examiner who examined the body for the Floyd family's civil case, both questioned whether the incisions that were made in Baker's department were truly deep enough to assess whether Chauvin had choked Floyd to death. The assessment called into question untold numbers of police cases. How often were police excused for their actions because the medical examiner did not cut deep enough to see a problem?

Those ideas would be supported by a 2021 study from the University of Washington that contended medical examiners had misclassified or covered up nearly seventeen thousand deaths that involved police between 1980 and 2018. The researchers combed through open-source data and media websites that have tracked police shootings—compensating for the absence of the comprehensive federal police database that was being advocated for in the policing bills. The study concluded that these mislabelings were slightly more likely to happen if the victim was Black. The report contended that this pointed to a systemic tendency for the medical examiner to give particular weight to an officer's description of the incident and an incentive to support their fellow government officials. In a 2011 survey, 22 percent of medical examiners had admitted to feeling pressure from government officials at some point to change the reported cause of death during their investigations.

Prosecutors determined they wanted to give less prominence to the assessment of the medical examiner. Instead of focusing on the body after death, Velazquez-Aguilu led a search to find experts who could describe what was happening in real time as Chauvin dug his knee into Floyd's neck. They wanted people who could describe how Chauvin's actions—even if their result was not asphyxiation, technically—would have been responsible for limiting Floyd's ability to breathe in the most explicit, understandable way possible. They looked for experts who understood the way the heart and the lungs work. One name kept coming up: Dr. Martin Tobin, an Illinois-based pulmonologist who is widely considered to be the world's foremost expert on breathing.

Tobin was eager to jump on the case and told prosecutors he had been waiting for someone to reach out to him. He was willing to spend hours examining the tapes of Floyd's death to erase any reasonable doubt that it was Chauvin's actions that killed him. Velazquez-Aguilu and Blackwell had a new centerpiece for their case.

As he looked at the continued global support for his brother, Philonise felt Gianna's words to Biden might have been prophetic. One day he was testifying before the United Nations, the next day at a congressional hearing. Guiding him along the way was Sharpton, who he called frequently to go over his speeches. Sharpton helped him crystallize his arguments, reminding him to use the word "justice" often enough that it would ring in people's ears. Brandon started teasing him with the nickname "Baby Al."

Floyd's death also brought his maternal family in closer contact with his siblings on his father's side, Bridgett and Terrence Floyd. Even though they shared the Floyd name, they hardly knew each other. Away from the crowds, Philonise and Rodney peppered them with questions about their history.

"He looked just like my father," Bridgett told him. "He sounded just like him too."

Philonise remained in emotional pain. Nightmares persisted. At these formal hearings, he could not even bring himself to tie a tie—the very pinch on his neck would make him despair over what had happened to his brother. At the family's next major appearance—the March on Washington that was spearheaded by Al Sharpton—he was relieved that he'd be able to go into the late-August humidity in a T-shirt and shorts, nothing formal.

But five days before the rally, on August 23, the world would be rocked by another video. This time, it was of Jacob Blake, a twenty-nine-year-old Black man who police shot at least six times outside his apartment in Kenosha, Wisconsin. Blake, a father of six, lay in the hospital, paralyzed from the waist down. The shooting set off another round of intense protests—especially in majority-White Kenosha, where the violence became deadly. On August 25, a White seventeen-year-old named Kyle Rittenhouse shot three people, two fatally, claiming that he was protecting local businesses.

The shooting added another layer of tension to a nation already on edge. Those worries punctured the NBA quarantine bubble in Orlando, Florida, where the Milwaukee Bucks decided they were too distraught to play game five of their first-round series against the Orlando Magic. They tried to forfeit, which the Magic wouldn't accept because they felt the same way, leading the NBA to cancel all playoff games that night, with some WNBA and MLB teams following suit.

Tensions were still high when the Floyd family arrived in Washington for the rally on August 28. They had no idea how many people to expect, and Sharpton could not fully believe they had managed to pull it off in the middle of a pandemic. Organizers spent hundreds of thousands of dollars on thermometers and masks for attendees and prayed that no one would get sick. As the family settled into their hotel, they realized how sprawling and diverse their networks of support really were.

"I think we're going to have a good turnout tomorrow," Sharpton said to Philonise. He told Philonise that he had run into a White woman in her seventies who had come all the way from San Diego and a White couple from St. Louis. Sharpton had helped to coordinate commemoration marches for the fortieth and fiftieth anniversaries of the famous March on Washington, and he felt the energy was already exceeding those rallies.

Still, Bridgett warned Philonise not to be overtaken by simple affirmations.

"We've lost somebody, and the world still has not done a damn thing about it," she said.

"We've got Instagram justice," Brandon added. "That's not real justice."

On the day of the rally, Sharpton and the Floyd family peeked through a tent erected as a waiting area by the Lincoln Memorial and saw a crowd stretching past the reflecting pool.

"All these people are here for my brother?" Philonise asked. "I can't believe this."

In the sweltering heat, Senator Harris spoke about the importance of combining "the wisdom of longtime warriors for justice with the creative energy of the young leaders today." One of those young leaders was Yolanda Renee King, Martin Luther King Jr.'s only grandchild. At age twelve, she spoke of her generation being the one that "dismantles systemic racism once and for all, now and forever."

After about an hour and a half of speeches, it was Philonise's turn to address the crowd. With his family behind him, Philonise peered down at the lectern and saw a marker that noted the special significance of where he was standing. It was the same spot from which Yolanda's grandfather delivered his famous "I Have a Dream" speech exactly fifty-seven years earlier.

"I'm so overwhelmed," Philonise told the crowd. "Hey, I wish George was here to see this right now."

Philonise got choked up and took a deep breath. Sharpton and Keeta put their hands on his shoulders. The crowd chanted, "George Floyd! George Floyd!" He wiped the sweat off his brow.

"I got it," he said to himself.

Philonise looked back across the crowd.

"Y'all showing a lot of empathy and passion and I'm enjoying every last bit of it right now," Philonise said. "If it weren't for y'all, I don't know where I'd be right now because y'all are keeping me running. I have to advocate for everybody, man, because right now, Jacob Blake . . ."

Reflecting upon the latest video of police violence, Philonise lost control. The magnitude of the moment was too much to bear. He started to weep. He turned to Bridgett to finish his speech, reiterating the call for justice. Tears in his eyes, Philonise stepped away from the microphone.

"I'm done," he said.

CHAPTER 13

Testimony

As the summer of American activism settled into a winter of nervous anticipation, Philonise Floyd and the Floyd family had begun to dread going back to Minneapolis.

"There's just a dark cloud over this city," Rodney Floyd said.

"This is our job now," Philonise reminded him.

By mid-March 2021, with jury selection proceeding more quickly than expected in the criminal trial of the officer who killed their brother, it was time to return.

The air in Minneapolis was frigid when they arrived. Downtown was desolate and gloomy, full of boarded-up windows. They saw images of Perry everywhere, his name scrawled on lampposts and graffitied on walls. The city felt by turns hopeful and combustible, hinging on the feelings of activists and agitators who prepared to unleash more unrest if things did not go their way.

Hours after Philonise, Rodney, and Brandon Williams settled in, their lawyers Ben Crump and Antonio Romanucci insisted they gather in a hotel to watch a livestream of a city council meeting. They didn't question why; they had now grown used to following the schedules that their attorneys planned for them. The city council took a brief recess and then returned to the dais with an unexpected announcement: they had approved a settlement agreement in the Floyd estate's civil suit against the city.

Floyd's brothers and nephew had no idea this news was coming and nervously awaited the decision.

The negotiations had been going on behind the scenes for months. Romanucci's firm was considered the architect of that civil suit, in connection with Jeff Storms, an attorney who had represented the family of David Cornelius Smith after an officer killed him by pressing his knee into his shoulders. When that suit was settled in 2013 for $3 million, the number was considered a jaw-dropping amount for a case involving a police officer killing a civilian.

But that number seemed laughable after the family of Justine Ruszczyk Damond, the White woman killed by Black officer Mohamed Noor in 2017, received $20 million from the city in a 2019 settlement.

"It was ridiculous," Crump remembered thinking. "It actually put a number on White life being more valued than Black life."

For this case, Crump, Romanucci, and Storms all agreed that the Floyd family deserved significantly more than what Damond's family received. But despite the mayor's public apologies and the governor's call to seek police reform, the city's attorneys claimed at first that Chauvin's actions were so beyond the pale of acceptable behavior that they were no more culpable than they had been in the Noor case. The city offered to settle for exactly the same amount: $20 million.

Romanucci was furious. He let the city know that he was so confident in the suit that he wouldn't hesitate to try the case in the civil courtroom if they could not come up with a mutually agreed upon settlement. Over the summer, the Floyd family's attorneys had surreptitiously set up two mock trials in Des Moines, Iowa, a city they felt had demographic and cultural similarities to Minneapolis. They presented the evidence to two groups of eight Iowans to assess potential flaws in the case. The locals found the city at fault both times, even though they still had concerns about Floyd's behavior at the scene.

The city and the Floyd family's attorneys agreed to go into mediation.

"And as the numbers became closer, we could tell that we were becoming partners," Romanucci said. "We both wanted the same thing. I think they were eager to see Minneapolis get better."

That afternoon, the city council announced the city would pay the Floyd estate $27 million. It would be the largest amount ever paid by the city in a police-related death.

The number was too big to process. While the family was relieved that the city had asserted that their brother's life meant something, they were uneasy to have a number—any number—associated with Floyd's life. Money itself could not wipe away centuries of a Black family being cheated, ignored, and tortured by the institutions that were supposed to look out for its citizens. And for a working-class family from humble roots, one whose dreams of attaining wealth had faded for generations after Hillery Thomas Stewart's land was stolen from him, the settlement left them feeling a little empty. It was an unexpected emptiness, for they had hoped that institutional responsibility for Floyd's death would help ease the pain—that was why they had consistently called for justice, after all. But was this what justice felt like?

"Honestly, when I heard, I didn't even care for it," Rodney said as he had dinner with his family a few hours later. "It's a step in the right direction, but honestly, I don't want that money. I want my brother back. I'm thinking about it now, twenty-seven million dollars. I don't even register what that means."

"This is so sweet and sour," Philonise said. "The money is like something that you can do and live for the rest of your life with—it will be good for him and his kids. But my brother being gone, I'll never get that back."

"I wish our mother were here," Rodney said. "We could have given it all to her."

A television producer found a soul food restaurant to deliver food for the family. Over big plates of ribs, tilapia, greens, and mac and cheese, the family allowed themselves a moment to muse over their newfound financial freedom. They had agreed to set aside $500,000 for investments at the corner of Thirty-Eighth and Chicago. Philonise was starting a charitable foundation. They could book tickets to Louisville and support the family of Breonna Taylor, who received a $12 million settlement from the city even though the officer who killed her was never charged with a crime.

And they still had the opportunity to achieve justice through the legal system. Blocks away, lawyers were close to whittling down their list of 326 names to twelve jurors and two alternates in the criminal case against Chauvin. Chauvin's attorney, Eric Nelson, who was being paid by the Minnesota Police and Peace Officers Association to represent him, had tried to move the case out of Minneapolis and Hennepin County, arguing that it would be too hard to find jurors in the area who had no opinion about the encounter. In response,

Judge Peter Cahill instructed the attorneys to look for jurors who had not made up their minds about the merits of the case or, at the very least, were willing to have their minds changed.

Prosecutors were relieved when Cahill ruled that Nelson could not bring up Floyd's criminal record, given that Chauvin had had no way of knowing his past before he tried to pull him into a police car at CUP Foods. Similarly, the prosecution was barred from bringing up previous complaints about Chauvin, including the frequency with which he had used the prone-restraint technique.

The state's prosecutors had been feeling good about how jury selection was coming along. But the Floyd family's muted response to the civil settlement raised even more questions about whether one officer's conviction would help them feel like their brother hadn't died in vain. They needed to do something bigger, in a moment in which something transformative seemed possible. President Joseph R. Biden was in the White House after defeating Trump in November's election, buoyed by Black and suburban voters who were concerned about the state of race relations in the country.

"We're going to go to Washington one day and get that policing act passed," Philonise said. "We need to get justice for all."

"The president says he could do it," Crump said. "And wouldn't it be a great thing if he could sign the bill on the one-year anniversary?"

Rodney nodded his head and smiled wide. "Yes, yes, that would be a beautiful thing."

A little more than two weeks later, *State v. Derek Chauvin* was set to begin. The city became even more militarized.

Governor Tim Walz and Mayor Jacob Frey deployed more than two thousand troops from the National Guard and dispatched more than 1,100 law enforcement officers across the area. Guardsmen in camouflage took up posts on street corners, and military vehicles parked in the middle of intersections. They constructed barricades and ran razor wire around the county government center, forming a fortress to shield those going to the courthouse.

On the morning of Monday, March 29, the first day of opening statements, three men headed out on their mission. Philonise slapped on a mask emblazoned with "8:46," and Brandon donned a necklace with his uncle's face as a pendant. Rodney wore a black suit. As they made their way to the courtroom, a host of family joined them. They invited some of Floyd's closest friends, their lawyers, and the pastors and bodyguards who came to protect them. The presence of Reverends Al Sharpton and Jesse Jackson brought gravitas to the moment.

The entourage stopped by a small park where members of the media had been waiting for them. Crump, who evoked the image of a Black attorney during the civil rights era in a gray fedora and black trench coat, stepped in front of the microphone.

"Today starts a landmark trial that will be a referendum on how far America has come in its quest for equality and justice for all," he said.

"Make no mistake about it: Chauvin is in the courtroom, but America is on trial," Sharpton added. "America is on trial to see if we have got to the place to hold police accountable if they break the law."

Sharpton talked until about 8:46 a.m. He then called for

the Floyd family and those with them to take a knee for eight minutes and forty-six seconds to demonstrate the unique cruelty of the officer's actions.

The group locked arms and took the position, bowing their heads in silence.

"Two minutes! I'm tired already!" Sharpton said as photographers clicked away. "I ain't even halfway there and I'm ready to get up."

Three minutes passed, and Brandon lost so much feeling that he felt that he needed to switch knees.

"Chauvin didn't switch knees," Sharpton observed.

The kneeling gesture was an intentional photo op. But for Floyd's family, it was an illustration of the duality of personal pain and public responsibility. As the camera crews continued to jostle for the perfect shot of them mimicking Chauvin, Rodney thought of Perry, his face digging into the pavement.

"Can you imagine what his cheek must have felt like?" he said. "On that pavement? Damn."

Eight minutes and forty-six seconds finally passed, and the group made their way to the courtroom. Sharpton began the chants of "No justice! No peace!" As they continued their walk, Philonise considered the optics.

"Rev, how about we do this?" he asked Sharpton as he raised his hand into the fist representing black power.

His protégé was getting it. Sharpton raised his fist, too, as the family went inside the courthouse.

Pandemic restrictions made the tiny courtroom feel even more antiseptic. Masks were mandatory except for those speaking. Plastic partitions were placed between the defense, the prosecution, the judge, and the witness chair. Only two reporters could watch the hearings in person, and only one family member from each side was allowed to attend.

No one from Chauvin's side showed up at first. But there were so many members of the Floyd family there that they gathered in an overflow room on the twenty-third floor, filled with potato chips, candy bars, and fruit. The family decided to split courtroom duties between morning and afternoon sessions. Philonise had the first shift, so he made his way to courtroom C-1856. In came Derek Chauvin, wearing an ill-fitting suit and looking more gaunt than he had on that fateful day in May 2020. He was accompanied by his attorney, Eric Nelson, who had slicked-back hair, a closely shaved beard, a Midwestern twang, and a casual approach to his courtroom presentations.

Anticipating this moment, Philonise had practiced not reacting when seeing the man who killed his brother. He told himself, "If anything, he should be afraid of seeing me." He would not allow Chauvin to make him shrink.

Then came the state's legal team, led by Keith Ellison, with Jerry Blackwell and Steve Schleicher following him.

Judge Peter Cahill, a White man with big cheeks and glasses, took his seat at the bench.

"All rise for the jury," he said.

Prosecutors had believed the selection of the jury was the trial's first major success. The group was diverse, multigenerational, and open-minded—a far cry from the all-White juries that so often made a police brutality case a fait accompli. It included one Black woman, two multiracial women, two White men, three Black men, and four White women. They ranged in age from their twenties to their sixties, with eight jurors under the age of forty.

"They say you win the case at jury selection," Schleicher remembered thinking. "You can't. But you can lose a trial at jury selection."

Blackwell stood up. He had recognized the gravity of the task, the historic odds facing him. Still, Blackwell smiled easily and greeted the jury in a conversational style.

"I apologize for talking to you through this plexiglass," Blackwell opened, before discussing the sacred oath that came with being an officer with the Minneapolis Police Department. The department's motto, Blackwell told them, was "to protect with courage and to serve with compassion"—an ideal he said Chauvin did not live up to on May 25, 2020.

"You will learn what happened in that nine minutes and twenty-nine seconds," Blackwell told the jury. "The most important numbers you will hear in this trial are nine twenty-nine."

In the family room, members of the Floyd family gasped and began to whisper.

"Did you hear that, Rev?" Brandon Williams said to Sharpton. "They're saying nine minutes and twenty-nine seconds. It's not eight forty-six."

His uncle had suffered for forty-three seconds longer than they had thought.

Twenty miles north but a world away, on Monday, March 29, as the first witnesses took the stand, Courteney Ross leaned over a fence and stared at a herd of horses on the prairie.

"A few weeks after Floyd's death I heard his voice in my ear," Ross said. She lowered her voice to deliver an impression. "He was like, 'Baby, you need to go horseback riding.'"

A friend of a friend owned a horse farm, so she began

going there with her younger son, James. He was a natural. Riding a horse named Hercules had been the first time she had seen him really happy since Floyd died, so they kept coming back.

As the world grappled with Floyd's death, Ross was trying to make sense of her place in it. It was an uncomfortable position to have loved a person but be bound to him neither by law nor by blood. After the incident at the funeral, she had begun to treat Floyd's death as a private pain that did not intersect with the struggle it represented. She worried that her mourning could seem shortsighted, selfish, even out of place.

Shaken by sadness and depression, Ross had sought refuge in her therapist and a local psychic, in antidepressants and in Trevor Noah stand-up specials. She constantly replayed that last conversation she had had with Floyd, consumed by guilt that her final words to him were so harsh and unforgiving. She had been too unsettled to work, and James had stopped going to school. Sometimes, at home, she would open a plastic bin in her closet that contained some of Floyd's old security-guard uniforms, just to smell them, to feel his presence.

Ross's therapist instructed her to avoid watching the proceedings, to try to carry on as normally as possible. But what was normal these days? Every move she made felt like it threatened her inner peace.

"I've never felt more isolated," Ross said. "Everyone's got their own thing going because of Floyd, everyone's on this journey, and I still don't know what to do or what to feel."

Prosecutors did want her to be a part of the case, despite concerns from relatives who were still upset by her comments when Floyd first died. They hoped her testimony would present a fuller picture of the man she knew. These kinds of testimonies come from what are known as "spark of life" witnesses, a phrase that she liked. Prosecutors warned her not to speak in generalities, like calling Floyd a "gentle giant," because it might give the defense an opening to discuss Floyd's arrest record and history with drugs, as well as their use of opioids together.

Nelson, in his opening statement, had already made Floyd's drug use central to his defense, arguing that the fentanyl and methamphetamine found in his system had ultimately played a major role in his death. Prosecutors practiced cross-examining Ross on those topics, she said, but she would break down and cry or get defensive. They encouraged her to be patient about potentially aggressive questioning. "You don't have to win the case for us," they had told her.

Her phone buzzed. It was her victim's advocate, giving her an update on when she might be expected in court. She needed to be ready by Wednesday morning—two days later.

Ross headed to her old neighborhood, where her friend Leah Prehall worked at a hair salon. Prehall had known Ross's family since childhood, and she would always experiment on her hair growing up. For the trial, they decided Ross's hair should be cut in a simple bob, with red highlights—she wanted to feel confident but not ostentatious.

Ross told Prehall she was nervous about saying enough to make her relationship feel real. She understood why the Floyd family did not acknowledge the role she felt she played in Floyd's life, and a part of her hoped they'd acknowledge her contributions enough to clear the air between them.

"Everyone thinks I'm an actress, that I didn't love him," Ross told Prehall. "Or that I'm the White girl who took him down."

Ultimately, Ross had believed that her race would work in her favor during the trial. She knew there were four White women on the jury, and she hoped they might find a connection to her and her pain. That connection might shape how they perceived Floyd's opioid use, given how much more sympathetic Americans have been to the crisis since it took root in White suburbia.

With her hair done, Ross now focused on her nails. She gathered James, who was playing alone in the back of the salon, and headed over to see her niece, Josie Tucker, who had a nail-styling kit. They decided on black nails instead of red, because it felt more serious.

Tucker asked about the trial, then recalled the last time she had seen Floyd. He had been scared to approach her new floppy mutt of a dog, Ronnie. Floyd told her dogs were not really seen as house pets where he grew up in Houston—they were largely stray animals or there for security. Over time, Floyd tried to get over his nervousness. The last time they saw each other, he started to approach Ronnie gingerly, eventually crawling on the floor to touch her, his nose to her snout.

Tucker understood why Ross loved him. Their big personalities complemented each other. And Floyd had felt so warm, so interested in the world around him. And then, he was gone.

"Do you remember calling me?" Tucker asked as she painted Ross's nails.

"I remember seeing you there at the parking lot," Ross said. "And then I remember going to the park."

That was when Tucker realized how much Ross had blanked out—hours had passed between the time she heard the news from Floyd's nephew and an interview Ross gave to a local television station at a nearby park. In that time, Tucker had raced to the coffee shop where Ross was working and found her collapsed in the parking lot. Tucker had held her tight. Then she had taken Ross to her mother's house, where she sat for hours, catatonic.

"Wow," Ross said as her nails dried, absorbing the details she had blotted out. "Just wow."

"It's so weird because it's like there's two different George Floyds," Tucker observed. "There's this thing that I don't even know, a sign of this movement—and there's just this guy."

"How my therapist says it, she's like, 'There's George Floyd and there's Floyd,'" Ross said. "And if I don't keep that straight in my head, I'll go crazy. Because George Floyd is what people want him to be. Floyd is who he is."

Night fell, and Ross decided to make one more stop, a gesture to both the man who she loved and the symbol he became. After months of avoiding the place, she made her way to George Floyd Square.

Ross parked her minivan about two blocks away from the site. She took a deep breath and stepped out of the vehicle, and the blustering wind ran through her newly cut hair. From the trunk of her car she pulled out a box of forty-six red glasses and forty-six candles.

She trembled as she walked up to the spot where Floyd had lost his life. On this night, to her relief, a group of activists on the corner welcomed her. They had already begun to lay down their own candles, tracing the outline of a blue silhouette of Floyd's body painted on the street. But their candles were small, unable to withstand the wind. Ross's contribution could help guard the light.

Ross knelt and joined them, setting down the candles, one for each year Floyd was on earth. The wind grew stronger.

"I feel like he's here with me," she said.

She went home, and James climbed into her bed so they could snuggle. On her bedroom door was a note that he had placed with purple tape after hearing his mother wailing during a teletherapy session.

"Don't be worried about trial," it read.

Inside the courtroom, prosecutors were calling witnesses to establish the first plank of their case: that the use of force Chauvin exerted on Floyd was excessive and intentional. Eyewitnesses took the stand to describe the trauma of watching a man beg for his life and die in front of them.

"When I look at George Floyd, I look at my dad. I look at my brothers. I look at my cousins, my uncles, because they are all Black," Darnella Frazier, who recorded the viral video of Floyd's death, told jurors. "And I look at that and I look at how that could have been one of them."

Judeah Reynolds, Frazier's nine-year-old cousin, also took the stand. She told jurors what she saw made her "sad and kind of mad."

Charles McMillian, the neighborhood busybody who told Floyd he could not win, grabbed tissues to wipe his tears and tapped his hands on the table when prosecutors played portions of body cam footage of Floyd crying for his mother.

"I don't have a mama, either," McMillian said. "I understand him."

McMillian was so overwhelmed that Judge Cahill called for a break.

Nelson, Chauvin's attorney, didn't ask questions of those

witnesses. But with others, his cross-examination revealed a strategy. In Nelson's cross-examination of Donald Williams II, the mixed martial artist who repeatedly called Chauvin a "bum," the defense lawyer tried to depict a growing mob that could have left his client feeling threatened.

"After you called him a bum, you called him a fucking bum, is that right?" Nelson asked. "You were angry, right?"

Nelson would ask questions using "angry" and "angrier" at least seven times during his cross-examination. Outside observers watching the trial quickly sensed that Nelson was deploying the racist trope of Black men being too wild to contain. During the 1993 trial for the officers who beat up Rodney King, the victim was described as having "hulk-like strength" and compared to a "Tasmanian devil."

Genevieve Hansen, the firefighter who begged for officers to check Floyd's pulse, was already nervous about testifying before she got to the courthouse.

"I didn't want to do this," Hansen recalled. "You can never say anything right. I don't know, being a White person right now, opening your mouth is just scary."

In the morning, she lifted some weights at the gym and tried to pretend like everything was normal. She put on her EMT uniform, and her mother helped tie her tie. On the stand, Nelson asked her to read from a statement in which she had called Floyd a small person—which he, of course, was not. She became incensed. Not only did she feel like Nelson was grasping at straws, but she was also frustrated that he was trying to co-opt her testimony.

Nelson pointed out that she became "angry" at the scene.

"I don't know if you've seen anybody be killed, but it's upsetting," Hansen said.

As the cross-examination grew increasingly tense, Cahill dismissed the jury to admonish her.

"You will not argue with the court, you will not argue with counsel," Cahill said. "They have the right to ask questions. Your job is to answer them."

Hansen walked out so infuriated that she took a water bottle and chucked it against the wall so powerfully that it exploded.

"Genevieve, we cannot get you arrested," she recalled a lawyer saying to her.

"I don't give a fuck!" she responded, before storming home.

The bystanders' testimonies were supposed to illustrate the trauma and the brutality of Chauvin's actions from the perspective of the public. But the cornerstone of this section of the case came from law enforcement agents who testified that Chauvin's actions were a stain upon his badge.

Minneapolis police chief Medaria Arradondo told the court that Chauvin had failed to follow policies on de-escalation, use of force, and offering medical aid. Officers were supposed to use "light-to-moderate pressure" when employing a neck restraint, Arradondo said.

"When I look at the facial expression of Mr. Floyd, that does not appear in any way, shape, or form that is light-to-moderate pressure," Arradondo testified. "Clearly, when Mr. Floyd was no longer responsive—and even motionless—to continue to apply that level of force to a person proned out, handcuffed behind their back, that in no way, shape, or form is anything that is set by policy, is not part of our training, and is certainly not part of our ethics or values."

Romanucci, one of the Floyd family's personal lawyers, listened to the testimony, shocked.

"I don't think the country has ever seen a chief of police come up and speak up against one of his own officers like we saw," he said.

From the legal perspective, he thought the case was headed in the right direction.

On Wednesday, March 31, Ross jumped out of bed and turned on some music. She set out a necklace and earrings bearing Floyd's name on her coffee table, next to an unfinished cat puzzle. She had a special mask with images of Floyd's face, in contrast to the popular "I can't breathe" masks circulating around town. She wanted to remember his life, not his death.

"It's you and me today, Floyd," she said out loud.

Her psychic suggested she bring something of his to the courthouse, and she searched a bookshelf-turned-shrine for mementos. Between a bag of the Fritos he loved and a book he had been reading, she found a silver coin he had received from Alcoholics Anonymous that she took as a symbol of his fortitude.

Prehall stopped by to touch up Ross's hair and help her put on a pair of strappy heels. She gave Ross a green index card with Bible verses from the New World Translation that she had written down, in case Ross got nervous in the courtroom.

"Your strength will be in keeping calm and showing trust." Isaiah 30:15.

"The peace of God that excels all thought will guard your hearts and your mental powers by means of Christ Jesus." Philippians 4:7.

"But Jehovah is waiting patiently to show you favor and to rise up and show you mercy. For Jehovah is a God of justice.

Happy are all those keeping in expectation of him." Isaiah 30:18.

"The Rock, perfect is his activity, for all his ways are justice." Deuteronomy 32:4.

Ross hugged her friend and then called her sister, Brook, who promised to come with her to the courtroom.

"I'm ready," she said.

Courteney and her sister went into the courthouse. Ross had expected guards inside to treat her with some deference, but when she approached the metal detectors, she got mad when they asked her to take off her shoes to pass through security—like any other person. A lawyer told Ross that she could not wear her special mask of Floyd, so she had to flip it inside out.

"Is no one going to acknowledge how difficult this must be?" she asked, growing furious.

She and her sister were forced to sit in a room by themselves as witness after witness was called to the stand. Then, one of the prosecutors told her that an interview she had done with the FBI over the summer had recently been submitted as evidence. He asked that she reread the transcript because they figured Nelson would introduce it in cross-examination.

Ross freaked out. She remembered the interview. Agents investigating the case had pulled out a thick stack of papers from a briefcase. They told her the papers were all the text messages between her and Floyd, containing frank discussions about his drug use, her warnings about Maurice and Shawanda, the heroin overdose from March.

She also admitted to them that she was listed in Floyd's phone as "Moma," which was something that she vowed she would never say in public. It was unquestionable to her that

Floyd called out to Miss Cissy for help outside CUP Foods. But, in Ross's mind, Floyd had also uttered, "Moma, I love you" during his final moments, shortly before he had yelled, "Tell my kids I love them." Judging from the inflection in his strained voice as he said that word, Ross was certain that Floyd was crying out to her.

Ross didn't want to have that discussion on the stand. She worried that others might view that revelation as another attempt to center Floyd's death around their relationship, or that it might dilute her testimony. As she and her sister sat in the room alone, a newfound anger set in. She was not just a spark-of-life witness. She would shoulder one of the most difficult parts of the case.

"We've got to put his drug use back in time, for one thing, to suggest that he may have been habituated to taking opioids, and so could withstand more," Blackwell recalled thinking about Ross's testimony. "We also need to humanize this ... It did not hurt in the trial that one of the persons who talked about it, humanized the drug use, was his former girlfriend ... a White woman."

After four o'clock, Ross declared she had been in the courtroom long enough. Without telling prosecutors, she and Brook drove home.

"How am I supposed to do this?" she cried.

The next morning, Ross was even more subdued. In some ways, it might have been good for her not to testify the previous day. She had gotten some anger out of her system and now had a sense of what to expect.

When she reached the metal detectors this time, she took her shoes off and flipped her mask around without complaint. Inside the courthouse, she went over the plan. As she waited to testify, Ross reread the Bible verses on the green index card and held Floyd's old silver coin.

She stepped into the courtroom and smiled at the jury. The judge swore her in, and prosecutor Matthew Frank asked how she knew Floyd.

Ross's eyes widened.

"Can I tell you the story?" she asked Frank, before turning to the jury. "It's one of my favorite stories."

Ross talked about meeting at the Salvation Army, then cried as she explained how Floyd had reintroduced God back into her life by praying with her. She told the court how much of a mama's boy Floyd was, how heartbroken he had been when his mother died in 2018. She talked about his love of food and his love of basketball, his athleticism.

And then the prosecutor shifted gears.

"I have to ask you if, you know, drug use was a part of the relationship."

Ross's voice flattened and she fidgeted with the Floyd necklace she was wearing.

"Our story, it's a classic story of how many people get addicted to opioids," Ross said. "We both suffered from chronic pain. Mine was in my neck, and his was in his back. We both had prescriptions. But after prescriptions that were filled and we—we got addicted. And tried really hard to break that addiction, many times."

She would spend a half hour on the stand.

"I felt like I had people's hearts in my hands," Ross said after she came out, "and I could see some of the jurors tearing up. I could see them feeling my pain, and that's what I wanted."

She tried her hardest to frustrate the defense attorney when he cross-examined her. After expressing his sympathy for her opioid addiction, Nelson, as expected, dug into her FBI interview.

Prosecutors had prepared her to answer the questions simply and truthfully, confident they could prove that drug use had no connection to Floyd's death. She described her presumptions that Floyd was doing drugs with Hall as speculation. She tried to be calm, but then came the question she had dreaded the most.

Nelson asked how Ross was listed in Floyd's phone. Ross told him the truth: "Moma."

As soon as Ross walked out of the courtroom, her phone and her Facebook messages started to buzz. A stranger wrote: "Not only are black lives not expendable, neither are addicts. I live two hours south of Minneapolis . . . Let me know if you ever need anything."

Her therapist wrote: "I don't quite know how you kept your wits, but you were sharp and true and honest and elegant and loving and hurt and pained, all at once."

Her twenty-year-old son, Gavin, who until then had never heard her discuss her obvious addiction, wrote: "Thank you for telling the truth."

She finally felt like she had done her part.

"I feel lighter than I've felt in months," Ross said.

The first week of the trial exhausted the Floyd family. They had spent their lives trying to emulate Miss Cissy's hospitality, but this trial called for them to protect themselves. They received incessant calls from white supremacists threatening to kill them and had to get used to going out in public with bodyguards. They wore small air filters around their necks to help ward off infection from the coronavirus, given the stream of strangers offering them unsolicited hugs. They also needed to guard their emotions. They had watched Perry die count-less times in the courtroom, in live footage and in slow motion. From the body cam footage of four different officers, security cameras from the outside, from videos of bystanders. In charts and in animation.

They began to fully understand the emotional anguish and guilt that some of the eyewitnesses had been going through. One teenage bystander's entire body was shaking when she came to meet Brandon Williams.

"I'm so sorry I didn't do more," she said.

"You shouldn't have done more," Brandon assured her. "Otherwise, there could have been two dead people that day."

They had to get used to strangers constantly referring to their brother as George; it was like they were talking about a completely different man than Perry. Finding their meals in Minnesota to be bland and boring, each morning they woke up hoping to make it to a nearby steakhouse but were too tired by the end of each day to even leave their hotel rooms.

The family returned to Houston that Friday, eager to sleep in their own beds, hug their children, and collect clean clothes. In less than forty-eight hours, though, they would be back on the plane. As Philonise packed his bags to leave Texas again, he was struck by how much more difficult each trip back to Minneapolis seemed to become.

The first part of the state's case was to show that officers used excessive force against Floyd. The second part of the case had to prove that the use of force killed him.

Dr. Martin Tobin, the pulmonologist at a VA hospital near Chicago, approached the bench. He wore a navy-blue suit and red patterned tie. Blond bangs swept across his wrinkled face. After all the practicing with prosecutors, he had one mission: to deliver the clearest, most compelling explanation that there could be no reason for George Floyd's death other than Chauvin suffocating him.

When Blackwell started to ask questions, Tobin looked directly at the jury and spoke slowly with a melodic Irish lilt. He told the jurors that he had watched the body cam videos hundreds of times, stopping and starting them, to truly understand what was happening in Floyd's body.

"Mr. Floyd died from a low level of oxygen," he concluded. "And this caused damage to his brain, that we see, and it also caused a . . . arrhythmia that caused his heart to stop."

Blackwell tried to connect the arrythmia term with another word that had become synonymous with choking in the trial.

"Is this what some persons might refer to as asphyxia?" Blackwell asked.

"Yes, it has been called asphyxia," Tobin said.

Tobin approached the death as something you might read about in a textbook. He employed animated diagrams of the respiratory system to show the jury how breathing works in an unusual circumstance, then explained his calculation that Floyd's airways had been narrowed by 85 percent—a restriction far beyond what a man Floyd's age could sustain.

Tobin asked the jury to put their thumbs and index fingers on their own necks, so they could understand what Floyd was feeling when Chauvin's knee was on him. He asked them to touch their Adam's apples, a sturdy part of the neck, and then the lower rings of cartilage below that are known as the trachea. Both would be hard to compress. But above the

Adam's apple is an extremely vulnerable part of the neck with little cartilage to shield it from external forces. And that was the part of the neck where Chauvin placed his knee.

The jurors were gripped by Tobin's clear descriptions, the graphics, and the demonstrations.

They took notes and examined their necks when Tobin asked, even when the judge instructed that they did not have to.

Tobin calculated that Chauvin placed ninety-one and a half pounds of force on Floyd's neck, restricting his breathing. After four minutes and fifty-one seconds of being in the prone restraint, Floyd had stopped making any sounds. Tobin explained that was the moment he went unconscious. Yet the knee remained on Floyd's neck.

Prosecutors zoomed in a video in which the jury could see Floyd's eyes make a sudden flinch.

"One second he's alive, one second he's no longer," Tobin testified. He added, "That's the moment that life goes out of his body."

Nelson, the defense attorney, homed in on the use of fentanyl during his cross-examination. He insinuated the drug might have killed Floyd by asking repeatedly if fentanyl slowed down breathing, and Tobin affirmed it did. Blackwell stepped up again to help redirect the witness.

"Doctor, you're familiar with the way people die from fentanyl?" Blackwell said.

"Yes, very," Tobin responded.

"Do they or do they not go into a coma before they die from a fentanyl overdose?"

"Yes, they will."

"Was Mr. Floyd ever in a coma?"

Tobin answered definitively: "No."

The medical portion of the trial was supposed to be more clinical, less visceral than the emotional testimonies of bystanders from the week before. But it did not feel that way for the Floyd family members, and some opted out of going into the courtroom altogether. It was harder to be there without having a shoulder to cry on or another person who might make a quick joke to lighten the mood. Increasingly, they looked to Philonise to represent them in the courtroom. He sat in the chair as two medical examiners, Dr. Lindsey Thomas and Dr. Andrew Baker, led the jury through autopsy photos of his brother at the end of the second week. He saw pictures of Perry's insides and his exposed heart.

The bystander videos had a muted effect on Philonise; the nature of how his brother died already played over and over again in his dreams. But seeing his brother's body reduced to a cadaver was a different kind of nightmare. He could not stop crying even as he left the courtroom, returned to the overflow room, and started to make his way back to the hotel.

"I am breaking down," Philonise admitted that Friday, April 9.

Rodney and Brandon wondered if this new burden was becoming too much. PJ had been set to take the stand as a spark-of-life witness at the beginning of the trial's third week, but they considered that maybe they needed to prepare to take the stand in his stead.

"I used to think it was nice in Minnesota," Philonise said. "But they're killing Blacks."

Philonise and Keeta prayed together for peace. Tiffany Hall, Brandon's childhood-sweetheart-turned-wife, tried to remember what Perry used to tell them when things got stressful or felt like too much.

"One roof, one family," Hall said. "That's still our motto. We'll get through it together."

Adarryl Hunter had an idea. He felt obliged to help the family as a way of honoring his lost friend. But the truth was that having the Floyd family around gave him a sense of calm he had not felt since Floyd had died. They respected his past and looked to him for guidance, like Floyd always had. And after all these months on the margins, Hunter was eager to make himself useful.

"I know where to go," Hunter told the family. So that Saturday, Hunter rented an SUV to show the family the places that made the Twin Cities feel like home to him, starting with the Mall of America. Philonise emerged from the hotel in a yellow tracksuit and baseball cap; Rodney, a black T-shirt and some joggers; and Keeta in an orange sweatshirt. Brandon and Tiffany followed them in an Uber.

They ate Cinnabons and hot dogs and looked for new Nike Air Force 1s. They smelled expensive cologne and wondered how someone could ever spend that much money on a fragrance. As they passed a small area for laser tag, Rodney reminisced about earlier battles on the field. They walked by Relaxing Massage, and Keeta suggested returning there the next time the trial overwhelmed them.

The family marveled at the throngs of diverse and intergenerational shoppers, especially compared with the malls in Houston, many of which tended to cater to a specific race or ethnic group.

"Everyone wants to spend their stimmies," PJ said to Keeta, referring to the stimulus payments sent by the Biden administration to help Americans during the pandemic.

Of course, the Floyd family had also received a fairly big

check—the $27 million for the settlement with the city. Their outsize public presence, and the fortune that others presumed came with it, had yielded its own set of problems. More people asked them for money, to which PJ practiced saying, "Why do you think I got the money? You know he had kids."

"I'm not going to keep the money," he said about the settlement. "I'm going to spend it to improve my community. I'm going to spend it on mental health. All of this [post-traumatic stress disorder] going around."

"You just don't know who has PTSD," Keeta said. "When George lost his mother, he lost everything. And we were talking to him every day, right, PJ? He was over here drowning, and we didn't know."

"I guess it's something he couldn't tell us," he said. "When you're the big brother, you're supposed to be the strongest. It's hard to show you needed help."

Philonise was not sure if he was suffering from his own form of PTSD. He hadn't seen his brother since their mother's funeral, and he wished he could have done more to help get him on track after her death. He blamed himself.

"I should have done more," Philonise said, "but I was grieving too."

Hunter had been thinking about Philonise's new inclination toward activism when he planned the second stop, back in the city. Hunter had recently started working with a group of local "violence interrupters" that had formed after Floyd's death to reduce police intervention in Minneapolis.

The site leader, Muhammad Abdul-Ahad, an enthusiastic man with short locks and a big smile, greeted the family at a strip mall. He said the men were going to walk up and down the main corridor, so people would get used to their presence, allowing them to potentially intervene before local beefs escalated.

Philonise gazed at his surroundings. The apartment building next door seemed pretty tidy, the stores in the strip mall freshly painted and busy.

"This is a tough neighborhood?" he asked.

Abdul-Ahad explained why everything looked so new: The site had been rebuilt after the unrest that followed Floyd's death. This was Lake Street, the nexus of the action. "The street was burning," Abdul-Ahad said. "You see that building that's boarded up? That's the police station where Chauvin came from."

This was new. For all the time they had spent in Minneapolis, Philonise and his family rarely had the chance to see and talk with locals. They learned that the city's Black communities faced the same struggles in obtaining local investments as they did back in Houston. But Abdul-Ahad told them that Floyd's death inspired a new type of collective action, as they demanded better schools and housing.

"And how's mental health around here?" Philonise asked.

"A lot of people right now are suffering from PTSD," Abdul-Ahad said. "They don't know how to deal with everything. They've been through so much."

Rodney and Philonise found something to appreciate in Minneapolis: the activism and the unity of the community in desiring change. "Look at you all working together," Rodney said. "I used to think this place was pretty dark and gloomy, but you all are warming my heart."

Philonise stared at a high-rise tower in front of him as they walked back to the car.

"I can't believe you are telling me that this is a bad neighborhood," he said.

"And guess what?" another member of Abdul-Ahad's team said. "That building is affordable. They don't make housing like that in Texas? Do you have any land grants? Community benefits agreements?"

Philonise shook his head. There was so much he had to learn.

The next morning, Sunday, April 11, Philonise left his family in the hotel to attend Hunter's church. The Creative Church in Fridley, a local suburb, met in a building that looked like a refurbished high school gym.

The pastor began delivering his sermon on the fifth chapter of the Gospel according to John. It is the story of an invalid who begins to walk after Jesus instills him with a sense of power to overcome his sickness.

Hunter was volunteering for the church's audio-visual team and sat away from Philonise. But he felt something divine about that scripture. It was the same one he had referenced years earlier when he told Floyd he needed to work harder to achieve his dreams. "It's all in the stretch," Hunter remembered telling him.

And now that scripture was being used to inspire the brother who believed he had to take Perry's place. If justice could not come by the law, Philonise hoped peace could come through faith.

"When I got to this church, I could hear my brother telling me, 'Thank you, keep going,'" he said after the service. "I feel his presence . . . He's going to allow me to handle it."

Armed with faith and a rekindled connection to the place, Philonise felt like he was ready to testify. He asked one more favor of Hunter: he wanted to go suit shopping at a less expensive mall. Hunter knew of the perfect place in another suburb.

On that same Sunday afternoon, Ross, too, was deciding whether she should step out again. Toshira Garraway, the woman who had embraced her so tightly at Floyd's service, invited Ross to attend an annual memorial for her dead fiancé, Justin Teigen.

Ross was fearful that her blunt nature would lead her to say something that might cause a mistrial. And she was still self-conscious about taking up space as a White woman in the movement for Black lives.

But Garraway begged Ross to do something outside of her comfort zone. Eleven years after the death of her fiancé, Garraway found it hard to draw attention to his case. Ross figured her attendance might garner more buzz, raising awareness of how pervasive the issue of police violence was in Minnesota.

When Ross arrived in St. Paul, she saw hundreds of people gathered in the parking lot of a strip mall near where Teigen had been found. Ross felt a pain rising in her chest and opened her car door to throw up. It had been a long time since she had been around a crowd of this size, and she was nervous about how strangers might respond to her. She considered turning back home. And then, out of the corner of her eye, she saw a lanky young Black man with an uneven flat top and a familiar gait. It was DJ Hooker. The two of them embraced. They had known each other from Edison High School, where Hooker coached chess and Ross had worked as an administrator. They had not seen much of each other since Floyd died. Hooker commended her testimony earlier in the week, and Ross asked him about what it had been like to be protesting on the streets.

"Are you staying safe?" Ross asked.

"I'm trying to," Hooker told her. But the truth was, ever since the protests began, he felt increasingly unsafe. All his activism had led to white supremacist groups doxxing him, posting his name and address online. Friends had assured him that it was no big deal, but then some activists started telling stories about having their cars or homes broken into. Hooker lost weight and sleep. At a low point in January, he called the suicide hotline and was admitted for treatment.

When he shared that he feared for his safety, his evaluator in the ward told him how safe most Black men were from the police. She asked if he could see or hear the white supremacists, implying that he might be delusional. Hooker's response to the white supremacist question: "I think I'm looking at one right now."

Hooker told Ross none of this. Instead, he hugged her, jumped in the back of a truck, and started chanting, "Black Lives Matter! Black Lives Matter!"

Soon, Garraway picked up a microphone. She welcomed the crowd and called for the loved ones of those who had died in police interactions to join her in a circle. She invited them to say a few quick words.

As the relatives gathered, it became clear why she insisted on keeping the speeches short. There were just so many victim families. There was the mother of Demetrius Hill, who said her son died in a botched police raid in 1997. There was the best friend of Travis Jordan, who was killed in 2018 when police came to his house after his girlfriend reported he was suicidal—police said he threatened them with a knife. There was Jamar Clark's family, and Hardel Sherrell's family, and more.

Ross slowly made her way to the circle and caught Garraway's eye.

"We're going to have the girlfriend of George Floyd, Courteney Ross, who is here, speak," Garraway told the crowd. "She doesn't really come out too much . . ."

Ross choked up, but the crowd cheered her on.

"Floyd was my man," she said. "But George Floyd is a movement. And his name speaks for everyone who has been affected by police violence!"

The crowd erupted in applause.

"Say his name! George Floyd!"

Soon, Garraway led the march to the state capitol, where she would release balloons in honor of her beloved. Many of the mothers stayed behind. As Ross made her way to her car, the mother of Demetrius Hill approached her. She grabbed Ross's hand and told her that God would eventually take care of what the American justice system would not, offering as an example that someone ended up killing the cop who killed her son.

"Keep faith," the woman said.

Before Ross could unlock her door, another set of parents who'd lost a loved one approached her. John Garcia and Amity Dimock's autistic son, Kobe Dimock-Heisler, was killed by police in 2019. Officers said he lunged at them with a knife when they came for a wellness check.

Dimock told Ross that the families of victims needed to stick together. It helped them cope. It also allowed them to be more cohesive, so they could comfort the inevitable next victim.

As they talked, Garcia checked his phone.

"They've killed another one," he said. "We've got to go."

It had been an uneventful Sunday afternoon for Katie Wright, a White woman with a round face and stringy hair, in her home near the border of Brooklyn Center. She played with her grandson, watched some television, and caught up with the latest goings-on in the Chauvin case.

Floyd's death was changing how she understood this area, where she had spent her youth before leaving to raise her family in Hudson, Wisconsin. While the schools were good there and the houses affordable, neighbors couldn't seem to get over the fact that Katie was with a Black man, Aubrey Wright. Police profiled and searched him with uncomfortable frequency, and the couple worried about how that kind of environment might impact their little boy, Daunte.

They moved back to the Twin Cities in 2009. Daunte was now twenty years old, still figuring out what he wanted to do with his life. He had the same long face and full lips as his father but was fair-skinned, and Aubrey had hoped that his son's biracial identity would protect him from some of the racism that he had faced. "You know you're a Black man, but you don't have to worry too much because you mixed," Aubrey Wright told him.

After Floyd's death, the parents talked about changing their messaging around the police. Daunte was rambunctious and immature and loved hanging out with his friends on the streets. They warned him about what could happen if he ran into the wrong police officer on the wrong day.

On this Sunday afternoon, Katie turned off the television and set Daunte's two-year-old son down for a nap. Aubrey was at Walmart picking up chicken wings and brats for a barbecue. Daunte came down the stairs and asked for $50 to wash the 2011 white Buick his parents had just given him.

Katie handed him the money, and he called a friend over to accompany him. Twenty minutes later, Katie was lying down for a nap when she got a call on Facebook Messenger. It was Daunte.

"Hey Mom, the police just pulled me over," he said.

Daunte told his mother that an officer noticed an air-freshener tree hanging from the rearview mirror, which is against the law in Minnesota. The officer noticed the tags were expired and was asking him for insurance, but they had not yet received the insurance cards because the car was new.

"Everything's going to be fine," Katie told him. "When the officers get back up to the car, just let me talk to them and I can give them my insurance information."

About a minute passed, and Katie soon heard the officer returning.

"Okay, Daunte, I'm going to have you step out of the car," she heard the officer say. "Put the phone down and step out of the car."

"Am I in trouble?" Katie heard Daunte ask.

The next thing Katie heard was the officer instructing her son to put his hands behind his back. Daunte asked why. And then, Katie heard the officer yell, "Daunte, don't run!"

She heard a quick bang. And then the phone disconnected.

Katie panicked. Did a cop just shoot her son? She tried using Facebook Messenger to call Daunte back, again and again. No response. She tried FaceTime. No answer. And then, after the longest minute and a half she had ever experienced, the friend who was driving with Daunte answered Katie's call.

"They shot him!" she yelled. "They shot him." She panned the camera to the driver's seat, and Katie could see her son, unconscious, blood seeping through his clothing. Katie tried to figure out where they were, but she heard another officer instruct the passenger to hang up the phone.

Katie called her husband, who was still at Walmart.

"They killed Daunte!" she screamed.

"What are you talking about? Calm down. What's up?" Aubrey responded, thinking she was blowing something out of proportion.

"They shot him! The police shot him!"

"Baby, calm down, we don't know what's goin' on."

"I've seen him," Katie said. "He died. I've seen him."

And when Aubrey heard his wife say that she had seen their son dead, he abandoned the shopping cart and drove straight home. By the time he returned to their house, Katie had already taken her grandson and jumped in a neighbor's vehicle to head to Sixty-Third and Lee, where a police dispatcher had told her the incident had taken place.

Everything moved in slow motion for Katie: The drive to the site. Her running toward the police tape. Her husband's bellows when he finally got there. Investigators would not tell them what was going on, who shot their son, or why. No one could clarify how Daunte ended up inside the car—she had heard the sound of the gunshot when Daunte was already outside of his vehicle, running away. Katie and Aubrey stood behind the police tape while police officers walked inside the perimeter, talking to one another and taking pictures.

Everyone was moving but her son, his body covered by a white sheet.

Katie Wright wondered how this could be. In what kind of place, in what kind of country, with what kind of officer would a discussion about an air freshener end with a man's life being stolen? Hardly a man—their son wasn't even old enough to buy a beer. He was their Daunte, the boy they named after Daunte Culpepper, the former quarterback for the Minnesota Vikings. Daunte, the quick-footed basketball player and class clown whose learning disability made it difficult for him to graduate high school. Daunte, who'd borrow money from his father and then give it to a panhandler on the street; who took in a cat that he saw trapped in a tree one day because it was about to rain. He named her Stormy.

For two weeks Katie had watched the great efforts that the state had taken to attempt to persuade a jury that killing a defenseless Black man was wrong. In a country so acquainted with police killing unarmed Black men, Katie knew it was inevitable that some mother would mourn another son. She just didn't expect it to be her. Her son was half-Black, but that was Black enough to be killed recklessly, she thought. Aubrey questioned if he had coddled him too much to avoid being the stereotypical, disaffected Black dad.

Aubrey noticed a Black officer on the other side of the police tape, whom he swore was staring at him with a mix of pain and guilt. He hoped the officer's presence could yield justice—if he was the one who shot his son, Aubrey wondered, maybe a jury would more easily convict him because he was a Black man—just like they convicted Mohamed Noor. And if that officer wasn't the one who shot Daunte, maybe his racial identity would compel him to speak out against the coworker who did.

It was a callous, cruel, realistic calculation. And Aubrey knew he was descending into a racial panic that he had hoped to avoid in Minnesota all along.

Katie had talked to Daunte just before two p.m.; it was now approaching six p.m. His body was still on the ground.

Hooker and a small crowd of young people had left St. Paul and headed to Brooklyn Center, for another night of chanting and protesting as word spread about the shooting twenty miles away. After releasing balloons into the sky for her beloved Justin, Garraway arrived at a combustible scene: the crowd was overwhelmingly young and saw Daunte as one of their peers. Police officers approached, holding batons and wearing bulletproof vests and helmets. But the young activists did not budge.

"I'm going to get killed today," Garraway overheard a young woman say. "And I don't give a fuck because I'm tired of them killing our people."

Garraway tried to remain calm. Another day, another megaphone. She introduced herself to the crowd and told the story of what happened to Justin. She pointed to the families who had left their march to lend support in Brooklyn Center.

"I don't want someone to lose their child today," she said. "We can't give them what they want. We have to be smart."

Garraway explained who she was to Katie and Aubrey and shared her plans for the next day: she would arrive at the police station first thing to demand they immediately release the body cam footage.

Katie and Aubrey stayed on the street until police finally picked their son from off the ground. Hooker and the rest of the crowd kept chanting until ten p.m., at which point they marched toward the police department.

Unlike the Third Precinct in Minneapolis, officers were not willing to abandon this station. About forty-five officers in riot gear stood sternly in front of them.

After an hour or so, the officers advanced, initiating a now-familiar series of events for the activists: yelling, then flash-bangs, and then tear gas. But Hooker had grown so used to tear gas that it no longer fazed him.

Ross had been trying to relax at home that evening. Then she heard her phone ringing again. It was her sister, Brook, wondering if she had heard the news about the shooting in Brooklyn Center. She said she had.

"His name was Daunte," Brook added.

Ross gasped.

"Was he light-skinned?" she asked. When Brook said yes, she told her about their connection.

"Oh my God," Ross cried. "I knew him. He was one of my students."

Ross could no longer treat her pain as singular in its scope, divorced from the protests that were happening around the world. In less than a year, two Black men she had known suffered similar fates. They were two and a half decades apart, raised in communities separated by more than a thousand miles, and yet their lives ended the same way. A truth about Black men and police was becoming inescapable.

And now, old students who had known Daunte were leaving voice mails on her phone.

"He's dead, Ms. Ross!" one cried. "Ms. Ross, I don't know what to do."

"His son will never know his father!" another said. "Every man needs a father!"

"This is too much," Ross said.

That night, in his downtown Minneapolis hotel, Philonise tried again to get a good night's sleep before being called to testify. But he found himself awake at one a.m., tossing and turning. He switched on CNN, where a chyron announced that there were late-night protests because of a police shooting in Brooklyn Center.

"That's the same place I bought my suit," he said.

And then he saw the picture of Daunte Wright. He wanted to keep focus on his task—but the events of the day would not allow it.

He sat on the bed. He woke up Keeta and told her what had happened.

"It's too much," he said.

Philonise could not go back to sleep. He continued to repeat to himself the familiar and comforting phrase: "Justice for George means freedom for all."

But that phrase had consequences. Not even twenty miles away, there was a community crying for the type of justice he hoped to jump-start if he could help prosecutors convict Chauvin.

The following afternoon, attorney Steve Schleicher called Philonise to the stand. Philonise hadn't had much of a relationship with the prosecutors and did not really practice for this moment. His shoulders stiffened as he began to tell the old stories: the big brother who packed lunches and played

Double Dribble with him; the man who talked to him for hours about the finer points of being a truck driver; the mama's boy who wrapped his arms around her body.

"On May 24, I got married, and my brother was killed May 25, and my mother died on May 30," he said, thinking back over the years. "It's like a bittersweet moment when that month comes."

There was one question that surprised Philonise. Schleicher asked him the words his brother would use when he said he wanted to play basketball.

"He'd always say, 'Let's go hooping,' and I'd say, 'Come on, let's go,'" he replied.

Philonise stared at Nelson, awaiting his cross-examination, eager to defend his brother's honor. Chauvin looked down, as he had for most of the trial, scribbling notes. Nelson stood up.

"No questions, Your Honor," he said.

Just like that, Philonise's court testimony was finished. When he and Keeta got back to their hotel, he turned on the television and took calls from reporters.

Pundits remarked that his testimony was successful, and Schleicher could use it to patch up some holes that Nelson was trying to poke in the case. Unwittingly, Philonise also settled a debate over the term "hooping." When he learned that Nelson may have been planning to allude to a definition on Urban Dictionary that described "hooping" as inserting drugs into one's rectum, he was incredulous.

"Keeta, do you hear this?" Philonise said. "How dumb is that?"

Philonise turned his attention back to the other news of the day. There were more details that clarified what had happened to Daunte Wright. Police stated that the officer who stopped him, Kim Potter, was planning on arresting Daunte because he had missed a court case in connection with two misdemeanor charges that he had illegally possessed a gun and ran away from officers the previous June. When Potter tried to put the handcuffs on him, Wright twisted away from her and jumped into his car. Camera footage captured Potter yelling, "Taser! Taser! Taser!" but she reached for the gun on the other side of her belt, something she said she did not realize until after pulling the trigger. She had shot Daunte in the chest. Wounded, he pressed on the gas pedal, colliding with a moving vehicle before skidding onto the curb.

"How can a cop make that mistake?" Philonise asked. To him, it felt like the same kind of cover-up that police tried to commit when they killed Perry. Following the update on the Wright case, the television anchor dispatched to Georgia, where actor Will Smith and director Antoine Fuqua said they would no longer film their latest movie there to protest the state's new laws restricting access to voting.

"At this moment in time, the nation is coming to terms with its history and is attempting to eliminate vestiges of institutional racism to achieve true racial justice," Smith and Fuqua said in a joint statement. "We cannot in good conscience provide economic support to a government that enacts regressive voting laws that are designed to restrict voter access."

"Everything is changing," Philonise said to Keeta.

But then there was more. Crump had agreed to take on Aubrey and Katie Wright as his newest clients in pursuit of justice. He wanted Philonise and his family to meet them the following afternoon, at a press conference.

*

The next day, after the judge dismissed the court for lunch, Philonise prepared for another kind of testimony. He put on a gray hat, his 8:46 mask, and a camel-colored coat. Crump, Rodney, and Brandon Williams followed him out of the courthouse as mid-April snow circled in the sky. This time, though, the ubiquitous news photographers trained their cameras on the Wright family. Garraway and her support group had been waiting for the family too. She prayed over them, in the same way she had when Ross broke down at Floyd's memorial service.

"Give Katie the strength, Lord Jesus, that she needs," Garraway said, bellowing over the clicks of the cameras. "Give all of our families that's being retraumatized the strength that we need to make it through. And I know that you are a God of justice and truth, so they will not get away with this."

A blue minivan pulled up to the parking lot. Ross had resolved to come to the press conference after getting a text message from Amity Dimock about showing support for the latest grieving family. It was beginning to feel like a duty.

Garraway patted Ross on the back and brought her into the circle.

"This is Daunte's mom," Garraway said to her.

"I remember her," Ross said, shaking. "Now that I see you, I remember you from school."

Katie Wright, swaddled in a blanket, nodded, and her face turned red as she teared up. Ross held the mother's hands and leaned in.

"I'm so sorry," Ross said. "Your boy was so beloved. He was such a goofy, lovable boy."

Philonise hung back. He knew he was expected to deliver comfort to a grieving mother and provide passionate quotes to the news media. But the case, this activist life, was still so new to him that it made him nervous. He stood by a tree, trying to find the right words.

"Everyone expects me to know what to say," he remarked. "But this isn't my field. I'm still learning."

Philonise pulled out his cell phone to check the details of the Wright case. He stared at the family. He prayed for strength.

"We're about to start," Crump called out to him.

Crump made his way to the podium, with Philonise behind him. Crump told reporters how it was ridiculous that Wright was even stopped for expired tags in the middle of a pandemic—especially in an emotionally tense period.

"But, I guess," he said, "when you're driving while Black, people sometimes forget memos and initiatives about the realities of life. When you think about the fact that Daunte was trying to get away, he was not a threat to them. Was it the best decision? No. But young people don't [always] make the best decisions. As the mother says, he was scared."

Philonise spoke next.

"It's a shame," he said, shaking his head a little to fight off tears. His voice rose. "The world is traumatized, watching another African American man being slayed! Every day I wake up, I never thought that this world could be in so much disorder like it is now."

He thought about the inspiration he found in the violence interrupters patrolling the streets.

"Minneapolis! Y'all can't sweep this under the rug anymore," he said. "We're here. And we will fight for justice for this family, just like we are fighting for our brother."

*

The trial was picking up steam. On Tuesday, April 13, Nelson had begun to present his case defending Chauvin. He tried to establish Floyd's addiction by bringing in an officer and paramedic who stopped him in 2019, when he said he had taken seven Percocets. Shawanda Hill rolled her eyes throughout the testimony, upset that the legal team who tried to justify the death of her lover had called her. Maurice Hall, who was also in the car with Floyd and had spent more than eighty days in a mental institution to deal with his anxiety, had pleaded the Fifth.

Barry Brodd, a national use-of-force expert, asked the jury to consider the split-second nature of the officer's decision. Dr. David Fowler proposed a number of alternative reasons for Floyd's death. He stated his high blood pressure might have caused a heart attack, or that a type of tumor known as paraganglioma could have secreted adrenaline into his heart, causing an arrythmia, or that Floyd's weakened heart could have been influenced by his ingestion of drugs. He also theorized that Floyd could have died of carbon monoxide poisoning from the car exhaust.

As Blackwell listened to Fowler's theories, particularly around carbon monoxide, he thought to himself, "This is the stupidest thing I ever heard."

During cross-examination, Blackwell asked Fowler if there was any evidence of carbon monoxide in Floyd's system, or if the car had even been running. The answer was no. He got Fowler to agree that 90 percent of paragangliomas do not secrete adrenaline. And Blackwell asked a question to Fowler about how officers should have reacted if in fact Floyd was having a heart attack.

"Are you critical of the fact that he wasn't given

immediate emergency care when he went into cardiac arrest?" Blackwell asked.

"As a physician, I would agree," Fowler responded.

By Thursday, April 15, prosecutors had called thirty-eight witnesses. The defense had called seven. There was one more witness at the scene that would have piqued interest: Chauvin himself. Chauvin told the jury: "I will invoke my Fifth Amendment privilege today."

With that, the defense rested its case. The jury was set to hear closing statements the following Monday.

The third weekend of the trial had arrived, and an exhausted Philonise decided to go back home again. At this point, he realized what he really needed, what he really wanted, was some good food. Back in Houston he packed up some oxtails, okra, rice, sausage, and corn to bring to Minneapolis.

Still, he found himself fretting over the details of the case, unable to fully relax. Philonise told himself that his faith would allow him to will Chauvin's conviction into existence. But as the trial wore on, he could find little comfort in faith alone. The Till family had faith. The King family had faith. So did Mike Brown's family and Trayvon's family and Eric Garner's family. But Philonise told himself all their suffering might have led to this moment, where a team of lawyers led by a Black attorney general might attain a type of justice that had eluded his entire family, his race, for centuries.

There was no turning back now.

"This is just one round of the fight," Philonise said. "No matter what happens I have to keep fighting."

Ross woke up on Saturday morning, and her right side had gone stiff. She wanted to go see friends, but she could not bring herself to think about everything that might happen. She turned on some meditative hip-hop songs and cleaned her house again. She looked out the window and fretted.

Members of the state's legal team found themselves in their houses, trying to prepare the closing arguments. Schleicher was chosen to deliver the closing statement. His job would be to provide the technical instructions on how the jury should think about all three charges. It was an unglamorous part of the job, but Schleicher wanted to make the jury feel something. He cloistered himself in his home office with his Rottweiler, Ranger. His goal was to try to empower the jury in the grand way that his hero, Reverend Jesse Jackson, empowered people.

Schleicher decided he wanted to tell the story of two groups. The first group was the bystanders who happened upon CUP Foods on May 25, 2020. The other group was also random: they were the jury members who were selected to decide a case for the history books.

"One group powerless, the other group powerful," Schleicher thought. "One group could do nothing. Another group could do everything."

He thought about the defense that Nelson had tried to craft to justify Chauvin's actions, particularly the idea that the officer needed to assert such great force because he was trying to detain a large man who appeared to be on drugs. That idea played into the worry that Floyd might have been in a state of excited delirium, which would have given him superhuman strength. Schleicher wanted to dismantle the argument before Nelson could attempt it.

To an audience of Ranger, he tried out the line "George Floyd was not showing superhuman strength." But it didn't have enough zing.

Then, it came to him: "There are no superhumans. Only humans."

That was the type of line he hoped Jesse Jackson would love.

He arrived at the courthouse at six a.m. on Monday, April 19, 2021, the day of closing arguments. Two hours later, the family arrived in the park outside the courthouse, with a host of dignitaries, including Sharpton, Jackson, Representative Ilhan Omar of Minnesota, Representative Sheila Jackson Lee of Texas, and some of Crump's other clients. They made the familiar walk inside the building, raising fists in the air, as Philonise had suggested on that very first day.

In the family room, Sharpton again led the prayer. He prayed once more for wisdom, fairness, and justice. Jackson then asked if he could also pray. The family held hands tightly as one of the nation's most prominent civil rights leaders delivered a blessing. At seventy-nine, Jackson could hardly stand on his own without assistance. Parkinson's had robbed Jackson of his booming voice. He stuttered softly, and many in the room strained to hear what he was saying.

Then Jackson said: "Repeat the words after me: I am somebody. In all things, you must not lose hope. Keep hope alive."

And Philonise and the Floyd family followed his lead, amplifying the message so everyone in the room could hear. The family elected him again to go sit in the courtroom.

"His name was George Perry Floyd Jr.," Schleicher began.

"The defendant stayed on top of him for nine minutes and twenty-nine seconds," he continued. "So desperate to breathe, he pushed with his face to lift himself, to open his chest, to give his lungs room to breathe. The pavement tearing into his skin. George Floyd losing strength, not superhuman strength. There was no superhuman strength that day.

"There's no superhuman strength because there's no such thing as a superhuman. Those exist in comic books, and Thirty-Eighth and Chicago is a very real place."

Schleicher then focused on the defendant, who he described as a man who was too proud to listen to the crowd and unrelenting in his cruelty.

Schleicher's statement clocked in at about one hour and forty-five minutes. He finished with the prose that he had practiced before his dog.

"At his death [Floyd] was surrounded by strangers," Schleicher said. "They were strangers, but you can't say they didn't care . . . They were utterly powerless, because even they respected the badge.

"*You* got a summons in the mail," Schleicher continued. "And here you are, all converged on one spot. Now, our system, we have power . . . The state, we have power, but we cannot convict the defendant. The judge has power, but he cannot convict the defendant. That power belongs to you."

Nelson spoke next. He thanked the jury for their dedication and apologized in advance for being long-winded. "I only get one bite of the apple here," Nelson said, because Blackwell was scheduled to give a final rebuttal.

Nelson moved from analogies about apples to needing all the ingredients necessary to bake chocolate chip cookies. "Criminal law works the same way," he told them. And he then suggested they didn't have all the ingredients for a conviction because they were not considering the totality of the circumstances. He asked jurors not to consider only the nine minutes and twenty-nine seconds that Chauvin kept his knee on Floyd's neck, but the seventeen minutes that preceded them. He went through Fowler's alternative theories and asked jurors to view the case from the perspective of a training officer getting to a scene where two rookie cops were trying to detain a large man, the police car rocking back and forth.

Nelson then displayed an unflattering freeze frame of Floyd in the police car, his mouth gaping wide, brow furrowed, looking as menacing as possible.

Blackwell thought to himself, "This isn't a dog whistle; it's a bullhorn." Blackwell tried to keep notes to prepare his rebuttal but soon had to pinch his wrists to keep from falling asleep.

As Philonise listened to Nelson continue, it all sounded like excuses. "Why is he talking for so long?" he remarked to himself.

Nelson spoke for close to two hours, until Judge Cahill eventually interrupted to call a lunch break.

After lunch, Nelson spoke for another fifty minutes. He ended with hypotheses about others involved in the incident.

"There's lots of what-ifs that could have happened, what could have happened, what should have happened," Nelson continued. "When you as members of the jury conclude your analysis of the evidence, when you review the entirety of the evidence, when you review the law as written, and you conclude it all within this—all within a thorough, honest analysis—the state has failed to prove its case beyond a reasonable doubt, and, therefore, Mr. Chauvin should be found not guilty of all counts."

Given his own exhaustion, Blackwell figured his rebuttal should not go very long. And the role of race partly informed how he thought about it. Blackwell didn't think he could afford to try to use the booming, literary prose to which Schleicher had aspired. He was still a Black man—one who knew that the same stereotypes about seeming angry, or too aggressive, or even too uppity could apply to him as much as they did to George Floyd.

Blackwell reminded jurors that their instructions did not stipulate that Chauvin's actions had to be the sole cause of Floyd's death, but a substantial one. Ultimately, Blackwell told them the case was "so simple a child could understand it."

"In fact, a child did understand it, when the nine-year-old girl said, 'Get off of him,'" Blackwell said.

After about fifteen minutes, Blackwell concluded it was time to land the plane. He did not want to end with thankyous or niceties, but with a powerful statement that picked up on Schleicher's theme of humanity. It had been a line that he had been working on since he learned he would get the final word in the Chauvin trial.

"We were told, for example, that Mr. Floyd died because his heart was too big," he told the jury. "You heard that testimony. And now, having seen all the evidence, having heard all the evidence, you know the truth. And the truth of the matter is that the reason George Floyd is dead is because Mr. Chauvin's heart was too small."

When the trial was over, Ellison told Schleicher that the Floyd family wanted to thank him in person. They took the elevators downstairs. When Schleicher walked into the room, he saw a man with his arm extended. It belonged to Jesse Jackson.

"Good job," Jackson said.

"All my life I've wanted to talk like you!" Schleicher said, stifling the lump in his throat.

The family laughed. Meanwhile, Philonise kept noticing a strange number popping up on his phone every five minutes. Philonise was not particularly interested in answering, because he recognized the number as belonging to Donald Trump.

Then he remembered Trump had previously called him from the White House and that he was no longer there. The person calling Philonise was Joe Biden, wishing his family well as they waited for the verdict.

All they could do now was wait. Their lawyers had different theories. Romanucci anticipated the jury might take all week, but Crump kept telling people that the trial would soon be over.

"It's a straightforward case," Crump insisted.

The next day, April 20, the Floyd family milled about the hotel lobby, huddling around a big bar with overhead televisions or in side offices to conduct television interviews.

At one point, Romanucci brought them all into a side room to listen to a woman on a conference call.

"Hello, beautiful family, this is Nancy."

It was Nancy Pelosi, Speaker of the House.

Immediately, she began to talk about the passage of a police reform bill. "We're not giving up until we get something passed," Pelosi said. "Only if you think it's worthy of him. Beautiful George has given his life for justice, we all saw it."

Meanwhile, an anxious Keith Ellison headed to the courthouse to await word from the jury, where he joined Schleicher and Blackwell.

And far away from the brokers of power and change, Ross

stayed in her basement apartment trying to figure out how to avoid the verdict. She and James had tried to go back to the horse farm, but the owners warned them that they might see "White Lives Matter" signs on the way there. She gathered some disposable mops and a can of Scrubbing Bubbles and picked up some of her niece's jobs cleaning houses. She finished the cat puzzle. She played with LEGO sets.

The only thing that kept her calm was that she, too, had felt Floyd's spirit, which she said kept telling her everything would be fine.

Ross decided it was better for her and James to get out of the house. They ate at a Mexican restaurant and then stopped at a spiritual bookstore that she'd heard about a few doors down. It sold sage and mood rocks and books about inner peace.

"We have an astrologer and tarot-card reader today," the store manager told Ross when she walked in. Ross figured she could indulge. Near the front window of the store, Della D-Z sat with a deck of tarot cards under a translucent white canopy. Della, who uses "they" pronouns, wore a black T-shirt and sported a haircut with the sides shaved.

"Do you have anything in mind, or do you want a general reading?" the fortune-teller asked.

"Just general," Ross said.

Della set down three cards. "Past, present, future."

The fortune-teller flipped the first card. Past.

"This is temperance," Della said. "It's about balance, seeking balance ... Combining things that are not the same. It looked like in the past you had found that balance."

They flipped the second card. Present. It was the five of pentacles.

Della stared into Ross's eyes.

"You're grieving," they said. "It's about something you've already experienced or something that's pending. But usually something that you've experienced."

Ross's heart started to beat faster, and Della flipped the third card. Future.

"The future is the fool," the fortune-teller said. "You might be believing in something and coming off as foolish. This card is an encouragement that you're not wrong hoping about the future, and you're not being naive. The grief will be over. A lot of people ask, 'When?'" the fortune-teller continued. "It's hard to pinpoint the exact time when this grief will be over. But it looks like a lot of positive stuff is going to be happening for you in the future."

Ross raised her eyebrow and looked at the fortune-teller.

"You know we are all waiting on the verdict in the Derek Chauvin trial, right?" Ross asked. "George Floyd was my boyfriend. It's just nerve-racking to, kind of, like, sit here, having to wait and never know when we have to wait until . . ."

The fortune-teller nodded.

"And it's like, what am I waiting for? And then, like, what does that mean? What's that next step?"

Ross's phone buzzed. It was her mother. The verdict was in.

"Mom, why do you look so nervous if you know he's guilty?" James asked as Ross drove him home.

"It's a lot to take in right now," she said. She dropped him off, then headed to the courthouse downtown. "It's just a normal drive," she told herself.

On the opposite side of the highway, Ross observed cars

rushing to get out of downtown. Business owners were boarding up their shops.

"Look at all these White people running away," Ross yelled. "Why are White people always running away?"

She picked up Garraway, and the two women arrived in front of the courthouse and immediately found themselves swarmed by reporters. The afternoon sun glinted off buildings. Behind them, DJ Hooker had taken the bullhorn. He stood on a platform and started shouting, "Black lives, they matter here!"

The Floyd family, meanwhile, were also racing back to the courthouse. They passed the razor wire, the barricades, the guardsmen and tried to remember how to find the back exit in case all hell broke loose. They settled in the waiting room, and the family again agreed that Philonise should be their representative in front of the jury. By the time Philonise got to the courtroom, the attorneys were already there. Nelson sat with Chauvin, who wore a charcoal-gray suit and a periwinkle tie, looking as stoic as ever. Ellison took a seat behind Schleicher and Blackwell.

"All rise for the jury," Cahill said, and the twelve members made their way to the courtroom.

"We put on a great case," Ellison remembered thinking. "But history is on Derek Chauvin's side, not our side."

"Members of the jury, I understand you have a verdict," Cahill said. He picked up a manila envelope on his desk and opened it.

As the judge prepared to read the decision, Ellison bowed his head and closed his eyes. Philonise did, too, praying for a result that could make Gianna's wish come true.

In that moment, more than twenty-three million

households across the country tuned into cable and broadcast television, including Katie and Aubrey Wright, who had closed their eyes, silently praying for a verdict that could provide them a scintilla of hope. A raucous crowd near CUP Foods, including Marcia Howard, fell silent, bowing their heads and closing their eyes. And outside the courthouse, a hush fell over a throng that included David Embaye and Maurice Hall, and cameras centered on Ross, whose head was also bowed as she held Garraway's hand. And then, the decision moved from Cahill's lips and echoed outside by a person several feet away from her.

"Guilty!" they shouted. And as cheers reverberated through the park, Ross broke down in tears and started to shake, awaiting the last two charges.

"Guilty! Guilty!"

Hooker led the crowd in chanting, "All three counts! All three counts!"

Garraway hugged Ross.

"Courteney, this is what we've been praying for," she said.

A phalanx of cameras continued to close in and pushed microphones into her face. Ross gripped Garraway tightly.

"Toshira, I don't know what to say," Ross whispered. And then, after months of Ross wondering where she belonged, Garraway gave her a sense of a new mission—something to speak about beyond her sorrow.

"Tell them that it's not over," Garraway said. "The fight's not over in Minneapolis."

Ross took the microphone. She talked about the need to reopen cases like Teigen's in Minnesota, about the other girlfriends and wives and mothers who had yet to see justice for their loved ones.

"Floyd loved to pray," said Ross, before leading the group in prayer. "Father God, Father God, please, Father God. Heal us today."

She stood outside, talking to every media outlet that asked her a question, until the sky grew dark. Ross stepped back into her minivan.

"I'm stunned," she said as she drove past downtown. "Just stunned. It's great. I'm happy. I'm glad for a guilty verdict. I'm glad justice was served."

And then, she was back on the empty highway.

"When you hear 'guilty,' it's for everybody," Ross said. "It's for everybody that they did wrong. But I know the reality of things. Cases, as much as I would love for them to just get reopened and reexamined and for people [to] go to jail, it's not going to happen. It takes so long to make huge systematic changes."

Her phone buzzed.

"Joe Biden's talking about Floyd!" her sister yelled. Brook was listening to a press conference during which the president told reporters how this case was a step toward tackling systemic racism, but Ross couldn't make out his distant voice. Then the phone buzzed again, and she slammed it down. Ross's sister was waiting for her when she got home.

"Brookie," Ross said, her voice breaking, "I still miss him."

At the Floyds' hotel, the tense, frenetic morning energy had transformed into a night of celebration. Between Hennessy and Red Bulls, Philonise was telling the story to a group of family members and strangers of what it was like in the courtroom. He said he felt like he wanted to jump in the air with his fist up, like Super Mario in one of the Nintendo games he used to play with Perry. But he did not want to make the judge upset, because he knew he still needed his support for sentencing. Instead, he cried and cried. The court rose as officers placed handcuffs on the man who killed his brother. "He looked so uncomfortable in them," Philonise said.

In another part of the bar, Crump and Romanucci discussed just how much the prosecutors had going for them. They had a fortunate band of knowledgeable witnesses—a fighter who could recognize a blood choke, an EMT who was ignored when she demanded a pulse, a teenager unafraid to record a video, and a police chief who was willing to speak out. The defense's witnesses were scant, and they were decimated by prosecutors in cross-examination. On its face, in retrospect, it was an open-and-shut case.

"Isn't it amazing that even with all of that, we still weren't sure?" Romanucci said. "That tells us something."

The screens above the bar in the hotel were all on CNN, replaying the family's press conference after the verdict was reached. Adarryl Hunter saw himself in the footage, chanting, "Say his name!"

"I can't believe I was standing next to Jesse Jackson," he said. "He was there when Martin Luther King died. And now I'm there—history."

One of Crump's staff attorneys emerged from a side office waving a giant flag with the black power fist, framed by the names of so many Black men and women who had become hashtags during the Black Lives Matter movement, whose families never attained the same measure of justice that Floyd's had.

The Floyd family decided to stay in Minneapolis long enough to attend Daunte's funeral. Then, they planned to go to Washington to witness the signing of a bill that they hoped would fundamentally change policing in the United States. At this point, big dreams felt possible—especially when supported by the most powerful people in the world.

Across social media, a video was circulating of the family huddled outside the courthouse with Crump, who held a cell phone. President Biden was calling again.

He began to speak to the family: "Nothing is going to make it go away . . . But at least now, there's some justice. I think of Gianna's comment, 'My dad is going to change the world.' We're going to start to change it now . . . I'm anxious to see you guys. We're going to get a lot more done."

"Hopefully, this is the momentum for the George Floyd Justice in Policing Act to get passed and have it signed," Crump said.

"You've got it, pal," Biden said. "That, and a lot more. This is going to be our first shot at dealing with, genuinely, systemic racism."

The Floyd family's battle for racial justice had a new front, and it was in Washington. Eight days after the verdict, Biden stood before a joint session of Congress, his first address to its 535 members since being elected. Not only did he discuss the policing act, he pushed Congress to pass it on the timeline the Floyd family wanted.

"My fellow Americans, we have to come together to rebuild trust between law enforcement and the people they serve, to root out systemic racism in our criminal justice system, and to enact police reform in George Floyd's name that passed the House already," Biden said. "We need to work together to find a consensus. But let's get it done next month, by the first anniversary of George Floyd's death."

CHAPTER 14

American Hope

Reverend Jesse Jackson had a message for Philonise Floyd and his family after Derek Chauvin's conviction: "This is a first down, not a touchdown," he said. "We still have injustice in Ohio; we have injustice in Wisconsin and Louisiana. So we have to keep working."

At age seventy-nine, in the twilight of his life, Jackson still could not forget the sight of Emmett Till's mutilated body or get over the acquittal of the fourteen-year-old Black boy's murderers. Till and Jackson were born in the same year. When he witnessed how disgusted the world was after seeing images of Till's mutilated corpse in an open casket, he was optimistic that people would work more diligently toward ending racism. Jackson had not seen the world so moved again until George Floyd had died—not just because so many had watched the actual death of the victim, but also because bystander videos allowed the world to observe the nonchalant face of the killer. During the trial, Jackson was certain the country had made progress in the long struggle for racial justice. Nonetheless, he knew the path to a more perfect union would still be perilous, obstructed by detractors, doubters, and those who would prefer to move on. Jackson hoped that those who had been fighting for a fairer world would not lose track of the bigger picture.

"You have to believe that, ultimately, right will win," Jackson said. "When I was growing up, they would take civil rights leaders and lock them in jail. Today I can go to the White House. When I was a boy, the police seemed untouchable. We called them the law. Now an officer is in jail, and we have the chance to change the law. It's a huge difference. So we're winning."

Jackson remembered the demonstrations he used to lead in Pittsburgh, Birmingham, and Houston, three cities that now had Black leaders. A younger generation of activists had invigorated the American protest movement through the simple mantra of "Black Lives Matter." He looked at the millions of people who had taken to the streets and a president who felt obligated to do right by the Black community that vaulted him into the White House. Biden even won the state of Georgia—a cradle of the South—by a fraction of a percent, where Democrats also gained its two crucial Senate seats. He wanted the Floyd family to remember that, using the very tools and rights embedded in the U.S. Constitution, they could achieve something great.

"We've shaken the moral foundations of this country," Jackson said. "When George died, people were moved to march. They had to vote. You can't separate [Biden's] victory in Georgia from George Floyd's death. I always felt that if we could move people to vote, you could have victory in the South. Can you imagine if we had voted like that in the Reagan days? I have seen the power of the voter and the pain of the nonvote. George Floyd gave us so many options. So, no matter what comes next, remember: we're still winning."

*

President Biden had given the family a specific dream: instead of spending May 25, 2021, mourning their brother, they would board Air Force One and go to the White House to watch him sign the George Floyd Justice in Policing Act. Philonise was no political insider, so he turned on the news every morning like any other member of the public to check on the progress of the potential legislation. The sad truth was that, after a closely watched trial and a summer of frenzied interest in his brother, either the media's interest or the public's attention—or both—had waned.

There were no more surfboard prayer groups in the water; no moments of silence on TV. Journalists called the family less often and fewer demonstrations invoked George Floyd's name on the streets. The on-screen updates from Capitol Hill showed that lawmakers had become fixated on other matters. Democrats and Republicans fought over mask mandates and vaccination policies. Democrats couldn't agree among themselves on how much to spend on building roads and bridges or how to implement Biden's social agenda. And then lawmakers were sounding the alarm on that foundational part of democracy itself: the right to vote. As states such as Georgia and Texas restricted access to early voting and undermined other laws that facilitated the casting of ballots, Democrats increasingly worried about what might lie ahead without federal intervention to protect and expand access to the ballot box, especially in Black and brown communities.

With so many issues at stake, Philonise wondered whether getting justice for his brother—and all the other families that he had now met facing similar situations—would ever be a priority again for the most powerful people in the United States. And a part of him questioned if it was selfish to even think that it should be. But what happens when a worldwide moment of solidarity begins to slip away? A year after his brother's murder, he, like so many others in his orbit, wondered whether America's soul-searching over racism sustained enough momentum to make lasting change.

After the conviction, the Floyd family, too, had become more fragmented. At least five different foundations stemmed from the Floyd bloodline—a bloom of charity that caused some internal tension and raised the prospect of relatives competing against one another for attention and for resources. One benefit of the fragmentation, though, was that events for the anniversary of his death were being planned across the country. Philonise, Rodney, and Brandon planned a march in Third Ward. Terrence Floyd set up an event in New York. Bridgett intended to head to a rally and a workshop series in downtown Minneapolis. Angela Harrelson helped to organize a block party at George Floyd Square.

Meanwhile, an ensemble of civil rights leaders—Reverend Al Sharpton, Marc Morial of the Urban League, Derrick Johnson of the NAACP, Sherrilyn Ifill of the NAACP Legal Defense Fund, Melanie Campbell of Black Women's Roundtable, Johnnetta Cole of the National Council of Negro Women, and Wade Henderson from the Leadership Conference on Civil and Human Rights—continued to press lawmakers in Washington to come to some sort of agreement. They had supported the Democrats in rejecting a Republican police reform bill, known as the JUSTICE Act, in the Senate because they thought it did not do enough to hold police accountable for misconduct. They were in favor of the Democratic-led George Floyd Justice in Policing Act, which had passed through the House; the unanimous Democratic support in the Senate meant it could pass the chamber with a tiebreaking vote from the first Black vice president. But they needed ten Republicans to break a filibuster that would allow them to bring the legislation to a vote. The lead Republican negotiators on the bill—South Carolina senators Lindsey Graham and Tim Scott—were optimistic they might be able to muster that kind of support for a deal conservatives found acceptable, but they hadn't yet worked out an agreement with the Democratic lead negotiators—Senator Cory Booker, Senator Dick Durbin, and Representative Karen Bass. As the anniversary inched closer, the lawmakers told reporters that, despite their best efforts, they would not meet the family's—and the president's—desired deadline.

Philonise held out for a miracle. He knew reporters could sometimes overplay what they were hearing in Washington, so he awaited word directly from someone in the White House. A few days before the anniversary, Philonise got the call. Biden and Harris extended an invitation for the family to visit. For a fleeting moment, Philonise considered the possibility that there might be some surreptitious deal in the works that would surprise the world.

And then, on May 24, Philonise received a call from Sharpton. Sharpton told him that it was good news that the president wanted to see him. But he had also observed the inner workings of Washington long enough to know that there would be no such miracle.

"The bad news is Biden is not going to be able to sign a bill because the bill has not been passed," he said. "But let me tell you something else: We fought for the choke-hold bill in New York. It took us five years, but it's a state law now. Andrew Cuomo signed the bill and gave Gwen Carr and I the pen."

The family was beginning to accept the hard truth of what Carr had told them about the fight for racial justice in America: their brother's death would not change things overnight. Sharpton noted that while things might move faster today, there was still a process. After all, it had taken almost nine years between Rosa Parks refusing to give up her seat on the bus and the passage of the Civil Rights Act of 1964.

Before Philonise could state his disappointment, Sharpton shared a lesson that he'd learned from his role model, Reverend Jesse Jackson, after Jackson lost the Democratic primary in New York in 1988: "In the face of defeat, you have to keep hope alive."

About a decade later, it was Jackson who tried to keep Sharpton calm after police officers were acquitted in the murder trial of Amadou Diallo, a Guinean immigrant living in the Bronx. Police shot Diallo forty-one times after they claimed to mistake his wallet for a gun. The officers' acquittal caused outbursts of anger throughout New York City and beyond.

"At the end of the day, you're going to have to say what they did was wrong, but you have to find a way to give people hope," Jackson told Sharpton. "Because your job is to expose the wrong but to make the victims feel like they can keep going."

That sort of philosophy struck Philonise, but it was also true that Sharpton and Jackson had chosen the activist life. The Floyd family felt convicted by it. Sure, they wanted to expose wrong, but they also remained very much in pain. They were trying to figure out how to provide hope while still seeking hope themselves.

Sharpton again pointed to the arc of history. Rethinking policing in America was no small task. Even after cops brutally beat Rodney King in 1991, sparking a national conversation on race, police reform did not move to the fore.

Back in the 1970s, Sharpton said, Black leaders often deemed policing a local issue, and before then, combatting segregation was a greater priority. In fact, many Black pastors and lawmakers were in favor of more police to tackle crime during the war on drugs. They had supported Senator Joe Biden in the 1990s when he was passing the tough-on-crime laws that led to the overpolicing of Cuney Homes, the same laws that facilitated Floyd's frequent incarceration. Now Biden was urging Congress to pass a law in his name and inviting his family to the White House.

"I just want to get the legislation passed," Philonise said.

The day before their visit, President Biden called Sharpton to get insight on the Floyd family's headspace.

"How are they doing?" Biden asked. "I'm concerned about them."

Sharpton told Biden that he needed to shift his thinking, and that it would be wrong to think of them as a family that wanted easy comfort from famous friends.

"Talk to them about the deal," Sharpton insisted. "Talk to them about policy."

"I'm concerned about the little girl," Biden told him.

May 25, 2021, was a bright and breezy day in the city where George Floyd had died. Adarryl Hunter had spent a year being content to stay in the background while friends of Floyd and hangers-on jumped in front of cameras. He avoided reporters; he did not attend protests. It all still felt strange to him.

But after the Chauvin trial, once the Floyd family had left Minneapolis, he felt an emptiness return. He thought he might find some fulfillment if he drove downtown to the shelter run by the Salvation Army, where Darlene Phillips had put together an event for those who had known Floyd. It was supposed to be an intimate gathering, but a host of reporters found out and showed up as well. Phillips had ordered red shirts with an image of Floyd in the clouds and purchased some balloons. Friends had gathered on the sidewalk outside the front door, where Floyd had so often prayed with others.

People hugged and told stories about Floyd feeding the homeless and accompanying them on group trips to the movies. They talked about his sensitivity, the compassion he had for those who were struggling, the times they saw him cry. And, in private corners, they told one another new stories too. There was unresolved pain and anger all over the city, from those who knew Floyd well and those who didn't know him at all, those who saw him hanging around town and those who watched him in his final minutes. So many lives would never be the same: Sylvia Jackson's Benz was still in the possession of federal investigators, who were keeping it as evidence, and painful memories led her to move to another city. Shawanda Hill was so racked with guilt about leaving Floyd at the scene that she suffered mental breakdowns. Some friends tried to cope by going for a bottle of pills or alcohol, while others checked themselves in at Turning Point, as a sort of tribute to the man they had lost. Bystanders such as Charles McMillian and Genevieve Hansen were upset that Ellison's office did little to look after them once they had testified— offering no mental health counseling or protection from law enforcement, who they feared might harass them. Darnella Frazier, who first posted the video of Floyd's death on social media, moved from the neighborhood and rejected public accolades and appearances, hoping she could find some way to return to life as a normal teenage girl.

Outside the Salvation Army, Darlene Phillips opened the program by presenting a portrait of Floyd to Aubrey Rhodes, to thank him for inspiring Floyd to come to this city. Afterward, she handed the microphone to Adarryl Hunter, who had told himself he needed to speak more publicly about Floyd because his friend would have appreciated it. He chose words from the Bible that had brought him comfort, and began to read Psalm 23: "Yea, though I walk through the valley of the shadow of death, I will fear no evil; for thou art with me; thy rod and thy staff they comfort me."

Courteney Ross took the microphone soon after. She was feeling more at ease being out in public, empowered by the encouragement she had found with Toshira Garraway's group. A few days earlier, the women were talking about how often public officials wanted to give them plaques and flags, as if those would make them feel better. What they needed most was support, and, on this morning, Ross told those in attendance that the Salvation Army was the best support group Floyd had in Minneapolis.

"He loved the Salvation Army with all his heart," Ross said. "It was like his second home."

Phillips and others handed out balloons. And then someone began the call-and-response chant that now echoed across the world.

"Say his name!" someone shouted.

"Big Floyd!" they yelled back as the wind lifted orange, blue, and red balloons into the heavens.

Ross scanned across the crowd and saw Hunter. The two had never really interacted; she approached him and they hugged, brought together by the shared pain of Floyd's death. They exchanged numbers so they could comfort each other when they were down and tell stories about the man they knew. And yet, even so, Ross warned herself not to get too close to him because, for all the therapy sessions, she still partly blamed herself for Floyd's demise. In those moments, she'd break down and ask, "What if I hurt him next?"

Earlier that morning, planners finished preparing for the formal celebration at George Floyd Square a few miles away. Along the southeast side of the square, a local musician named Ananda Bates got ready to sing a protest song he wrote after Floyd's death called "We the People." Around the corner from CUP Foods, Samara Ferguson, thirty-one, had set up a folding table in front of the big windows of the barbershop where she worked. She and her ten-year-old daughter, Shamiyah Millon, brought out boxes of Snickers, Doritos, Capri Sun, and Powerade they planned to hand out for free.

"I think we'll need more," Ferguson told her daughter, before heading out to Target to pick up additional snacks.

Near the blue silhouette of Floyd's body painted on the street, someone placed an easel that instructed visitors on how to carry themselves over the course of the day. "Ask Questions! Conversate with those you don't know," it read. An elderly White couple carrying a box of flowers took the instructions seriously and walked toward a middle-aged Black man in a baseball cap, taking everything in.

"Our church decided we should come down here today," the man said, "and these instructions say we should have a conversation with someone we don't know . . . So."

The person they approached turned out to be Alvin Manago.

"Nice flowers," he said. "I was George Floyd's roommate."

"Oh my God," the woman said as the box of flowers shook in her hands. "I'm so sorry. We've got to do better in this world."

The couple set down the flowers by the silhouette and walked away. Manago smiled. Coming together could be awkward. But he appreciated that it felt like people in Minneapolis were making an effort.

He and Theresa Scott still lived in the townhome he'd rented with Floyd. Posters and portraits of his old roommate now hung alongside the African art that once brought him calm. Scott's emotions remained raw, and she would sometimes yell to herself, "They killed my boy ... That White man killed my boy." Manago said the only thing they could do for comfort was to go over the Bible verses they used to discuss with Floyd. Scott couldn't bear the idea of coming out for the anniversary, so Manago had stopped by alone on the way to work. The memorial brought him a sense of tranquility.

"I know Big Floyd made a change," Manago said. "I am glad to be a small part of it."

Minutes later, gunshots rang out. A stray bullet pierced through the big windows of the barbershop, whizzing right past ten-year-old Shamiyah. Her father swept her up and ran inside, where shards of glass littered the floor.

The crowd scattered into nearby alleyways. Another bullet tore through the tires of Bates's tour bus. This type of activity was not unheard of at George Floyd Square—gunshots were a fact of life in the neighborhood. But to have it happen this early, on this particular day, invited all kinds of concern: Was it a person having a bad day in a country where mass shootings are a daily occurrence? Was it a white supremacist looking to make a statement? Was it a domestic dispute or a neighborhood beef?

"What's the procedure?" Bates asked inside the bus. "Do we call the police?"

Someone told him no—not here. Despite the commotion, no police car came. Everyone aboard waited inside for about fifteen minutes until it felt safe to step out again. There were no bodies or injured people around, and no one could conclusively say what happened. Visitors gradually returned to the square, hugging and conducting wellness checks. Ferguson had rushed back from Target, concerned for her daughter, but felt that the plans for the day should carry on as normally as possible. She placed the rest of the snacks on the folding table.

"We're going to keep going," Ferguson said.

On the other end of the street, news cameras huddled around a fair-skinned young man approaching the memorial. Damik Bryant, Daunte Wright's older brother, had come to pay his respects. He was greeted by Jay Webb, a seven-foot-tall man with dreadlocks who tended a nearby greenhouse.

"Let me show you something," Webb told him.

He walked him to the intersection at Thirty-Eighth and Chicago, where an activist-made traffic circle sat in the middle of the road. An iron black power fist stood in the middle of it, surrounded by a garden bed covered in wood chips. The wood came from the plywood and the debris of businesses that had burned in the aftermath of Floyd's murder. Now they helped the flowers grow.

"We started one way," Webb told Bryant. "But we're turning into something new."

Like Floyd's other siblings, Bridgett Floyd had an appointment with the president, but she decided to skip it to attend a protest in downtown Minneapolis. Over the course of the year, Bridgett had become more skeptical that public officials were willing to generate real, substantive change. This deepened an internal split between Floyd's relatives about their political approaches, the familiar divide between activists debating whether they wanted to work within existing power structures or break them down from the outside. Bridgett had chosen the more radical approach.

"He didn't do what he promised to do, so why am I going there?" she said. "I will see him when there is something to sign."

Bridgett's decision to skip the visit to Washington came as a surprise to White House officials; she had informed reporters before she had told them. And as White House staff prepared the Oval Office for the rest of the family's arrival, Philonise, Terrence, and Rodney Floyd, together with Brandon Williams, were being shuffled around congressional offices with their legal team. The morning had already been difficult—another day putting on suits, another early-morning barrage of phone calls expressing condolences after another sleepless night. But their job today was to work the Hill. And this time, they came with Roxie Washington, Gianna's mother. The young girl wore a blue dress with a big white bow atop her head. One of their stops was at House Speaker Nancy Pelosi's office; she was there with Karen Bass, the congresswoman who helped write the policing act in the House.

Bass told the family that they needed a little more time to get Republicans to agree to the terms but that they were basically at the finish line. Pelosi thanked the family for being an example of strength in a tumultuous time. She told them not to be too concerned about the timeline; it was better to have robust legislation than to have shallow laws delivered on a deadline. Philonise said he understood.

"We want the bill to be meaningful," Philonise told her. "It has my brother's name on it."

Crump asked Pelosi to continue pushing for legislation, reminding her that it had been more than a half century since a major civil rights bill passed through Congress. He and Antonio Romanucci let her know they were willing to do whatever they could to help pass this legislation, calling it the honor of their lives.

They walked out of Pelosi's office for a brief press conference. Positioning herself next to Gianna Floyd, who was playing with her mother's hair, Pelosi told the press that no honor had surpassed inviting the family to her office, and that she had confidence that the Senate would pass a bill to honor Gianna's wishes.

Representative Bass then introduced Philonise to the assembled media. "We need to get this [bill] taken care of," he said, "because just like Gianna said—your daddy's gonna do what?"

"Change the world!" she replied.

The family then jumped into a black van and made their way to the White House. They hadn't been inside before, but Philonise immediately tried to downplay the importance of the building. "It's just a house," he told himself as they walked in. And President Biden was just a man, a friend who called on the phone sometimes. He was waiting for them in the Oval Office, standing next to Vice President Harris.

They shook hands and took seats on the beige couches. Staff offered them cookies with the presidential seal in frosting and brought ice cream for Gianna. Biden didn't ignore Sharpton's advice; he talked to the family about policy. He told them that the biggest sticking point in the Senate was on the issue of eliminating qualified immunity, which would allow an officer to be sued for violating someone's civil rights.

"If we didn't have that in the bill, we could get it done tomorrow," Biden told them.

Nonetheless, Biden said that he was unwavering in his commitment to making sure Floyd's death would not be in vain. And Philonise and Rodney expressed a wish that police reform would become more than a political message. They wanted it to serve as a way to bring all leaders and all races together.

The talk did not stay political for very long.

"It's been a year," Biden said. "How are you doing?"

"It's devastating," Philonise said.

The family talked with the president and vice president for more than an hour. They shared private, raw stories about the nature of grief. More so than with any other politician he had met, Philonise marveled at the president's warmth and genuine concern about this family from Houston.

As they walked out of the Oval Office, Philonise stared at the large eagle emblem in the center of the rug. The sacredness of that symbol, and what it stood for, stirred him in an unexpected way. Philonise's mind turned to the Black men who grew up being told that in America they were "an endangered species." In contrast to the national bird, Philonise realized that there were too few laws to safeguard Black people from police officers who felt justified in killing them.

After that moment, he started repeating a line to the press: "If you could make federal laws to protect the bird, which is the bald eagle, you can make federal laws to protect people of color."

The last people to leave the room were Washington and Gianna.

"Daddy did change the world," Biden said to Gianna. "And it's up to us to continue advocating for that change."

Before they walked out, Washington patted her daughter on the head and said, "You know, Gianna, Grandmother's probably looking down and saying, wow, look at where we are . . . Look at what we did."

Meanwhile, on Capitol Hill, legislative momentum proved fleeting. At first, with the 2020 election cycle behind them, Booker and Scott were confident they could make some sort of deal, using as a template the prison reform law they had worked together to pass in 2018. They embraced the idea of doing something transformative, not just for the country but for themselves as Black men, as each had told colleagues stories over the years about interactions with the cops that were demeaning, demoralizing, and dangerous.

There seemed to be consensus on several key provisions: The federal government would not provide grants to local departments unless they banned neck restraints and stopped using no-knock warrants. There was also broad agreement to provide funding for body cameras and to maintain databases that would track use-of-force events and officers who had been removed from their jobs because of misconduct. Even the police unions were willing to consider supporting such changes.

But, as Biden told the family, talks started to devolve over discussions about ways to curtail criminal conduct from officers. In addition to eliminating qualified immunity, the bill aimed to loosen the tough standards under which federal prosecutors could convict officers of misconduct if they violated civil rights, changing the "willful" standard to a "reckless" one.

The discussion set up the first major conflict of the bill.

Republicans, as well as police unions, claimed the changes would cast an unfair burden on officers, criminalizing the individual more than the system from which they came. But for Democrats and civil rights advocates, there was no part of the law that was more important. They hoped that harsher penalties would cause officers to think twice before they fired a gun at another unarmed Black person.

Negotiators tried to come up with some solution that could thread the needle. Among other changes, they discussed setting up insurance funds, making municipalities liable instead, and limiting the "reckless" standard to only the most heinous crimes—ideas that the Fraternal Order of Police said they would consider.

But Booker's staff grew increasingly frustrated with aides on the Republican side. As the one-year anniversary of the murder approached, they accused Scott's aides of walking back on parts of the bill he originally signaled that he would support. Scott's aides said they did no such thing—they were just trying to hash out details beyond the "top-level" items. Then, Republicans also pitched a half-million-dollar cap on how much an officer could be sued for—an idea that would not sit well with attorneys such as Crump who had secured their victims millions of dollars through civil suits. By June 2021, Graham started commenting on a leaked draft of the bill, casting it as legislation that was clearly antipolice. Scott complained that Democrats were conditioning federal funding on too many areas.

"The devil's in the details," Scott told *The New York Times*. "And we're now meeting the devil."

A clear-eyed agenda for reforming policing in the United States descended into the morass of national politics, as lobbyists became involved and staff grew frustrated, pointing fingers at one another. And as the group missed self-imposed deadlines in July and August, it became clear that this piece of legislation would not be a law that captured the public's original desire for urgent change—if it even passed at all. It risked dying a slow death, hardly different from the continued attempts to pass broadly popular measures on gun control. The Sharpton-led coalition of activists begged Biden to use his bully pulpit and jump into negotiations on the Hill, but the president told them he wanted to see what the legislative branch could figure out on its own.

There was a way to avoid the bipartisan bickering. Democrats likely had enough votes to pass the bill on their own—if they chose to jettison the filibuster. But lawmakers were split on whether the impact of the bill was worth the political fallout that would ensue, so they chose not to upend the system.

The fate of the act now largely rested on two of the only three Black senators in Congress. For Scott and Booker, the debate came down to the principles of practical change. Did the bill really need to be transformative if it could do a few good things? Scott suggested that they work to pass a "skinny bill"—its least controversial parts. Booker argued that such a compromise would dishonor the name of Floyd and dismiss the seriousness of the problem.

The squabbling continued and, reflecting the strained politics of the moment, the two sides could not come to an agreement on even the most basic facts.

There had at least been a definitive shift in American culture and discourse. Within those twelve months, calls for change did not only come from chants on the street; they came from executives on Wall Street. The chief executive of

JPMorgan Chase took a picture of himself kneeling with his staff, mirroring the pose made famous by Colin Kaepernick, the quarterback who was blacklisted from the NFL when he took that position during the national anthem. NFL commissioner Roger Goodell reversed the league's position after Floyd's death, saying that "we were wrong for not listening" to players who peacefully protested police brutality.

Workplaces pushed to make Juneteenth—a day commemorating when the last American slaves were freed—an official holiday, and the federal government would soon follow. News organizations debated whether they should capitalize the "b" in "Black," and the Associated Press, the standard-bearer for journalistic practice, decided that it would no longer release mug shots or the names of suspects involved in minor crimes because of the lasting impact on those who might be falsely accused.

Walmart, the country's largest retailer, pledged to stop locking up "multicultural" beauty products in display cases, and Sephora committed to devoting at least 15 percent of its shelf space to Black-owned beauty brands. Even toymaker LEGO suspended marketing for police-themed sets. *The Washington Post* found that, taken together, the country's fifty biggest companies pledged at least $49.5 billion to address racial inequality.

With Floyd's death, some long-standing controversies that defined the culture wars were suddenly resolved. Quaker Oats abandoned the venerable but stereotypical mammy of a mascot, Aunt Jemima, and Disney announced it would reimagine one of its most popular rides, Splash Mountain, from being an homage to its racist 1946 paean to Dixie, *Song of the South*, into one for *The Princess and the Frog*, its only animated film featuring a Black princess. The Washington Redskins took the slur out of its name, the Cleveland Indians became the Cleveland Guardians, and more than 160 Confederate statues or symbols around the country were removed or replaced, including on the Mississippi state flag.

Some state governments took measures to increase police accountability on their own, even as Congress debated what to do on the federal level. A *New York Times* analysis in April 2021 found that sixteen states had restricted the use of the neck restraint and five limited the use of no-knock warrants.

But there was a burgeoning backlash about whether the country's amplified concern over race had gone too far. By September 2020, a study from the Pew Research Center found that support for the Black Lives Matter movement decreased from 67 percent to 55 percent overall, where it would remain into the next year, driven by a precipitous drop in support from Whites, Hispanics, and Asian Americans. The fascination with the phrase appeared to be a ceremonial, summertime fling.

This backlash had made its way to school boards and to state capitals, which manifested a growing anxiety about the movement's psychological impact on White Americans. That worry made itself clear as the term "critical race theory" moved from the corridors of the academy onto segments of *The View* and *Tucker Carlson Tonight*.

The critical race theory framework originally examined racism as a systemic problem embedded in institutions rather than an assessment of individual actions. After Floyd's death, opponents of the term used it as a catch-all to describe any policy or position that had to do with race, including affirmative action and diversity training. They worried that all this talk about racism and America's original sin—most notably highlighted in *The New York Times*' 1619 Project, which recast American history through the lens of slavery's legacy—would imbue children with feelings of guilt and shame. Eleven days before the anniversary of Floyd's death, a group of eleven Republicans in Congress introduced a bill to ban critical race theory in schools.

"Critical Race Theory, like all its racist derivations, is a direct affront to our core values as Americans," Texas representative Chip Roy said in a statement introducing the bill. "No one in America—be they students, servicemen and -women, government employees, or anyone—should be indoctrinated to hate our country, its founding, or our fellow citizens. Worse yet is the continued effort to 'divvy us up by race' and perpetuate the lie that we should be treated differently by virtue of our skin color."

The legislation was dead on arrival in the Democrat-held House of Representatives. But five Republican state legislatures passed laws banning critical race theory from being taught in college classrooms.

People like Katie Wright wondered what a ban would even mean—no lessons about slavery, no discussions on Martin Luther King Jr.? And how would teachers then tell the story of what happened to her son Daunte, or to George Floyd, or to all the others who died in Minnesota and beyond?

While the political drama played out behind the scenes, the Floyd family and their lawyers continued coming to Washington in hopes of pressuring legislators to move faster. During this process, Crump remained unusually tempered in his public comments. Politics was a new sphere and he was cautious about offending those who were on the fence.

Although he had mastered how to extract outrage from the public and win millions of dollars for wronged families, the legal game was different from the legislative one.

As Crump and Romanucci pushed for a federal ban on qualified immunity doctrines, similar attempts failed in thirty-five states. Faced with these legislative setbacks, Crump sought other ways to garner public attention. When an unarmed seventeen-year-old was fatally shot by a White sheriff's deputy during a traffic stop in the suburbs of Little Rock on June 23, 2021, Crump and Sharpton headed to Arkansas to do what they usually did when such instances occur.

There was a key difference: Hunter Brittain was White. The two hoped that drawing attention to this case might influence some who considered police violence to solely be a Black person's issue; perhaps the policing act would engender more support if it were thought of as a public health crisis disassociated from race.

"Brittain's death will start to change the narrative and perception of the problem of police violence as the country sees that children of all races and ethnicities can be victims," Crump said.

The act was righteous, but the intentions were clear: the narrative about police reform was slipping away from the murder of Floyd, and Crump and others were desperate to find some way to reclaim it.

Those fighting in Minneapolis felt they, too, needed to try different, and sometimes more drastic, measures. During the last weekend of June 2021, days after Brittain had been killed, a pride event centering on the contributions of queer people of color turned from joyous to alarming. For all their protests and meetings with city officials, activists like DJ Hooker were frustrated that the city had refused to defund the police or agree to keep George Floyd Square as a sacred space permanently closed to vehicle traffic. Hooker was so furious that he felt compelled to confront city councilwoman Andrea Jenkins, who he hoped would have been an ally. Hooker accused Jenkins of showing up to the event as a photo op without truly doing enough to address the community's most pressing issues. "We can agree to disagree," Jenkins told him, trying to defuse the argument. But then Hooker told her that her support for the police department especially put the lives of Black transgender women in danger.

As the first Black transgender person to be elected to a city council in the entire country, she found Hooker's accusation offensive and hurtful. Being the councilwoman whose district included George Floyd Square had been stressful enough; since Floyd's death she said her multiple sclerosis had worsened, which she attributed to the events of the last year taking a profound physical and mental toll. She tried to disengage from the argument and headed toward her car, at which point Hooker told her his next move was going to be protesting peacefully outside her home.

"If you show up at my house, I'm calling the police on your Black ass," she said.

Now it was Hooker who was hurt and offended. After Floyd and Daunte Wright, after the tear gas and rubber bullets, after the suicidal thoughts, Hooker could not bear the idea of someone threatening to call the police on him. His activist friends backed him up, and they decided to try a new tactic. They surrounded Jenkins's car, refusing to let her leave until she signed a scribbled sheet of their demands for George

Floyd Square to remain open, and calling for the immediate resignation of the mayor.

Jenkins was effectively held hostage: the interaction went on for ninety minutes before she agreed to sign. The activists cheered and let her go.

Jenkins would later say she signed under duress, and an editorial in the *Star Tribune* used the incident as an example to show how protesting had gone too far. Hooker offered no apologies. He wrote in a Facebook post that the lack of progress on the issues had given him few choices. Even the activist movement wouldn't be immune from the fissures threatening to derail Floyd's legacy.

"When I say I support a diverse pool of tactics and by any means necessary I MEAN IT," Hooker wrote. "That cause the tactics we been using the last 400 years don't seem to work on there [*sic*] own. So we need to develop new tools."

Meanwhile, another sort of standoff was taking place at the state capitol in St. Paul. Governor Tim Walz had told the state legislature that he was willing to keep them beyond the July 1 end of the legislative session if they could not figure out some way to pass police reform.

Walz had followed through on his promise to Garraway, meeting with her group and vowing to support legislation that honored their stories. Garraway's group worked with other social justice organizations to draft a list of demands for the bill. Some mirrored the proposals in Congress: an end to qualified immunity, a ban on no-knock warrants. But they also proposed legislation that would ban pretext traffic stops—such as driving with an expired tag—and no longer require officers to arrest drivers at traffic stops if they had missed a court date, two laws that would have saved Daunte

Wright. They called for new standards for mental and physical health care for those in police custody—something that could have saved Hardel Sherrell. They called for police body cam video to be released to families within two days, something they hoped would prevent officers from colluding and covering up malfeasance. And they asked to lift the statute of limitations on investigations into killings by police, which would allow lawyers and the police department to get to the truth of what happened to Garraway's partner, Justin Teigen.

Garraway and the families spent the early summer lobbying for themselves at the state capitol, trying to rally support. While they found some champions, they also encountered a lot of blank stares from lawmakers from both parties who did not seem to connect to the issues. Opponents worried that these bills were an opening act to defunding the police. Conservatives talked about how these bills might hurt police morale at a time when officers were leaving in droves—in Minneapolis alone, about 588 officers remained in a department that received funding for 888.

By the session's end, the legislature had agreed to limit no-knock warrants and allow sign-and-release warrants at traffic stops. They banned choke holds and passed a bill named for Hardel Sherrell. But they rejected the accountability measures the group had pushed, such as strengthening civilian oversight, ending qualified immunity, and the two-day release of body cam footage.

"The state has failed Black people once again," said Nekima Levy Armstrong, the former head of the local NAACP, who noted that Minnesota had a history of "admiring the problem" when it came to race.

"The fact that the bill didn't get passed is classic

Minnesota," Levy Armstrong said. "There's always an excuse, always a reason why these things don't get passed. But it just has more to do with the mentality of a lot of the people in positions of power who think that things are fine the way that they are."

As the legislation arrived on the governor's desk, Garraway pleaded with him to find some way to do more.

"You listen to our stories. You watch us break down. You watch us cry," she said. "So how can you make a deal? How can you make a deal to say this is okay?"

Walz felt he had little choice but to sign the bills. The further the country got from Floyd, the less likely it was that he would be able to pass any legislation at all.

"I feel like I failed Toshira," Walz admitted. He ended up using executive action to add $15 million for violence-prevention programs, and then stipulated that families could receive body camera footage within five days, not the proposed two. But there would be no justice for Justin Teigen—the statute of limitations would remain.

In part, Walz wondered if his legislature was even at the point where they truly understood the plight of these new activists. He theorized that what the country really needed was a truth and reconciliation commission, like they had in post-apartheid South Africa, in which victims told stories about the cruelty of racism as a way to acknowledge and heal a broken system.

Walz's worry was that the country was not actually getting to the core of the issue, the roots of its internal prejudices. And he was not sure how to achieve racial healing when White men like him wanted to debate the nuances, while Black women like Garraway wanted urgent, immediate change, recognizing that their lives and the lives of their families were at stake.

It was that kind of tension that Walz worried could pull the country apart. The polarized aftermath of Floyd's death had revealed how differently Americans perceived the subject of race.

"I worry about what I'm seeing at the national level," Walz said. "I'm seeing our democracy under threat, and I'm seeing the community here that's losing faith ... We may not get another shot at this."

Biden had thought the biggest challenge was to persuade White Americans that they should not be threatened by addressing the inequalities that exist between them and other races, a result of a "cramped view that America is a zero-sum game" in which progress for one group had to come at the expense of another.

"At our best, the American ideal wins out," Biden said. "It's never a rout, it's always a fight. And the battle is never fully won. That's because the hate never goes away—it only hides."

It was that lurking hate that Levy Armstrong and Garraway knew could yield disastrous consequences for Black people in America. Their hope was that, one day, lawmakers would understand that racist systems would not be dismantled with righteous words alone—the governor's pessimism was a marker of privilege that they could not afford. They had to be optimistic that things could change; the alternative was far too bleak. For them, continuing the fight was not some glib turn of phrase. Optimism was their American hope, their defense mechanism, a way of survival.

Levy Armstrong encouraged her sisters in the struggle to

take comfort in Harriet Tubman, and in Homer Plessy and Dred Scott, who thought well enough of the legal system that they took their concerns to court. She thought about Fannie Lou Hamer and Rosa Parks. All those leaders were now gone, but she looked to their memory as inspiration that she could outlast any pundit or politician who stood in her way. There was no turning back from fighting for change.

"Even though it seems like it's a never-ending fight sometimes, even though it seems like it's a hopeless fight sometimes, at least we have a chance of winning," Garraway recalled. "But if we don't fight, we don't even have a chance."

There was a memory of Perry that kept flashing in Philonise's head. He was a kid, back at Cuney Homes, playing catch with his football star brother. They'd stand at opposite ends of a sidewalk and Perry would launch a spiral that kept going askew, forcing PJ to run to catch the ball.

"You can't throw," he complained to his brother. Perry responded by saying that PJ needed to prepare for the times when the ball wouldn't come directly to him—he had to put in extra effort to complete the play.

Now Perry was gone, and the great racial reckoning was beginning to wane. Yes, Chauvin had been sentenced to twenty-two and a half years in prison and would later plead guilty to federal charges. The other officers involved would also be sent to prison, albeit with lighter sentences. Majority-White juries would also convict the officer who killed Daunte Wright and the neighborhood vigilantes who killed Ahmaud Arbery. Still, legislative action had stalled. Philonise reached out again to Sharpton to figure out what was left for him to do.

Sharpton and his cohort of civil rights leaders had felt

forced to focus on other matters. The Supreme Court upheld two Arizona laws that observers thought further diluted the Voting Rights Act, allowing election officials to throw out ballots cast in the wrong district and restricting the collection and delivery of votes to polling places. Civil rights leaders feared a systematic effort was afoot to disenfranchise voters, particularly those of color. Attention soon turned to attempting to strengthen voter laws in Congress, including a bill named in honor of the late civil rights hero John Lewis. Whenever Sharpton got on the phone or had a meeting with the White House or a moderate Democrat who could break the impasse, he found himself making similar arguments to the ones that John Lewis had to make more than a half century earlier.

"When we won the Chauvin trial, I expected there was going to be backlash," Sharpton recalled telling Philonise. "They're doing these restrictive laws. Don't forget, after the March on Washington in '63, it was the four girls bombed in Birmingham. So, imagine the jubilation that Doctor King and Roy Wilkins had, leaving Washington in August, and then a few weeks later, they bombed this church in Birmingham."

"For every step forward, they're going to try to step back," Philonise said.

"Absolutely," Sharpton replied. "I call it the Newton Law of Civil Rights. For every action, there's going to be a reaction. So, brace yourself. But keep going."

Sharpton's next destination was the nation's capital for another rally on the same day as the original March on Washington, this time to draw attention to the assault on voting rights.

He invited Philonise to speak again at the rally. Even though the event did not directly have to do with Floyd, Philonise had come to realize that justice for his brother could not be separated from the larger call for racial justice. He headed back to the National Mall on August 28, 2021, where the swells of support had overwhelmed him exactly one year earlier.

This time, though, he and his nephew Brandon Williams chatted in the waiting area with so many faces who had now become familiar, including Martin Luther King III and his thirteen-year-old daughter, Yolanda Renee.

Philonise found a quiet corner to review the notes he had scribbled for his speech.

"Let me know if I left anything out," he called out to Sharpton.

Sharpton scanned the notes, then glanced up at Philonise and raised his eyebrow.

"Who wrote this for you?" Sharpton joked. The speech felt perfect.

"I know what to do," Philonise told him.

Philonise took to the stage, this time facing the Lincoln Memorial. He looked out over the audience, a smaller gathering of sixty thousand than the hundreds of thousands who had packed the Mall the previous summer.

"I wanna thank everybody for coming out to support," Philonise began. He encouraged the audience to support voting rights laws in Congress, and DC statehood. And then he spoke about his personal case.

"Everyone needs to understand: the ground that we stand on is soaked in blood, and it will continue to be that way until we pass the George Floyd Justice in Police policy," he said.

"Change needs to be now, because we're going to

continue to see young men and young women murdered every day."

Philonise found himself beginning to feel overwhelmed again. He took a deep breath and uttered, "Man, this is crazy." But this time, he would not stop.

"The dead cannot cry for justice, so it's up to us to do that. The only weapon they had was the color of their skin."

He spoke about the history of protesting peacefully in this country, and the need to honor those who fought for the right to vote. He talked about keeping pressure on government until lawmakers agreed to their demands. He used the line about protecting the bald eagle, and the audience cheered.

"The bald eagle, it symbolizes freedom," Philonise continued. "So if I can't walk to the store—George Floyd—or even jog—Ahmaud Arbery—or sleep in the comfort of my own home—Breonna Taylor—or eat ice cream on my couch—Botham Jean—what can I do? Where can I live? How can I be the person I want to be?"

A year earlier, Philonise Floyd was not sure who he wanted to be. Neither were his siblings, his cousins, nor his nephew. But they knew they were in the middle of a singular moment in American history, that Perry's murder had the potential to change everything. They hoped, as Vice President Harris once did, that the lessons learned in the aftermath of his death could allow the country to sing a new song when it came to racial justice. But the summer of George Floyd did not dismantle systemic racism in America. Racism remained a pernicious force, a living nightmare that could disenfranchise voters, divide communities, snuff out a life.

In his life, Philonise did not like the way the ball had

been thrown to him. But he was steeled to catch the pass, just like the man who touched the world had taught him to do.

"Say his name!" Philonise yelled.

"George Floyd!" the crowd responded.

Philonise stood, trying to find a way to breathe. He knew that the police reform bill might not pass soon, or maybe ever. And even if it did become law, there was no guarantee that the stroke of a pen could stop the nightmares. There was still so much more to do, and all he had left to cling to was the belief that the heavy burden that had befallen his people could be lifted. It was the same belief that animated Toshira Garraway, Gwen Carr, and Valerie Castile; the same struggle that affected Reverend Martin Luther King Jr.'s son and his granddaughter, who had yet to see the fulfillment of their patriarch's dream. There was no new song to sing.

At the end of the program, Sharpton asked everyone on the stage to hold hands. A keyboard started to play. And then the group began to sing a prayer that spoke to the aspirations of a weathered people:

> *We shall overcome,*
> *We shall overcome, some day.*
> *Deep in my heart, I do believe that we shall overcome*
> *some day.*

Acknowledgments

We were in the basement of a Minneapolis hotel when attorney Ben Crump had to manage a standoff—a cordial one, but a standoff nonetheless—between us and the producers for a network news show who had been double-booked for sit-down interviews with his clients, the relatives of George Floyd.

"You have to go last," Crump said to us. "Their questions are easy; yours are hard."

Crump had a point. What we were asking four of Floyd's siblings—Philonise, Rodney, Terrence, and Bridgett—and his nephew Brandon Williams to do was emotionally draining. It had been merely four months since Floyd's brutal death, leaving them with little choice but to grieve publicly. Going an hour beyond their scheduled time, they shared memories that were funny, thrilling, heartwarming, and sad. Even when grief overwhelmed them, they soldiered on, wanting to make sure we fulfilled our mission: to help the world to see Perry as they saw him.

Upon our return to Minneapolis in March 2021, the Floyds welcomed us at their dinner tables, chatted with us after each day of testimony, and allowed us to tag along on their trips around the city, insisting that they pay for our Cinnabons at the mall. We are tremendously grateful for the trust that the Floyd family put in us to get this story right—answering even the thorniest questions with insight, graciousness, and honesty. As our reporting journey continued, we saw that those traits spanned across his family, whether it was Floyd's sisters Zsa Zsa and LaTonya; his sister-in-law, Keeta; three of his aunts, Angela Harrelson, Mahalia Jones, and Kathleen McGee; his uncle Selwyn Jones; or his cousins Shareeduh Tate and Tera Brown. They each helped us understand Floyd with profound intimacy.

Floyd's cadre of friends, lovers, and acquaintances both in Minneapolis and in Houston helped us develop a fuller appreciation of his personality. Travis Cains, Tiffany Cofield, Jacob "Fathead" David, Milton "PoBoy" Carney, Vaughn Dickerson, Becky Johnson, Robert Fonteno, Jonathan Veal, De'Kori Lawson, Ortierre Lawson, Walter Jefferson, Michael Riggs, and many others were instrumental in allowing us to understand his life in Houston. Peter Hayden and Woodrow Jefferson opened up so many doors to us at Our Turning Point. We thank Courteney Ross for helping us frame his last few years in Minneapolis and for showing us the difference between Floyd the man and George Floyd the movement. And much appreciation to Adarryl Hunter, who answered so many questions and willingly let us rummage through his family storage unit to find photographs and letters from Floyd. Sylvia Jackson, Maurice Hall, and Shawanda Hill showed great courage as they walked us through Floyd's last moments on what remains the hardest day of their lives.

There were also several people who did not know George Floyd personally but who offered us great insight into this singular moment in American history. They include activists such as Donald Hooker Jr.; advocates such as Toshira Garraway; academics such as Sherman James, Ayana Jordan, and Samuel Myers; public officials such as Mayor Jacob Frey, Attorney

General Keith Ellison, and Governor Tim Walz; public figures such as Reverend Al Sharpton, Reverend Jesse Jackson, and Ben Crump; and the hundreds of others who talked with us along the way. This book also builds off the groundbreaking reporting and writing about systemic racism in the past few years, notably by Nikole Hannah-Jones, Isabel Wilkerson, Richard Rothstein, and Ibram X. Kendi. It also builds off the great local reporting done at the *Star Tribune*, which led in covering the immediate aftermath of Floyd's death.

The more we learned about Floyd and how systemic racism shaped his life, the more complex our mission became. Our editor at Viking, Ibrahim Ahmad, was indefatigable and curious, continually pushing us. The dozens of hours he spent with us on Zoom calls, polishing this narrative and asking thoughtful questions, made us better writers and made this a better book. His assistant, Marissa Davis, approached the text with vigor and clarity. To the rest of the team at Viking— including Lindsay Prevette, Carolyn Coleburn, Bel Banta, Kate Stark, Mary Stone, Lydia Hirt, Linda Friedner, Tricia Conley, Tess Espinoza, Chelsea Cohen, Alan Walker, Paul Buckley, Andrea Schulz, and Brian Tart—thank you for taking such great care of this project.

We are also thankful for the support of Steven Ginsberg, managing editor at *The Washington Post*, and former *Post* editor Simone Sebastian. Both shepherded "George Floyd's America," the news organization's award-winning series that provided the foundational reporting for this text. In addition to the lead reporters of that series who were named in the Introduction, we extend our heartfelt thanks to a host of other journalists who helped to make that reporting successful. They include Julie Vitkovskaya, Junne Alcantara, Reem Akkad, Drea

Cornejo, Jake Crump, Nicki DeMarco, Karly Domb Sadof, Alice Li, Travis Lyles, Robert Miller, Suzette Moyer, Linah Mohammad, Ted Muldoon, Martine Powers, Maggie Penman, and Kanyakrit Vongkiatkajorn. *Post* reporters Mike DeBonis, Steven Rich, and Neena Satija, as well as freelancer Jared Goyette, also contributed important reporting for these pages. A special shout-out to *Post* photojournalist Joshua Lott, who was a steadfast companion throughout the reporting, as well as editors Matea Gold and Peter Wallsten for their unflagging advocacy.

Ginsberg stayed with us through the completion of this book, offering guidance with his annoyingly innate sense of reporting judgment and perceptive edits. Thanks to Alice Crites, our newsroom researcher, and fact-checker Lucy Shackelford, both of whom solved reporting mysteries with dizzying speed. Thanks to Jim Webster for his eagle-eyed proofread. We are also grateful for the institutional support at the *Post* from its leaders—including from managing editors Cameron Barr, Tracy Grant, and Krissah Thompson; our former executive editor, Marty Baron; and Baron's successor, Sally Buzbee, who eagerly embraced a project she inherited. And thank you to the *Post*'s agents at Aevitas Creative Management, Karen Brailsford and Todd Shuster, for their indispensable guidance in helping two first-time authors draft a book proposal.

Robert Samuels

My first attempts at writing literature were indulged by my fourth-grade teacher, Mrs. Lorene Lindahl. I think about her a lot, as she worked educational wonders with a group of motivated Black and Hispanic students attending a Title I school in the Bronx, and I rarely forget how fortunate I was to have had the opportunity of a great teacher at a crucial age when so many others in my community would not have. I promised her nearly thirty years ago that she would be the first person I'd acknowledge in a published book—and it is particularly fitting to acknowledge her on such a topic. My thoughts are also on two college professors, Mary Ann Weston and the late Richard Iton, who inspired the sense of critical analysis about public policy and American ambition that has become a bedrock of my reporting style. And Tolu, whose reporting and writing instincts were nothing short of a marvel to witness in real time, has been a wonderful coauthor, harmonious in even the most stressful moments.

I owe so much to the wide network of friends and family who have been indelible parts of this process. Thank you to my longtime journalism junta—Kenny Malone, Patricia Mazzei, Yedi Kaleem, and Hannah Sampson—for their continued insight, courtesy reads, and humor. Thank you to my spiritual support network—Aashish Abraham, Ashley Close, Bekki Fahrer, Angela Kissel, Richard Kelley, Kevin Lum, Adam Watson, and Andy Wessbecher—who never stopped praying for me. A special acknowledgment to my dear friends in the Midwest who opened their homes to me in the middle of a pandemic—Andrew and Elizabeth Bentley (who went into labor and continued serving me dinner!) and Misuzu and Alvin Miyashita Schexnider, as well as Tania Ganguli and Chris deLaubenfels, who offered me lodging for weeks at a time and whose dog, L. Boogie, decided on her own to become my personal alarm clock. Erin Ailworth, a friend from college and fellow journalist, took the time off from work to make key introductions. Mom and Dad taught me to think big. And through everything, my love, Jocylynn, has been a never-ceasing fount of patience, tolerance, and support. I'm lucky to have you all in my life.

Toluse Olorunnipa

In the Yoruba language of my ancestors, "Olorunnipa" means "God is powerful." I would be remiss if I did not start by thanking an awesome God whose power has been my strength and the source of my confidence. "God's got us" became my go-to motto while writing this book, and many times when my tank was empty, a higher power came to my rescue and made a way.

To my incredible wife, Tobore, I could not have done this without your love, your support, and your serene assurances that I could, indeed, do this. I am so blessed to have you as a partner, and I love you with all my being. To my son, Bami, you are my heartbeat and my greatest source of peace and inspiration. Thank you for choosing me.

To my dad, Zacchaeus Isenewa Olorunnipa, you have been the rock of our family. You arrived in this country with nothing but faith, a strong work ethic, and a hunger for knowledge. You have instilled all those qualities in your children and grandchildren, and we owe so much of our success to your steady, righteous leadership.

To my mother, Florence Omotade Olorunnipa, there are few jobs in this country that you have not taken on as you strived to carve out a slice of the American dream for your children—from hairstylist to gas station clerk, from babysitter to home health aide, from cook to counselor. I have always marveled at your immigrant superwoman powers. Even as you raised four kids while studying to become a nurse, you always took time to make me feel special. My love for you is something divine.

To my siblings, Funmi, Shola, and Yemi, I have watched in awe as you each charted a path from the little house on Nannas Loop to the Ivy League and beyond, always making excellence seem effortless. Thank you for modeling intelligence and integrity, and for always showing up for me.

To Robert, I count myself lucky to have been able to collaborate with you to tell this story with nuance, care, and moral clarity. Your dedication to the mission never wavered, and you handled the wrangling of this complex narrative with wisdom, precision, and aplomb. Your good-humored stories about the randomness of life never ceased to bring cheer and levity to a difficult, high-pressure task.

To my nieces, Orin, Jiri, Riri, and Nori, and nephews, Duro, Sayo, Isaiah, Elijah, and Jomi, your smiles bring me unspeakable joy. As you grow up to touch the world, your uncle Toto will be cheering you on.

I have the privilege of being connected by marriage to a large and amazing set of in-laws. First, to Mr. Vincent and Mrs. Stella Edema, thank you for raising such a fierce, graceful, intelligent, and beautiful daughter, and for welcoming me into your home with love. *Migwo. Do!*

To my sisters-in-law, Yewande and Abi, and my brothers-in-law, Tunde, Ochuko, Efe, Kevwe, and Ese, you each have added to the happiness of our growing clan.

I owe a debt of gratitude to the hundreds of relatives in my extended family, each hailing from the ancestral villages that helped send my parents to America. To the communities of Igbo, Bunu, Iyara, Edumo, and Kabba in Nigeria, I'm proud to carry your flag high. To my grandma, Mummy Olle, and my uncle Isaac, *E se gan ni, eku ise.*

Growing up in Tallahassee, Florida, an even larger tribe of family friends and warrior "aunties" formed a hedge of protection around me, keeping trouble away from me and keeping me away from trouble. I can't even begin to express my thanks to aunties Elizabeth Ojo, Felicia Oguntoye, and Abi Latinwo, and to the Agboolas, Kumuyis, Ipinmorotis, Joneses, Ebubes, Oyinloyes, Elebiyos, Okojies, Salaus, Jemisaiyes, Kalus, Gbadebos, Somorins, Bradleys, Zions, Mintas, Dadas, Campses, Adenikinjus, Toloruntomis, Johnsons, Olorunfemis, Fapohundas, Badejos, Alemikas, and so many more.

To my Stanford crew, Reyna, Daniel, Jared, Jonathan, Brittani, Cassie, Nana, Anna, Ade, Eki, and all of your spouses, you all get me, and the easy laughs of our group chats and gatherings were fresh air throughout this process.

To my Go Ye family in Tallahassee, and my New Wine family in Washington, your love, support, and prayers mean the world to me.

In addition to everyone at *The Washington Post* already listed, I am indebted to my colleagues who served on the indomitable White House reporting team during the turbulent Trump years: Josh Dawsey, Anne Gearan, Seung Min Kim, David Nakamura, Damian Paletta, Ashley Parker, and Philip Rucker. Thank you for picking up the slack when I had to duck out during the height of the 2020 presidential campaign to tell the story of George Floyd's America. To Dan Eggen and Dave Clarke, thank you for being such sharp-minded and cool-under-pressure editors.

To Joyce Peterside, you never stopped encouraging me to write, even when I doubted myself. It breaks my heart that the pandemic took you away before you could see this book published, but I know you are smiling down from heaven as proud as you have always been.

Finally, to my uncle Joseph Osanaiye and aunt Grace Adeola Motoni, who passed away during the writing of this book, may your gentle souls rest in heavenly peace.

Authors' Note

Zsa Zsa Floyd was napping in her Houston home when the phone rang one Sunday afternoon in the fall of 2021.

One of us was on the other end of the line, hoping she might once again indulge us as we asked her a series of personal questions about her deceased brother.

"Phew . . . okay, yes," she said after answering the phone, gathering her bearings as she stretched herself awake. "You know, I've had a couple other reporters call me and, for some reason, I just felt comfortable with you . . . So, what's going on? Talk to me."

In the conversation that followed, she described George Perry Floyd Jr. as few know him, recalling memories that traced back to his earliest moments. It was a continuation of a dialogue that began during a protest march months earlier in Houston's Third Ward, when Zsa Zsa and Floyd's other siblings took time between chants of "Say his name!" to tell us about what their brother was like in the years before he became a global icon for racial justice.

Those conversations were among the more than four hundred interviews we conducted over the course of more than a year as we put together this biography. In those discussions, including with the friends and family members who knew Floyd best, we heard intimate details about his ambitions, his triumphs, his trials, and his failures.

And, with a clarity that exceeded our expectations, we heard his voice.

The dialogue presented in this book reflects hundreds of hours of recorded interviews in which people who were close to Floyd, those who were familiar with the systems he tried to navigate, and those who have joined the movement to change those systems helped describe his journey, his America, and the fight for racial justice sparked by his death.

Floyd's relatives and friends willingly shared their most indelible memories, recalling with vivid detail the time they spent with him.

While the process of re-creating conversations that took place years ago can be complex, as journalists we worked to obtain a comprehensive and truthful account of the scenes depicted in this book. We used the exact words relayed to us by people who were directly involved in the conversations. On numerous occasions, our sources reenacted exchanges by mimicking Floyd's Southern drawl and verbal tics, enabling us to present dialogue as it happened at the time.

Where possible, we conducted separate interviews with others who were present to confirm details, quotes, and scenes. We also verified dates and contextual information using various elements of the public record.

Some of our interviews lasted for more than twelve hours as Floyd's friends showed us around his old neighborhoods in Houston's Third Ward and Minneapolis, took us to his favorite restaurants, and welcomed us into the places he called home.

These lengthy discussions gave us the opportunity to go over certain scenes moment by moment, as Floyd's confidants relived key episodes by retracing the steps he had taken and repeating the words he had spoken. They provided a road map that we could use to explore his worlds on our own. We spent hours hanging outside the Blue Store in Third Ward and inside Our Turning Point, Conga, and Floyd's old apartment in Minneapolis, as well as his old workplaces and local haunts, to get a feel for the places he frequented.

In addition to the interviews, we conducted a thorough review of public and private records related to Floyd. These include his diary entries, rap lyrics, poems, medical records, historical documents, cell phone videos, social media postings, personal photos, arrest reports, mug shots, court documents, job applications, text messages, love letters, and more.

In the handful of cases where there were conflicting accounts of scenes and occurrences, we relied on that extensive set of records and follow-up interviews to reconcile any discrepancies.

Floyd's friends and family were candid in sharing his many struggles and in describing their own challenges, from addiction to poverty to criminal activity and other symptoms or causes of despair. In almost every case, they did so on the record, in the interest of contributing to an accurate portrayal of Floyd's story.

In rare cases, we depicted scenes where Floyd was the only person present or engaged with another person who has also passed away. Those descriptions are based on interviews with people he subsequently spoke to about the set of events.

We have largely avoided speculating on Floyd's private emotions, feelings, and innermost thoughts. In those instances where we have described his mindset, we relied on interviews with the people in whom he confided or the text of his own writings.

In addition to our interviews with dozens of experts,

researchers, activists, policymakers, and public officials, we read thousands of pages of social science research and relevant literature to bolster our understanding of the institutions at play in Floyd's life. That research, which informed our portrayal of the environment in which Floyd came of age, is listed in the Notes and Bibliography.

There are a few sections of the book where we feel compelled to provide an even more thorough explanation of our methodology.

In tracing more than three hundred years of American history to reveal the ancestral lines of Floyd and Derek Chauvin in Chapters 3 and 6, respectively, we relied on thousands of pages of historical records as well as more than a dozen hours of interviews in which family oral history was relayed by Floyd's relatives. In almost every case, family lore was confirmed by a review of the public record, which included Census documents, marriage records, death certificates, mortgage deeds and other property records, financial and tax records, family Bibles, wills, trusts, probates, ship manifests, governmental documents, local news reports, and more. In Chapter 3 and elsewhere throughout the book, there are periodic references to offensive, insensitive, or outright racist terms used by others at the time. We opted to present the language as it was used during the period in question, to provide an authentic historical account. Throughout the book, we have followed the capitalization conventions for the terms "Black" and "White" as outlined in the style guide of *The Washington Post*.

Several chapters, especially Chapter 5, include scenes of Floyd engaged in allegedly criminal behavior. We did not rely solely on police and court records, also conducting interviews with people who had direct knowledge of the events in question or who spoke with Floyd around the time of his arrests.

Floyd's conviction for armed robbery in 2007 has taken on outsize importance in the public consciousness since his death, in part due to the rapid spread of misinformation about the case. In re-creating that scene, we reviewed legal records and spoke with several people with knowledge of the situation. Our *Washington Post* colleague Arelis R. Hernández conducted several interviews in Spanish with the victim in the case, Aracely Henriquez. We believe we have presented the turn of events before, during, and after the robbery as accurately as possible.

The last day of Floyd's life, outlined in Chapters 1 and 10, has also been the subject of intense public debate. Our portrayal reflects an amalgamation of a wide range of source material, including court testimony, police records, 911 transcripts, investigative interviews, body camera footage, cell phone and security camera videos, autopsy reports, toxicology reports, other medical records, and news reports. Most of the dialogue and action in these chapters comes directly from this trove of source material, and most of the quotes were recorded by one of the more than a dozen cameras that captured Floyd's final moments. The others come from the recollections of Genevieve Hansen, Maurice Hall, Shawanda Hill, Sylvia Jackson, and Charles McMillian, based on several interviews and interactions with us.

Because Part III of the book deals with the period after George Floyd's death, we were present for many of the scenes that took place in 2020 and 2021. Some of the events we portray in this section were captured on livestreams and many reflect our own direct knowledge of key moments. For example, we had dinner with the Floyd family the night they learned about the $27 million settlement, accompanied them on trips to the Mall of America and to the church in Fridley, and were present at the bar with them following the Chauvin verdict. We conducted interviews with them about their visit to the White House and their travels to Washington. We were with Courteney Ross throughout the Chauvin trial, traveling with her on the day she testified as well as on the day jurors reached a verdict. The behind-the-scenes look at deliberations with prosecutors was based on interviews held after the trial was completed. Derek Chauvin did not respond to requests seeking his comments, and Eric Nelson, Chauvin's attorney in the criminal trial, declined interviews with us on multiple occasions. We were in ongoing communication with congressional aides throughout negotiations over the George Floyd Justice in Policing Act.

In very rare cases, we granted anonymity to allow sources to speak freely off the record. Otherwise, all names that appear in this book are the true names of the people described.

Notes

Introduction: Flowers

ix **Floyd had grown up singing:** Wendy Grossman Kantor, "George Floyd's Sister Says Brother Was 'Best Friend,' Recalls Favorite Song They'd Sing Together," *People*, March 5, 2021, https://people.com/crime/george-floyd-sister-brother-best-friend-sing-reo-speedwagon -song.

ix **"And I'm gonna keep":** "Keep on Loving You" by REO Speedwagon, released November 4, 1980. Songwriter: Kevin Patrick Cronin; lyrics © BMG Rights Management. Lyrics via https://genius.com/Reo-speedwagon-keep-on-loving-you-lyrics.

x **"Reese, I love you!":** Hall is listed in some public documents as Morries Lester Hall, but his given name is Maurice.

xiii **"I've got my shortcomings":** Luis Andres Henao, Nomaan Merchant, Juan Lozano, and Adam Geller, "For George Floyd, a Complicated Life and a Notorious Death," Associated Press, June 10, 2020, https://apnews.com/article/death-of-george-floyd-houston-hip-hop-and-rap-cb9a406e27abb071191875cfd d89cdbf.

xiv **"people quick to count you out":** Brandon Jenkins, "Season 3, Part 4: Big Floyd," *Mogul*, podcast audio, July 14, 2021, https://gimletmedia.com/shows/mogul/v4h6zle/s3-part-4-big-floyd.

Chapter 1: An Ordinary Day

8 **six foot six:** Although Floyd's autopsy placed him at six foot four, his friends and family, and most public records, all refer to him as being six foot six.

Chapter 2: Home

14 **On their marriage certificate:** Copy of March 28, 1969, marriage certificate for George Perry Floyd and Larcenia Jones, obtained from the Office of the City Clerk of New York, Marriage Bureau.

15 **The twin girls thought he resembled:** Mel Watkins, "Flip Wilson, Outrageous Comic and TV Host, Dies at 64," *The New York Times*, November 27, 1998, https://www.nytimes.com/1998/11/27/arts/flip-wilson-outrageous-comic-and-tv-host-dies-at-64.html.

17 **Chocolate Buttermilk Band:** Gabrielle Banks, Julian Gill, John Tedesco, and Jordan Rubio, "George Floyd: 'I'm Gonna Change the World,'" *Houston Chronicle*,

June 4, 2020, https://www.houstonchronicle.com/news/houston-texas/houston/article/George-Floyd-Houston-Texas-change-the-world-15322149.php.

17 **Residents had nicknamed:** Claudia Feldman, "Third Ward: The Epicenter of Houston's Fight for Racial Equality," *Houston Chronicle*, August 22, 2014, https://www.houstonchronicle.com/life/article/Third-Ward-The-epicenter-of-Houston-s-fight-for-5706658.php; and U.S. Census Bureau records from 1970–1980.

17 **one of the poorest wards:** Feldman, "Third Ward: The Epicenter of Houston's Fight for Racial Equality"; and U.S. Census Bureau records from 1970–1980.

17 **almost everyone living:** "Census Tracts: Houston Tex. Standard Metropolitan Statistical Area: 1970 Census of Population and Housing," U.S. Department of Commerce, Bureau of the Census, May 1972, https://www2.census.gov/library/publications/decennial/1970/phc-1/39204513p9ch02.pdf.

18 **When Houston was first incorporated:** Calvin Blair, "The Story of Houston's Third Ward and Emancipation Avenue," *Main Street Matters*, September 2018, 4–6, https://www.thc.texas.gov/public/upload/MS%20Matters%20september.pdf#page=4.

18 **After World War I:** Blair, "The Story of Houston's Third Ward and Emancipation Avenue," 5, https://www.thc.texas.gov/public/upload/MS%20Matters%20september.pdf#page=5.

18 **The 564-unit complex:** *Public Housing Needs and Conditions in Houston: Hearings Before the Subcommittee on Housing and Community Development of the Committee on Banking, Finance, and Urban Affairs*, House of Representatives, Ninety-Ninth Congress, First Session, Part 1 (Washington, DC: U.S. Government Printing Office, 1986), 135, https://books.google.com/books?id=bNk26Ufvn_wC&pg=PA135&lpg=PA135&dq=cuney+homes&source=bl&ots=pZP8bGWpGu&sig=ACfU3U1BI27j94ezMsp1P3YHuxJfXaSdtw&hl=en&sa=X&ved=2ahUKEwj3j5Pa2MP0AhU7kWoFHe1LAm0Q6AF6BAgjEAM#v=snippet&q=cuney&f=false.

21 **She pitched Houston:** Census records cited by "Historical Population: 1900 to 2013," City of Houston's Planning & Development Department, accessed November 14, 2021, https://www.houstontx.gov/planning/Demographics/docs_pdfs/Cy/coh_hist_pop.pdf.

22 **Teacher Corps, a federal program:** Sarah Anne Eckert, "The National Teacher Corps," *Urban Education* 46, no. 5 (March 23, 2011): 932–52, https://doi.org/10.1177/0042085911400340; Martin Wal-dron, "Houston Moves to Desegregate Schools amid Clamor of Protest," *The New York Times*, March 1, 1970, https://www.nytimes.com/1970/03/01/archives/houston-moves-to-desegregate-schools-amid-clamor-of-protest-angry.html.

24 **The responses gave insight:** Personal records of Waynel Sexton, shared with the authors, "Future Famous Americans, Mrs. Sexton's Class, 1981–1982."

24 **"When I grow up":** Personal records of Waynel Sexton, shared with the authors, "Future Famous Americans, Mrs. Sexton's Class, 1981–1982."

25 **Floyd had earned a 3.1:** Personal records of Waynel Sexton, shared with the authors.

26 **Originally named Third Ward School:** Ezell Wilson, "Third Ward, Steeped in Tradition of Self-Reliance and Achievement," *Houston History* 8, no. 2 (March 25,

2011): 32, https://houstonhistorymagazine.org/wp-content/uploads/2011/04/wilson-third-ward.pdf.

26 **The establishment of the first colored school:** Richard Rothstein, *The Color of Law: A Forgotten History of How Our Government Segregated America* (New York: Liveright Publishing Corporation, 2017), 136, Kindle.

27 **They named the project:** Joe Holley, "Norris Wright Cuney Never Stopped Fighting," *Houston Chronicle*, June 14, 2020, https://www.houstonchronicle.com/news/columnists/native-texan/article/Norris-Wright-Cuney-never-stopped-fighting-15338633.php.

27 **When Cuney Homes opened:** Tracy Jan and Arelis R. Hernández, "George Floyd's America: Segregated from Opportunity," *The Washington Post*, October 15, 2020, https://www.washingtonpost.com/graphics/2020/national/george-floyd-america/housing.

27 **University for Negroes:** Jeannie Kever, "Little-Known Lawsuit Creating TSU Is Still Opening Doors," *Houston Chronicle*, October 1, 2010, https://www.chron.com/news/houston-texas/article/Little-known-lawsuit-creating-TSU-is-still-1607278.php.

27 **In response to a Supreme Court ruling:** "Sweatt v. Painter," Oyez, accessed December 6, 2021, https://www.oyez.org/cases/1940-1955/339us629.

27–8 **Redlining and restrictive covenants:** Jan and Hernández, "George Floyd's America: Segregated from Opportunity."

28 **Much of the discrimination was sanctioned:** Rothstein, *The Color of Law*, preface.

28 **An almost thirty-point disparity:** Heather Long and Andrew Van Dam, "The Black-White Economic Divide Is as Wide as It Was in 1968," *The Washington Post*, June 4, 2020, https://www.washingtonpost.com/business/2020/06/04/economic-divide-black-households.

28 **the typical White family:** Long and Van Dam, "The Black-White Economic Divide."

28 **Shortly before the Federal Housing Administration:** Rothstein, *The Color of Law*, 72.

28 **The vicious cycle:** Aaron Williams and Armand Emamdjomeh, "America Is More Diverse Than Ever—but Still Segregated," *The Washington Post*, May 10, 2018, https://www.washingtonpost.com/graphics/2018/national/segregation-us-cities.

28 **African Americans remained the most segregated:** Williams and Emamdjomeh, "America Is More Diverse Than Ever."

28 **President Richard Nixon decried:** Richard Nixon, "Special Message to the Congress Proposing Legislation and Outlining Administration Actions to Deal with Federal Housing Policy," September 19, 1973, via the American Presidency Project, accessed November 18, 2021, www.presidency.ucsb.edu/documents/special-message-the-congress-proposing-legislation-and-outlining-administration-actions.

33 **Things were especially tight:** Jonathan Harsch, "Reagan Cuts Eat into School Lunches," *The Christian Science Monitor*, September 17, 1981, https://www.csmonitor.com/1981/0917/091746.html.

34 **During his inauguration:** Ronald Reagan, Inaugural Address, January 20, 1981, via Ronald Reagan Presidential Foundation and Institute, accessed November 17, 2021, https://www.reaganfoundation.org/media/128614/inaguration.pdf#page=2.

34 **It was "morning again":** Martin Schram, "Reagan Narrates Ticket's Positively Pitched Campaign Ads," *The Washington Post*, September 18, 1984, https://www. washingtonpost.com/archive/politics/1984/09/18/reagan-narrates-tickets-positively-pitched-campaign-ads/2669830c-7db3-4b86-83a9-c1daa468f74b.

34 **The nation's economy expanded:** U.S. Department of Commerce, Bureau of Economic Analysis, "Table 1.1.1. Percent Change from Preceding Period in Real Gross Domestic Product," accessed November 16, 2021, https://apps.bea.gov/ iTable/iTable.cfm?reqid=19&step=3&isuri=1&1921=survey&1903=1#reqid=19&st ep=3&isuri=1&1921=survey&1903=1.

34 **In fact, much of the growth:** Gillian Brockell, "She Was Stereotyped as the 'Welfare Queen.' The Truth Was More Disturbing, a New Book Says," *The Washington Post*, May 21, 2019, https://www.washingtonpost.com/history/2019/05/21/ she-was-stereotyped-welfare-queen-truth-was-more-disturbing-new-book-says.

34 **Reagan's tax legislation eliminated:** Staff writers, "Tax Bill Is Signed into Law," *The Washington Post*, October 21, 1986, https://www.washingtonpost.com/archive/ politics/1986/10/23/tax-bill-is-signed-into-law/0d8b2dc7-2c07-4a93-94ec-c25231b15df2.

34 **the minimum wage held steady:** U.S. Department of Labor, "History of Federal Minimum Wage Rates Under the Fair Labor Standards Act, 1938–2009," accessed November 18, 2021, https://www.dol.gov/agencies/whd/minimum-wage/history/ chart#fn4.

34 **Reagan opposed the kind of increases:** George Lardner Jr., "Business Gets Cold Feet on Subminimum Wage," *The Washington Post*, March 20, 1981, https://www. washingtonpost.com/archive/politics/1981/03/20/business-gets-cold-feet-on-subminimum-wage/7a1f10fe-9acc-4c11-a818-3e4fb2ab2720.

34 **While the wage gap between:** Peter Baker and Susan Glasser, *The Man Who Ran Washington: The Life and Times of James A. Baker III* (New York: Doubleday, 2020), chapter 14, Libby e-book.

37 **Nationwide, the homicide rate:** Roland G. Fryer Jr., Paul S. Heaton, Steven D. Levitt, and Kevin M. Murphy, "Measuring Crack Cocaine and Its Impact," Harvard University Society of Fellows, April 2006, 6, https://scholar.harvard.edu/ files/fryer/files/fhlm_crack_cocaine_0.pdf#page=6.

37 **Houston's Fox television affiliate:** Fox KRIV biography page for reporter Randy Wallace, accessed November 23, 2021, https://www.fox26houston.com/person/w/ randy-wallace.

Chapter 3: Roots

40 **Born enslaved in 1857:** U.S. Census Bureau, 1870 United States Census, Grove, Harnett, North Carolina; Roll: M593_1142; Page: 51B, digital image s.v. "Hiley Stewart," Ancestry.com. Authors also interviewed Stewart's descendants to compile family oral history. While historical records show multiple spellings of Stewart's first name, his family spells it as "Hillery."

40 **he had managed to amass:** Property records from Harnett County Register of Deeds: Grantor Index to Real Estate Conveyances, Old Index Book, pages 124-A,

124-B, 124-F, 124-G, and 124-H; and authors' interviews with Stewart's descendants.

40   **less than 2 percent:** Guion Griffis Johnson, *Ante-Bellum North Carolina: A Social History* (Chapel Hill: University of North Carolina Press, 1937), 54, https://docsouth.unc.edu/nc/johnson/menu.html; U.S. Census Bureau, "Agriculture of the United States in 1860," https://www2.census.gov/library/publications/decennial/1860/agriculture/1860b-09.pdf#page=27; page 210 of "Agriculture of the United States in 1860" includes a county-by-county breakdown of all farms in North Carolina with more than three acres of land in 1860. Only nine farms in Harnett County had five hundred acres or more.

40   **Working alongside his twelve siblings:** U.S. Census Bureau, 1870 United States Census, Grove, Harnett, North Carolina; Roll: M593_1142; Page: 51B, digital image s.v. "Abram Stewart" and family, Ancestry.com.

41   **In 1888, Stewart married:** U.S. Census Bureau, 1910 United States Census, Grove, Harnett County, North Carolina; Roll: T624_1116; Page: 3A; digital image s.v. "Hilery Stewart," "Larcenia Stewart," and family, Ancestry.com; and family oral history via authors' interviews with Stewart's descendants.

41   **Behind his back:** Family oral history, via authors' interviews with Stewart's descendants.

42   **In 1748:** Family history of the White Stewarts was obtained via written and oral family history, local newspaper articles, family Bible records, and Census records. Authors reviewed North Carolina archivist James Mark Valsame's family history of Charles Stewart and Hannah Kirk, found at https://www.familysearch.org/service/records/storage/das-mem/patron/v2/TH-904-70438-404-62/dist.txt?ctx=ArtCtxPublic.

   Additionally, several of Charles and Hannah Stewart's descendants provided written histories of their ancestry in the family tribute section at the back of Mary Alice Hasty's *The Heritage of Harnett County, North Carolina.*

43   **The list of properties Charles granted:** Deed from Charles Stewart to James Stewart, May 7, 1805, accessed via Consolidated Real Property Index, Register of Deeds, Wake County, North Carolina, Book 00000U, Page 280, http://services.wakegov.com/booksweb/PDFView.aspx?DocID=108487232&RecordD ate=03/08/1808. The deed was recorded on March 8, 1808, after Charles Stewart's death.

43   **His net worth increased tenfold:** U.S. Census Bureau, 1850 United States Census, Western Division, Wake County, North Carolina; Roll: 647; Page: 179b, digital image s.v. "James Stewart" and family, Ancestry.com; and U.S. Census Bureau, 1860 United States Census, Southern Division, Wake County, North Carolina; Roll: M653_916; Page: 36; digital image s.v. "James Stewart" and family, Ancestry.com.

   Stewart's real estate holdings were listed as $2,040 in 1850. By 1860, his real estate was worth $1,500 and the value of his personal property was listed as $14,965.

43   **though his jump in wealth:** U.S. Census Bureau, 1860 United States Census, Slave Schedules, Southern Division, Wake County, North Carolina, digital image, s.v.

"James Stewart," Ancestry.com. The record lists James Stewart as the owner of nineteen enslaved people, ages two to eighty.

43 **Stewart used his fortune:** Wills and Estate Papers for James Stewart, dated 1867 (Wake County, North Carolina), 1663–1978; North Carolina Division of Archives and History (Raleigh, North Carolina); digital images, s.v. "James Stewart," Ancestry.com.

43 **while making money as a slaver:** *Federal Writers' Project: Slave Narrative Project, Vol. 11, North Carolina, Part 2, Jackson-Yellerday*, 1936, 321, https://www.loc.gov/ resource/mesn.112/?sp=321. Sam T. Stewart, a formerly enslaved man on James Stewart's plantation in Wake County, North Carolina, told interviewers from the Federal Writers' Project in 1936, "When I was two years old James Arch Stewart sold my father to speculators, and he was shipped to Mississippi. I was too young to know my father."

43 **By 1860, Charles Stewart's grandson:** U.S. Census Bureau, 1860 United States Census, Slave Schedules for Harnett County, North Carolina, digital image, s.v. "Joseph Stewart," Ancestry.com.

44 **In 1862, he left his home:** U.S. Civil War Soldier Records and Profiles, 1861–1865, "Joseph Stewart," Ancestry.com.

44 **enlisting as a corporal:** National Park Service, The Civil War Soldiers and Sailors System database, entry for Joseph A. Stewart, accessed December 5, 2021, https:// www.nps.gov/civilwar/search-soldiers-detail.htm?soldierId=E84E57D5-DC7A-DF11- BF36-B8AC6F5D926A.

44 **Since the first Africans had arrived:** J. David Hacker, "From '20. and Odd' to 10 Million: The Growth of the Slave Population in the United States," *Slavery & Abolition* 41, no. 4 (May 13, 2020): 840–55, https://doi.org/10.1080/01440 39x.2020.1755502.

45 **But almost all the government-funded provisions:** National Archives and Records Administration report on Freedmen's Bureau's activities in North Carolina between 1865 and 1872. Rations data comes from "Records of the Assistant Commissioner for the State of North Carolina Bureau of Refugees, Freedmen, and Abandoned Lands, 1865–1870," https://www.archives.gov/files/ research/african-americans/freedmens-bureau/north-carolina.pdf.

45 **Despite the lack of federal aid:** U.S. Census Bureau, 1870 United States Census, Grove, Harnett County, North Carolina.

45 **In his book Black Property Owners:** Loren Schweninger, *Black Property Owners in the South, 1790–1915* (Urbana: University of Illinois Press, 1990), 160.

45 **only forty-one thousand of the South's:** Schweninger, *Black Property Owners in the South*, 3.

45 **or less than 5 percent:** Schweninger, *Black Property Owners in the South*, 161.

45 **an increasing number of Black landowners:** Waymon R. Hinson, "Land Gains, Land Losses: The Odyssey of African Americans since Reconstruction," *American Journal of Economics and Sociology* 77, no. 3–4 (May–September 2018): 893–939, https://doi.org/10.1111/ajes.12233.

46 **In a series of transactions:** Property records from Harnett County Register of Deeds: Grantor Index to Real Estate Conveyances, Old Index Book, pages 124-A,

124-B, 124-F, 124-G, and 124-H; tax auction announcements in the *Harnett County News*; and authors' interviews with descendants of the Stewarts.

46 **"But if default shall be made":** Record of Hillery Stewart Mortgage Deed, March 14, 1904, Harnett County Register of Deeds, Deed Book 101, page 26.

47 **The April 15, 1920, edition:** W. H. Turlington, "Land Sale for Taxes," *Harnett County News*, April 15, 1920, https://www.newspapers.com/image/63242528/.

47 **His descendants have disputed:** Leo McGee and Robert Boone, *The Black Rural Landowner—Endangered Species: Social, Political, and Economic Implications* (Westport, CT: Greenwood Press, 1979), 104–05, 146–47.

47 **An ad placed in the same:** England Realty and Auction Co. ad, *Harnett County News*, April 15, 1920, https://www.newspapers.com/image/63242535.

47 **The average cost of an acre:** Charles H. Barnard and John Jones, *Farm Real Estate Values in the United States by Counties, 1850–1982* (Washington, DC: U.S. Department of Agriculture, Economic Research Service, 1987), http://hdl.handle.net/2027/uiug.30112046854219.

48 **If Stewart had not lost:** Turlington, "Land Sale for Taxes." Turlington, the Harnett County sheriff, announced in the newspaper that a 230-acre property owned by Hillery Thomas Stewart would be "sold at auction in front of the courthouse door in Lillington, for 1918 taxes, Monday, May 5, 1919." Stewart allegedly owed $37.15 for the property.

48 **Between 1910 and 1997:** Jess Gilbert, Spencer D. Wood, and Gwen Sharp, "Who Owns the Land?: Agricultural Land Ownership by Race/Ethnicity," *Rural America* 17, no. 4 (Winter 2002): 1, https://www.ers.usda.gov/webdocs/publications/46984/19353_ra174h_1_.pdf?v=0.

48 **More than two thousand people:** Staff writers, "Rally at Grove," *The County Union* (Dunn, NC), November 9, 1898, https://www.newspapers.com/image/61501655.

49 **"Whenever a man was found":** D. H. McLean, "Joseph A. Stewart," *Harnett County News*, July 17, 1919, https://www.newspapers.com/image/63242370.

49 **"Negro and pie":** Staff writers, "Rally at Grove."

50 **but the very same week:** LeRae Umfleet, *1898 Wilmington Race Riot Report: 1898 Wilmington Race Riot Commission* (Raleigh, NC: Research Branch, Office of Archives and History, NC Department of Cultural Resources, 2006), 88, https://digital.ncdcr.gov/digital/collection/p249901coll22/id/5443.

50 **"Declaration of White Independence":** Umfleet, *1898 Wilmington Race Riot Report*, 115.

52 **Led by a Wilmington legislator:** Umfleet, *1898 Wilmington Race Riot Report*, 209.

52 **"This, Mr. Chairman":** The Committee on House Administration of the U.S. House of Representatives, *Black Americans in Congress, 1870–2007* (Washington, DC: U.S. Government Printing Office, 2008), 169, https://www.govinfo.gov/content/pkg/GPO-CDOC-108hdoc224/pdf/GPO-CDOC-108hdoc224.pdf#page=177.

52 **No other Black person from the South:** "Black-American Members by Congress, 1870–Present," History, Art & Archives, United States House of Representatives, accessed December 5, 2021, https://history.house.gov/Exhibitions-and-

Publications/BAIC/Historical-Data/Black-American-Representatives-and-
Senators-by-Congress.

53 **Driving home the skewed:** Joseph A. Stewart, "A Card. For Register of Deeds," *The County Union* (Dunn, NC), August 3, 1898, https://www.newspapers.com/clip/54252608/joseph-a-stewart-runs-for-register-of. Stewart wrote, "I hereby announce myself a candidate for the office of Register of Deeds for Harnett County, subject to the action of the Democratic County Convention to be held in Lillington on August 15."

53 **He was defeated:** Special Staff of Writers, *History of North Carolina. Vol. VI. North Carolina Biography* (New York: The Lewis Publishing Company, 1919), 56, https://play.google.com/books/reader?id=AEU4AQAAMAAJ&pg=GBS.PA56&hl=en.

53 **Though he lost his bid:** "All Known NC Post Offices—1785 to 1971, Alphabetical Order M–Z," accessed December 5, 2021, https://www.carolana.com/NC/Towns/NC_POs_1785_to_1971_M_thru_Z.htm; R. F. Winter, "Postmark Catalog: Harnett County," North Carolina Postal History Society, May 23, 2017, 54, http://www.ncpostalhistory.com/wp-content/uploads/2017/05/PostmarkCatalog_harnett_county-20170523.pdf#page=54.

53 **His descendants and relatives:** Local news reports, *Coats Museum News*, December 5, 2011, http://www.coatsmuseum.com/december-5-2011.html. Other modern-day descendants of Charles and Hannah Stewart appear in the family tribute section at the back of Mary Alice Hasty's *The Heritage of Harnett County, North Carolina* (Erwin, NC: The Heritage of Harnett Book Committee, in Cooperation with Delmar Printing, 1993).

53 **Hillery Thomas Stewart soon fell ill:** Standard Certificate of Death, Hillery Thomas Stewart, filed December 20, 1937, with the North Carolina State Board of Health, Bureau of Vital Statistics, North Carolina State Archives, Raleigh, North Carolina, digital image, Ancestry.com. Authors also interviewed Stewart's descendants.

55 **Towering over the five-foot-eight Jones:** Family oral history and World War II Draft Registration Cards listing the men's heights.

55 **"You messed that girl up":** Family oral history relayed to the authors by the children of H. B. and Laura Ann Jones.

56 **On the White-owned farms of Goldsboro:** The description of the Jones family's experience as sharecroppers was relayed to the authors during interviews with several of George Floyd's aunts, uncles, and other relatives, who spent time working the tobacco fields as children.

59 **Despite scientific studies:** U.S. Department of Health and Human Services, Centers for Disease Control and Prevention, "History of the Surgeon General's Report on Smoking and Health," CDC.gov, October 19, 2021, https://www.cdc.gov/tobacco/data_statistics/sgr/history/index.htm.

60 **Researchers later found:** Joseph G. L. Lee et al., "A Systematic Review of Neighborhood Disparities in Point-of-Sale Tobacco Marketing," *American Journal of Public Health* 105, no. 9 (September 2015): e8–18, https://doi.org/10.2105/ajph.2015.302777; Tess Boley Cruz, La Tanisha Wright, and George Crawford, "The Menthol Marketing Mix: Targeted Promotions for Focus Communities in

the United States," *Nicotine & Tobacco Research* 12, Supplement 2 (December 1, 2010): S147–S153, https://doi.org/10.1093/ntr/ntq201.

60 **Upward of 60 percent:** U.S. Department of Health and Human Services, *Tobacco Use Among U.S. Racial/Ethnic Minority Groups: African Americans, American Indians and Alaska Natives, Asian Americans and Pacific Islanders, and Hispanics: A Report of the Surgeon General* (Atlanta: U.S. Department of Health and Human Services, Centers for Disease Control and Prevention, National Center for Chronic Disease Prevention and Health Promotion, Office on Smoking and Health, 1998), 23, Figure 1, https://www.cdc.gov/tobacco/data_statistics/sgr/1998/complete_report/pdfs/complete_report.pdf#page=36.

60 **North Carolina farms yielded:** Staff writers, "North Carolina & Tobacco: A Timeline," PBS's *Bright Leaves*, a point-of-view documentary on the tobacco industry, aired August 23, 2005, http://archive.pov.org/brightleaves/timeline.

60 **Americans smoked more than 350 billion:** Laverne Creek, Tom Capehart, and Verner Grise, *U.S. Tobacco Statistics, 1935–92* (Washington, DC: U.S. Department of Agriculture, Economic Research Service, Commodity Economics Division, 1994), 5, https://www.ers.usda.gov/webdocs/publications/47092/59808_sb869.pdf#page=19.

60 **spending more than $3.5 billion:** Creek, Capehart, and Grise, *U.S. Tobacco Statistics, 1935–92*, 51.

60 **By 1963, when over 40 percent:** Creek, Capehart, and Grise, *U.S. Tobacco Statistics, 1935–92*, 5.

60 **or more than 4,300:** Creek, Capehart, and Grise, *U.S. Tobacco Statistics, 1935–92*, 14. American adults smoked 4,325 cigarettes per capita in 1963, the highest total on record. Tobacco producers sold more than $7 billion worth of cigarettes in the U.S. that year.

60 **It was so politically powerful:** W. P. Hedrick and J. H. Cyrus, "North Carolina Tobacco Report, 1964–1965" (Raleigh, NC: Tobacco Section, Division of Markets, North Carolina Department of Agriculture, 1965), 5, https://digital.ncdcr.gov/digital/collection/p249901coll22/id/306767.

61 **In 1924, James Buchanan "Buck" Duke:** "About the Duke Endowment," The Duke Endowment, accessed December 6, 2021, https://www.dukeendowment.org/about/about-the-endowment.

63 **His death certificate said:** Standard Certificate of Death, Frank Jones, filed January 15, 1958, with the North Carolina State Board of Health, Bureau of Vital Statistics, North Carolina State Archives, Raleigh, North Carolina, digital image, Ancestry.com. Authors also interviewed Frank Jones's siblings.

65 **"Welcome to Ku Klux Klan country":** Bruce Siceloff, "Signing Off: Klan Greeting Topples After 10 Years," *The News and Observer* (Raleigh, NC), March 27, 1977, https://www.newsobserver.com/latest-news/90xc6p/picture232986937/alternates/FREE_768/Klan1977.JPG; Mary Ann Lachat, "Desegregation in Goldsboro, North Carolina: A Case Study" (Washington, DC: Office of Education, 1973), 9, https://files.eric.ed.gov/fulltext/ED117278.pdf.

67 **In a metropolis of almost:** "Total Population—New York City & Boroughs, 1900 to 2010," Population Division, New York City Department of City Planning,

accessed December 6, 2021, https://www1.nyc.gov/assets/planning/download/
pdf/planning-level/nyc-population/historical-population/nyc_total_pop_1900-
2010.pdf.

67 **a man whose family history:** George Perry Floyd Sr.'s family history was obtained
via Census records, marriage records, news reports, and oral history from his
descendants.

67 **His owner, a wealthy man:** Will and probate records of Francis Floyd, North
Carolina, 1856–1859, Division of Archives and History, Probate Place: Robeson
County, North Carolina, Ancestry.com.

67 **Because Francis Floyd's thirty-two slaves:** Francis Floyd's will and probate records
include a November 1858 court petition made on behalf of his heirs, who wished
to sell off two enslaved people and split the proceeds equally. They wrote: "Your
petitioners further show that they desire to have the said slaves divided among
them according to their respective rights and interests in the same but that a
division in kind cannot be made without injury to the parties concerned. Your
petitioners therefore pray your worships to order a sale . . ." The court approved
and, in February 1859, a twenty-four-year-old man from the Floyd plantation was
taken to the auction block to be sold to the highest bidder. White men haggled
during the auction until a man named Williams put forward the top bid: $1,196.
The sold man's name happened to be George Floyd.

67 **Five years after the Civil War:** U.S. Census Bureau, 1870 United States Census,
White House, Robeson County, North Carolina, Roll: M593_1157; Page: 198B,
digital image, s.v. "Carlyle Floyd," Ancestry.com.

68 **Two years later, Carlyle married:** Indexed Register of Marriages, Robeson County,
listing March 24, 1872, marriage between Carlyle Floyd and Kitty Pittman,
Ancestry.com.

68 **the Black Floyds would be mainstays:** Staff writers, "Deaths and Funerals: Archie
Floyd," *The Robesonian* (Lumberton, NC), November 29, 1955, https://www.
newspapers.com/image/42046330/?terms=%22archie%20floyd%22&match=1.
Family oral history was also relayed to the authors by descendants of Carlyle
Floyd.

CHAPTER 4: LESSONS

71 **The minimetropolis:** Thomas D. Snyder and Charlene M. Hoffman, *Digest of
Education Statistics 1994* (Washington, DC: U.S. Department of Education, Office
of Educational Research and Improvement, National Center for Education
Statistics, 1994), 217, https://books.google.com/books?id=WSurcCkIzvEC&pg=
PA217&lpg=PA217&d.

72 **Floyd looked out over:** Richard Pennington, "Darrell K Royal-Texas Memorial
Stadium," Texas State Historical Association Handbook of Texas, September 1,
1995, https://www.tshaonline.org/handbook/entries/darrell-k-royal-texas-
memorial-stadium.

72 **"In short, you face":** George H. W. Bush, "Remarks at the University of Texas
Commencement Ceremony in Austin," The American Presidency Project, May

19, 1990, https://www.presidency.ucsb.edu/documents/remarks-the-university-texas-commencement-ceremony-austin.

74   **The Temple High School Wildcats:** "Population Estimates of Texas Cities, 1990–99, Arranged in Alphabetical Order," Texas State Library and Archives Commission, citing U.S. Census records, October 20, 2000, https://www.tsl.texas. gov/ref/abouttx/popcity2.html.

76   **During Floyd's time in high school:** John Werner, "Texas Sports Hall of Fame: Dynamic Bailey Left Lasting Legacy," *Waco Tribune-Herald*, February 28, 2018, https://wacotrib.com/sports/texas_sports_hall_of_fame/texas-sports-hall-of-fame-dynamic-bailey-left-lasting-legacy/article_17deec32-dbf8-57b1-af8d-d7805b780a04. html. This article includes a photo with the caption: "Three members of the 1990 Chicago Bears—(from left) linebacker John Roper, running back Johnny Bailey and receiver Quintin Smith—were also teammates in high school at Houston Yates." *The Great Yates: Thursday Night Lights and the Magical Season*, produced by Donald M. Pinkard and Jocelyn Pinkard (Dallas: Urban Aggregate LLC, 2019), accessed September 4, 2021, https://jpink98701.gumroad.com. Bailey, Roper, Smith, and other Yates players who advanced to the NFL were featured in this documentary.

77   **Named after a formerly enslaved:** Ezell Wilson, "Third Ward, Steeped in Tradition of Self-Reliance and Achievement," *Houston History* 8, no. 2 (March 25, 2011): 32, https://houstonhistorymagazine.org/wp-content/uploads/2011/04/wilson-third-ward.pdf.

77   **The 1896 Supreme Court decision:** Plessy v. Ferguson, 163 U.S. 537 (1896).

78   **After the Supreme Court reversed:** The Texas Advisory Committee on Segregation in the Public Schools, "Report of the Legal and Legislative Subcommittee of the Texas Advisory Committee on Segregation in the Public Schools," September 1, 1956, 1–58, https://lrl.texas.gov/scanned/interim/54/54_SegregInPubSchools.pdf.

78   **In its final report in 1956:** The Texas Advisory Committee on Segregation in the Public Schools, "Report," 8.

78   **Texas legislators passed:** Charles Waite, "Price Daniel, Texas Democrats, and School Segregation, 1956–1957," *East Texas Historical Journal* 48, no. 2 (2010): 110–19, https://scholarworks.sfasu.edu/ethj/vol48/iss2/10.

79   **In Houston, school administrators:** Delores Ross, et al., Plaintiffs-appellants, v. Houston Independent School District, et al., Defendants-appellees, 699 F.2d 218 (5th Cir. 1983).

79   **Determined to prevent:** William Henry Kellar, *Make Haste Slowly: Moderates, Conservatives, and School Desegregation in Houston* (College Station: Texas A&M University Press, 1999), 138.

79   **Courts rejected the measures:** Kellar, *Make Haste Slowly*, 127. In an August 3, 1960, ruling, district court judge Ben Connally ruled that a desegregation plan submitted by Houston's school district "does not constitute a good faith attempt at compliance with previous orders of the court but is a palpable sham and subterfuge designed only to accomplish further evasion and delay."

Notes

79 **By 1970, when Houston:** Laura Meckler, "George Floyd's America: Looking for His Ticket Out," *The Washington Post*, October 12, 2020, https://www.washingtonpost. com/graphics/2020/national/george-floyd-america/education.

79 **judges had grown tired:** Martin Waldron, "Houston Moves to Desegregate Schools amid Clamor of Protest," *The New York Times*, March 1, 1970, https://www. nytimes.com/1970/03/01/archives/houston-moves-to-desegregate-schools-amid-clamor-of-protest-angry.html.

79 **And with few White parents willing:** Texas Education Agency, "Yates High School, Final 1990–91 Campus Performance," accessed September 12, 2021, https://rptsvr1.tea.texas.gov/perfreport/aeis/91/campus/101912020.html.

79 **Months before Floyd enrolled:** Associated Press, "18-Year-Old Texas Mother Is a Valedictorian," *The New York Times*, June 11, 1989, https://www.nytimes. com/1989/06/11/us/18-year-old-texas-mother-is-a-valedictorian.html.

79 **"Where did they go?":** Associated Press, "18-Year-Old Texas Mother Is a Valedictorian."

81 **August 8, 1991:** Except where otherwise noted, all details and quotes about Carl Owens's death were obtained by the authors during interviews with multiple witnesses and via police records.

85 **"Yates Athlete's Murder Stuns":** James T. Campbell, "Yates Athlete's Murder Stuns Coaches, Friends; Community Mourns Senseless Tragedy," *Houston Chronicle*, August 12, 1991, A11.

85 **Some were willing to say:** Waldron, "Houston Moves to Desegregate Schools."

86 **The city's school district:** Meckler, "George Floyd's America: Looking for His Ticket Out"; and Delores Ross, et al., Plaintiffs-appellants, v. Houston Independent School District, et al., Defendants-appellees, 699 F.2d 218 (5th Cir. 1983).

86 **Between 1970 and 1983:** Delores Ross, et al., Plaintiffs-appellants, v. Houston Independent School District, et al., Defendants-appellees, 699 F.2d 218 (5th Cir. 1983).

86 **On the west side:** Ross v. Houston Independent Sch. Dist, 457 F. Supp. 18 (S.D. Tex. 1977), https://law.justia.com/cases/federal/district-courts/FSupp/457/18/2347735. In this ruling, Judge Finis E. Cowan wrote that the proposed Westheimer Independent School District was essentially a "protest movement" seeking to combat integration by creating a "white break-away district" on Houston's west side.

87 **Like Detroit, Atlanta, St. Louis, Wilmington:** Ross v. Houston Independent Sch. Dist, 457 F. Supp. 18 (S.D. Tex. 1977). In this ruling, Judge Cowan wrote: "One of the most serious problems with which HISD must contend is the fact that HISD is surrounded by predominantly white school districts which serve as areas for white flight and bear none of the burdens of eliminating the effects of the previously existing dual system." Cowan added that Detroit, Atlanta, St. Louis, Wilmington, and "virtually every urban metropolitan area in our nation" were bedeviled by this "serious problem."

87 **In the first such challenge:** Spencer Rich, "School Integration Sought by U.S. in Houston, Suburbs," *The Washington Post*, May 16, 1980, https://www.

washingtonpost.com/archive/politics/1980/05/16/school-integration-sought-by-us-in-houston-suburbs/0f90f3cf-cef8-48d9-a4f2-ebf42b1f3042.

87   **A federal judge sided:** Meckler, "George Floyd's America: Looking for His Ticket Out."

87–8   **One declared that Houston:** Delores Ross, et al., Plaintiffs-appellants, v. Houston Independent School District, et al., Defendants-appellees, 699 F.2d 218 (5th Cir. 1983). Judge Alvin B. Rubin's ruling affirmed the lower court's finding that HISD had achieved "unitary status."

88   **Specifically citing the impact:** Rubin's 1983 ruling in Delores Ross, et al., Plaintiffs-appellants, v. Houston Independent School District, et al., Defendants-appellees, 699 F.2d 218 (5th Cir. 1983).

88   **The court rulings helped:** Delores Ross, et al., Plaintiffs-appellants, v. Houston Independent School District, et al., Defendants-appellees, 699 F.2d 218 (5th Cir. 1983). In his 1983 ruling, Judge Alvin Rubin wrote, "The student population in twenty-two of the 226 schools in the system has been 90% or more black continuously since 1960. And there are now thirty-three more schools whose student population is 90% or more black."

90   **The Supreme Court had:** Luke Records v. Navarro, 960 F.2d 134 (11th Cir. 1992). The U.S. Supreme Court denied certiorari in this case, blocking efforts by Florida authorities to appeal the circuit court's ruling in favor of 2 Live Crew.

91   **"If you love someone":** "Poor Georgie" by MC Lyte, released September 17, 1991. Songwriters: Dee Jay Doc/Lana Moorer; lyrics © BMG Rights Management. Lyrics via https://genius.com/Mc-lyte-poor-georgie-lyrics.

95   **Almost thirty of the thirty-six seniors:** David Barron, "Yates Looks to Settle the Score with History," *Houston Chronicle*, May 29, 2005, https://www.chron.com/sports/article/Yates-looks-to-settle-the-score-with-history-1949167.php; *The Great Yates: Thursday Night Lights and the Magical Season*.

97   **Maybe the magic:** Sam Khan Jr., "Yates May See Its Football Playoff Streak End," *Houston Chronicle*, October 24, 2008, https://www.chron.com/sports/high-school/article/Yates-may-see-its-football-playoff-streak-end-1764766.php. A chart in the article showed that Yates had the most consecutive playoff appearances in Texas high school football history, a thirty-one-year streak that began in 1977. The streak would have been fifteen years long in 1992.

98   **In 1970, as federal courts condemned:** Waldron, "Houston Moves to Desegregate Schools."

98   **The reassignments were designed:** Waldron, "Houston Moves to Desegregate Schools."

102   **A photographer:** Richard Carson/*Houston Chronicle* file photo, November 11, 1992. The photo appeared in an article by Gabrielle Banks, Julian Gill, John Tedesco, and Jordan Rubio, "George Floyd: 'I'm Gonna Change the World,'" *Houston Chronicle*, June 6, 2020, https://www.houstonchronicle.com/news/houston-texas/houston/article/George-Floyd-Houston-Texas-change-the-world-15322149.php.

105   **A thick fog:** University Inter-Scholastic League, "1992 State Championship Conference 5A Division 2," box score, https://www.uiltexas.org/files/athletics/

state-football/boxscores/19925AD2FBBOX.pdf. The description of the state championship game comes from authors' interviews with several players, school officials, and fans and the official box score, along with a video of the 1992 game broadcast by Home Sports Entertainment, available at https://vimeo.com/424586915.

106 **But the game slipped:** University Inter-Scholastic League, "1992 State Championship Conference 5A Division 2."

108 **State officials had introduced:** GI Forum v. Texas Education Agency, Civil Action No. SA-97-CA-1278-EP (W.D. Tex. Jan. 7, 2000), https://casetext.com/case/gi-forum-v-texas-education-agency-wdtex-2000/case-details.

108 **In 1999, a suit:** GI Forum v. Texas Education Agency, Civil Action No. SA-97-CA-1278-EP (W.D. Tex. Jan. 7, 2000).

109 **had failed to adequately prepare them:** Mark A. J. Fassold, "Disparate Impact Analyses of TAAS Scores and School Quality," *Hispanic Journal of Behavioral Sciences* 22, no. 4 (November 2000): 460–80, https://doi.org/10.1177/0739986300224006.

109 **Despite agreeing with the plaintiffs:** GI Forum v. Texas Education Agency, Civil Action No. SA-97-CA-1278-EP (W.D. Tex. Jan. 7, 2000).

109 **In 1983, a federal education commission:** The National Commission on Excellence in Education, "A Nation at Risk: The Imperative for Educational Reform," April 1983, https://www2.ed.gov/pubs/NatAtRisk/title.html.

109 **It recommended more rigorous standardized testing:** Andrew P. Huddleston and Elizabeth C. Rockwell, "Assessment for the Masses: A Historical Critique of High-Stakes Testing in Reading," *Texas Journal of Literacy Education* 3, no. 1 (2015): 38–49, https://files.eric.ed.gov/fulltext/EJ1110955.pdf.

109 **Texas—which at the time ranked fortieth:** Michael Isikoff and David Von Drehle, "Perot-Schools Shootout," *The Washington Post*, June 28, 1992, https://www.washingtonpost.com/archive/politics/1992/06/28/perot-schools-shootout/03e8c3ea-4baf-4a8b-9581-01f43b47c444.

109 **A 2000 study:** NewsEditor, "Studies Find High Stakes Tests Threaten Disadvantaged Students in Texas," Harvard Graduate School of Education, January 5, 2000, https://www.gse.harvard.edu/news/00/01/studies-find-high-stakes-tests-threaten-disadvantaged-students-texas.

114 **"Look, man. I'm just":** Details from this 1997 arrest were documented in Houston Police Department records obtained by the authors, including HPD OLO Incident Report 098848797.

CHAPTER 5: THE STATE OF TEXAS VS. GEORGE FLOYD

124 **The nation's incarceration rate:** Jeremy Travis, Bruce Western, and Steve Redburn, eds., *The Growth of Incarceration in the United States: Exploring Causes and Consequences* (Washington, DC: The National Academies Press, 2014), 33, https://www.nap.edu/read/18613/chapter/4.

124 **President Richard Nixon had declared:** David Farber, "The War on Drugs Turns 50 Today. It's Time to Make Peace," *The Washington Post*, June 17, 2021, https://

www.washingtonpost.com/outlook/2021/06/17/war-drugs-turns-50-today-its-time-make-peace.

124 **Nixon's assertion that drugs were:** "President Nixon Declares Drug Abuse 'Public Enemy Number One,'" Richard Nixon Foundation, June 17, 1971, YouTube video, uploaded April 29, 2016, 4:37, https://www.youtube.com/watch?v=y8TGLLQlD 9M&t=1s.

124 **A top aide to Nixon admitted:** David Baum, "Legalize It All: How to Win the War on Drugs," *Harper's Magazine*, April 2016, https://harpers.org/archive/2016/04/ legalize-it-all. The article quotes Nixon's domestic policy advisor John Ehrlichman, who said, "The Nixon campaign in 1968, and the Nixon White House after that, had two enemies: the antiwar left and black people. You understand what I'm saying? We knew we couldn't make it illegal to be either against the war or black, but by getting the public to associate the hippies with marijuana and blacks with heroin, and then criminalizing both heavily, we could disrupt those communities. We could arrest their leaders, raid their homes, break up their meetings, and vilify them night after night on the evening news. Did we know we were lying about the drugs? Of course we did."

125 **Floyd had just started middle school:** Ronald Reagan, "September 14, 1986: Speech to the Nation on the Campaign Against Drug Abuse," The Miller Center, University of Virginia, https://millercenter.org/the-presidency/presidential-speeches/september-14-1986-speech-nation-campaign-against-drug-abuse.

125 **A few days after Floyd enrolled:** Michael Isikoff, "Drug Buy Set Up for Bush Speech: DEA Lured Seller to Lafayette Park," *The Washington Post*, September 22, 1989, https://www.washingtonpost.com/wp-srv/local/longterm/tours/scandal/ bushdrug.htm.

125 **"All of us agree that":** George H. W. Bush, "Public Papers: Address to the Nation on the National Drug Control Strategy," George H. W. Bush Presidential Library, September 5, 1989, https://bush41library.tamu.edu/archives/public-papers/863.

125 **Both Bush and Reagan touted:** Michael Isikoff, "Drug Plan Allows for Use of Military," *The Washington Post*, September 10, 1989, https://www.washingtonpost. com/archive/politics/1989/09/10/drug-plan-allows-use-of-military/e5093198-7d79-4301-a1ea-529d393672cc/.

125 **Funding for federal drug enforcement:** Reagan, "September 14, 1986: Speech to the Nation on the Campaign Against Drug Abuse."

125 **In 1994, President Bill Clinton:** Ann Devroy, "Crime Bill Is Signed with Flourish," *The Washington Post,* September 14, 1994, https://www.washingtonpost.com/ archive/politics/1994/09/14/crime-bill-is-signed-with-flourish/650b1c2f-e306-4c00-9c6f-80bc9cc57e55.

126 **The legislation funded:** U.S. Department of Justice, Office of Justice Programs, "1994 Violent Crime Control and Law Enforcement Act," February 14, 2020, https://www.ojp.gov/ojp50/1994-violent-crime-control-and-law-enforcement-act# 1994-violent-crime-control-and-law-enforcement-act.

126 **money that incentivized states:** Glenn Kessler, "Joe Biden's Defense of the 1994 Crime Bill's Role in Mass Incarcerations," *The Washington Post*, May 16, 2019,

https://www.washingtonpost.com/politics/2019/05/16/joe-bidens-defense-crime-bills-role-incarceration-trend.

126 **The crime bill's impact disproportionately fell:** Michelle Alexander, *The New Jim Crow: Mass Incarceration in the Age of Colorblindness* (New York: New Press, 2010), Chapter 1, Kindle.

126 **While studies show that Whites and Blacks:** Substance Abuse and Mental Health Services Administration, *Results from the 2013 National Survey on Drug Use and Health: Summary of National Findings*, NSDUH Series H-48, HHS Publication No. (SMA) 14-4863 (Rockville, MD: Substance Abuse and Mental Health Services Administration, 2014), 41, https://www.samhsa.gov/data/sites/default/files/NSDUHresultsPDFWHTML2013/Web/NSDUHresults2013.pdf#page=41.

126 **By the time Floyd returned from college:** Staff writers, "U.S. Prison Population Exceeded 1.2 Million in '97," *The Washington Post*, August 3, 1998, https://www.washingtonpost.com/archive/politics/1998/08/03/us-prison-population-exceeded-12-million-in-97/49f17f46-de5f-44ca-bd11-14aa25cc84ea/.

126 **Drug offenders made up the vast majority:** Megan T. Stevenson and Sandra G. Mayson, "The Scale of Misdemeanor Justice," *Boston Law Review* 98 (March 2018): 731–77, https://ssrn.com/abstract=3146057.

126 **Between 1986 and 1999:** Jason Ziedenberg and Vincent Schiraldi, "Race and Imprisonment in Texas: The Disparate Incarceration of Latinos and African Americans in the Lone Star State," Justice Policy Institute, 2005, 7, https://justicepolicy.org/wp-content/uploads/justicepolicy/documents/05-02_rep_txraceimprisonment_ac-rd.pdf#page=7.

126 **Texas was on the bleeding edge:** Dana Kaplan, Vincent Schiraldi, and Jason Ziedenberg, "Texas Tough?: An Analysis of Incarceration and Crime Trends in the Lone Star State," Justice Policy Institute, October 2000, 6, https://web.archive.org/web/20210128130151/https:/www.justicepolicy.org/uploads/justicepolicy/documents/texas_tough.pdf#page=6.

126 **As the state's prison system tripled:** Allen J. Beck and Paige M. Harrison, "Prisoners in 2000," *Bureau of Justice Statistics Bulletin*, August 2001, 9, https://bjs.ojp.gov/content/pub/pdf/p00.pdf#page=9.

126 **it overtook California's:** Robert Perkinson, *Texas Tough: The Rise of America's Prison Empire* (New York: Metropolitan Books, 2010), 4.

127 **By the time Floyd began cycling:** Kaplan, Schiraldi, and Ziedenberg, "Texas Tough?," 6.

127 **Floyd's undercover drug bust:** Criminal records from the Houston Police Department and Harris County District Clerk, obtained by authors.

128 **Floyd's jail stint:** Arelis R. Hernández, "Police Were a Part of George Floyd's Life from Beginning to End," *The Washington Post*, October 26, 2020, https://www.washingtonpost.com/graphics/2020/national/george-floyd-america/policing.

130 **DJ Screw's technique:** IYO Visuals, "All Screwed Up | Visual Tribute (Official Version)," YouTube video, November 18, 2020, 33:12, https://www.youtube.com/watch?v=Dh3rz4sE5vg.

131 **"What you want me to say":** Brandon Jenkins, interview with Cal Wayne, in "Season 3, Part 4: Big Floyd," *Mogul*, podcast audio, July 14, 2021, https://gimletmedia.com/shows/mogul/v4h6zle/s3-part-4-big-floyd.

131 **While Floyd's freestyles:** DJ Screw, Big Floyd, Chris Ward, and AD, "Sittin' on Top of the World Freestyle," released 1996, https://genius.com/Dj-screw-sittin-on-top-of-the-world-freestyle-lyrics.

131 **"Damn, little Wayne":** Jenkins, "Season 3, Part 4: Big Floyd."

132 **The success of chopped-and-screwed:** Timothy Bella, "Hip-Hop's Unlikeliest Icons: Promethazine Codeine Syrup Manufacturers," *Bloomberg News*, March 9, 2017, https://www.bloomberg.com/news/features/2017-03-09/hip-hop-s-unlikeliest-icons-promethazine-codeine-syrup-manufacturers.

132 **Floyd's petty dealing landed him:** The account of this arrest is based on criminal records from the Houston Police Department and Harris County District Clerk, obtained by authors.

133 **When Floyd got to the station:** Harris County intake and triage documents, obtained by *The Washington Post*.

133 **"When I talk, people listen":** Harris County intake and triage documents, obtained by *The Washington Post*; Hernández, "Police Were a Part of George Floyd's Life from Beginning to End."

134 **As Floyd battled his inner demons:** Polly Ross Hughes, "State Budget Shortfall May Hit \$12 Billion by 2003," *Houston Chronicle*, August 30, 2002, https://www.chron.com/news/houston-texas/article/State-budget-shortfall-may-hit-12-billion-by-2003-2110490.php; R. G. Ratcliffe, "How the Legislature Might Address the Less-Than-Dire Budget Shortfall," *Texas Monthly*, January 11, 2021, https://www.texasmonthly.com/news-politics/texas-budget-deficit-hegar/.

134 **in part due to the ballooning cost:** Paige M. Harrison and Jennifer C. Karberg, "Prison and Jail Inmates at Midyear 2003," *Bureau of Justice Statistics Bulletin*, May 2004, https://bjs.ojp.gov/content/pub/pdf/pjim03.pdf.

134 **Other nations that prioritized treatment:** Alexander, *The New Jim Crow*, 9.

134 **The tough-on-crime policies:** Alexander, *The New Jim Crow*, preface.

135 **Over the course of Floyd's lifetime:** Alexander, *The New Jim Crow*, 7; Travis, Western, and Redburn, eds., *The Growth of Incarceration in the United States*, 41.

135 **By 2002, states were spending:** United States Census Bureau, Annual Survey of State Government Finances Tables, 2002, https://www.census.gov/data/tables/2002/econ/state/historical-tables.html; Perkinson, *Texas Tough*, 343.

135 **Many state legislatures:** Perkinson, *Texas Tough*, 343–44.

135 **But Texas opted to stay:** Perkinson, *Texas Tough*, 344–45.

135 **As the inmate population continued:** Tracey Kyckelhahn, "State Corrections Expenditures, FY 1982–2010," U.S. Department of Justice, Office of Justice Programs, Bureau of Justice Statistics, December 2012 Bulletin, 6, https://bjs.ojp.gov/content/pub/pdf/scefy8210.pdf#page=6.

135 **Texas reported reducing per-inmate:** Kyckelhahn, "State Corrections Expenditures, FY 1982–2010," 7, https://bjs.ojp.gov/content/pub/pdf/scefy8210.pdf#page=7.

135 **The state also set a caloric:** Robert Perkinson, "Rick Perry, Criminal Justice Reformer? The Governor's Surprisingly Complicated Record," *The New Republic*,

September 16, 2011, https://newrepublic.com/article/95046/perkinson-prison-texas-perry-death-penalty-justice-reform; Associated Press, "Cost Cutters Slash Prison Food Budgets," May 14, 2003, https://www.cbsnews.com/news/cost-cutters-slash-prison-food-budgets.

135 **During his term, Bush:** Perkinson, *Texas Tough*, 340–41.

136 **George W. Bush had himself:** "Book Excerpt: Mark Updegroves' 'The Last Republicans,'" ABC News, November 12, 2017, https://abcnews.go.com/Politics/book-excerpt-mark-updegroves-republicans/story?id=51088011; Melina Delkic, "George W. Bush 'Chased a Lot of Pussy and Drank a Lot of Whiskey' in His Youth, He Says in a New Book," *Newsweek*, November 10, 2017, https://www.newsweek.com/george-w-bush-chased-pussy-drank-whiskey-708653.

136 **He had survived his encounters:** Staff and wire reports, "Bush Acknowledges 1976 DUI Charge," CNN, November 2, 2000, https://www.cnn.com/2000/ALLPOLITICS/stories/11/02/bush.dui; Lois Romano and George Lardner Jr., "Bush: So-So Student but a Campus Mover," *The Washington Post*, July 27, 1999, https://www.washingtonpost.com/wp-srv/politics/campaigns/wh2000/stories/bush072799.htm.

The article about Bush's collegiate experience states, "Several times Bush got into minor trouble. Once it was for pulling down a goal post at Princeton with a bunch of friends while celebrating a Yale football victory.

"'The game ended and we all poured out and George was on the goal post. I remember it like it was yesterday,' recalled his friend Clay Johnson. 'We tore that sucker down and the campus police said, "You all are coming with us." So we went marching over to the campus police station and they said, "You've got 10 minutes to get out of town."'

"On another occasion, Bush got caught with some friends 'borrowing' a Christmas wreath from a store door in New Haven. He was arrested for disorderly conduct, but the charges were dropped."

136 **Instead, he passed the time:** Maya Rao, "George Floyd's Search for Salvation," *Star Tribune* (Minneapolis), December 27, 2020, https://www.startribune.com/george-floyd-hoped-moving-to-minnesota-would-save-him-what-he-faced-here-killed-him/573417181.

136 **After being stopped by Houston police:** Arrest records from Houston Police Department, obtained by authors, and interviews with members of Floyd's family.

137 **In their report, officers said:** Houston Police Department Archived OLO Incident Report No. 11827701, August 29, 2001, and Harris County District Court records, obtained by authors.

137 **"I'll take it. It's mine":** This arrest was relayed to the authors during an interview with Rodney Floyd and other members of George Floyd's family who witnessed the event.

138 **The officer who had arrested Floyd:** Hernández, "Police Were a Part of George Floyd's Life from Beginning to End."

138 **On February 5, 2004:** Houston Police Department records, including Archived OLO Incident Report No. 19342804, February 5, 2004, obtained by authors.

138   **The narcotics officer, a Black man:** Manny Fernandez, "Probe of Old Drug Cases Raises Questions About 2004 George Floyd Arrest," *The New York Times*, June 19, 2020, https://www.nytimes.com/2020/06/19/us/unrest-george-floyd-houston-goines.html.

139   **Goines, the only witness:** Nicole Hensley, "Slamming Disgraced Cop's Involvement in Case, DA Kim Ogg Backs Posthumous Pardon for George Floyd," *Houston Chronicle*, April 28, 2021, https://www.houstonchronicle.com/news/houston-texas/houston/article/Ogg-pens-formal-plea-for-George-Floyd-posthumous-16137063.php.

139   **Goines targeted impoverished minority men:** Kim Ogg, Office of District Attorney, Harris County, Texas, "Harding Street Supervisors Charged in Probe of Houston Police Narcotics Division," Official Statement, July 1, 2020, https://app.dao.hctx.net/harding-street-supervisors-charged-probe-houston-police-narcotics-division.

    In the statement, District Attorney Kim Ogg said her office's civil rights division was reviewing thousands of cases filed by Squad 15 of HPD's narcotics division, a group that disproportionately arrested minorities for petty drug crimes. "This investigation is peeling back layers of a narcotics-enforcement system gone array [*sic*]," Ogg said. "It calls into question the way HPD has been enforcing narcotics laws, especially in communities of color. The lion's share of arrests made by this squad were minority men for low-level drug crimes."

140   **Prosecutors offered him:** Fernandez, "Probe of Old Drug Cases Raises Questions About 2004 George Floyd Arrest."

140   **Texas prosecutors were known to:** Robert Walters, Michael Marin, and Mark Curriden, "Jury of Our Peers: An Unfulfilled Constitutional Promise," *SMU Law Review* 58, no. 2 (2005): 319, https://scholar.smu.edu/smulr/vol58/iss2/5.

141   **He ultimately signed his name:** Harris County District Clerk plea documents for George Perry Floyd from 1997, 1998, 2001, 2003, 2004, 2005, and 2007, obtained by authors.

141   **In an examination of Harris County:** Neel U. Sukhatme and Jay Jenkins, "Pay to Play? Campaign Finance and the Incentive Gap in the Sixth Amendment's Right to Counsel," *Duke Law Journal* 70 (2020): 43–45, https://ssrn.com/abstract=3611209.

141   **In 1999, a Democratic state senator:** Neena Satija, "How Judicial Conflicts of Interest Are Denying Poor Texans Their Right to an Effective Lawyer," *Texas Tribune*, August 19, 2019, https://www.texastribune.org/2019/08/19/unchecked-power-texas-judges-indigent-defense.

141   **Eight days after launching:** George W. Bush, "Official Memorandum, State of Texas, Office of the Governor," Veto of Senate Bill 247, June 20, 1999, https://lrl.texas.gov/scanned/vetoes/76/sb247.pdf#navpanes=0; Adam Nagourney, "Bush Iowa Trip Signals Real Start of 2000 Race for the Presidency," *The New York Times*, June 13, 1999, https://www.nytimes.com/1999/06/13/us/bush-iowa-trip-signals-real-start-of-2000-race-for-the-presidency.html.

147   **There are conflicting recollections:** Except otherwise noted, the depiction of the 2007 robbery and the ensuing criminal investigation is based on Houston Police

Department records and multiple interviews, including several interviews with Aracely Henriquez, who was in the home during the robbery, by *Washington Post* reporter Arelis R. Hernández.

153 **"I don't know if the defense":** Van Terrell Dickerson and Vaughn Terrell Dickerson, Appellants, vs. the State of Texas, Appellee, Court of Appeals of Texas, Fourth District, San Antonio, 87 S.W. 3rd 632 (Tex. App. 2002), June 26, 2002, https://casetext.com/case/dickerson-v-state-33.

155 **During initial processing:** Texas Department of Criminal Justice, *Offender Orientation Handbook*, November 2004, http://www.law.umich.edu/special/ policyclearinghouse/Documents/Texas%20-%20Offender_Orientation_ Handbook_English.pdf.

155 **In 1967, a thirty-two-year-old:** Shane Bauer, *American Prison: A Reporter's Undercover Journey into the Business of Punishment* (New York: Penguin Books, 2019), 461–79; Bruce Jackson, *Inside the Wire: Photographs from Texas and Arkansas Prisons* (Austin: University of Texas Press, 2013).

156 **Its ascendancy ran parallel:** Bauer, *American Prison*, 691.

156 **When CCA was awarded a contract:** Alex Friedmann, "Apples-to-Fish: Public and Private Prison Cost Comparisons," *Fordham Urban Law Journal* 42, no. 2 (April 2016): 544, https://ir.lawnet.fordham.edu/cgi/viewcontent.cgi?article=2565&cont ext=ulj#page=43.

157 **During the time Floyd:** Texas Department of Criminal Justice, "Annual Review 2010," July 2011, 7, https://www.tdcj.texas.gov/documents/Annual_Review_2010. pdf#page=7. In 2010, Texas Department of Criminal Justice officials reported identifying $55 million in savings at the request of the governor. In 2011, TDCJ officials agreed with the governor's office on an additional $40 million in savings. A portion of the reductions were attributed to prison privatization; Texas Department of Criminal Justice, "Summary of Fiscal Year 2011 Budget Reductions," 1.

157 **The state faced a projected budget shortfall:** Dave Mann, "The Budget Deficit from Hell," *Texas Observer*, January 11, 2011, https://www.texasobserver.org/ the-budget-deficit-from-hell.

157 **sought to rein in its prison budget:** Texas Department of Criminal Justice, "Annual Review 2010," 56, https://www.tdcj.texas.gov/documents/Annual_Review_2010. pdf#page=56; Texas Department of Criminal Justice, "Annual Review 2011," 54, https://www.tdcj.texas.gov/documents/Annual_Review_2011.pdf#page=54. TDCJ officials reported that Texas Correctional Industries sold $83.5 million in products made by inmates in 2010, and $77.4 million in 2011.

158 **While Floyd was at Bartlett:** Cleve R. Wootson Jr., "Profiting from Prisoners," *The Washington Post*, October 19, 2020, https://www.washingtonpost.com/ graphics/2020/national/george-floyd-america/criminal-justice; Chris Rogers, "Local City Faces Financial Crisis After Jail Closes," KCEN-TV, July 6, 2017, https://www.kcentv.com/article/news/local/local-city-faces-financial- crisis-after-jail-closes/454768963.

158 **CCA hired locals:** U.S. Census Bureau, "Texas: 2010, Population and Housing Unit Counts," September 2012, 76, https://www.census.gov/prod/cen2010/cph-2-45. pdf#page=120; Rogers, "Local City Faces Financial Crisis After Jail Closes."

158   **The city had wooed:** Wootson, "Profiting from Prisoners."

158   **The benefits accrued quickly:** James C. Dillard, "Facility Focus: Bartlett State Jail," *InsideCCA*, February 11, 2015, https://web.archive.org/web/20210228152206/ http://staging.cca.com/insidecca/facility-focus-bartlett-state-jail. In this company publication, the writer noted, "Led by Warden Michael Phillips, the facility is a major employer and strong corporate citizen in the Bartlett community, providing more than 200 jobs, $868,000 in annual utility use and fees and more than $166,000 in local spending for goods and services."

158   **Even with the upgrades:** Rogers, "Local City Faces Financial Crisis After Jail Closes."

159   **The jail, Grant wrote:** Wootson, "Profiting from Prisoners."

159   **While Floyd was locked up:** Corrections Corporation of America, Form 10-K 2010, accessed January 6, 2022, 2, http://ir.corecivic.com/static-files/940963bd-f49c-435b-8910-58fec39c8c8d.

159   **Its investors, which included:** Yahoo! Finance data on stock price of CoreCivic between December 31, 2009, and January 1, 2011, https://finance.yahoo.com/ quote/CXW/history?period1=1262304000&period2=1296518400&interval=1mo &filter=history&frequency=1mo&includeAdjustedClose=true.

159   **CCA, which changed its name:** David Boucher, "CCA Changes Name to CoreCivic amid Ongoing Scrutiny," *The Tennessean*, October 28, 2016, https:// www.tennessean.com/story/news/2016/10/28/cca-changes-name-amid-ongoing-scrutiny/92883274.

160   **The motivational book:** Rick Warren, *The Purpose Driven Life* (Chagrin Falls, OH: Zondervan, 2006), Kindle.

162   **In fact, most of the people:** Legislative Budget Board Staff, "Statewide Criminal and Juvenile Justice Recidivism and Revocations Rates," January 2017, 12, https:// www.lbb.state.tx.us/Documents/Publications/Policy_Report/3138_Stwide_ Crim_Just_Recid_Revoc.pdf#page=19.

Chapter 6: The Use of Restraint

164   **Those use-of-force techniques:** Neena Satija, "How Minneapolis Police Handled the In-Custody Death of a Black Man 10 Years Before George Floyd," *The Washington Post*, August 29, 2020, https://www.washingtonpost.com/ investigations/2020/08/29/david-smith-death-minneapolis-police-kneeling.

165   **The officer's name was Derek Chauvin:** The description of the training for the prone restraint comes from training materials and sign-in sheets, obtained by the authors.

165   **Chauvin's great-great-great-grandparents:** Manifest of the *Antarctic*, "New York, U.S., Arriving Passenger and Crew Lists (including Castle Garden and Ellis Island), 1820–1957," August 16, 1855, digital image, s.v. "Anton Neideck," Ancestry.com.

165   **Unlike George Floyd's family:** This accounting of Derek Chauvin's family history is based on public records, including Census documents, business registrations, school yearbooks, marriage certificates, death records, and newspaper accounts. Many of the records were obtained via Ancestry.com.

165   **Anton was employed as a stonecutter:** U.S. Census Bureau, 1860 United States Census, Place: Detroit Ward 4, Wayne, Michigan; Roll: M653_565; Page: 249, digital image, s.v. "Antony Neideck," Ancestry.com.

165   **The Chauvins had traced a similar pattern:** Staff, "The Chauvin Murder," *The Detroit Free Press*, September 11, 1894, https://www.newspapers.com/image/119555548/?terms=charles%20b.%20chauvin&match=1.

165   **By 1925, he had amassed:** *Michigan Manufacturer and Financial Record* 35 (Detroit: Manufacturer Publishing Company, January 25, 1935), 66, https://books.google.com/books?id=JuUTAQAAMAAJ&lpg=RA25-PA66&dq=cadillac%20book%20binding%20co%20williams&pg=RA25-PA66#v=onepage&q&f=false; "Summary for: A. R. Chauvin Co.," Michigan Department of Licensing and Regulatory Affairs, accessed November 1, 2021, https://cofs.lara.state.mi.us/CorpWeb/CorpSearch/CorpSummary.aspx?token=nBxILn58HwVtv4JMRDwTm1cW blopjmzIgq3FCQzRMH7Z0mRAdeXC1NI5kwbxmQNL5P1KV/usstRZI5w/XS2yLZDgDwmI49hGwZxc85AcGOHl/NQDjiiMvmoEwGtNYKPm OvkICO2EqSq0VJNRGjV/z2OZFZKxwTN64yF1m0zzMeglc0MUvk Qu767ehDc0iTKO27BiTLZdR9pDTzEEldcwWbBExz5YuLHlG3yIIO3Kk DrlLTNPBBEEI1AXlCvA2UdyGy45G8cXJPHZHMkEOmRLPVWnoNeU4+ Q209bTREKwYja0FRwyto+1VBDRM4dpOsEcCpnno GwBesy1LF8WDavDvN1ykQbRnxN8.

165   **Richard's son Arthur:** World War II Draft Registration Card for Arthur Richard Chauvin, October 16, 1940, U.S., World War II Draft Cards Young Men, 1940–1947, digital image, s.v. "Arthur Richard Chauvin," Ancestry.com.

165   **The company grew alongside Detroit:** Kurt Metzger and Jason Booza, "African Americans in the United States, Michigan and Metropolitan Detroit," Center for Urban Studies, Wayne State University, February 2002, 9, https://web.archive.org/web/20060620081451/http://www.cus.wayne.edu/content/publications/AAwork8.pdf#page=9.

166   **at the cusp of the Motown era:** Metzger and Booza, "African Americans in the United States, Michigan and Metropolitan Detroit," 9.

166   **In 1972, Robert Chauvin:** Simley High School Yearbook, 1966, U.S., School Yearbooks, 1900–1999, digital image, s.v. "Carolyn Runge," Ancestry.com.

166   **As a teenager, Chauvin:** These details are drawn from Chauvin's school yearbooks, his personnel file at the Minneapolis Police Department, and interviews with family and friends who declined to be named out of fear for their safety. Some interviews were conducted by Minneapolis-based freelancer Jared Goyette.

168   **His records show that:** Communities United Against Police Brutality, "Derek M. Chauvin, badge #1087," accessed December 11, 2021, http://complaints.cuapb.org/police_archive/officer/2377.

169   **"Don't stick me with it":** "Derek Chauvin Sentencing Hearing," CNN, June 25, 2021, http://www.cnn.com/TRANSCRIPTS/2106/25/cnr.09.html.

170   **Some of those allegations:** "Janee Harteau Resigns: A Timeline," *Star Tribune* (Minneapolis), July 22, 2017, https://www.startribune.com/janee-harteau-resigns-a-timeline/435917263; "Lieutenant Medaria Arradondo, Lieutenant Donald Harris, Sergeant Charles Adams, Sergeant Dennis Hamilton, and Lieutenant Lee

Edwards, Plaintiffs, v. City of Minneapolis, the Minneapolis Police Department, and Timothy Dolan, an, individual, Defendants," Minnesota Public Radio, accessed December 11, 2021, https://minnesota.publicradio.org/features/2007/12/03_williamsb_copslawsuit/complaint.pdf.

171 **With a marginal Black population:** "Timeline," MPD 150: A People's Project Evaluating Policing, accessed September 14, 2021, https://www.mpd150.com/report-old/timeline.

171 **In response, Mayor Art Naftalin:** National Advisory Commission on Civil Disorders, Report (1967), U.S. Department of Justice, accessed December 11, 2019, https://www.ojp.gov/ncjrs/virtual-library/abstracts/national-advisory-commission-civil-disorders-report.

172 **Still, a grand jury decided:** Karren Mills, "City Image Tarnished by Allegations of Police Racism," Associated Press, March 21, 1989, https://apnews.com/article/962eed0dea6d4ccdadbbe151564b7413.

173 **No matter what the crime:** Tim Murphy, "Keith Ellison Is Everything Republicans Thought Obama Was. Maybe He's Just What Democrats Need," *Mother Jones*, March/April 2017, https://www.motherjones.com/politics/2017/02/keith-ellison-democratic-national-committee-chair.

174 **They saw a beloved community center:** Kirsten Delegard, Michael Lansing, and Kristen Zschlomer, "The Way Community Center: 1913 Plymouth Avenue North," Augsburg Digi-Tours, accessed December 11, 2021, https://digitours.augsburg.edu/items/show/29.

177 **"Under all that uniform":** S. M. Chavey, "Refugee Once Shamed for Her Looks Vying to Be the First Hmong Mrs. Minnesota," *Pioneer Press* (Minnesota), June 2, 2018, https://www.twincities.com/2018/06/02/refugee-who-was-shamed-for-her-looks-as-a-child-is-vying-to-be-the-first-hmong-mrs-minnesota.

178 **When Santamaria asked Chauvin:** Holly Bailey, "Derek Chauvin: Officer's Aggressive Behavior Raises Questions About Excessive Off-Duty Police Work as Trial Approaches," *The Washington Post*, March 5, 2021, https://www.washingtonpost.com/national/derek-chauvin-george-floyd/2021/03/05/cd6d37b8-782e-11eb-948d-19472e683521_story.html.

180 **He also complained to:** The details of these incidents involving Chauvin are based on interviews with the complainants. Details regarding citizen complaints are not public record in Minneapolis if they do not result in disciplinary action.

180 **And among the 570 complaints:** Office of Justice Programs Diagnostic Center, "Diagnostic Analysis of Minneapolis Police Department, MN," January 2015, accessed November 15, 2021, https://mn.gov/mdhr/assets/2015.01%20OJP%20Minneapolis%20Police%20Report_tcm1061-457047.pdf.

181 **a 2006 federal study estimated:** Bureau of Justice Statistics: Special Report, "Citizen Complaints About Police Use of Force," June 2006, https://bjs.ojp.gov/content/pub/pdf/ccpuf.pdf.

181 **In Minneapolis, publicly available data:** "Police Use of Force," Open Minneapolis, accessed Nov. 15, 2021, https://opendata.minneapolismn.gov/datasets/police-use-of-force/explore.

181 **During the period of slavery:** Angela Saini, *Superior: The Return of Race Science* (Boston: Beacon Press, 2019), 30–31.

182 **They were on display again:** Carroll Bogert and Lynnell Hancock, "Superpredators: The Media Myth That Demonized a Generation of Black Youth," *The Marshall Project*, November 11, 2020, https://www.themarshallproject. org/2020/11/20/superpredator-the-media-myth-that-demonized-a-generation-of-black-youth.

182 **"Excited delirium is a condition":** "Excited Delirium Syndrome" (PowerPoint presentation, Minnesota Police Department), accessed November 15, 2021, https://lims.minneapolismn.gov/download/Agenda/1858/MPDExcitedDelirium SyndromePowerPointPresentation.pdf/54462/2328/MPD%20Excited%20 Delirium%20Syndrome%20PowerPoint%20Presentation.

183 **One study of the period:** A. J. Ruttenber et al., "Fatal Excited Delirium Following Cocaine Use: Epidemiologic Findings Provide New Evidence for Mechanisms of Cocaine Toxicity," *Journal of Forensic Sciences* 42, no. 1 (1997): 25–31.

183 **A 2017 article:** Philippe Gonin, Nicolas Beysard, Bertrand Yersin, and Pierre-Nicolas Carron, "Excited Delirium: A Systematic Review," *American Emergency Medicine* 25, no. 5 (May 2018): 552–65, https://doi.org/10.1111/acem.13330.

183 **Critics were also disturbed:** Jason Szep, Tim Reid, and Peter Eisler, "How Taser Inserts Itself into Investigations Involving Its Own Weapons," Reuters, August 24, 2017, https://www.reuters.com/investigates/special-report/usa-taser-experts.

184 **The Department of Justice had warned:** National Law Enforcement Technology Center, "Positional Asphyxia—Sudden Death," June 1995, https://www.ojp.gov/ pdffiles/posasph.pdf/.

184 **Neck restraints represented:** Jeff Hargarten, "Stark Racial Disparities Remain as Police Use-of-Force Rate Rises," *Star Tribune* (Minneapolis), June 5, 2020, https:// www.startribune.com/stark-racial-disparities-remain-as-minneapolis-police-use-of-force-rate-rises/568966861.

186 **The family did not file:** State of Minnesota, "State's Supplemental Memorandum of Law in Support of Other Evidence," November 16, 2020, accessed July 12, 2021, https://mncourts.gov/mncourtsgov/media/High-Profile-Cases/27-CR-20-12646/ Memorandum11162020.pdf.

187 **The report does not note:** These incidents were based on police records obtained by authors, as well as the recollections of Monroe Skinaway.

187 **Between the time the Minneapolis Police Department:** This analysis of publicly available data was conducted by Steven Rich of *The Washington Post*; data available at https://opendata.minneapolismn.gov/datasets/police-use-of-force/ explore.

CHAPTER 7: YOU'RE ON YOUR OWN

192 **But staying out of prison:** The State of Texas Legislative Budget Board Staff, "Statewide Criminal and Juvenile Justice Recidivism and Revocations Rates," January 2017, 12, https://www.lbb.state.tx.us/Documents/Publications/ Policy_Report/3138_Stwide_Crim_Just_Recid_Revoc.pdf#page=19.

195 **Former felons were barred:** Mike Ward, "Second Chances Blocked by State Licensing Rules," *Houston Chronicle*, December 26, 2014, https://www. houstonchronicle.com/politics/texas/article/Second-chances-blocked-by-state-licensing-rules-5980367.php.

195 **With about a third of all jobs:** Ward, "Second Chances Blocked."

196 **The state also had:** Rebecca Beitsch, "States Rethink Restrictions on Food Stamps, Welfare for Drug Felons," *Stateline*, The Pew Charitable Trusts, July 30, 2015, https://www.pewtrusts.org/en/research-and-analysis/blogs/stateline/2015/07/30/ states-rethink-restrictions-on-food-stamps-welfare-for-drug-felons.

196 **Some public housing authorities blocked:** Austin/Travis County Reentry Roundtable, "Locked Out: Criminal History Barriers to Affordable Rental Housing in Austin & Travis County, Texas," October 2016, 10, https://www. reentryroundtable.org/wp-content/uploads/2013/10/Criminal-Background-White-Paper.final_.pdf#page=10.

196 **And Texans with criminal records:** L. M. Sixel, "Working: Ex-Offenders Need Not Apply for Many State Jobs," *Houston Chronicle*, March 26, 2014, https://www. houstonchronicle.com/business/columnists/sixel/article/Working-Ex-offenders-need-not-apply-for-many-5352145.php.

196 **excluding them from a sector:** Texas Workforce Commission, "Equal Employment Opportunity and Minority Hiring Practices Report, Fiscal Years 2017–2018," 2018, 5, https://www.twc.texas.gov/files/twc/equal-employment-opportunity-minority-hiring-practices-report-2017-2018-twc.pdf#page=6.

196 **The same year that Floyd was released:** Lance Murray, "State of Texas Sues over EEOC Guidelines on Hiring Felons," *Dallas Business Journal*, November 4, 2013, https://www.bizjournals.com/dallas/news/2013/11/04/state-of-texas-sues-over-eeoc.html.

196 **Guidelines issued by:** Sixel, "Working: Ex-Offenders Need Not Apply."

197 **Floyd, one of almost five million:** Helen Gaebler, "Criminal Records in the Digital Age: A Review of Current Practices and Recommendations for Reform in Texas," William Wayne Justice Center for Public Interest Law, The University of Texas School of Law, March 2013, 2, https://law.utexas.edu/wp-content/uploads/ sites/27/Criminal-Records-in-the-Digital-Age-Report-by-Helen-Gaebler. pdf#page=3.

198 **Floyd held her:** Stephanie Wash, Sabina Ghebremedhin, and Eva Pilgrim, "George Floyd's 6-Year-Old Daughter Speaks Out About Her Dad: 'I Miss Him,'" ABC News, June 3, 2020, https://abcnews.go.com/GMA/News/george-floyds-daughter-speaks-dad-time/story?id=71031800.

199 **"I love what y'all out here doing":** Rapzilla.com, "Corey Paul Did Ministry with George Floyd, Legin Talks Safe House, Mitch Darrell on Next Gen Leaders," YouTube video, October 22, 2020, 1:22:35, https://youtu.be/ GCJp6O-Y5H8?t=2939.

200 **Ngwolo also planned:** Kate Shellnut, "George Floyd Left a Gospel Legacy in Houston," *Christianity Today*, May 28, 2020, https://www.christianitytoday.com/ news/2020/may/george-floyd-ministry-houston-third-ward-church.html.

201   **"I just want to say, man":** Brandon Jenkins, "Season 3, Part 4: Big Floyd," *Mogul*, podcast audio, July 14, 2021, https://gimletmedia.com/shows/mogul/v4h6zle/s3-part-4-big-floyd.

212   **"Your changing station":** Maya Rao, "George Floyd's Search for Salvation," *Star Tribune* (Minneapolis), December 27, 2020, https://www.startribune.com/george-floyd-hoped-moving-to-minnesota-would-save-him-what-he-faced-here-killed-him/573417181.

213   **In 1995, Texas:** Robert Samuels, "Racism's Hidden Toll," *The Washington Post*, October 22, 2020, https://www.washingtonpost.com/graphics/2020/national/george-floyd-america/health-care.

213   **A decade later:** Nate Blakeslee, "Hooked on Hard Time," *Texas Observer*, February 16,2001,https://www.texasobserver.org/19-hooked-on-hard-time-perrys-budget-feeds-the-prison-construction-industry-while-drug-treatment-goes-hungry.

213   **Texas had declined to expand Medicaid:** "Who Could Medicaid Reach with Expansion in Texas?," Kaiser Family Foundation, accessed October 28, 2021, https://files.kff.org/attachment/fact-sheet-medicaid-expansion-TX.

CHAPTER 8: TURNING POINT

227   **Sherman James, then an epidemiologist:** Sherman A. James, Curriculum Vitae, Duke University, https://sanford-files.cloud.duke.edu/sites/default/files/2021-07/Sherman_James_CV_July_19_2021.pdf.

228   **A future colleague of his:** Gene Demby, "Making the Case That Discrimination Is Bad for Your Health," *Code Switch*, January 14, 2018, https://www.npr.org/sections/codeswitch/2018/01/14/577664626/making-the-case-that-discrimination-is-bad-for-your-health.

228   **In their studies, African Americans tended:** James S. Jackson, Katherine M. Knight, and Jane A. Rafferty, "Race and Unhealthy Behaviors: Chronic Stress, the HPA Axis, and Physical and Mental Health Disparities over the Life Course," *American Journal of Public Health* 100, no. 5 (2010): 933–39, https://doi.org/10.2105/AJPH.2008.143446.

229   **A 2019 analysis of federal data:** Sirry M. Alang, "Mental Health Care Among Blacks in America: Confronting Racism and Constructing Solutions," *Health Services Research* 54, no. 2 (2019): 346–55, https://doi.org/10.1111/1475-6773.13115.

230   **But Jordan said:** Elana K. Schwartz et al., "Exploring the Racial Diagnostic Bias of Schizophrenia Using Behavioral and Clinical-Based Measures," *Journal of Abnormal Psychology* 128, no. 3 (2019): 263–71, https://doi.org/10.1037/abn0000409.

230   **For example, the 1994 law:** Office of Legislation and Regulations, Office of General Counsel, "Housing and Urban Development Authorities," February 8, 2001, 16, https://www.huduser.gov/portal/Publications/pdf/HUD-11646.pdf.

230–1   **At least $2.5 billion:** Public Law 114-255, 114th Congress, December 13, 2016, https://www.govinfo.gov/content/pkg/PLAW-114publ255/pdf/PLAW-114publ255.pdf.

231 **the Comprehensive Addiction and Recovery Act:** "Implementation of the Provision of the Comprehensive Addiction and Recovery Act of 2016 Relating to the Dispensing of Narcotic Drugs for Opioid Use Disorder," Federal Register, January 23, 2018, https://www.federalregister.gov/documents/2018/01/23/2018-01173/implementation-of-the-provision-of-the-comprehensive-addiction-and-recovery-act-of-2016-relating-to.

231 **The continued and aggressive police presence:** Sirry Alang, Donna D. McAlpine, and Rachel Hardeman, "Police Brutality and Mistrust in Medical Institutions," *Journal of Racial and Ethnic Health Disparities* 7 (2020): 760–68, https://doi.org/10.1007/s40615-020-00706-w.

231 **Even more, a 2017 study:** Shervin Assari et al., "Racial Discrimination During Adolescence Predicts Mental Health Deterioration in Adulthood: Gender Differences Among Blacks," *Frontiers in Public Health* 5 (2017), https://doi.org/10.3389/fpubh.2017.00104.

231 **A 2013 review published:** Earlise Ward and Maigenete Mengesha, "Depression in African American Men: A Review of What We Know and Where We Need to Go from Here," *The American Journal of Orthopsychiatry* 83, no. 2, part 3 (April–July 2013): 386–97, https://doi.org/10.1111/ajop.12015.

231 **Six years later, Science Advances magazine:** Travis A. Hoppe et al, "Topic Choice Contributes to the Lower Rate of NIH Awards to African-American/Black Scientists," *Science Advances* 5, no. 10 (October 2019), https://doi.org/10.1126/sciadv.aaw7238.

234 **Floyd marveled at the cavernous place:** Lily, "How Big Is the Mall of America? 10 CRAZY Stats," *Discover the Cities*, April 2, 2021, https://discoverthecities.com/how-big-is-the-mall-of-america.

243 **When he walked downstairs:** This scene was re-created through interviews with friends of Floyd and public records obtained from the St. Louis Park Police Department.

Chapter 9: The Real Comes In

249 **the state university system enrolled:** Emma Carew, "U's First Black Graduate and 1880s Race Relations," *The Minnesota Daily*, February 8, 2006, https://mndaily.com/198401/uncategorized/us-first-black-graduate-and-1880s-race-relations.

249 **restrictive racial covenants:** University of Minnesota, "Mapping Prejudice: Data & Maps," accessed December 11, 2021, https://mappingprejudice.umn.edu/data-and-map-launch-page/index.html.

249 **Even so, this longtime egalitarianist state:** Samuel L. Myers Jr., "The Minnesota Paradox," University of Minnesota Hubert H. Humphrey School of Public Affairs, accessed December 11, 2021, https://www.hhh.umn.edu/research-centers/roy-wilkins-center-human-relations-and-social-justice/minnesota-paradox.

249 **Yet researchers and doctors:** Rachel R. Hardeman, "Black Maternal Health: Getting at the Root Cause of Inequity," Testimony to Minnesota House Health Finance and Policy Committee, February 10, 2021, https://www.house.leg.state.mn.us/comm/docs/jxcJts0rmE6fMILpfcbbcw.pdf.

249 **Minneapolis is a prosperous city:** Tracy Jan, "Minneapolis Had Progressive Policies, but Its Economy Still Left Black Families Behind," *The Washington Post*, June 30, 2020, https://www.washingtonpost.com/business/2020/06/30/ minneapolis-had-progressive-policies-its-economy-still-left-black-families-behind.

250 **Of the nation's hundred largest:** Christopher Ingraham, "Racial Inequality in Minneapolis Is Among the Worst in the Nation," *The Washington Post*, May 30, 2020, https://www.washingtonpost.com/business/2020/05/30/minneapolis- racial-inequality/.

250 **Overall, Minnesota boasts:** Rob Grunewald and Anusha Nath, "A Statewide Crisis: Minnesota's Education Achievement Gaps," Federal Reserve Bank of Minneapolis, October 11, 2019, https://www.minneapolisfed.org/~/media/assets/ pages/education-acheivement-gaps/achievement-gaps-mn-report.pdf.

251 **More than six hundred Black families:** Jane McClure, "Rondo Neighborhood," *Saint Paul Historical*, accessed December 11, 2021, https://saintpaulhistorical.com/ items/show/160?tour=41&index=11; Myron Medcalf, "Racism, Not a Highway, Tore Apart St. Paul's Rondo Neighborhood," *Star Tribune* (Minneapolis), February 20, 2021, https://www.startribune.com/a-racism-reckoning-in- rondo/600025477.

251 **A similar dynamic:** Robert Samuels, "In Syracuse, a Road and Reparations," *The Washington Post*, October 20, 2019, https://www.washingtonpost.com/ nation/2019/10/20/how-crumbling-bridge-syracuse-is-sparking-conversation- about-reparations.

251 **Their sense of civic pride dwindled:** "Living near Highways and Air Pollution," American Lung Association, updated January 5, 2021, https://www.lung.org/ clean-air/outdoors/who-is-at-risk/highways.

252 **Of the 395,000 Black people:** Heather Brown, "What Is the History Behind Minnesota's Somali-American Community?," WCCO 4, July 23, 2019, https:// minnesota.cbslocal.com/2019/07/23/minnesota-somali-american-population- good-question.

252 **When police killed twenty-two-year-old Terrance Franklin:** Karl Vick and Josiah Bates, "Minneapolis Police Were Cleared in the Killing of Terrance Franklin. Franklin's Family Says a Video Proves He Was Executed—and Now the Case May Be Reopened," *Time*, June 25, 2021, https://time.com/6075094/terrance-franklin- shooting.

253 **Police said that Clark:** Mark Berman, "Minneapolis Police Officers Who Fatally Shot Jamar Clark Won't Face Federal Civil Rights Charges," *The Washington Post*, June 1, 2016, https://www.washingtonpost.com/news/post-nation/wp/2016/06/01/ minneapolis-officers-who-fatally-shot-jamar-clark-wont-face-federal-civil-rights- charges.

253 **"His DNA is all over that gun":** FOX 9 Minneapolis–St. Paul, "Mike Freeman: 'DNA Is Truth Serum' in Jamar Clark Case," April 1, 2016, 2:25, https://www.fox9. com/news/mike-freeman-dna-is-truth-serum-in-jamar-clark-case.

254 **Nonetheless, a jury acquitted Yanez:** Mark Berman, "Minn. Officer Acquitted in Shooting of Philando Castile During Traffic Stop, Dismissed from Police Force," *The Washington Post*, June 17, 2017, https://www.washingtonpost.com/news/

post-nation/wp/2017/06/16/minn-officer-acquitted-of-manslaughter-for-shooting-philando-castile-during-traffic-stop.

259 **As prescription pills flooded:** Bella, "Hip-Hop's Unlikeliest Icons: Promethazine Codeine Syrup Manufacturers."

259 **What started as a trend:** Kim Painter, "Sizzurp: What You Need to Know About Cough Syrup High," *USA Today*, January 23, 2014, https://www.usatoday.com/story/news/nation/2014/01/23/sizzurp-cough-syrup-drug/4793865/.

259 **But living in the Midwest:** Keturah James and Ayana Jordan, "The Opioid Crisis in Black Communities," *The Journal of Law, Medicine & Ethics* 46, no. 2 (June 2018): 404–21, https://doi.org/10.1177/1073110518782949.

260 **The disparity was yet another example:** Mary DeLaquil, "Differences in Rates of Drug Overdose Deaths by Race," Minnesota Department of Health, 2019, https://www.health.state.mn.us/communities/opioids/documents/raceratedisparity2019prelimfinal.pdf.

260 **In 2019, only nine other states:** "Opioid Overdose Deaths by Race/Ethnicity," Kaiser Family Foundation, 2019, https://www.kff.org/other/state-indicator/opioid-overdose-deaths-by-raceethnicity/?currentTimeframe=0&sortModel=%7B%22colId%22:%22Location%22,%22sort%22:%22asc%22%7D.

260 **By 2020, the federal government:** U.S. Department of Health and Human Services Substance Abuse and Mental Health Services Administration, Office of Behavioral Health Equity, "The Opioid Crisis and the Black/African American Population: An Urgent Issue," accessed December 11, 2021, https://store.samhsa.gov/sites/default/files/SAMHSA_Digital_Download/PEP20-05-02-001_508%20Final.pdf.

268 **This wave of death:** Holly Hedegaard, Merianne Rose Spencer, and Matthew F. Garnett, "Increase in Drug Overdose Deaths Involving Cocaine: United States, 2009–2018," NCHS Data Brief 384 (2020), https://www.cdc.gov/nchs/products/databriefs/db384.htm.

268 **in Floyd's age group:** "Leading Causes of Death—Males—Non-Hispanic Black—United States, 2017," Centers of Disease Control and Prevention, accessed December 11, 2021, https://www.cdc.gov/healthequity/lcod/men/2017/nonhispanic-black/index.htm.

269 **As officers approached the vehicle:** Holly Bailey, "Judge in George Floyd Case Allows Evidence of Prior Arrest, an Incident That Ended Without Violence," *The Washington Post*, October 15, 2020, https://www.washingtonpost.com/national/george-floyd-minneapolis-previous-arrest-evidence/2020/10/15/8471e296-0f2b-11eb-b1e8-16b59b92b36d_story.html.

270 **They included finding higher rates:** Ayana Jordan et al., "An Evaluation of Opioid Use in Black Communities: A Rapid Review of the Literature," *Harvard Review of Psychiatry* 29, no. 2 (March–April 2021): 108–130, https://doi.org/10.1097/HRP.0000000000000285.

274 **McRaven would eventually be convicted:** State of Minnesota v. Jeffrey Alan McRaven, 27-CR-20-1792, accessed December 30, 2021, https://www.mncourts.gov/Access-Case-Records.aspx.

276 **Floyd found himself unemployed:** Kavita Kumar, "Half of Black Workers in Minnesota Have Lost Work During Pandemic," *Star Tribune* (Minneapolis), July 18, 2020, https://www.startribune.com/half-of-black-workers-in-minnesota-have-lost-work-during-pandemic/571820441.

CHAPTER 10: MEMORIAL DAY

279 **A Palestinian immigrant:** Aymann Ismail, "The Store That Called the Cops on George Floyd," *Slate*, October 6, 2020, https://slate.com/human-interest/2020/10/cup-foods-george-floyd-store-911-history.html.

279 **Initially favored by Swedish immigrants:** Community Design Group, LLC, "The 38th Street and Chicago Avenue Small Area / Corridor Framework Plan," adopted March 21, 2008, 16–17, https://minneapolis2040.com/media/1496/38th-st-chicago-ave-small-area-corridor-framework-plan.pdf#page=16.

280 **Still, by the early twenty-first century:** Community Design Group, LLC, "38th Street and Chicago Avenue," 21.

280 **He was almost as tall as Floyd:** Ismail, "The Store That Called the Cops on George Floyd."

280 **"Um someone comes our store":** Peter Martinez, "Minneapolis Releases Transcript of George Floyd 911 Call," CBS News, May 29, 2020, https://www.cbsnews.com/news/george-floyd-death-911-transcript-minneapolis-police.

281 **The son of a White single mother:** Kim Barker, "The Black Officer Who Detained George Floyd Had Pledged to Fix the Police," *The New York Times*, June 27, 2020, https://www.nytimes.com/2020/06/27/us/minneapolis-police-officer-kueng.html.

281 **Lane tapped his flashlight:** Except where otherwise noted, the depiction of Floyd's killing comes from authors' interviews with witnesses, police records, court documents and testimony, recorded investigative interviews, body camera footage, autopsy records and other medical reports, cell phone camera video, security camera footage, and news reports.

291 **Three white supremacists:** Sue Anne Pressley, "Black Man Dragged to Death," *The Washington Post*, June 10, 1998, https://www.washingtonpost.com/wp-srv/national/longterm/jasper/charges061098.htm.

294 **She lived just a short walk:** Jennifer Brooks, "Hero of Her Own Story: A Young Eyewitness to George Floyd's Killing Is Writing a Children's Book," *Star Tribune* (Minneapolis), July 5, 2020, https://www.startribune.com/hero-of-her-own-story-a-young-eyewitness-to-george-floyd-s-killing-is-writing-a-children-s-book/571630222.

300 **"They killed him":** Darnella Frazier, "They killed him right in front of cup foods over south on 38th and Chicago!!," Facebook, May 26, 2020, https://www.facebook.com/darnellareallprettymarie/videos/1425398217661280.

302 **Man Dies After Medical Incident:** Bill McCarthy, "What the First Police Statement About George Floyd Got Wrong," *PolitiFact*, April 22, 2021, https://www.politifact.com/article/2021/apr/22/what-first-police-statement-about-george-floyd-got.

CHAPTER 11: WE HAVE NOTHING TO LOSE BUT OUR CHAINS

307 **"Chief," he recalled it saying:** "Derek Chauvin Trial Week Two," CNN, April 5, 2021, http://www.cnn.com/TRANSCRIPTS/2104/05/cnr.11.html.

309 **According to a video posted:** Libor Jany (@StribJany), "MPD/Mayor Frey news conference re the in-custody death," Twitter, May 26, 2020, https://twitter.com/i/broadcasts/1YqKDEkAWpBGV.

315 **He had recently taken on:** David A. Fahrenthold, "A Woman Killed. An Officer Shot. No One Legally Responsible," *The Washington Post*, September 24, 2020, https://www.washingtonpost.com/politics/breonna-taylor-castle-doctrine/2020/09/24/44e41eba-fe90-11ea-b555-4d71a9254f4b_story.html.

315 **Crump was also working:** Hannah Knowles, "Georgia's Attorney General Asks DOJ to Investigate Handling of Ahmaud Arbery's Killing," *The Washington Post*, May 11, 2020, https://www.washingtonpost.com/nation/2020/05/10/ahmaud-arbery-doj-investigation.

318 **"Every person is entitled to fairness":** Max Nesterak, "Minneapolis Mayor Calls for Charges Against Officer Who Killed George Floyd," *Minnesota Reformer*, May 27, 2020, https://minnesotareformer.com/briefs/minneapolis-mayor-calls-for-charges-against-officer-who-killed-george-floyd.

319 **"Ask the family of Jamar Clark":** Libor Jany (@StribJany), "Afternoon George Floyd newser," Twitter, May 26, 2020, https://twitter.com/StribJany/status/1265358407344754689.

320 **a long, arduous battle:** Holly Bailey, "Reconstructing Seven Days of Protests in Minneapolis After George Floyd's Death," *The Washington Post*, October 9, 2020, https://www.washingtonpost.com/graphics/2020/national/live-stream-george-floyd-protests.

321 **In November 2012:** 27-CR-12-27954 Complaint, Scribd, accessed December 30, 2021, https://www.scribd.com/doc/115096002/Police-report.

321 **He fell onto his stomach:** Nicole Norfleet, "Suspect Is Taken to HCMC After Trading Shots with Minneapolis Police," *Star Tribune* (Minneapolis), November 29, 2012, https://www.startribune.com/suspect-is-taken-to-hcmc-after-trading-shots-with-minneapolis-police/181317301.

326 **Online, celebrities:** Christi Carras, "Ava DuVernay and John Boyega Lead Hollywood's Charge Against George Floyd's Killing," *Los Angeles Times*, May 28, 2020, https://www.latimes.com/entertainment-arts/story/2020-05-28/george-floyd-celebrity-reactions-twitter-instagram.

327 **"If you had done it":** ABC News (@ABC), "BREAKING: Minneapolis Mayor Jacob Frey calls for officer seen in video with his knee on George Floyd's neck to be charged," Twitter, May 27, 2020, https://twitter.com/ABC/status/1265708290362785792.

328 **Frey in turn reached out:** Jennifer Bjorhus and Liz Navratil, "Mayor Frey: Gov. Walz Hesitated to Deploy National Guard During Minneapolis Riots," *Star Tribune* (Minneapolis), August 4, 2020, https://www.startribune.com/mpls-mayor-says-walz-hesitant-to-deploy-guard-During-riots/571999292.

328 **Buildings smoldered:** Bailey, "Reconstructing Seven Days of Protests in Minneapolis After George Floyd's Death."

333 **His office had also named:** Dan Cooney, "Read the Complaint Charging Ex-Officer Derek Chauvin with George Floyd's Death," *PBS NewsHour*, May 29, 2020, https://www.pbs.org/newshour/nation/read-the-complaint-charging-ex-officer-derek-chauvin-with-george-floyds-death.

333 **The man with the umbrella:** Libor Jany, "Minneapolis Police Say 'Umbrella Man' Was a White Supremacist Trying to Incite George Floyd Rioting," *Star Tribune* (Minneapolis), July 28, 2020, https://www.startribune.com/police-umbrella-man-was-a-white-supremacist-trying-to-incite-floyd-rioting/571932272.

333 **Federal agents said:** "George Floyd Protests: 'Boogaloo' Member Held in Precinct Attack," BBC News, October 24, 2020, https://www.bbc.com/news/world-us-canada-54670557.

337 **"So, let's be very clear":** "Minnesota Gov. Tim Walz Press Conference Transcript: Mobilizes Full National Guard," *Rev*, May 30, 2020, https://www.rev.com/blog/transcripts/minnesota-gov-tim-walz-press-conference-transcript-mobilizes-full-national-guard.

337 **Around the country, protests:** Ben Westcott, Brett McKeehan, Laura Smith-Spark, Fernando Alfonso III, Amir Vera, and Daniella Diaz, "May 30 George Floyd Protests News," CNN, May 31, 2020, https://www.cnn.com/us/live-news/george-floyd-protests-05-30-20/index.html.

337 **"This is chaos":** Tim Craig and Vanessa Williams, "Atlanta Mayor Keisha Lance Bottoms Says She Won't Seek Reelection," *The Washington Post*, May 7, 2021, https://www.washingtonpost.com/politics/georgia-democrats-atlanta-mayor/2021/05/07/34c3bf9e-af2b-11eb-acd3-24b44a57093a_story.html.

338 **"rat- and rodent-infested mess":** Colby Itkowitz, "Trump Attacks Rep. Cummings's District, Calling It a 'Disgusting, Rat and Rodent Infested Mess,'" *The Washington Post*, July 27, 2019, https://www.washingtonpost.com/politics/trump-attacks-rep-cummingss-district-calling-it-a-disgusting-rat-and-rodent-infested-mess/2019/07/27/b93c89b2-b073-11e9-bc5c-e73b603e7f38_story.html.

338 **civil rights hero, Representative John Lewis:** Cleve R. Wootson Jr., "In Feud with John Lewis, Donald Trump Attacked 'One of the Most Respected People in America,'" *The Washington Post*, January 15, 2017, https://www.washingtonpost.com/news/the-fix/wp/2017/01/15/in-feud-with-john-lewis-donald-trump-attacked-one-of-the-most-respected-people-in-america.

338–9 **Now in the throes of a pandemic:** Jose A. Del Real, Robert Samuels, and Tim Craig, "How the Black Lives Matter Movement Went Mainstream," *The Washington Post*, June 9, 2020, https://www.washingtonpost.com/national/how-the-black-lives-matter-movement-went-mainstream/2020/06/09/201bd6e6-a9c6-11ea-9063-e69bd6520940_story.html.

339 **A study from the Brookings Institution:** Valerie Wirtschafter, "How George Floyd Changed the Online Conversation Around BLM," *Brookings*, June 17, 2021, https://www.brookings.edu/techstream/how-george-floyd-changed-the-online-conversation-around-black-lives-matter.

340   **And in the nation's capital:** Carol D. Leonnig, "Protesters' Breach of Temporary Fences near White House Complex Prompted Secret Service to Move Trump to Secure Bunker," *The Washington Post*, June 3, 2020, https://www.washingtonpost. com/politics/secret-service-moved-trump-to-secure-bunker-friday-after-protesters-breached-temporary-fences-near-white-house-complex/2020/06/03/e4ae77c2-a5b9-11ea-b619-3f9133bbb482_story.html.

340   **Soon, Trump was being mocked:** Robert Costa, Seung Min Kim, and Josh Dawsey, "Trump Calls Governors 'Weak,' Urges Them to Use Force Against Unruly Protests," *The Washington Post*, June 1, 2020, https://www.washingtonpost.com/ politics/trump-governors-george-floyd-protests/2020/06/01/430a6226-a421-11ea-b619-3f9133bbb482_story.html.

340   **while sending out tough-guy tweets:** Peter Baker and Maggie Haberman, "As Protests and Violence Spill Over, Trump Shrinks Back," *The New York Times*, May 31, 2020, https://www.nytimes.com/2020/05/31/us/politics/trump-protests-george-floyd.html.

341   **But the country would soon understand:** Dalton Bennett, Sarah Cahlan, Aaron C. Davis, and Joyce Sohyun Lee, "The Crackdown Before Trump's Photo Op," *The Washington Post*, June 8, 2020, https://www.washingtonpost.com/investigations/ 2020/06/08/timeline-trump-church-photo-op.

CHAPTER 12: HEAR MY CRY

343   **"I can't believe":** MSNBC, "Floyd's Brother: Trump 'Didn't Give Me the Opportunity to Even Speak," YouTube video, May 30, 2020, 5:47, https://www. youtube.com/watch?v=hQvb0sfHDX0.

344   **Biden tried to connect with them:** Tim Ott, "Joe Biden: The Heartbreaking Car Accident That Killed His Wife and Daughter," Biography.com, September 28, 2020, https://www.biography.com/news/joe-biden-first-wife-daughter-car-accident-story.

344   **"I know what it means to grieve":** President Joseph R. Biden answered questions from authors through email, January 10, 2021.

346   **The Floyds' request:** Mark Berman, "Minn. Officer Acquitted in Shooting of Philando Castile During Traffic Stop, Dismissed from Police Force," *The Washington Post*, June 17, 2017, https://www.washingtonpost.com/news/ post-nation/wp/2017/06/16/minn-officer-acquitted-of-manslaughter-for-shooting-philando-castile-during-traffic-stop.

346   **A former world history teacher:** U.S. Census Bureau, "QuickFacts, Minnesota," accessed September 14, 2021, https://www.census.gov/quickfacts/MN/.

347   **The Star Tribune had calculated:** Jeff Hargarten, Jennifer Bjorhus, MaryJo Webster, and Kelly Smith, "Every Police-Involved Death in Minnesota Since 2000," *Star Tribune* (Minneapolis), updated January 3, 2022, https://www.startribune.com/ every-police-involved-death-in-minnesota-since-2000/502088871.

347   **Only one of those officers:** Dana Theide, "Mohamed Noor Receives Maximum Sentence in Death of Justine Ruszczyk," KARE 11, October 21, 2021, https://www. kare11.com/article/news/crime/mohamed-noor-resentencing-justine-ruszczyk/ 89-273c6951-4a3f-4431-8dbf-f84e8696651c.

349 **In Minneapolis, the team:** 27-CR-20-12646 Complaint, Document Cloud, accessed December 9, 2021, https://www.documentcloud.org/documents/6933248-27-CR-20-12646-Complaint.

350 **Neighboring Washington County:** Jennifer Mayerle, "Derek Chauvin and Wife Kellie Charged with Multiple Felony Tax Crimes," WCCO 4, July 22, 2020, https://minnesota.cbslocal.com/2020/07/22/derek-chauvin-and-wife-charged-with-multiple-felony-tax-crimes.

351 **The unrelated charges:** Rochelle Olson, "Derek Chauvin and His Ex-Wife Plead Not Guilty to Tax Evasion," *Star Tribune* (Minneapolis), November 5, 2021, https://www.startribune.com/derek-chauvin-and-his-ex-wife-plead-not-guilty-to-tax-evasion/600113433.

351 **The other three officers:** 27-CR-20-12646 Complaint, Document Cloud, accessed December 9, 2021, https://www.documentcloud.org/documents/6933248-27-CR-20-12646-Complaint.

352 **"give grace" to the police:** Reg Chapman, "'He Was Kind, He Was Helpful': Friends, Family Say George Floyd Was a Gentle Giant," WCCO 4, May 26, 2020, https://minnesota.cbslocal.com/2020/05/26/he-was-kind-he-was-helpful-friends-family-say-george-floyd-was-a-gentle-giant.

354 **Police maintained they were chasing:** Associated Press, "Police Identify Body Found in Inver Grove Heights Recycling Center," MPR News, August 20, 2009, https://www.mprnews.org/story/2009/08/20/body-found-recycling-center.

355 **Another woman, Paulette Quinn:** Mara H. Gottfried, "St. Paul Family of Troubled Man Killed by Police Wants Answers," *Pioneer Press* (Minnesota), December 15, 2015,https://www.twincities.com/2015/12/22/st-paul-family-of-troubled-man-killed-by-police-wants-answers/.

355 **His slow death:** Brandon Stahl, A.J. Lagoe, and Steve Eckert, "KARE 11 Investigates: Records Reveal Multiple Failures to Prevent Inmate's Death," KARE 11, July 23, 2020, https://www.kare11.com/article/news/investigations/kare-11-investigates-records-reveal-multiple-failures-to-prevent-inmates-death/89-e9a811bc-0828-4de6-9a10-3a88bab7a420.

356 **"They followed me":** Unicorn Riot, "[LIVE] Families, Victims of Police Terror Speak Out at MN Governor's Residence," Facebook, June 1, 2020, https://www.facebook.com/watch/live/?ref=watch_permalink&v=542002096471608.

361 **"Since he had a Bible":** KARE 11, "Full George Floyd Memorial Service in Minneapolis," YouTube video, June 4, 2020, 2:35:57, https://www.youtube.com/watch?v=EKIFFIRa9zs.

362 **There had been protests in all fifty states:** Lara Putnam, Erica Chenoweth, and Jeremy Pressman, "The Floyd Protests Are the Broadest in U.S. History—and Are Spreading to White, Small-Town America," *The Washington Post*, June 6, 2020, https://www.washingtonpost.com/politics/2020/06/06/floyd-protests-are-broadest-us-history-are-spreading-white-small-town-america.

362 **In Santa Monica, California:** "Surfers Hold 'Paddle Out' Memorial for George Floyd," *Today*, June 6, 2020, https://www.today.com/video/surfers-hold-paddle-out-memorial-for-george-floyd-84562501803.

362 **Around the world, oppressed groups:** Jennifer Hassan and Rick Noack, "How George Floyd's Killing Sparked a Global Reckoning," *The Washington Post*, May 25, 2021, https://www.washingtonpost.com/world/2021/05/25/george-floyd-anniversary-global-change/.

362 **In Kenya, protesters:** "Kenya: Police Brutality During Curfew," Human Rights Watch, April 22, 2020, https://www.hrw.org/news/2020/04/22/kenya-police-brutality-during-curfew#.

363 **and in New Zealand:** Michael Neilson, "Police Use of Force Report: Taser Used on Three 15-Year-Olds in 2018, Māori Disproportionately Affected," *New Zealand Herald*, November 11, 2019, https://www.nzherald.co.nz/nz/police-use-of-force-report-taser-used-on-three-15-year-olds-in-2018-maori-disproportionately-affected/2JNABU7ZGXCYBNLTIVJGXQVMAU.

363 **Amy Klobuchar, Minnesota's senior senator:** This anecdote comes from an interview with Senator Amy Klobuchar, conducted October 5, 2021.

363 **Mitt Romney joined:** Michelle Boorstein and Hannah Natanson, "Mitt Romney, Marching with Evangelicals, Becomes First GOP Senator to Join George Floyd Protests in D.C.," *The Washington Post*, June 8, 2020, https://www.washingtonpost.com/dc-md-va/2020/06/07/romney-protest-black-lives-matter.

364 **Biden looked in their eyes:** This scene was re-created with the memories of the Floyd family, attorneys, and advisors to the Biden campaign who witnessed the interaction.

364 **He had seen an interview:** *Good Morning America*, "George Floyd's 6-Year-Old Daughter Opens Up about Her Dad | GMA," YouTube video, June 3, 2020, 3:34, https://www.youtube.com/watch?v=jxvxYoATF2E.

365 **In Los Angeles:** Derek Hawkins, Katie Mettler, and Perry Stein, "'Defund the Police' Gains Traction as Cities Seek to Respond to Demands for a Major Law Enforcement Shift," *The Washington Post*, June 7, 2020, https://www.washingtonpost.com/nation/2020/06/07/protests-defund-police.

366 **"I've been coming to grips":** Sana Saeed (@SanaSaeed), "Minneapolis Mayor Jacob Frey showed up today at the protests . . . ," Twitter, June 6, 2020, https://twitter.com/SanaSaeed/status/1269407893406826496.

368 **including Jenny Durkan:** Chris Daniels, "Seattle Mayor Jenny Durkan Will Not Seek Re-election, Prompting Reaction and Speculation," King5, December 7, 2020, https://www.king5.com/article/news/local/seattle/durkan-wont-week-re-election/281-594c83dc-3564-43d5-8a1b-4ace0c246758.

368 **and Keisha Lance Bottoms:** Keisha Lance Bottoms (@KeishaBottoms), "dearatl.com," Twitter, May 6, 2021, https://twitter.com/KeishaBottoms/status/1390494737967235074.

368 **They'd provide money for racial bias training:** Office of Cory Booker, "Booker Announces Framework for Comprehensive Police Reform Legislation," June 1, 2020, https://www.booker.senate.gov/news/press/booker-announces-framework-for-comprehensive-police-reform-legislation.

368 **"The chants and the marches":** "Cory Booker & Kamala Harris Speech Transcript on George Floyd & Racial Injustice," *Rev*, June 2, 2020, https://www.rev.com/blog/

transcripts/cory-booker-kamala-harris-speech-transcript-on-george-floyd-racial-injustice.

369 **"That doesn't happen in my church":** Paul Kane, "In Shift, Key Republicans Talk Openly of Police Reforms After George Floyd's Death," *The Washington Post*, June 3, 2020, https://www.washingtonpost.com/powerpost/in-shift-key-republicans-talk-openly-of-police-reforms-after-george-floyds-death/2020/06/03/e6a29454-a5ba-11ea-b619-3f9133bbb482_story.html.

369 **"The actual problem is not":** "Sen. Tim Scott Speech Transcript on Police Reform After JUSTICE Act Vote," *Rev*, June 25, 2020, https://www.rev.com/blog/transcripts/sen-tim-scott-speech-transcript-on-police-reform-after-justice-act-vote.

372 **strangulation in autopsies:** Dr. Baker declined a request for his participation in this project.

372 **And then there was a statement:** Shaila Dewan and Tim Arango, "How the Medical Examiner's Previous Statements May Help the Defense," *The New York Times*, April 9, 2021, https://www.nytimes.com/live/2021/04/09/us/derek-chauvin-trial/how-the-medical-examiners-previous-statements-may-help-the-defense.

372 **Freeman maintained that his office:** This quote comes from emailed responses from the Hennepin County Attorney's Office to authors' questions, November 24, 2021.

373 **Those ideas would be supported:** GBD 2019 Police Violence US Subnational Collaborators, "Fatal Police Violence by Race and State in the USA, 1980–2019: A Network Meta-Regression," *The Lancet* 398, no. 10307 (October 2021): S1239–55, https://www.thelancet.com/journals/lancet/article/PIIS0140-6736(21)01609-3/fulltext#%20.

373 **The study concluded that these mislabelings:** Peter Neufeld, Keith Findley, and Dean Strang, "Opinion: Thousands of Missed Police Killings Prove We Must Address Systemic Bias in Forensic Science," *The Washington Post*, October 15, 2021, https://www.washingtonpost.com/opinions/2021/10/15/medical-examiners-forensics-bias-police-killings.

373 **In a 2011 survey, 22 percent:** Julie Melinek et al., "National Association of Medical Examiners Position Paper: Medical Examiner, Coroner, and Forensic Pathologist Independence," ME Independence Position Paper, accessed December 9, 2021, https://name.memberclicks.net/assets/docs/00df032d-ccab-48f8-9415-5c27f173cda6.pdf.

376 **In the sweltering heat, Senator Harris:** "2020 March on Washington Event Transcript," *Rev*, August 28, 2020, https://www.rev.com/blog/transcripts/2020-march-on-washington-event-transcript.

377 **"I'm so overwhelmed":** CBC News, "Thousands Rally in D.C. for March on Washington 2020," YouTube video, August 28, 2020, 3:17:06, https://www.youtube.com/watch?v=BZvNNjXuF2Q.

CHAPTER 13: TESTIMONY

379 **But that number seemed laughable:** Andy Mannix, "Minneapolis Agrees to Pay $20 Million in Death of Justine Ruszczyk Damond," *Star Tribune* (Minneapolis),

May 4, 2019, https://www.startribune.com/minneapolis-agrees-to-pay-20-million-in-fatal-police-shooting-of-justine-ruszczyk-damond/509438812.

379 **The city offered to settle:** This information was provided to the authors by city officials.

381 **Blocks away:** Mark Berman and Holly Bailey, "The Jurors Who Decided Derek Chauvin's Fate," *The Washington Post*, April 20, 2021, https://www.washingtonpost.com/nation/2021/03/28/jury-chauvin-trial-george-floyd.

383 **Guardsmen in camouflage:** Holly Bailey, "Boarded Up and Lined with Barbed Wire, Minneapolis Braces for Murder Trial in George Floyd's Death," *The Washington Post*, March 7, 2021, https://www.washingtonpost.com/national/minneapolis-derek-chauvin-trial-george-floyd/2021/03/07/35b37c0a-7a92-11eb-b3d1-9e5aa3d5220c_story.html.

384 **"Two minutes!":** Sky News, "Chauvin on Trial: George Floyd's Family Take the Knee for Eight Minutes and 46 Seconds," YouTube video, March 29, 2021, 9:41, https://www.youtube.com/watch?v=AYwfw7aYJT8.

386 **"I apologize for":** Law&Crime Network, "MN v. Derek Chauvin Trial – Opening Statements – Prosecution Jerry Blackwell, Defense Eric Nelson," YouTube video, March 29, 2021, 1:35:10, https://www.youtube.com/watch?v=dvCv-soaifo.

390 **an interview Ross gave:** WCCO – CBS Minnesota, "'He Was Kind, He Was Helpful': Family Says George Floyd Was Beloved," YouTube video, May 26, 2020, 1:58, https://www.youtube.com/watch?v=y6x-NFvpVrk.

392 **During the 1993 trial:** Lateshia Beachum, "Chauvin's Lawyer Asked a Black Witness About Anger, Conjuring Centuries-Old Tropes, Scholars Say," *The Washington Post*, March 30, 2021, https://www.washingtonpost.com/nation/2021/03/30/chauvin-trial-donald-floyd-witness.

415 **About forty-five officers:** WCCO-TV Staff, "Protesters Clash with Police in Brooklyn Center After Deadly Officer-Involved Shooting," April 12, 2021, https://minnesota.cbslocal.com/2021/04/12/bca-reporting-to-officer-involved-shooting-in-brooklyn-center/.

418 **Camera footage captured:** *Good Morning America*, "New Video of Ex-cop Fatally Shooting Daunte Wright Shown in Court | GMA," YouTube video, December 9, 2021, 5:00, https://www.youtube.com/watch?v=P-nTPADiaBs.

418 **"At this moment in time":** Steven Zeitchik, "Apple and Will Smith Move Their New Film 'Emancipation' About Slavery out of Georgia to Protest Voting-Rights Law," *The Washington Post*, April 12, 2021, https://www.washingtonpost.com/business/2021/04/12/georgia-voting-rights-boycott-apple-film.

419 **"Give Katie the strength":** KARE 11, "Attorney Ben Crump, Wright and Floyd Families Meet with Reporters," YouTube video, April 13, 2021, 1:10:01, https://www.youtube.com/watch?v=m35bmCrrZQg.

421 **Dr. David Fowler proposed:** Hannah Knowles, Timothy Bella, Marisa Iati, and Meryl Kornfield, "Defense Expert Says Derek Chauvin Did Not Cause George Floyd's Death as Cross-Examination Grows Tense," *The Washington Post*, April 14, 2021, https://www.washingtonpost.com/nation/2021/04/14/derek-chauvin-trial.

422 **The defense had called seven:** Paul Walsh, Abby Simons, and Hannah Sayle, "Who Were the Witnesses in the Derek Chauvin Trial?," *Star Tribune* (Minneapolis),

April 15, 2021, https://www.startribune.com/who-are-the-witnesses-in-the-derek-chauvin-trial-for-the-killing-of-george-floyd-in-minneapolis/600042794.

424 **"His name was George Perry Floyd Jr.":** "Prosecution Closing Argument Full Transcript: Derek Chauvin Trial for Murder of George Floyd," *Rev*, April 19, 2021, https://www.rev.com/blog/transcripts/prosecution-closing-argument-full-transcript-derek-chauvin-trial-for-murder-of-george-floyd.

431 **"Members of the jury":** FOX 9 Minneapolis–St. Paul, "Judge Cahill Reads Verdict, Derek Chauvin Found Guilty on All Three Counts," YouTube video, April 20, 2021, 3:13, https://www.youtube.com/watch?v=Z5kpgMdRY7M.

435 **a video was circulating:** KHOU 11, "Raw Video: President Biden, Vice President Harris Call Attorney Ben Crump, George Floyd's Family Aft," YouTube video, April 20, 2021, 3:37, https://www.youtube.com/watch?v=P6eb2uNUHlU.

435 **"My fellow Americans":** The White House, "Remarks by President Biden in Address to a Joint Session of Congress," April 29, 2021, https://www.whitehouse.gov/briefing-room/speeches-remarks/2021/04/29/remarks-by-president-biden-in-address-to-a-joint-session-of-congress.

Chapter 14: American Hope

437 **"This is a first down":** Jackson is referring to the police killings of Ma'Khia Bryant in Columbus, Ohio, Jacob Blake in Kenosha, Wisconsin, and Roland Greene, outside Monroe, Louisiana.

450 **They walked out of Pelosi's office:** "Speaker Pelosi and Representative Bass Meeting with George Floyd Family Members," C-SPAN, May 25, 2021, https://www.c-span.org/video/?512087-1/speaker-pelosi-representative-bass-meeting-george-floyd-family-members.

453 **"The devil's in the details":** Nicholas Fandos and Catie Edmondson, "Policing Reform Negotiations Sputter in Congress amid Partisan Bickering," *The New York Times*, June 10, 2021, https://www.nytimes.com/2021/06/10/us/politics/policing-reform-congress.html.

454 **The squabbling continued:** These negotiations reflect interviews with aides conducted by authors and Mike DeBonis of *The Washington Post*.

455 **NFL commissioner Roger Goodell:** Tracy Jan, Jena McGregor, Renae Merle, and Nitasha Tiku, "As Big Corporations Say 'Black Lives Matter,' Their Track Records Raise Skepticism," *The Washington Post*, June 13, 2020, https://www.washingtonpost.com/business/2020/06/13/after-years-marginalizing-black-employees-customers-corporate-america-says-black-lives-matter.

455 **News organizations debated:** John Daniszewski, "Why We're No Longer Naming Suspects in Minor Crime Stories," Associated Press, June 15, 2021, https://blog.ap.org/behind-the-news/why-were-no-longer-naming-suspects-in-minor-crime-stories.

455 **Walmart, the country's largest retailer:** Abha Bhattarai, "Walmart Will Stop Locking 'Multicultural' Hair and Beauty Products," *The Washington Post*, June 11, 2020, https://www.washingtonpost.com/business/2020/06/11/walmart-will-stop-locking-multicultural-hair-beauty-products/.

455 **The Washington Post found:** Tracy Jan, Jena McGregor, and Meghan Hoyer, "Corporate America's $50 Billion Promise," *The Washington Post*, August 24, 2021, https://www.washingtonpost.com/business/interactive/2021/george-floyd-corporate-america-racial-justice/.

456 **The Washington Redskins:** Giulia McDonnell, Neito del Rio, John Eligon, and Adeel Hassan, "A Timeline of What Has Happened in the Year Since George Floyd's Death," *The New York Times*, May 25, 2021, https://www.nytimes.com/2021/05/25/us/george-floyd-protests-unrest-events-timeline.html.

456 **A New York Times analysis:** Steve Eder, Michael H. Keller, and Blacki Migliozzi, "As New Police Reform Laws Sweep Across the U.S., Some Ask: Are They Enough?," *The New York Times*, updated October 10, 2021, https://www.nytimes.com/2021/04/18/us/police-reform-bills.html.

456 **By September 2020, a study:** Deja Thomas and Juliana Menasce Horowitz, "Support for Black Lives Matter Has Decreased Since June but Remains Strong Among Black Americans," Pew Research Center, September 16, 2020, https://www.pewresearch.org/fact-tank/2020/09/16/support-for-black-lives-matter-has-decreased-since-june-but-remains-strong-among-black-americans; Juliana Menasce Horowitz, "Support for Black Lives Matter Declined After George Floyd Protests, but Has Remained Unchanged Since," Pew Research Center, September 27, 2021, https://www.pewresearch.org/fact-tank/2021/09/27/support-for-black-lives-matter-declined-after-george-floyd-protests-but-has-remained-unchanged-since.

456 **That worry made itself clear:** Marisa Iati, "What Is Critical Race Theory, and Why Do Republicans Want to Ban It in Schools?," *The Washington Post*, May 29, 2021, https://www.washingtonpost.com/education/2021/05/29/critical-race-theory-bans-schools.

457 **New York Times' 1619 Project:** The 1619 Project, *The New York Times Magazine*, accessed December 7, 2021, https://www.nytimes.com/interactive/2019/08/14/magazine/1619-america-slavery.html.

457 **"Critical Race Theory, like all":** "Owens Introduces Legislation to Combat Critical Race Theory," Office of United States Congressman Burgess Owens, press release, updated May 14, 2021, https://owens.house.gov/media/press-releases/owens-introduces-legislation-combat-critical-race-theory.

458 **As Crump and Romanucci:** Kimberly Kindy, "Dozens of States Have Tried to End Qualified Immunity. Police Officers and Unions Helped Beat Nearly Every Bill," *The Washington Post*, October 7, 2021, https://www.washingtonpost.com/politics/qualified-immunity-police-lobbying-state-legislatures/2021/10/06/60e546bc-0cdf-11ec-aea1-42a8138f132a_story.html.

458 **There was a key difference:** Paulina Villegas, "Sharpton and Crump, High-Profile Advocates for Black Rights, Take on White Teen Shot by Police," *The Washington Post*, July 15, 2021, https://www.washingtonpost.com/nation/2021/07/15/sharpton-crump-case-hunter-brittain.

459 **Hooker was so furious:** Donald Hooker Jr., Facebook, June 27, 2021, https://www.facebook.com/ZD126/videos/10219355414538608.

460   **an editorial in the Star Tribune:** Editorial Board, "Abuse of Public Officials Doesn't Further Causes," *Star Tribune* (Minneapolis), June 30, 2021, https://www.startribune.com/abuse-of-public-officials-doesnt-further-causes/600073719.

460   **Governor Tim Walz had told the state:** Nicholas Bogel-Burroughs and Jack Healy, "Minnesota Lawmakers Vowed Police Reform. They Couldn't Agree on Any," *The New York Times*, June 20, 2020, https://www.nytimes.com/2020/06/20/us/minnesota-police-george-floyd.html.

461   **Conservatives talked about how these bills:** Holly Bailey, "A Ballot Initiative on Overhauling Police After George Floyd's Death Is Tearing Minneapolis Apart," *The Washington Post*, October 22, 2021, https://www.washingtonpost.com/nation/2021/10/22/minneapolis-police-reform-ballot-initiative.

462   **"You listen to our stories":** Johnathon McClellan, "Post Legislative Press Conference June 31st 2021," YouTube video, uploaded July 1, 2021, 38:25, https://www.youtube.com/watch?v=XKqm4-oArXM.

464   **Yes, Chauvin had been sentenced:** Holly Bailey, "Derek Chauvin Sentenced to 22½ Years in Prison for the Murder of George Floyd," *The Washington Post*, June 25, 2021, https://www.washingtonpost.com/nation/2021/06/25/derek-chauvin-sentencing-george-floyd.

465   **Civil rights leaders feared:** Robert Barnes, "Supreme Court Upholds Arizona Voting Laws That Lower Court Found Were Unfair to Minorities," *The Washington Post*, July 1, 2021, https://www.washingtonpost.com/politics/courts_law/supreme-court-arizona-voting-laws/2021/07/01/5fef7800-da6b-11eb-9bbb-37c30dcf9363_story.html.

466   **He looked out over the audience:** "March On for Voting Rights Rally," C-SPAN, August 28, 2021, https://www.c-span.org/video/?514285-1/march-voting-rights-rally.

Bibliography

Alexander, Michelle. *The New Jim Crow: Mass Incarceration in the Age of Colorblindness*. New York: New Press, 2010.

"All Screwed Up | Visual Tribute (Official Version)." Directed by Isaac Yowman. Houston: Iyo Visuals, 2020. Accessed October 15, 2021. https://www.youtube.com/watch?v=Dh3rz4sE5vg.

Austin, James, and Garry Coventry. *Emerging Issues on Privatized Prisons*. U.S. Department of Justice, Bureau of Justice Assistance. February 2001. https://www.ojp.gov/pdffiles1/bja/181249.pdf.

Baker, Peter, and Susan Glasser. *The Man Who Ran Washington: The Life and Times of James A. Baker III*. New York: Doubleday, 2020.

Baptist, Edward E. *The Half Has Never Been Told: Slavery and the Making of American Capitalism*. New York: Basic Books, 2014.

Bassett, John Spencer. *Slavery in the State of North Carolina*. Baltimore: Johns Hopkins Press, 1899. https://docsouth.unc.edu/nc/bassett99/bassett99.html.

Bauer, Shane. *American Prison: A Reporter's Undercover Journey into the Business of Punishment*. New York: Penguin Books, 2019.

Blackmon, Douglas A. *Slavery by Another Name: The Re-enslavement of Black Americans from the Civil War to World War II*. New York: Doubleday, 2008.

Brill, Steven. *Class Warfare: Inside the Fight to Fix America's Schools*. New York: Simon & Schuster Paperbacks, 2012.

Bush, George W. *Decision Points*. New York: Crown Publishers, 2010.

The Committee on House Administration of the U.S. House of Representatives. *Black Americans in Congress, 1870–2007*. Washington, DC: U.S. Government Printing Office, 2008. https://www.govinfo.gov/content/pkg/GPO-CDOC-108hdoc224/pdf/GPO-CDOC-108hdoc224.pdf.

Creek, Laverne, Tom Capehart, and Verner Grise. *U.S. Tobacco Statistics, 1935–92*. Washington, DC: U.S. Department of Agriculture, Commodity Economics Division, Economic Research Service, 1994. https://www.ers.usda.gov/webdocs/publications/47092/59808_sb869.pdf.

Desmond, Matthew. *Evicted: Poverty and Profit in the American City*. London: Penguin Books, 2017.

Edmonds, Helen G. *The Negro and Fusion Politics in North Carolina, 1894–1901*. Chapel Hill: University of North Carolina Press, 1951.

Federal Writers' Project: Slave Narrative Project, Vol. 11, North Carolina, Part 1, Adams–Hunter. 1936. Manuscript/Mixed Material. https://www.loc.gov/item/mesn111.

Federal Writers' Project: Slave Narrative Project, Vol. 11, North Carolina, Part 2, Jackson–Yellerday. 1936. Manuscript/Mixed Material. https://www.loc.gov/item/mesn112.

Fowler, Malcolm. *They Passed This Way: A Personal Narrative of Harnett County History*. Lillington, NC: Friends of Harnett County Library, Inc., 1992.

The Great Yates: Thursday Night Lights and the Magical Season. Produced by Donald M. Pinkard and Jocelyn Pinkard. Dallas: Urban Aggregate LLC, 2019. Accessed September 4, 2021. https://jpink98701.gumroad.com.

Hasty, Mary Alice. *The Heritage of Harnett County, North Carolina*. Erwin, NC: The Heritage of Harnett Book Committee, in Cooperation with Delmar Printing, 1993.

Hinson, Waymon R. "Land Gains, Land Losses: The Odyssey of African Americans Since Reconstruction." *American Journal of Economics and Sociology* 77, no. 3–4 (May 2018): 893–939. https://doi.org/10.1111/ajes.12233.

Hobbs, Jeff. *The Short and Tragic Life of Robert Peace: A Brilliant Young Man Who Left Newark for the Ivy League*. New York: Scribner, 2015.

Jackson, Bruce. *Inside the Wire: Photographs from Texas and Arkansas Prisons*. Austin: University of Texas Press, 2013.

Johnson, Guion Griffis. *Ante-Bellum North Carolina: A Social History*. Chapel Hill: University of North Carolina Press, 1937. https://docsouth.unc.edu/nc/johnson/johnson.html.

Kellar, William Henry. *Make Haste Slowly: Moderates, Conservatives, and School Desegregation in Houston*. College Station: Texas A&M University Press, 1999.

Kendi, Ibram X. *Stamped from the Beginning: The Definitive History of Racist Ideas in America*. New York: Vintage, 2021.

Leonnig, Carol, and Philip Rucker. *I Alone Can Fix It: Donald J. Trump's Catastrophic Final Year*. London: Bloomsbury, 2021.

Lincoln, Abraham, Stephen A. Douglas, and Edwin Erle Sparks. *The Lincoln-Douglas Debates*. Mineola, NY: Dover Publications, 2018.

Lowery, Wesley. *"They Can't Kill Us All": Ferguson, Baltimore, and a New Era in America's Racial Justice Movement*. New York: Little, Brown & Company, 2017.

McGee, Leo, and Robert Boone. *The Black Rural Landowner—Endangered Species: Social, Political, and Economic Implications*. Westport, CT: Greenwood Press, 1979.

Meacham, Jon. *Destiny and Power: The American Odyssey of George Herbert Walker Bush*. New York: Random House, 2016.

Moore, Wes. *The Other Wes Moore: One Name, Two Fates*. New York: Spiegel & Grau Trade Paperbacks, 2011.

Oliver, Melvin L., and Thomas M. Shapiro. *Black Wealth/White Wealth: A New Perspective on Racial Inequality*. New York: Routledge, 2006.

Palmer, John Logan, and Isabel V. Sawhill. *The Reagan Record: An Assessment of America's Changing Domestic Priorities*. Cambridge, MA: Ballinger Publishing Co., 1984.

Perkinson, Robert. *Texas Tough: The Rise of America's Prison Empire*. New York: Metropolitan Books, 2010. Kindle.

Rothstein, Richard. *The Color of Law: A Forgotten History of How Our Government Segregated America*. New York; London: Liveright Publishing Corporation, 2017. Kindle.

Schottenstein, Allison E. *Changing Perspectives: Black-Jewish Relations in Houston during the Civil Rights Era*. Denton: University of North Texas Press, 2021.

Schweninger, Loren. *Black Property Owners in the South, 1790–1915*. Urbana: University of Illinois Press, 1990.